War & Conflict in Africa

For Ariela, with love

War & Conflict in Africa

PAUL D. WILLIAMS

polity

First published in 2011 by Polity Press
Reprinted 2012 (twice), 2013, 2014 (twice), 2015 (twice)

Polity Press
65 Bridge Street
Cambridge CB2 1UR, UK

Polity Press
350 Main Street
Malden, MA 02148, USA

ISBN-13: 978-0-7456-4544-5
ISBN-13: 978-0-7456-4545-2 (pb)

A catalogue record for this book is available from the British Library.

Typeset in 9.5 on 13 pt Swift Light
by Toppan Best-set Premedia Limited
Printed and bound in USA by RR Donnelley

The publisher has used its best endeavours to ensure that the URLs for external websites referred to in this book are correct and active at the time of going to press. However, the publisher has no responsibility for the websites and can make no guarantee that a site will remain live or that the content is or will remain appropriate.

Every effort has been made to trace all copyright holders, but if any have been inadvertently overlooked the publisher will be pleased to include any necessary credits in any subsequent reprint or edition.

For further information on Polity, visit our website: www.politybooks.com

Contents

List of Tables

List of Figures

List of Abbreviations

ADC	*Alliance Démocratique du 23 Mai 2006 pour le Changement* (Mali)
ADF	Allied Democratic Forces (Uganda)
AFDL	Alliance of Democratic Forces for the Liberation of Congo–Zaire
AFRC	Armed Forces Revolutionary Council (Sierra Leone)
AMIB	AU Mission in Burundi
AMIS	AU Mission in Sudan
AMISEC	AU Mission for Support to the Elections in the Comoros
AMISOM	AU Mission in Somalia
APC	All People's Congress (Sierra Leone)
APSA	African Peace and Security Architecture
ASF	African Standby Force
ATNMC	*Alliance Touareg Nord-Mali pour le Changement* (Mali)
AU	African Union
CAR	Central African Republic
CDF	Civil Defence Force (Sierra Leone)
CDR	*Coalition pour la Défense de la République* (Rwanda)
CEN-SAD	Community of Sahel-Saharan States
CEWARN	Conflict Early Warning and Response mechanism (IGAD)
CEWS	Continental Early Warning System (AU)
CIJ	Coalition for International Justice
CNDP	*Congrès National pour la Défense du Peuple* (DRC)
CPA	Comprehensive Peace Agreement (Sudan, 2005)
CPAG	Commonwealth Peacekeeping Assistance Group
CPDTF	Commonwealth Police Development Task Force
DDR	disarmament, demobilization and reintegration
DLF	Darfur Liberation Front
DRC	Democratic Republic of Congo
EASBRIG	East African Standby Brigade
ECCAS	Economic Community of Central African States
ECOFORCE	ECOWAS Force in Côte d'Ivoire
ECOMICI	ECOWAS Mission in Côte d'Ivoire
ECOMIL	ECOWAS Mission in Liberia
ECOMOG	ECOWAS Monitoring Group
ECOWARN	ECOWAS Early Warning and Response Network

ECOWAS	Economic Community of West African States
EIJM	Eritrean Islamic Jihad Movement
EPLF	Eritrean People's Liberation Front
EPRDF	Ethiopian People's Revolutionary Democratic Front
ESF	ECOWAS Standby Force
EU	European Union
EUFOR	EU Force
EUFOR RD	EU Reserve Deployment Force
EUPOL	EU Police Mission
EUSEC	EU Security Sector Reform Mission
FAC	Congolese Armed Forces
FARDC	*Forces Armées de la République Démocratique du Congo* (DRC)
FDLR	*Forces Démocratiques de Libération du Rwanda*
FIS	*Front Islamique du Salut* (Algeria)
FLEC	Front for the Liberation of the Cabinda Enclave
FLN	*Front de Libération Nationale* (Algeria)
FN	*Forces Nouvelles* (Côte d'Ivoire)
FNI	Nationalist and Integrationist Front (DRC)
FOMAC	Central African Multinational Force
FOMUC	CEMAC Multinational Force in the Central African Republic
GAF	Guinean Armed Forces
GDP	gross domestic product
GNI	gross national income
GSPC	Salafist Group for Preaching and Combat
GTZ	German Development Agency
HIPC	heavily indebted poor countries
HRW	Human Rights Watch
HSM	Holy Spirit Movement (Uganda)
HSR	Human Security Report
ICC	International Criminal Court
ICG	International Crisis Group
ICRC	International Committee of the Red Cross
IFI	international financial institution
IGAD	Intergovernmental Authority on Development
IGNU	Interim Government of National Unity (Liberia)
IISS	International Institute for Strategic Studies (UK)
IMF	International Monetary Fund
IR	International Relations
IRC	International Rescue Committee
JEM	Justice and Equality Movement (Sudan)
LRA	Lord's Resistance Army (Uganda)
LURD	Liberians United for Reconciliation and Democracy
MAES	AU Electoral and Security Assistance Mission to the Comoros
MCA	Millennium Challenge Account (US)

MEND	Movement for the Emancipation of the Niger Delta (Nigeria)
MFDC	Movement of Democratic Forces of Casamance (Senegal)
MICOPAX	Mission for the Consolidation of Peace in Central African Republic
MINUCI	UN Mission in Côte d'Ivoire
MINURCA	UN Mission in the Central African Republic
MINURCAT	UN Mission in the Central African Republic and Chad
MINURSO	UN Mission for the Referendum in Western Sahara
MIOC	AU Military Observer Mission in the Comoros
MISAB	Inter-African Peace Force (Central African Republic)
MJP	Patriotic Youth Movement (Côte d'Ivoire)
MLC	Movement for the Liberation of Congo (DRC)
MNJ	*Mouvement des Nigériens pour la Justice* (Niger)
MODEL	Movement for Democracy in Liberia
MONUA	UN Observer Mission in Angola
MONUC	UN Mission in the Democratic Republic of Congo
MOSOP	Movement for the Survival of the Ogoni People (Nigeria)
MPCI	*Mouvement Patriotique de Côte d'Ivoire*
MPIGO	Ivorian Movement of the Great West
MPLA	*Movimento Popular de Libertação de Angola*
MRND	National Revolutionary Movement for Development (Rwanda)
MSF	Médecins Sans Frontières
NASBRIG	North African Standby Brigade
NATO	North Atlantic Treaty Organization
NCP	National Congress Party (Sudan)
NGO	non-governmental organization
NIF	Neutral International Force (Rwanda)
NPFL	National Patriotic Front of Liberia
OAU	Organization of African Unity
ODA	overseas development assistance
OECD	Organization for Economic Cooperation and Development
OLF	Oromo Liberation Front (Ethiopia)
OLMEE	OAU Liaison Mission in Ethiopia–Eritrea
OMC	Observation and Monitoring Centre (ECOWAS)
OMIB	UN Observer Mission in Burundi
ONLF	Ogaden National Liberation Front (Ethiopia)
ONUB	UN Operation in Burundi
ONUMOZ	UN Operation in Mozambique
PGE	Provisional Government of Eritrea
PITF	Political Instability Task Force (US)
POLISARIO	Popular Front for the Liberation of Saguia el-Hamra and Río de Oro (Western Sahara)
PSC	Peace and Security Council (of the AU)

RCD	Congolese Rally for Democracy (DRC)
RECs	Regional Economic Communities (Africa)
RENAMO	the Mozambican Resistance Movement
RFDG	Rally of Democratic Forces of Guinea
RPF	Rwandan Patriotic Front
RUF	Revolutionary United Front (Sierra Leone)
SAC	structural adjustment credit
SADC	Southern African Development Community
SADCBRIG	SADC Brigade
SADR	Sahrawi Arab Democratic Republic
SEA	sexual exploitation and abuse
SLA	Sierra Leone Army
SLM/A	Sudan Liberation Movement/Army
SNM	Somali National Movement
SPLM/A	Sudan People's Liberation Movement/Army
SRRA	Sudan Relief and Rehabilitation Association
SSR	security sector reform
TFG	Transitional Federal Government (Somalia)
TPLF	Tigray People's Liberation Front
TRC	Truth and Reconciliation Commission
TSZ	temporary security zone (Ethiopia–Eritrea)
UCDP	Uppsala Conflict Data Programme
UIC	Union of Islamic Courts (Somalia)
UK	United Kingdom
ULIMO	United Liberation Movement of Liberia for Democracy
UN	United Nations
UNAMID	AU/UN Hybrid Operation in Darfur
UNAMIR	UN Assistance Mission for Rwanda
UNAMSIL	UN Mission in Sierra Leone
UNASOG	UN Aouzou Strip Observer Group
UNAVEM	UN Angola Verification Mission
UNCTAD	UN Conference on Trade and Development
UNDP	UN Development Programme
UNEP	UN Environment Programme
UNITA	National Union for the Total Independence of Angola
UNITAF	Unified Task Force (Somalia)
UNMEE	UN Mission in Ethiopia and Eritrea
UNMIL	UN Mission in Liberia
UNMIS	UN Mission in Sudan
UNOCI	UN Operation in Côte d'Ivoire
UNOMIL	UN Observer Mission in Liberia
UNOMSIL	UN Observer Mission in Sierra Leone
UNOMUR	UN Observer Mission in Rwanda–Uganda

UNOSOM   UN Mission in Somalia
UPDA   Ugandan People's Democratic Army
UPDF   Ugandan People's Defence Force
US   United States of America
WHO   World Health Organization
ZANU-PF   Zimbabwe African National Union-Patriotic Front

Acknowledgements

In the course of writing this book I have accrued a number of debts and I am pleased to acknowledge them here. First of all, the generosity, support and constructive criticism of two good friends, Alex Bellamy and Ian Taylor, have been invaluable. Over the past fifteen years Alex and I have collaborated on numerous projects, and my thinking on a whole range of issues, especially peace operations, owes a great deal to his insights. Once again, he provided extensive comments on the draft manuscript. It is also well over a decade since Ian welcomed a strange PhD student into his home in South Africa, and he has been teaching me things about politics in Africa ever since. We have also worked together on various projects related to Africa's international relations and I have learned a great deal in the process. Ian too offered suggestions about how to improve the draft manuscript.

Many of the ideas in this book have been discussed with the MA students who took my 'War and Conflict in Africa' class at the Elliott School of International Affairs. Whether or not they appreciated it at the time, I learned a great deal during our seminars. I hope they did too and that the finished product might prove useful in the important work many of them are doing related to Africa. The book also benefited from the research assistance provided by three Elliott School students: Matthew Hughes compiled the index; Matthew Hickey collected documentation related to Africa's sub-regional arrangements; and Katrina Timlin located and summarized various studies relevant to the chapter on religion and provided feedback on the Introduction.

At Polity, I am pleased to acknowledge the help and advice I received from Emma Hutchinson, David Winters, Caroline Richmond and especially Louise Knight. I am proud that this book is being published by the team at Polity – they are consummate professionals and a model for what political publishing should be about.

Conducting research on African issues can be expensive, and while writing this book I was fortunate to receive financial support which facilitated travel, research assistance and relevant interviews from the UK's Economic and Research Council's New Security Challenges programme and the Elliott School of International Affairs. I also want to say thank you to the many people within governments, international organizations, NGOs, academia and the general public who provided me with relevant documents or took the time to discuss with me issues of war and peace in Africa.

Whatever its shortcomings, this book is definitely better than it would have been due to the helpful comments I received on earlier drafts from Alex Bellamy, Stuart Croft, Jon Elliott, Lee Ann Fujii, Linda Melvern and Ian Taylor. Polity's two anonymous readers also deserve a special mention for providing many constructive suggestions on how to improve the manuscript. Thank you. Naturally, I am solely responsible for any remaining errors.

Finally, I want to thank my wife, Ariela Blätter, whose love and support has made it all possible. This one's for you!

PDW
Washington, DC, November 2010

Introduction

In its 2003 *Human Development Report*, the UN Development Programme described the 1990s as 'a decade of despair'. During this time it noted that fifty-four countries around the world, many of them African, underwent development in reverse, ending up less developed at the start of the twenty-first century than they had been in 1990. Twenty-one states had a larger proportion of people going hungry; fourteen had more children dying before the age of five; twelve had seen primary school enrolments shrink; and, in thirty-four, life expectancy had fallen.[1] Warfare played a significant part in these dire outcomes.

Africa's wars have cost the continent dear in many respects: they have killed many millions of people, most through the effects of disease and malnutrition exacerbated by displacement; they have left in their wake a traumatized generation of children and young adults; they have broken bonds of trust among and across local communities that will be immensely difficult to repair; they have shattered education and healthcare systems; they have disrupted transportation routes and infrastructure; and they have done untold damage to the continent's ecology, from its land and waterways to its flora and fauna. In financial terms, one estimate suggested that these wars have cost Africa well over $700 billion in damages since 2000 alone.[2] Yet, for all the powerful statistics, there are still no clear answers as to *why* these terrible things happened. As Krijn Peters and Paul Richards concluded, unfortunately, 'much of the hard work in explaining recent African wars remains to be done.'[3]

The first aim of this book therefore is to try and understand why Africa experienced so many armed conflicts after the Cold War. The second aim is to examine how international society tried to end those wars and reduce the risk of future conflicts on the continent. To do this, the book addresses three central questions: first, What were the main trends in Africa's armed conflicts after the Cold War (1990–2009)?, second, What accounts for those armed conflicts?, and, third, How did international society try and bring them to an

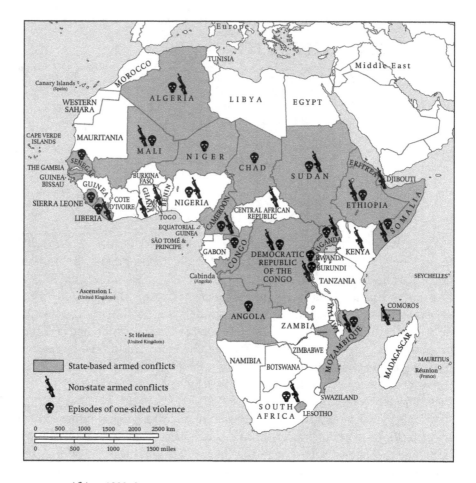

Africa, 1990–9

end? The book's three parts – contexts, ingredients and responses – reflect these central concerns.

With regard to terminology, I define conflict as the pursuit of incompatible goals by different groups. My focus here is on a subset of conflict, namely, warfare, defined as the use of organized violence by collectivities for political purposes which results in casualties. Warfare is not characterized solely by violence but is a social and political condition which affects the lives of those touched by it in many different ways, not all of which relate directly to acts of violence.[4] By politics, I mean the process through which individuals and groups decide who gets what, when and how.[5]

My central argument draws on the major insight of the war and society approach, namely, that the nature of armed conflict in post-Cold War Africa is in many respects a consequence of state–society relations and the particular dynamics associated with the politics of regime survival across much of the

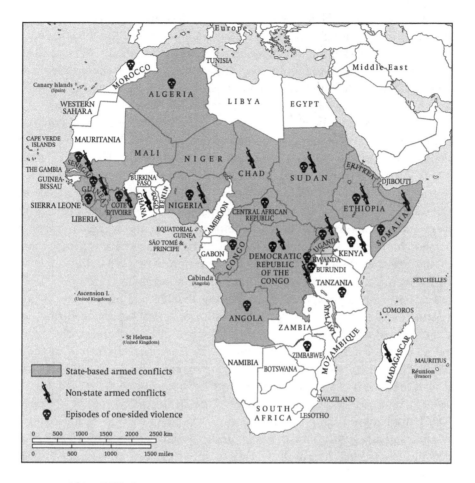

Africa, 2000–9

continent.[6] Specifically, regime survival strategies often provided the crucial intersection between local political dynamics and international networks, structures and processes.[7] Particularly when a regime's legitimacy was challenged, these strategies frequently involved instrumentalizing disorder and using violence to assert authority. It is in this sense that many of Africa's wars owe a great deal to the combustible mix of state institutions which struggled to maintain legitimacy among the domestic population and the political strategies of regimes seeking to preserve their privileged status within this context.

Why Africa?

In this book, Africa refers to the territory of the fifty-three members of the African Union (AU) plus Morocco. My focus on the continent is not meant to suggest there is something exceptional about the reasons why Africans fight

– indeed, as one scholar noted, 'African conflicts are remarkably unexceptional'.[8] They are fought for reasons as complex as those fought elsewhere. As even a cursory examination of recent conflicts in the Balkans, the Caucasus, South and Southeast Asia, Colombia, Afghanistan and elsewhere illustrates, debates about how governance structures, resources, sovereignty, ethnicity or religion are related to warfare are certainly not restricted to Africa.

The first reason to focus on Africa is the sheer volume of armed conflicts the continent experienced over the last two decades. In addition, two trends make post-Cold War Africa a particularly interesting case. First, during the 1990s it suffered from a rise in the number of armed conflicts as other parts of the developing world were experiencing a significant reduction. Thus, by the start of the twenty-first century, more people were being killed in Africa's wars than in the rest of the world combined.[9] Second, the average number of armed conflicts in Africa starting each year during the 1990s was twice that of the previous decade.[10] This begs the question, why? What happened in Africa before or during the 1990s that can account for these trends?

The news was still appalling during the first decade of the twenty-first century. Between 1999 and 2008, for instance, Africa experienced thirteen major armed conflicts, the highest total for any region of the world.[11] And yet some good news did start to emerge. By 2006 more than half of these conflicts had come to an end and, according to one estimate, the toll of battle deaths dropped by 98 per cent from the peak of about 100,000 reached during 1999 (primarily on account of the wars in the Democratic Republic of Congo [DRC] and between Ethiopia and Eritrea).[12] The news was also more positive when comparing Africa to the rest of the world: whereas in 1999 Africa accounted for nearly half of the world's major armed conflicts, by 2008 it was home to just one in five.[13] (The continent represents just over one-quarter of the UN's member states and just under one-sixth of the world's population.)

Two areas where the news remained decidedly bad, however, concerned non-state armed conflicts and one-sided violence (see chapter 1).[14] With regard to the former, Africa suffered more non-state armed conflicts after the Cold War than any other region of the world. With regard to the latter, between 1997 and 2006, 42 per cent of actors engaged in one-sided violence anywhere in the world were in Africa. This type of violence occurred before, during and after armed conflicts and was carried out by both non-state groups and governments.

A second reason to focus on Africa is that it challenges some of the standard conceptual frameworks used by students of contemporary war. Not least, it raises difficult questions for the trinitarian view of warfare popularized by Carl von Clausewitz's unfinished classic *On War*.[15] African cases often blurred the distinctions between Clausewitz's central categories of the government, the military and society. Consequently, they rarely sat comfortably within the nationalist frame of reference with which Clausewitz was operating and require different tools of analysis which capture today's more tangled and transnationalized state–society relations.[16]

A third rationale is that Africa's wars commonly suffered from rather simplistic explanations or – even worse – depictions that verged on the racist. Too many outsiders have looked at African war zones and seen little other than an inexplicable and exotic blend of modern technology and pre-modern (often irrational) barbarism. A closer look, however, reveals that, while psychotic individuals were usually present, as they are across the world's conflict zones, their presence alone does not explain why Africa's wars occurred or why these conflicts assumed the forms they did.

Finally, Africa suffers from some of the most intractable conflicts on the planet. The difficulty of resolving them was particularly evident if measured by the number of peace agreements warring parties signed but which either collapsed or failed to produce anything remotely resembling stable peace. The conflicts in Liberia and Somalia, for example, both resulted in the collapse of over a dozen peace agreements of one sort or another. Africa's conflict zones therefore posed severe headaches for the world's mediators and its peacekeepers with missions involving over 15,000 personnel deployed at various times to five African states (Liberia, Somalia, Sierra Leone, the DRC and Sudan). These conflict zones also proved to be some of the most difficult laboratories for international attempts to provide humanitarian assistance and promote development.

Understanding Africa's Wars: From Causes to Recipes

Accounting for Africa's glut of armed conflicts is a daunting task. First, there is the huge problem of gathering accurate information. Not only is it sometimes dangerous to collect, there is also no consensus on what analysts should be looking for. Simply put, our data about what goes on before, during and after Africa's wars are poor. It is therefore important to acknowledge at the outset that when it comes to Africa's war zones the foundations of our knowledge are distinctly shaky. This is a particularly important – and usually under-acknowledged – issue for quantitative studies about the continent's wars. As discussed in chapter 1, analysts have regularly disagreed on the basic question of how many armed conflicts were going on at any given time. In part, this problem came down to different analysts adopting different definitions of war and civil war.[17] But it was exacerbated by the difficulties of collecting accurate information about what was happening on the ground.

A second, more philosophical challenge is that there is always more than one story to tell about why a particular armed conflict occurred. The search for a single, all-encompassing theory of what causes warfare, or even what caused a particular war, has been a source of controversy for a long, long time. Indeed, there is probably much to be said for the historian's preference to limit oneself to understanding the origins of particular wars rather than searching for the causes of warfare in general. Dissatisfaction with a focus on direct causation has led a variety of analysts to frame their theories of violence in terms of increasing/decreasing probabilities and greater/lesser levels of risk.[18] Nevertheless, the search for a general theory of warfare has persisted, with two approaches proving particularly durable: those which frame the causes of war as a level-of-analysis problem and those which locate the fundamental cause of organized violence in human biology/genetics.[19] While I think the former approach is far more useful for this book (see chapter 2), I agree with Michael Brown's conclusion that 'the best scholarly studies of internal conflict are powerful precisely because they do not rely on single-factor explanations. Instead they try to weave several factors into a more complex argument.'[20]

With this in mind, it is useful to recall several broad distinctions which have been used to help think about complex stories of war occurrence. The first is between necessary conditions and sufficient conditions. In relation to warfare, necessary conditions are those things which must exist in order for war to occur – i.e. without X, war cannot occur. At a very basic level, the capacity for humans to form political communities and demonstrate the ability to kill one another is necessary in the sense that it is logically presupposed by the definition of war used here.[21] We might also say that, because war is a matter of choice, acts of belligerence and acts of resistance are necessary conditions for war.[22] Sufficient conditions, in contrast, are phenomena which, if present, we know war will break out – i.e. if X, then war will follow. At the abstract level, we might suggest that the existence of several factors simultaneously might meet the definition of a sufficient condition for war. For example, when groups of humans with the ability to kill one another exist, and when one group's belligerent act is met with an act of resistance by another group, war will occur. In more practical terms, however, to my knowledge, the vast literature on the causes of war has failed to identify any convincing examples of empirical phenomena which satisfy the definition of being a sufficient condition for war. In this sense, the distinction between necessary conditions and sufficient conditions is not particularly useful for tackling the questions posed in this book.

A more useful distinction is between underlying or permissive factors and catalytic or trigger factors.[23] While the former identify dispositions which make organized violence more likely, they do not allow us to explain why wars break out in some cases where these underlying factors are present but not in others. Trigger factors, on the other hand, emphasize the fact that, to engage in warfare/armed conflict, particular actors must choose to do so – i.e. at a basic level one must choose to go on the offensive or to resist attack rather than surrender. Triggers thus refer to those forces or factors which generate actions or policies that represent the conscious choices of particular actors to engage in political violence.

In one sense, therefore, this book can be seen as a challenge to some of the more popular approaches to thinking about Africa's wars which reduce their complexity to a single issue or binary problems. Among the most common of these 'big ideas' is the tendency to blame Africa's wars on colonialism, postcolonial elites, ethnicity and greedy criminals, respectively.

Especially within Africa, colonialism is often identified as the root cause of the continent's current wars. As one analyst recently argued, 'There is hardly any zone of conflict in contemporary Africa that cannot trace its sordid violence to colonial history.'[24] The usual mechanisms of colonial responsibility were said to be the favouring of particular local groups over others and the drawing of arbitrary borders which forced different peoples to live together – or split similar peoples apart – thus sowing the seeds of discord and exacerbating the likelihood of war. The basic problem with this argument is that, while colonialism is an important underlying factor, it is not a principal cause or trigger of contemporary conflicts. In this sense, colonialism certainly represents a piece of Africa's war puzzle, but as an explanation for the continent's contemporary conflicts it is flimsy. Among its biggest problems are the fact that colonialism was far from monolithic in both its practices and legacies and that significant portions of postcolonial Africa (and elsewhere) have remained free from armed conflicts; it does not explain why the 1980s and 1990s in particular proved to be such devastating decades for the continent; and it almost entirely eliminates African agency and responsibility from wars fought predominantly by Africans.

A second common argument, this time at the opposite end of the colonial responsibility spectrum, was to put the blame firmly on Africa's postcolonial ruling elites.[25] It was hardly surprising that Tony Blair's Commission for Africa, for example, suggested that Africa's fundamental problem was its lack of 'good governance' – the polite way of saying that peace would require stamping out the continent's 'big man culture' which was the root cause of its wars and underdevelopment.[26] But African initiatives have also blamed local politicians. Sierra Leone's Truth and Reconciliation Commission, for instance, concluded that the primary cause of its civil war 'was years of bad governance, endemic corruption and the denial of basic human rights that created the deplorable conditions that made conflict inevitable'.[27] Other variants of this view suggested that neighbouring regimes and diasporas were often more responsible for Africa's contemporary wars than former colonial powers. While this perspective brought African agency back in, its focus on local triggers downplayed the international forces and structures which increased the risks of war on the continent, such as the global trade in conflict goods, the deeply divisive policies promoted by international financial institutions, and the practice of adopting international business as usual with what Robert Jackson famously described as 'quasi-states' – those political entities granted juridical sovereignty despite their lack of domestic legitimacy (see chapter 5).[28]

A third big idea was that, in Africa, ethnicity kills. According to this view, Africa's wars were basically tribal conflicts fought between competing ethnic groups.[29] This tended to appear in two main varieties: the 'ethnic hatreds' and 'ethnic fears' perspectives.[30] The former suggested that hatred of different ethnic groups persisted over generations but remained dormant or simmered until something triggered an explosion of mass violence against the hated group. In the second variant, political leaders and other elites stoked mass fear of some ethnic 'other' using media, organized riots, arbitrary arrests, etc., in order to further their political agendas. The ensuing insecurity dilemma pushed ordinary people to react violently. As discussed in chapter 6, the big problems here were twofold. First, ethnic difference explained virtually nothing – and certainly not why groups went to war. Even in the hatreds and fears versions noted above, it was emotions (hatred and fear) that were doing at least as much explanatory work as ethnic solidarity. Second, even when understood as an underlying condition for violence, the fact remained that, during the post-Cold War period, Africa's most ethnically diverse states were among its most peaceful. On the other hand, African countries where ethnic differences were minimal (e.g. Rwanda) or virtually non-existent (e.g. Somalia) were among the bloodiest.

A fourth popular explanation for Africa's wars put the blame squarely on greedy warlords. Championed by a group of economists associated with the World Bank, this approach argued that civil wars were caused either by political grievances or by economic opportunities and, since grievances were virtually omnipresent in Africa but civil wars were not, the answer must lie on the economic/greed side of the equation. Africa's wars were therefore blamed on greedy criminals – indeed, insurgency itself was conceptualized as being like any other criminal activity, except that it was rarer than petty theft because of the greater risks and the significant start-up costs incurred.[31] This greed thesis proved hugely popular with policymakers but it too suffered from many serious problems (see chapter 4). Perhaps its most fundamental errors were to suggest the study of the causes of war was synonymous with the study of individual motivations and that greed and grievance were clearly separable categories when in fact there has never been such a thing as an apolitical war.[32] Indeed, it was revealing that the main advocates of this approach, Paul Collier and Anke Hoeffler, changed their tune: after years of apparently proving that civil wars were all about economic motives they launched their new 'feasibility thesis' – the idea that 'where civil war is feasible it will occur without reference to motivation'.[33]

In light of these points, it would be better to discard these 'big ideas' about the principal cause of Africa's wars and instead think about the many different recipes for making wars and the multiple ingredients which go into them.[34] Thinking of warfare in culinary terms may sound odd, but the metaphor is useful for several reasons. First, wars are complex social systems and, like particular dishes, are comprised of multiple ingredients. Second, because the ingredients can be combined in a variety of different ways, recipes, like wars, don't always turn out as planned and, as with wars, it pays to have the correct instruments to hand at the right time. Third, like wars, recipes don't make themselves – there must be cooks, and it is important to know whether one is dealing with a novice or a master chef. As any beginner in the kitchen will testify, a list of ingredients is little use without details about the proportions, preparation techniques and cooking instructions through which separate items should be combined to produce the dish in question. So it is with the causes of war. Moreover, there is always scope to develop new twists on old recipes or invent new dishes, just as humans have proved inventive at finding different things to fight about.

Darfur's Recipe for War

Take the case of the war in Darfur, Sudan. Clearly the immediate trigger was the formation of insurgent organizations which had the motives, means and opportunity to engage in armed resistance against the government's belligerence. But what were the factors that made this possible? What were the main ingredients and who were the principal chefs in Darfur's recipe for war?

One perspective suggested the key ingredient was the oppressive nature of the longstanding relationship between the dominant core of Khartoum and Sudan's marginalized peripheral zones. The key chefs were the military and theocratic elites which propped up President al-Bashir's regime. As Douglas Johnson put it, in many respects, Sudan was little more than 'a constellation of underdeveloped regions'.[35] After decades of marginalization, Darfur's war was triggered by local resistance groups who demanded a greater say in the region's governance and a better deal from the country's repressive centre.

A related argument described the war as an almost inevitable consequence of the 'turbulent' nature of the Sudanese state.[36] Specifically, it was the product of a Sudanese state governed by a hyper-dominant but politically unstable centre characterized by competing elite factions in Khartoum, none of which had been able to establish complete dominance over the others. The result of this longstanding and inherently turbulent state of affairs was that 'provincial war and destabilization' became 'the habitual modus operandi of the Khartoum elites'.[37]

A third view saw the key ingredient as ethnic tensions between Darfur's 'Arab' and 'African' populations, but once again they were manipulated by Khartoum's war chefs. The local 'lighter-skinned' 'Arab' fighters, commonly labelled as the *janjawiid*, were aroused, armed and supported by the government of Sudan and promised various rewards, mainly land and plunder, in exchange for their efforts to put down the rebellious 'black' 'Africans'.[38]

A fourth perspective pointed to religious ingredients, specifically the intra-Islamic dimensions of the conflict and the struggle over what should count as the authentic version of Islam and what its relationship should be to the apparatus of the Sudanese state.[39] These disputes rose to a new level of intensity with the distribution in May 2000 of *The Black Book: Imbalance of Power and Wealth in Sudan*. The book was heavily critical of the ruling National Islamic Front and its inability to govern Sudan according to appropriate Islamic codes.[40] Calling themselves 'The Seekers of Truth and Justice', the authors of *The Black Book* were members of the Islamist movement aligned against President Bashir and who would later go on to become influential architects of the rebel group Justice and Equality Movement (JEM).

A fifth set of views emphasized that war in Darfur could not have been cooked up without the longstanding system of regional conflicts that had developed since the 1960s between the Sudan, Chad, Libya and, to a lesser extent, the Central African Republic. From this perspective, the current conflict was simply the latest episode in which Darfur became involved in a violent cycle of cross-border dynamics. This time around, the principal chefs of various proxy wars were the regimes in Khartoum and N'djamena.[41]

Finally, there were those who argued that war was precipitated by a structural brew of resource scarcity and changing environmental conditions. This resource-based argument had many variants. One version saw the key ingredient as being 'land envy' rather than 'ethnic hatred'.[42] The UN's Special Envoy to Darfur, for example, said this was in essence a 'fight about grass' between Arab nomadic herders and African pastoralists.[43] A second variant saw climate change as a key ingredient, with UN Secretary-General Ban Ki-moon concluding that the underlying problem was an 'ecological crisis, arising at least in part from climate change'.[44]

The war in Darfur was thus framed simultaneously as a war about governance, the state and issues of self-determination; as an ethnic conflict; as religious fratricide; and as a resource war. Were all these explanations equally accurate? Were all these factors equally significant? Were any of them sufficient or even necessary to have caused the war? The answer to all three questions is almost certainly 'no'. But they were all arguably ingredients in Darfur's recipe for war.

Structure of the Book

With this in mind, the book's structure revolves around the three central questions noted above. Part I, 'Contexts', provides an overview of the statistical, conceptual and political background on which I base the subsequent analysis of the key ingredients in, and international responses to, Africa's wars. Chapter 1 analyses several attempts to count the number and scale of Africa's armed conflicts, focusing particularly on the post-Cold War period. Chapter 2 provides a conceptual and political sketch of the terrain of struggle upon which they were waged. Conceptually, it concentrates on social forces and state–society complexes and frames Africa's wars as a levels-of-analysis problem. The chapter then summarizes and explains the central political characteristics of Africa's post-Cold War conflict zones.

Part II, 'Ingredients', reflects upon the period between 1990 and 2009 in order to understand the relationship between five issues and Africa's armed conflicts. These chapters do not provide an exhaustive list of ingredients, but I believe they address the most widely debated issues related to Africa's wars during this period, namely, governance, resources, sovereignty, ethnicity and religion. Chapter 3 analyses the extent to which governance was related to Africa's armed conflicts by focusing on dynamics within the neopatrimonial regimes found in many of the continent's weak states. In chapter 4, I assess the extent to which so-called natural resources were a key ingredient in Africa's wars. Chapter 5 tackles the key issues related to statehood and armed conflict, namely sovereignty and the associated concept of self-determination. In chapter 6, I examine the construction and manipulation of ethnic identities as an ingredient in warfare, while chapter 7 discusses the relationship between warfare and one of the most powerful belief systems known to humans: religion.

Part III, 'Responses', also reflects on the two decades since the end of the Cold War but this time analysing the major international efforts to end Africa's wars. Chapter 8 examines international efforts to build a new African Peace and Security Architecture (APSA), which despite its title was a collaborative enterprise between African and non-African states and organizations. After providing an overview of this architecture and some of its limitations, the focus of chapters 9 and 10 is on its two main policy instruments: peace-making initiatives and peacekeeping operations. The former discusses international attempts to build stable peace through mediation, while the latter examines the major challenges that confronted the scores of peace operations which were deployed to the same end. Finally, chapter 11 analyses the main challenges faced by the two principal forms of external aid to Africa's war zones: humanitarian relief and development assistance.

The conclusion briefly summarizes the main findings from parts II and III and reflects upon what they might mean for designing more effective responses to warfare in the future.

PART I

Contexts

CHAPTER ONE

Counting Africa's Conflicts (and their Casualties)

'Wars', the Political Instability Task Force concluded, 'can not be measured exactly but only estimated'.[1] This is certainly true in Africa, where information about the continent's conflicts is notoriously incomplete, unreliable and usually part of somebody's propaganda machine. There are, of course, basic obstacles to data-gathering such as personal safety and security, but part of the problem is that analysts are often looking for different things. Most of the attempts to count Africa's wars have been based on information produced by governments and international organizations. But this is not without its problems. First of all, most African states have lacked stable and effective bureaucracies charged with collecting relevant information. Second, much of these data apply to the national level and hence can conceal huge differences across different parts of a country. Third, reliance on government statistics has produced data-sets which have tended to be state-centric, looking at what governments did rather than how violence enters into societal interactions more broadly. As I discuss below, shifting our collective gaze from states to social forces, specifically to take account of armed non-state actors, could be the single most important factor in rethinking and recalculating the statistics of war and conflict in Africa (and probably in many other parts of the world as well). Certainly, the preliminary data collected by the Uppsala Conflict Data Programme about 'non-state armed conflicts' should change the way we think about, and count, organized violence in post-Cold War Africa.

The purpose of this chapter is to provide an overview of the patterns of armed conflict in Africa, thereby providing a broader historical context of warfare in post-colonial Africa in which to situate the analysis that follows in parts II and III of the book.[2] In particular, I examine how analysts have answered such basic questions as what counts as an armed conflict – and hence what is the universe of relevant cases? Where does Africa fit into global conflict trends? And, how many people have died as a result of Africa's wars?

I do this by approaching questions about the statistics of Africa's conflicts from two directions. First, at a macro-level, I compare three frameworks and data-sets that have catalogued the number, type and intensity of Africa's armed conflicts. Second, at a more micro-level, I look at the problems and politics of trying to develop rigorous and comprehensive information about Africa's wars by examining attempts to count the casualties of the war in

Darfur, Sudan (2003–present) and the Democratic Republic of Congo (1998–present). For different reasons, both these wars attracted unprecedented efforts to measure the human death toll, but in neither case did clear answers emerge.

The basic argument can be summarized quickly. At the macro-level, not only is there no consensus over how to count Africa's armed conflicts but analysts have ignored the non-state dimensions of organized violence for too long. At the micro end of the spectrum, all statistics are political and unreliable, and core assumptions about levels of baseline mortality can have drastic effects on the conclusions reached.

Counting Armed Conflicts in Africa

There is no simple and uncontested answer to the question: 'How many armed conflicts has Africa witnessed in the post-Cold War period?'. Nevertheless, a good place to start is with the answers provided by three relevant efforts to compile data: the Political Instability Task Force (PITF), Monty Marshall's 2006 study for the UK government and the Uppsala Conflict Data Programme (UCDP).

The Political Instability Task Force version

The PITF was originally formed in 1994 at the request of senior policymakers in the US government. It comprised a core group of ten to fifteen leading scholars from various US universities, and its remit was 'to assess and explain the vulnerability of states around the world to political instability and state failure'. The Task Force's aspiration was to 'develop statistical models that can accurately assess countries' prospects for major political change and can identify key risk factors of interest to US policymakers'. Regardless of the predictive quality of its subsequent models, the PITF's data-set provides a useful starting point for studying the broad contours of armed conflict in postcolonial Africa. It catalogues a variety of 'state failure events' which encompass a range of severe political conflicts and regime crises, specifically, revolutionary wars, ethnic wars, adverse regime changes, and genocides and politicides.[3]

The Task Force's concept of 'complex events', such as those in Sudan between 1983 and the present and Chad between 1965 and 1994, is particularly useful in the African context. These complex events are understood as being 'made up of two or more temporally linked wars and crises. If events overlap or if five years or less separate the end of one event and the onset of the next distinct event, they are combined into complex events (subsequent flareups of events are considered continuations).' This concept is useful precisely because Africa's wars rarely have neat beginnings or endings. As David Keen observed, in Africa as elsewhere, 'peacetime' and 'wartime' share some

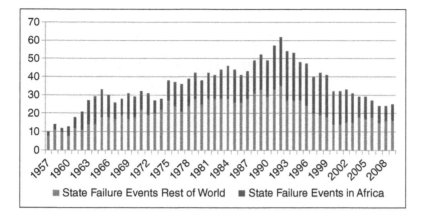

Figure 1.1 *Number of state failure events, 1955–2009*

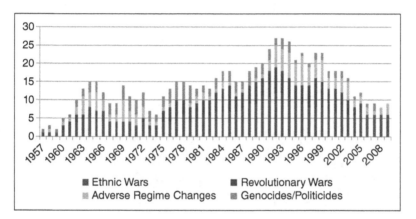

Figure 1.2 *State failure events in Africa, 1955–2009*

important characteristics, not least the existence of significant numbers of violent deaths and the willingness to use violence to accumulate resources and repress opponents.[4]

Using the PITF data, figure 1.1 demonstrates that during the period 1955–2009 approximately 40 per cent of all state failure events globally took place in Africa. Of the four categories of PITF state failure events, most of these were either ethnic or revolutionary wars, although, especially during the 1990s, adverse regime changes account for a significant percentage (see figure 1.2).

Given my focus on armed conflicts, it seems appropriate to discard the PITF category of adverse regime changes and concentrate instead on those events that are defined by a degree of organized violence: ethnic and revolutionary wars, as well as genocides and politicides. At its peak, in 2000, Africa accounted for 67 per cent of revolutionary wars worldwide (see figure 1.3). Moreover, between 1997 and 2003 the continent was consistently home to at least 50 per cent of the world's revolutionary wars. In 2006–9, however, there were

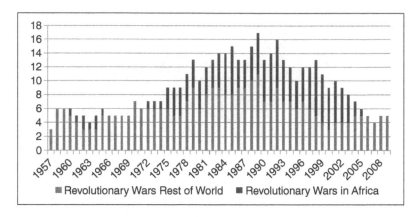

Figure 1.3 *Number of revolutionary wars, 1955–2009*

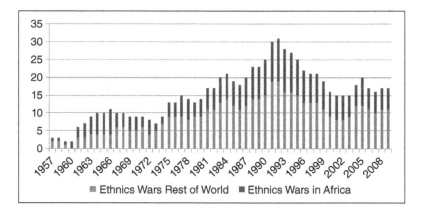

Figure 1.4 *Number of ethnic wars, 1955–2009*

no such wars taking place within Africa. A similar picture is evident in relation to ethnic wars. At its peak in 2001 and 2002, Africa accounted for 47 per
cent of the world's ethnic conflicts, and from 1990 to 2009 the continent
consistently endured more than one-third of the world's ethnic conflicts (see
figure 1.4). The picture is even starker in relation to genocides and politicides
(see figure 1.5). For long periods (1996–7 and 2000–7) Africa was the only
continent to experience such forms of violence, and between 1993 and 2007
the continent never suffered less than 50 per cent of the world's genocides
and politicides.

Monty Marshall's version

In 2006 one of the members of the PITF conducted a study for the UK government's Africa Conflict Prevention Pool that focused specifically on the incidence and magnitude of armed conflict in sub-Saharan Africa.[5] Interestingly,

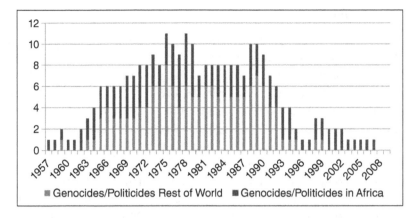

Figure 1.5 *Number of genocides and politicides, 1955–2009*

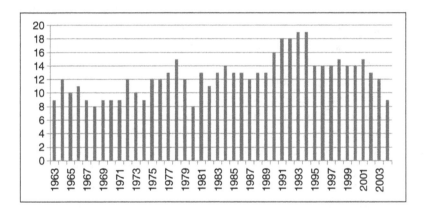

Figure 1.6 *Number of major armed conflicts in sub-Saharan Africa, 1963–2004*

Marshall departed from the PITF framework by identifying eighty-five epi-sodes of major armed conflict in the region between 1963 and 2004. These were defined as 'episodes of organized and sustained, collective violence during the course of which there occur at least 500 direct, battle-related deaths at a rate in excess of 100 deaths per annum'. Episodes include wars of independence, interstate warfare, civil warfare and political mass murder (all of which involve direct action by state authorities) and intercommunal vio-lence (in which the state is not directly involved). It should be noted that Marshall's data-set was not only restricted to sub-Saharan Africa but it focused on 'major armed conflicts' rather than wars and hence operated with a lower threshold of battle-related deaths (at least 500) compared with the PITF data-set (which required at least 1,000 for a violent episode to count as an ethnic or revolutionary war). Figure 1.6 shows the distribution of major armed con-flicts in sub-Saharan Africa between 1963 and 2004 according to Marshall's calculations.

The Uppsala Conflict Data Programme version

A third source of relevant data is the Uppsala Conflict Data Programme (UCDP).[6] Particularly since the end of the Cold War, the UCDP has developed different types of data as more and more questions have arisen about how to count and classify episodes of organized violence and how to think about conflict management. It is organized around two types of armed conflict: state-based (where one of the warring parties is a government) and non-state (where organized, collective armed violence occurs but where a recognized government is not one of the parties). The UCDP defines an armed conflict as a contested incompatibility that concerns government or territory, or both, where the use of armed force between two parties results in at least twenty-five battle-related deaths. Wars involve at least 1,000 battle-related deaths in a calendar year. The complete UCDP list of state-based armed conflicts in Africa between 1990 and 2009 is provided in Appendix A.

Using UCDP data, post-Cold War Africa experienced approximately one-third of the world's state-based armed conflicts (see figure 1.7). Calculated by the number of states, Africa represents fifty-three out of the now 192 UN members, or 28 per cent. Calculated with reference to human population, the continent has approximately 930 million out of the global total of 6,600 million, or 14 per cent. By either measure, Africa has suffered more than its fair share of armed conflicts. In absolute terms, Africa often endured more than a dozen state-based armed conflicts, almost all of which have been of the intra-state or internationalized intra-state variety.

Comparing these three data-sets is difficult in one sense because each of them operates with a different definition of a relevant armed conflict. Nevertheless, it is worth undertaking a comparison because all of them set out to measure episodes of organized violence in Africa and elsewhere. When the data-sets are compared, several conclusions become apparent (see figure 1.8). First, while

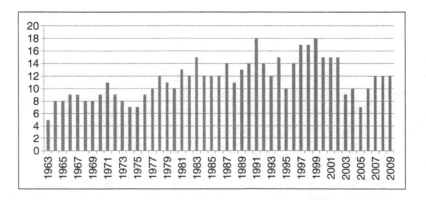

Figure 1.7 *Number of state-based armed conflicts in Africa, 1963–2009*

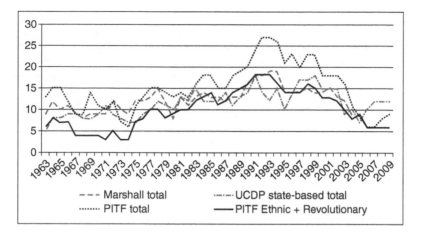

Figure 1.8 *Number of armed conflicts in Africa compared, 1963–2009*

they diverge over the exact numbers of armed conflicts in Africa, they agree on broad trends. For our purposes, two are particularly relevant: (1) there was a significant increase in armed conflicts during the 1980s; and (2) there has been a substantial decline (of approximately 50 per cent) in the number of armed conflicts during the post-Cold War period after the peak in 1991–2.

On occasion (i.e. 1991 and 1996) the three data-sets converge exactly. At other times, however, there are serious discrepancies of up to six armed conflicts remaining (e.g. 1992, 1993, 2007). In 1992, for example, table 1.1 shows the discrepancies for particular conflicts across the data-sets. It is particularly difficult to understand why the UCDP list is smaller than the other two data-sets, given its much smaller threshold for inclusion (twenty-five battle-related deaths).

While many factors may help explain these discrepancies, several issues stand out as noteworthy. First, given the low threshold of twenty-five or more battle-related deaths used by the UCDP, it is surprising that from 1990 to 1996 its data are lower than those of both the other approaches. Then again, it does not include incidents of one-sided violence which might figure in the other data-sets. In relation to Marshall's study, on the one hand, we should expect his data to produce slightly lower figures because they are restricted to sub-Saharan Africa (i.e. excluding North Africa) rather than taking in the entire continent. On the other hand, we would expect his data to include more episodes of armed conflicts than the PITF approach because his threshold of battle deaths for 'major armed conflicts' is half as much as that of the PITF for inclusion as an ethnic or revolutionary war. It would appear that the latter factor is more significant because Marshall's figures are often higher than those of the original PITF approach.

In sum, these data-sets show that, even on such a basic macro-level issue as 'How many ongoing armed conflicts are there?', the conclusions that follow

TABLE 1.1 List of armed conflicts in Africa for 1992

PITF (Ethnic + revolutionary)	Monty Marshall	UCDP
Algeria	X	Algeria
Angola (UNITA)	Angola (UNITA)	Angola (UNITA)
X	Angola (Cabinda)	X
Burundi	X	Burundi
Chad	Chad	Chad
Djibouti	Djibouti	Djibouti
Egypt	X	X
X	X	Ethiopia
Kenya	Kenya	X
Liberia	Liberia	X
Mali	Mali	X
Mozambique	Mozambique	Mozambique
X	Niger	Niger
X	Nigeria	X
Rwanda	Rwanda	Rwanda
Senegal	Senegal	Senegal
Sierra Leone	Sierra Leone	Sierra Leone
Somalia	Somalia	Somalia
South Africa	South Africa	South Africa
Sudan	Sudan	Sudan
Uganda	Uganda	Uganda
Zaire	Zaire	X

are built on contested foundations. Indeed, it might be more accurate not to talk of foundations for knowledge but instead recognize that our analysis is at best anchored to certain (contestable and potentially shifting) definitions and assumptions. That said, these approaches do agree on the broad trends in the number and type of armed conflicts in Africa after the Cold War.

A further limitation with these data is the lack of precise information about conflicts 'whose distinguishing feature is that none of the warring parties is a government'.[7] This is a problem because it has long been clear that non-state actors have played important roles in postcolonial Africa, including in relation to armed conflict.[8] Yet it was only in 2004 that the UCDP started to collect systematic data on what it called non-state armed conflicts.

The UCDP has now collected data on non-state armed conflicts in Africa between 1990 and 2009. The results are very instructive. During this period,

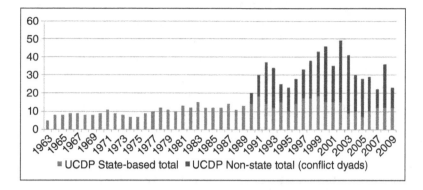

Figure 1.9 *State-based and non-state armed conflicts in Africa, 1963–2009*

the UCDP counted 287 non-state armed conflict dyads in twenty-four different states. These dyads and the fatalities they caused are listed in Appendix B. Somalia had the most non-state armed conflicts, with fifty-nine, while, overall, approximately 84 per cent of these conflicts occurred in just seven states (DRC, Ethiopia, Kenya, Nigeria, Somalia, Sudan and Uganda). The UCDP's best estimate for the combined total of fatalities for the 287 conflicts is 59,008. While Sudan experienced the highest number of these, with 12,451, it is interesting to note that approximately 77 per cent of all these fatalities occurred in just five states (DRC, Ethiopia, Nigeria, Somalia and Sudan). These figures mean that, on average, each of these non-state armed conflicts killed more than 205 people. Hence, with reference to the UCDP categories of armed conflict intensity, the vast majority count as minor or intermediate armed conflicts. Nevertheless, nine of them would register as wars, with over 1,000 fatalities. These took place in seven states (DRC x2, Ghana, Liberia, Nigeria, Somalia, South Africa and Sudan x2), with the two most deadly being the conflict between the SPLM/A and the South Sudan Defence Force (which killed 4,428 people) and the conflict between the Hema and Lendu peoples in the DRC (which killed 4,267 people).

These figures should significantly alter the way analysts think about organized violence in Africa. As figure 1.9 demonstrates, if the new sample of non-state armed conflicts is added into the UCDP's original list of state-based armed conflicts, it becomes obvious that analysts are missing a great deal by focusing solely on the latter category.

Counting the Casualties

How analysts count the casualties of war is important for both scholarly and political reasons. Intellectually, it is necessary to have at least a rough idea of the magnitude of the conflict and the numbers of casualties involved. Politically, efforts to count the dead and dying are important for attracting international attention and humanitarian assistance and for debates about possible intervention. But, inevitably, any estimates become entangled in the propaganda wars of the belligerents (and other groups). As Douglas Johnson noted in the case of Sudan, when it comes to producing casualty estimates the point of the exercise is often to attract attention to one's cause.[9] Without exception, the process of estimating the casualties in Africa's armed conflicts is incredibly daunting and potentially very dangerous work. Not only do analysts usually lack comprehensive and reliable demographic data (such as census information and birth and mortality rates) about life before the armed conflict started, they will be extremely hard pressed to gather it after the outbreak of hostilities, especially in the areas most prone to violence.

The most recent war in Darfur, Sudan, provides a good illustration of the ways in which casualty estimates emerge, develop, become contested, subsequently fluctuate and then get recycled across various media outlets and political organizations. Table 1.2 sets out a (far from comprehensive)

TABLE 1.2 Measuring the death toll in Darfur

30 October 2003	Andrew Natsios, USAID administrator, says that between February and October 2003 the war has left 7,000 people dead.
22 March 2004	The UN estimates the death toll at 10,000.
23 April 2004	Richard Williamson, US Ambassador to the UN, suggests the death toll is 30,000.
26 April 2004	Andrew Natsios says reports of 30,000 killed cannot be confirmed.
13 May 2004	Sudanese Foreign Minister Mustafa Osman Ismail says only 1,000 have been killed.
4 July 2004	The *Washington Post* estimates that 30,000 people have been killed in the war.
23 July 2004	US Congressman Donald Payne says that 30,000 people have been killed.
23 July 2004	Jan Egeland, UN Head of Emergency Relief Coordination, says the death toll could be as high as 50,000.
9 August 2004	The UN estimates 30,000 to 50,000 dead. Sudanese Foreign Minister Ismail denies this, saying the number is 5,000, including 500 policemen.
2 September 2004	The International Rescue Committee estimates that there could be 200,000 to 300,000 deaths if the aid and security situation in Darfur does not improve.
13–14 September 2004	The World Health Organization (WHO) estimates that at least 50,000 people have been killed in attacks since February 2003.
1 October 2004	The WHO estimates that 6,000 to 10,000 civilians in Darfur are dying each month from violence and disease.

TABLE 1.2 *Continued*

6–7 October 2004	While UK Prime Minister Tony Blair visits Khartoum, news reports suggest that more than 50,000 have been killed in Darfur since February 2003.
15 October 2004	David Nabarro, the top WHO crisis official, estimates 70,000 people have died in Darfur displacement camps since March 2004 from malnutrition and disease.
17 October 2004	Mohammed Yusuf Ibrahim, Sudanese State Minister of Humanitarian Affairs, disputes the WHO claim and says that no more than 7,000 people have died.
20 January 2005	The Coalition for International Justice (CIJ) says that, in a survey conducted for the US State Department, 61 per cent of the 1,136 refugees surveyed had witnessed a family member killed. Eric Reeves, a professor of English language and literature at Smith College (USA), argues that, if this ratio holds for all of Darfur's 2 million displaced people, then 200,000 would be killed.
21 January 2005	The US government says more than 70,000 people have been killed.
9 March 2005	Jan Egeland declares that many more people than the 70,000 reported last year have died in Darfur, largely from preventable causes such as pneumonia and diarrhoea. Egeland maintains that the 70,000 figure was released when there were 1 million internally displaced in Darfur, but that number has since doubled. He is quoted as saying: 'Is it three times that? Is it five times that? I don't know, but it's several times the number of 70,000 that have died altogether.'
11 March 2005	Eric Reeves releases his twelfth assessment of mortality in Darfur and claims 380,000 dead.
16 March 2005	The UN revises its death toll estimate to 180,000 dead.
30 March 2005	The UK House of Commons International Development Committee estimates the death toll in Darfur to be 'somewhere around 300,000'.
21 April 2005	The Coalition for International Justice estimates the death toll in Darfur could be as high as 400,000 (140,000 directly from violence and 250,000 deaths from disease, starvation and other causes).
November 2006	After reporting at the time that the total deaths in Darfur from February 2003 to January 2005 were between 98,000 and 181,000, the US State Department concluded later that between 63,000 and 146,000 excess deaths had occurred.[10]
January 2010	An independent study based on a review of sixty-three different mortality surveys concluded that, for the period between March 2003 and December 2008, a reasonable estimate of the total deaths was 486,121 and 298,271 excess deaths. Of these, 62,305 (or less than 20 per cent) were said to be violence related.[11]

Source: CIJ, *Chronology.*

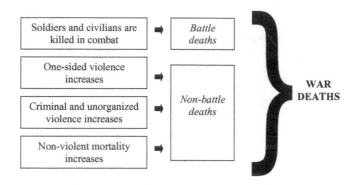

Source: Lacina and Gleditsch, 'Monitoring trends', p. 149.

Figure 1.10 *Sources of war deaths*

chronological overview of when different organizations and individuals produced estimates of the death toll in Darfur's war. It highlights not only the
contested and rather haphazard nature of the process but also how the casualty estimates are often used explicitly to justify a particular way of framing
the situation and/or the appropriate response(s). In addition, most organizations did not take the time to distinguish between total deaths and excess
deaths, with most using the former category.

Arguably, the most sophisticated framework and data-set for classifying
and estimating the human costs of war has been compiled by Bethany Ann
Lacina and Nils Petter Gleditsch (see figure 1.10). It covers the period 1946–
2005 and has been designed to be compatible with the information compiled
by the UCDP. Their data-set distinguishes between combatant deaths, battle
(or combat) deaths and non-battle deaths. Battle deaths are defined as 'deaths
resulting directly from violence inflicted through the use of armed force by
a party to an armed conflict during contested combat'.[12] This tells us how
many people were killed in military operations and provides the best measure
of combat intensity. However, it does not account for all losses in any given
armed conflict. To arrive at a more complete estimate of all war deaths, they
suggest that analysts need to include one-sided violence, criminal violence
and non-violent deaths.

In Lacina and Gleditsch's framework, battle is conceived as an encounter
involving at least two sides engaged in combat. One-sided violence, as the
name suggests, involves one side using violence and the other side suffering
the consequences. It might be soldiers firing on unarmed protestors, summary
executions of prisoners or genocide. The UCDP define one-sided violence as
'the use of armed force by the government of a state or by a formally organized group against civilians which results in at least 25 deaths. Extrajudicial
killings in custody are excluded.' The importance of including one-sided violence is highlighted by the UCDP's data on the phenomenon. Between 1990

and 2009, it identified around 100 campaigns of one-sided violence in Africa, far more than any other region of the world (listed in Appendix C). These were conducted by approximately eighty-five different actors (governments and non-state groups) in twenty-seven different states and resulted in an estimated 589,840 fatalities. The vast majority of the fatalities occurred in the 1994 Rwanda genocide, which, according to the UCDP, resulted in approximately 500,000 deaths. Of the remaining fatalities, approximately 47 per cent occurred in just two countries – DRC and Sudan.

Based on their data-set, Lacina and Gleditsch drew several general conclusions. First, since 1945, the military scale and combat intensity of armed conflicts has declined, in part because the number of large interstate wars has significantly reduced. In Africa, large-scale interstate wars have been notable for their absence, with the exception of Tanzania's invasion of Uganda (1978–9) and, more importantly, the Ethiopian–Eritrean war (1998–2000). Since then, the conflicts that come closest to being traditional interstate wars are those in the DRC (1998–2003) and Ethiopia's invasion of Somalia (2006–9). This should not, however, obscure the prevalence of African governments engaging in cross-border support for favoured rebel groups and periodic raids against rebel bases in neighbouring states.[13]

Second, they note that, from 1990 to 2002, approximately 93 per cent of all battle deaths resulted from intra-state conflicts, principally in sub-Saharan Africa and Central and South Asia. The numbers of battle deaths in Africa and the rest of the world between 1990 and 2005 are depicted in figure 1.11. This also highlights the dramatic decline in battle deaths in sub-Saharan Africa after the end of the Ethiopian–Eritrean war in 2000.

Their third conclusion was that non-battle causes of mortality, especially the effects of displacement, malnutrition and disease, account for more fatalities than battles. As table 1.3 demonstrates, this conclusion is borne out from their data on various conflicts in sub-Saharan Africa, where battle deaths

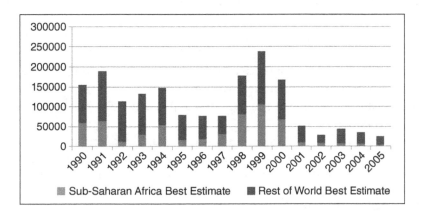

Figure 1.11 *Battle deaths in armed conflicts, 1990–2005*

TABLE 1.3　Deaths in selected African conflicts

Country	Years	Estimates of total war deaths	Battle deaths	Percentage of battle dead
Sudan (Anya Nya rebellion)	1963–73	250,000–750,00	20,000	3–8
Nigeria (Biafra rebellion)	1967–70	0.5–2 million	75,000	4–15
Angola	1975–2002	1.5 million	160,475	11
Ethiopia (excluding Eritrean insurgency)	1976–91	1–2 million	16,000	+42
Mozambique	1976–92	0.5–1 million	145,400	15–29
Somalia	1981–96	250,000–350,000 (to mid-1990s)	66,750	19–27
Sudan	1983–2002	2 million	55,500	3
Liberia	1989–96	150,000–200,000	23,500	12–16
Democratic Republic of Congo	1998–2001	2.5 million	145,000	6

Source: Lacina and Gleditsch, 'Monitoring trends', p. 159.

generally accounted for only a small proportion of overall war deaths. Since the factors causing non-battle mortality will continue long after combat has ceased, analysts face a problem of timeframe – i.e. deciding when the effects of a particular armed conflict can be said to have ended. Lacina and Gleditsch conclude that these causes of non-battle mortality are particularly prevalent when warfare destroys a state's economy, infrastructure (especially health and human services) and public safety systems. This makes them especially pertinent when analysing many of Africa's armed conflicts, which often take place against a backdrop of state weakness and where there are generally low levels of infrastructure and healthcare to start with. Given the relative importance of the causes of non-battle mortality, it is demographers, public health specialists and epidemiologists who probably hold the key to calculating the human costs of armed conflicts. As Lacina and Gleditsch note, 'The tools of scientific studies of population have already been used to provide data on a few recent conflicts that is of a precision and clarity far beyond that offered by other sources.'[14]

The problems and politics of counting the casualties of war are exemplified in the case of the DRC since 1998. This is a particularly important case study, not only because it is commonly thought to involve the most deadly of Africa's wars, but also because it is one of the few cases where sophisticated epidemiological studies have been conducted and then exposed to rigorous critique. Unfortunately, most armed conflicts in Africa do not attract such thorough attention. As noted in table 1.3, Lacina and Gleditsch estimated that the number of battle deaths in the DRC between 1998 and 2001 were 145,000, while the total number of war deaths for the same period was 2.5 million. These figures are based upon the surveys undertaken by the International Rescue Committee (IRC). Between 2000 and 2007, the IRC published five reports of mortality rates in the DRC. Initially these focused on the eastern part of the country but the last three were nationwide in coverage. The IRC surveys represent arguably the most sophisticated and certainly the most sustained attempt to count the casualties of any of Africa's major armed conflicts. It is thus worth summarizing their claims and methods in some detail before outlining the problems raised by their critics.

Between 18 April and 27 May 2000, the IRC conducted a series of five mortality surveys in sites representing three of the DRC's five eastern provinces.[15] These sites had a collective population of 1.2 million people. The 1,011 households visited contained 7,339 living residents, who reported 606 deaths among their members since 1 January 1999. Extrapolating from this data, the IRC concluded that 1.7 million 'excess deaths' had occurred in the previous twenty-two months, or approximately 77,000 per month, of which some 26,000 (or 34 per cent) were children younger than five years of age. In spite of this huge number, the IRC concluded that their 'projection of 1.7 million deaths due to this war in eastern DRC is a very conservative estimate'.[16] There were a number of reasons for this, including the fact that the surveys occurred in safer and more accessible areas than the average location in eastern DRC. The IRC also noted that,

> If entire families were killed, they would not have representatives to be included in our survey, resulting in a survivor bias in our surveys and an underestimate of mortality. Unfortunately, this is most likely to occur in the areas where the most violence occurred, and these locations are the most important in estimating the excess mortality.[17]

Although the IRC did produce figures that distinguished between violent and non-violent deaths, it emphasized the point that violence and deaths from infectious disease are inseparably linked. Specifically, the researchers concluded that there was 'an apparent association between the areas with the most violence-related mortality and the most "other" mortality. . . . In eastern DRC, war means disease'.[18]

During March–April 2001 the IRC conducted a second set of five surveys in eastern DRC (defined as the provinces of North Kivu, South Kivu, Orientale, Maniema and Katanga).[19] These interviewed members of a further 1,340 households and the results were then combined with the five surveys conducted for the 2000 IRC report and an earlier one from 1999. The eleven surveys encompassed a total of 18,450 people. Based on these data, the IRC estimated that 2.5 million excess deaths had occurred during the 32-month period between August 1998 and March 2001 (this is above and beyond the approximately 1 million deaths that the IRC estimated would have occurred in stable circumstances). Again, the overwhelming majority of deaths were related to disease and malnutrition. The number of violent deaths was estimated at 350,000.

The IRC undertook a third round of surveys – this time nationwide – between September and November 2002. In its subsequent report, published in April 2003, the organization drew several conclusions.[20] First, the mortality rate in eastern DRC had decreased from 5.4 deaths/1,000/month between August 1998 and April 2001 to 3.5 deaths/1,000/month for 2002. Without the war, the IRC estimated that the expected baseline mortality rate would have been 1.5 deaths/1,000/month. Second, the rate of death from violence in the east had 'decreased dramatically' – that is, it was approximately one-tenth of that seen in previous years. Finally, the IRC estimated that '3.3 million excess deaths occurred between August 1998 and December 2002 in the five eastern provinces of the DRC'.[21] Depending on assumptions made about the populations excluded from the survey, the IRC suggested that this estimate could range from 3 to 4.7 million people.

The IRC conducted its fourth survey between April and July 2004.[22] This was the IRC's second nationwide survey, although on this occasion approximately 5 million people were deemed inaccessible because of the security situation. In this effort, 19,500 households were visited (13,500 in eastern DRC and 6,000 in the west), accounting for a total population of 119,378 people. The heads of each household were asked about all deaths of household members during January 2003 to April 2004. Building on the previous IRC surveys, this one estimated that the total death toll from the war (August 1998 to April 2004) was 3.9 million (although reasonable estimates could range between 3.5 to 4.4 million). Again, most deaths were the result of 'easily preventable and treatable illnesses rather than violence'.[23] Not surprisingly, deaths due to violent injury were concentrated in the east. Men over fifteen years of age were 'at greater risk of being killed, constituting 71% of all violent deaths, although women (18%) and children younger than 15 years (10%) were not exempt'.[24]

The IRC's fifth survey covered the period from January 2006 to April 2007 using a three-stage cluster sampling technique to survey 14,000 households (defined as a group of persons who eat and sleep together) in thirty-five health zones across all eleven provinces – i.e. a wider geographic coverage than any of the previous IRC surveys.[25] Wherever possible, the questionnaire was conducted with a senior female member of the household. The IRC team concluded that 5.4 million excess deaths had occurred between August 1998 and April 2007 (by this stage the DRC's total population was estimated at 69.9 million people). An estimated 2.1 million of those deaths were thought to have occurred after the formal end of the war in 2002 and an estimated 4.6 million of them occurred in the five insecure eastern provinces. In addition, while the mortality levels in the east of the country had improved, at 2.6

deaths/1,000/month, this was still 85 per cent higher than the sub-Saharan average. The survey also concluded that only 0.4 per cent of the deaths in the DRC could be attributed directly to violence, most being caused by fever/malaria, diarrhoea, respiratory infections, tuberculosis, neonatal conditions and measles. The IRC's overall analysis of mortality trends is depicted in figure 1.12.

The IRC surveys have not been the only attempt to estimate casualties of the DRC's war, but to my knowledge they are the most concerted and sustained effort to date. In early 2010, however, the *Human Security Report* (HSR) published a critique of the IRC's findings on excess death estimates in the DRC.[26] The HSR team did not conduct their own surveys within the DRC but instead questioned the IRC's methodology – that is, they disputed how the IRC turned the data it collected in the surveys into an overall estimate of excess war deaths. Specifically, the HSR argued that two serious methodological problems rendered the IRC's estimate 'far too high'. First, it contended that, in the two surveys in 2000 and 2001, the 'IRC's researchers did not select the areas to be surveyed in a way that ensured they were representative of the region as a whole'. These errors 'led to large and unwarranted inflations of the excess death estimates.' More precisely, the HSR estimated that when these errors were corrected the excess death estimates were 678,600 instead of the IRC's figure of 1.6 million.[27]

The second problem was that, in the final three surveys (2002, 2004, 2007), the baseline mortality rate used by the IRC to determine the excess death rate was too low. Here, the HSR argued that it was wrong for the IRC to use the sub-Saharan average of 1.5 deaths/1,000/month as its baseline mortality rate for all but the very last survey (when the sub-Saharan average dropped to 1.4) because the DRC was not an average country in sub-Saharan Africa. In fact, the DRC was near the bottom of most cross-African measures of development before the war, and so the HSR asserted that it would be reasonable to expect that the baseline mortality rate for the country as a whole should be considerably higher than the sub-Saharan African average. It therefore ran the same numbers using a higher baseline rate of 2.0 deaths per 1,000 instead of the IRC's rate of 1.5. When this was done, it 'sharply' reduced 'the estimated excess death toll attributable to the war throughout the entire period, with the decreases being greatest for the three most recent [IRC] surveys.'[28] Table 1.4 compares the different estimates of excess mortality figures generated by the IRC and the HSR calculations. It shows that changing the baseline rate from 1.5 to 2.0 deaths/1,000/month generates a total of excess deaths only one-third the size of the IRC estimate – 863,000 down from 2.83 million. Naturally, this critique generated a response from within the IRC and counter-arguments from the HSR.[29] My sense of the subsequent exchanges and debates is that the HSR critique has stood up to the scrutiny it has received.

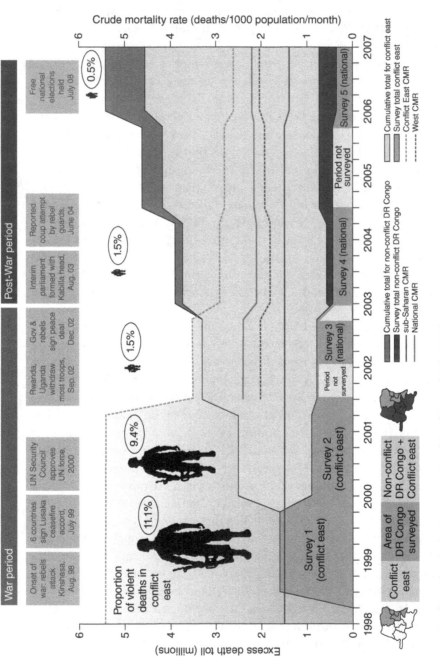

Source: IRC, *Mortality in the Democratic Republic of Congo* (IRC, 2007), p. 13.

Figure 1.12 *International Rescue Committee estimates of trends in mortality and deaths from violence in the Democratic Republic of Congo, 1998–2007*

TABLE 1.4 Excess deaths in the Democratic Republic of Congo, 2001–7: International Rescue Committee (IRC) and Human Security Report Project (HSRP) estimates

Period	IRC (best)	HSRP (best)	IRC (low)	HSRP (low)	IRC (high)	HSRP (high)
May 2001 – December 2001	418,400	209,200	180,800	29,800	654,500	402,300
January 2002 – December 2002	343,200	257,400	120,100	34,300	583,400	497,600
January 2003 – April 2004	607,000	101,200	101,200	–404,700	1,112,900	607,000
May 2004 – December 2005	735,000	136,600	419,300	–179,700	1,138,100	539,100
January 2006 – April 2007	727,000	158,600	522,000	–31,800	1,050,000	371,300
May 2001 – April 2007	2,830,600	863,000	1,343,400	–552,100	4,538,900	2,417,300

Source: *Human Security Report 2009*, p. 42.

Conclusions

Counting armed conflicts and their casualties is never an exact science. But without such attempts we would have no idea of the potential universe of cases we are dealing with or any understanding of the varying intensity and scale of these different conflicts. While the first point is important for drawing comparative insights across the continent, the second is crucial for framing particular episodes and giving relative weight to particular wars. Even so, since statistics are always produced for someone and for some purpose, any such exercises will inevitably become entangled in the propaganda wars and blame games that swirl around all armed conflicts. Because some form of statistics is a necessary point of departure for any analysis, their limitations are best acknowledged and addressed explicitly. By looking at the trends identified in three sophisticated attempts to gather relevant data, this chapter showed that, whether measured in terms of its population or the number of its states, post-Cold War Africa has suffered more than its fair share of organized violence. It is this troubling fact that makes the search to explain and understand its causes so important.

In one sense, the recent signs are encouraging. All three data-sets analysed here confirm that, from a peak in the early 1990s, the number of state-based conflicts has roughly halved. Almost all of these conflicts were intra-state, although all of them had transnational dimensions of one sort or another. On the other hand, Africa's armed conflicts accounted for a large proportion of the violent campaigns worldwide that targeted non-combatants – i.e. the

PITF categories of genocide and politicide and the UCDP's notion of one-sided violence. Some of the major reasons behind this uncomfortable fact are discussed in subsequent chapters of this book.

Perhaps the most striking point of all, however, is what might be called the 'known unknown' of non-state armed conflict. As the UCDP data from 1989–2009 demonstrates, any attempt to grapple with the causes of organized violence in post-Cold War Africa cannot focus solely on the activities of governments. While state behaviour is clearly an important part of the story on many occasions, we need to situate our understanding of organized violence in an ontological framework that locates governments within the wider social, political and economic contexts in which they are embedded. Chapter 2 aims to do this by placing socio-political complexes at the centre of its attempt to understand the political terrain on which Africa's armed conflicts were waged.

CHAPTER TWO

The Terrain of Struggle

As chapter 1 demonstrated, Africa's wars cannot be adequately understood using state-centric perspectives. But trying to understand the entire range of actors, institutions and processes that influence the course of Africa's wars is daunting, if not practically impossible. Part of the challenge is that events in world politics are interconnected in complicated ways. Indeed, the increasing number, complexity and intensity of interconnections between humans, and between humans and planet earth, are arguably *the* defining features of the contemporary era. Consequently, one of the most useful ways to approach the mega-concept of globalization is to see it as essentially about circulation – the processes through which people and places become interconnected. Understood in this manner, warfare has been a historically pervasive and significant form of interconnection between societies. 'In and through war', Tarak Barkawi observed,

> people on both sides come to intensified awareness of one another, reconstruct images of self and other, initiate and react to each other's moves. To be at war is to be interconnected with the enemy. Such connections involve social processes and transformations that should be understood under the rubric of globalization. . . . From a war and society perspective, war can be seen as an occasion for interconnection, as a form of circulation between combatant parties. In and through war, societies are transformed, while at the same time societies shape the nature of war.[1]

Warfare thus exists in a symbiotic relationship with society: wars shape societies but societies also influence the shape of wars. Thus, to 'abstract the conduct of war from the environment in which it was fought', Michael Howard concluded, is 'to ignore dimensions essential to its understanding.'[2] This is as true of Africa's wars as anywhere else.[3]

Life's interconnections also raise the fundamental question of what phenomena need to be put under our analytical microscopes to understand Africa's wars. Carolyn Nordstrom captured the essence of this challenge when she asked: Where are the battlefields? Who are the players? And, where should we locate the study of war?[4] Unfortunately, there is no easy or formulaic answer. As complex social processes, wars are not isolated events. But, once we recognize the importance of interconnections, where does one stop? Since the war in eastern DRC, for example, is influenced by the scramble for minerals used in the production of high-tech computers, telephones and games consoles, should our analysis of that war include the manufacturers and consumers of those items, most of whom have never set foot in the Congo? In sum, do we need what Richard Jackson called 'a new ontology of contemporary warfare in Africa'?[5]

The short answer is 'yes': we need a conceptual framework that can tell us which phenomena to focus upon and how they interrelate. To understand which phenomena to study, Robert Cox's neo-Gramscian approach is useful because it focuses on the different types of state–society complexes which form within particular historical structures.[6] First of all, this approach offers a relevant corrective to the traditional state-centric accounts which have dominated International Relations (IR) theorizing. As such, it is well suited to the African context because the continent's 'power constellations are not entirely state-centric'.[7] Second, Cox's framework is built around the issue of social change. This is useful because it is during periods of war that social change occurs most intensely. 'War', as Morten Bøås observed, 'is by its very nature an instrument for social and economic restructuring. It is a site for innovation, which reorders social, economic, and political life.'[8] By focusing on the actors, institutions and processes through which social change occurs, Cox's ontology provides a useful starting point for thinking about the dynamics of warfare.

To understand how such phenomena interrelate, I revisit what IR scholars refer to as the 'levels-of-analysis' problem.[9] This allows us to recognize that Africa's wars are complex social processes which are *simultaneously*, but to varying degrees, local, national, regional and global. In the rest of this chapter I discuss Africa's wars as a levels-of-analysis problem before examining some of the major characteristics of the African terrain on which these struggles have been waged. This provides the conceptual and historical backdrop for the analysis of the ingredients of Africa's war recipes conducted in part II of the book.

Africa's Wars as a Levels-of-Analysis Problem

The terrain of struggle on which African wars have been waged is multi-levelled and populated by a variety of actors, structures and processes. I use the term 'levels' in an ontological sense to refer to distinct contexts – generally organized on the principle of spatial scale – 'where both outcomes and sources of explanation can be located'.[10] As Barry Buzan has explained, within IR the levels-of-analysis *problem* is generally thought to revolve around 'how to identify and treat different types of location in which sources of explanation for observed phenomena can be found.'[11] In this sense, there are actually two problems: first, how to locate and identify the relevant levels and, second, deciding how explanatory weight should be distributed among them.

TABLE 2.1 Levels of analysis in Africa's armed conflicts

Level-of-analysis	Description
Local	Relations between individuals and their immediate (sub-state) politico-geographic context
National	Focused on the institutions of state power
Regional	Geographically coherent, sub-global security complexes which involve the agents of at least two states
Global	De-territorialized networks, structures, processes, institutions or belief systems (with the potential to be global in scope)

Consequently, there exists what might be called a 'levels-of analysis' problem and a 'levels-of-explanation' problem.[12]

My answer to the first problem (of analysis) is to offer a framework based on the four distinct levels which are of most direct relevance for understanding the dynamics of Africa's armed conflicts: local, national, regional and global.[13] These are summarized in table 2.1. There is no 'individual level' because, as Colin Wight has persuasively argued, there is no need for one, 'since individuals feature in every level and are tied into their social contexts'.[14] Nor is there a 'bureaucratic level' about which a similar point could be made: all social formations – including tribes, religious sects, insurgencies, firms, states and international institutions – could be understood as involving some type of formal or informal officials, administrators and bureaucrats.

With regard to the second 'levels-of-explanation' problem, the challenge is complicated by the fact that, in contemporary Africa, and elsewhere, the four levels are not completely separate from one another. As Kassimir and Latham have observed, since 'considerable amounts of social power and political outcomes are being generated where international, local and national forces operate coterminously . . . it becomes impossible at times even to identify a set of dynamics as squarely part of one level or another.'[15] In light of this pertinent observation I suggest that the concept of distinct *levels* of analysis with rigid spatial divides between them paints an unhelpful mental image. While the different levels are, by definition, not completely reducible to one another, the idea of fluid 'scapes' that bleed into one another provides a more useful mental image. As used by the anthropologist Arjun Appadurai, the notion of scapes captures the essence of a 'world in motion' rather than static relationships.[16]

Recognizing the interrelationships between different levels or scapes is useful, but it does not tell us how, or if, they might be combined to arrive at one overall explanation of the armed conflict in question.[17] As discussed in the Introduction, my approach is to reject mono-causal explanations of warfare in the sense that there is always more than one story to tell about the causes of particular conflicts (as well as the phenomenon of warfare in general) and that these stories differ depending on the level of explanation prioritized. If the individual levels are not reducible to one another then, logically, neither can our explanations of warfare be collapsed into a single, all-encompassing causal account. This means the levels-of-explanation problem cannot be resolved at the purely abstract level. Instead, the most sophisticated accounts will be those that provide a rich historical description of how the different levels interacted to produce a particular conflict. With this caveat in mind, the rest of this section briefly summarizes and illustrates these four distinct levels or what might be referred to as 'warscapes'.

Local wars

Africa's wars all have local roots. Here, 'local' refers to the relationship between individuals and their immediate politico-geographic context (Cox's state–society complexes). In spatial terms this immediate context is defined as sub-state to separate it from national level dynamics discussed below.

In many of Africa's wars, local agendas and the contours of domestic politics played decisive roles in their onset, their sustenance and, ultimately, their endings.[18] These agendas have taken a variety of forms, including a sense of entitlement to land and other resources, attempts to control systems of governance, and questions about identity, belonging and citizenship.

With regard to the onset of war, analysts have convincingly used statistical data across a range of cases to demonstrate the importance of sub-state factors. Østby, Nordås and Rød, for instance, used data collected from first-level administrative units in twenty-two African states (rather than national-level data) to show that armed conflict was more likely to occur in sub-state regions that lacked education services, were relatively deprived compared to the country mean, had strong intra-regional inequalities, and combined the presence of natural resources and relative deprivation.[19]

Sub-state factors were also important in sustaining warfare and in shaping its dynamics. The ways in which armed groups mobilize and endure, for example, were significantly affected by local-level factors such as people deciding to take up arms after personal and localized experiences of humiliation suffered at the hands of government soldiers or rebels, or out of a desire to avenge similar acts meted out to their friends or families.[20] In an analysis of African civil wars from 1970 to 2001, Buhaug and Rød used data related to 100 x 100 km grid cells (rather than national-level data) to conclude that armed conflict clustered unevenly in spatial terms. Specifically, they found that conflicts over territory (secessionist conflicts) were more likely in sparsely populated regions near the state border, at a distance from the capital and without significant rough terrain, while conflict over governance issues was more likely in regions that are densely populated, near diamond fields and near the capital city.[21] The burgeoning literature analysing the micro-foundations of violent conflict – i.e. the causes and effects of conflict at the community, household and individual levels – has also shown that it is particularly useful in accounting for heterogeneity across individuals and groups within the same conflict.[22]

Recent studies of particular African wars have drawn similar conclusions to these general hypotheses. In eastern DRC, for example, Séverine Autesserre has convincingly argued that it is impossible to understand violence in the Kivus without paying attention to some very local antagonisms, such as leadership struggles over specific militias, disagreement over who controls the resources won by the group and who gets appointed to local administrative positions, and opposing claims on land, mining sites, and traditional positions among villagers, as well as tensions arising over ethnicity and clan affiliations.[23] Detailed studies of Sudan's wars have made similar points. In the conflict between the government of Sudan and the SPLM/A, for example, the government's tactic of recruiting local militias from within the south hardened local ethnic and social divides, which in turn made local identity dynamics crucial to understanding the conflict's twists and turns.[24] The same was true for Darfur's most recent war, with analysts emphasizing the ways in which ethnic/tribal rifts at local levels lay at the heart of conflict.[25]

The preceding points suggest there is considerable evidence that Africa's wars have been fought over and involved changing configurations of power, authority and identity in the relationships between local actors. Indeed, as shown in chapter 1, it is notable how many recent African conflicts have been fought between two or more localized non-state actors.[26] Thus, although Africa's conflicts occur within the confines of an international society of states, in an important sense they are not always *of* that society. As important as local dynamics are, however, they are not the whole story.

National wars

Regimes in Africa's weak states often found it difficult to effectively broadcast their power far beyond the capital city and other strategic locales.[27] Yet struggles to control state institutions have at times been crucial for understanding why wars began and how they unfolded. With regard to the outbreak of conflict, as Christopher Clapham put it, 'The place to start trying to understand any political crisis is always with the government in power.'[28]

This insight also finds support in more quantitative studies. For example, one recent analysis of all ethnic groups worldwide between 1946 and 2005 concluded that exclusion from state power was a crucial factor in whether ethnic groups started rebellions, especially if this was combined with prior experience of conflict and the group's potential to mobilize support was high.[29] Similarly, as discussed in more detail in chapter 3, the PITF concluded that regime type was the most reliable predictor of instability, with 'partial democracies with factionalism' being the most unstable.[30] Recent qualitative research using examples from conflicts in Sierra Leone and Nigeria placed similar emphasis on state power, concluding that the 'critical juncture' in the outbreak of armed conflict appeared when national rulers were 'no longer able to assert their dominance over local strongmen in their patronage network'. At that point, armed groups were utilized 'for their own commercial and political benefit without the ruler's authorization'.[31]

As discussed in more detail in chapters 3 to 5, the principal explanations for the state's importance revolve around the importance of juridical sovereignty and its role as a source of resources – both the local resources which the state's functionaries are able to bring under their control and external resources procured from a variety of actors, including international financial institutions, other international organizations, donor states and private corporations.[32] External resources in particular have tended to accrue to groups which controlled the capital city, producing what Clapham called 'letterbox sovereignty' – the idea 'that whoever opened the letters in the presidential palace received the invitation to represent the state concerned in the United Nations and other international bodies.'[33] In cases where this applied, the conflict might bypass considerable swathes of the country which were considered of little strategic consequence in the struggle.

Contests over state power are also important for understanding the dynamics of warfare in more peripheral zones. As William Reno observed, ties to patronage politics in the capital influenced armed groups across Sierra Leone as a whole. In particular, variation in the way they treated civilians was influenced by the patronage networks from which they emerged before the war broke out. First of all, Reno concluded that, 'the closer the connection of local authorities to capital-based patronage politics, the more likely are local armed groups to behave in a predatory fashion vis-à-vis the interests of their home communities.'[34] Second, he observed that 'armed groups in communities where the local political elite were relatively marginal to pre-conflict patronage networks tend to behave in a much more protective fashion vis-à-vis the interests of their home communities.'[35] Consequently, he predicted that 'most predatory and socially destabilizing violence should develop in areas where the political establishment was most closely linked to the patronage networks of the capital.'[36] This suggests that, if an armed group's patron was not locally based, it did not need to treat the local population with respect and win its support. Moreover, the loss of a distant patron may force once predatory commanders to heed local interests and make deals with local people.[37]

Regional wars

Particularly since the end of the Cold War, regional developments have been identified as crucial for understanding contemporary security dynamics in

Africa and elsewhere.[38] Thus the regional dimensions of Africa's armed conflicts constitute a third distinct warscape. Specifically, the disjuncture
between the processes of warfare and Africa's political borders helped form
a series of 'regional security complexes' characterized by 'durable patterns of
amity and enmity taking the form of subglobal, geographically coherent patterns of security interdependence'.[39]

Regional wars can assume many forms, but among the most common
African variants have been government forces crossing into neighbouring
states to eliminate rebel bases and supply lines and/or intimidating countries
which gave sanctuary to rebels; or, conversely, neighbouring governments
acting in support of the incumbent regime; neighbouring states supporting
insurgencies in order to weaken and destabilize regional rivals; and refugee
flows producing camps that become potential pools for rebel recruitment.[40]
The archetypal example of such regional dynamics was the war fought in the
DRC (1998–2003) between Rwanda, Uganda, Burundi, Zimbabwe, Angola,
Namibia, Chad and Sudan.[41]

The importance of Africa's regional political geography was intensified by
three main factors: military inefficiency, the disjuncture between political
identities and state boundaries, and the combination of weak states and
porous borders. First, the region became important in part because most
African militaries could operate efficiently only over relatively short distances
(if they could operate efficiently at all).[42] This meant that most African states
usually engaged in significant military interactions with their neighbours or
states nearby.[43] Regional warfare thus became a real possibility in a way that
continental warfare did not.

The significance of the regional level was also partly a consequence of
prominent kinship and other cross-border identity ties which facilitated all
sorts of transnational relations in Africa's war zones.[44] They also gave governments in neighbouring states incentives to become actively engaged in those
conflicts.[45] Examples of such transnational actors are cross-border insurgencies, mercenaries, corporations engaged in various forms of resource extraction, and organized criminal gangs, as well as humanitarian and development
NGOs and the displaced populations they assist.[46] A particularly notorious
example emerged during the West African wars of the 1990s where Human
Rights Watch identified the formation of an 'insurgent diaspora' – a pool of
professional warriors who moved from one conflict to the next and exemplified the transnational dimension of warfare.[47] Another good example from
Central Africa is the increasingly multinational Lord's Resistance Army, a
roaming insurgent group that sparked a war in which an estimated 65,000
civilians have been killed over the last twenty years in northern Uganda,
southern Sudan, the DRC and the Central African Republic (see chapter 7).[48]

Finally, the relatively porous state borders evident in many of Africa's war
zones combined with the inability of many regimes to effectively project
power over all their official territory meant that there were often relatively

few impediments to spillover effects or the unwanted interference of external powers. The frequent criss-crossing of the Sudan–Chad border by armed groups engaged in the war in Darfur is only one of the more prominent recent examples.

Global wars

Despite the stubborn prevalence of the view that Africa is the place that globalization forgot, in reality the continent and its conflicts have all been deeply affected by an array of globalizing structures, networks, processes, institutions and belief systems.[49] At an abstract level, as Ann Hironaka has argued, international processes have long played a crucial role in perpetuating (and often escalating) conflicts in three main ways: they have affected the dynamics of state behaviour and civil wars by conferring statehood on some entities and not others, by sustaining particular models of appropriate state structures, and by diffusing cultural scripts which have informed and guided state behaviour.[50]

The type of phenomena that exemplify globalizing dynamics include what Thomas Callaghy and his colleagues called 'transbounday formations', which link the local to the global through an array of structures, networks and discourses that ultimately produce and/or sustain forms of authority and order.[51] These phenomena constitute the fourth and final warscape identified here. From the deep structures of global capitalism and the more fickle policies of the international financial institutions, from the diffusion of Christianity and Islam across the continent to the uncertain impact of rapidly globalizing norms about humanitarianism, human rights, anti-imperialism and racial equality, Africa's conflicts have been intimately bound up with the ebb and flow of globalizing trends in world politics.

In the political economy sector, one significant example has been the way in which the international relief/development industry has interacted with Africa's war zones (see chapter 11).[52] Indeed, the quintessential displacement camp often came to represent an intensified encounter between the global forces of the humanitarian relief industry and the local participants in the conflict concerned. As sites where belligerents often tried to recruit, resupply and reorganize, as well as places of shelter for the victims, displacement camps administered by aid agencies became a symbol of globalized warfare *par excellence*. Other good examples are the human networks which facilitated the licit and illicit markets for arms and conflict goods such as diamonds, oil, coltan, rubber, timber, etc.[53]

In the social sector, a relevant example is the organized diaspora groups that funded or advocated for particular belligerents from many of the world's important political centres, such as Washington, DC, New York, Brussels, Geneva, London, Paris, etc. One of the most infamous contemporary cases was the *Forces Démocratiques de Libération du Rwanda* (FDLR), which emerged from the remnants of Rwanda's genocidal regime in 1994. The FDLR's operations in the DRC were orchestrated by leadership networks in Europe, especially in Germany and France. In other cases, such as the multiple attempts to assemble an effective transitional government for Somalia, individuals were plucked from the exiled or diaspora communities to become senior politicians in their country of origin.

In the ideological realm, local conflicts have been caught up in more global currents, if only for the instrumental purpose of extracting resources from particular external constituencies. As the rivalry between the communist and capitalist blocs subsided, these were more likely to be found in regimes claiming to defend democracy from its enemies or, especially in North Africa and the Horn, religious networks espousing Islamic *jihad* (see chapter 7).[54]

To be clear, I am not suggesting that 'the global' level automatically exercises power over 'the local' or other levels. If that were true there would be homogeneous patterns of behaviour across the entire globe. In reality, wars around the world look different precisely because there are interconnections between the local and the global and the various places in between rather than a situation where one level dominates all the others. In the African cases of wars waged in the name of Islamic *jihad*, for example, the specific movements which emerged in Algeria, Egypt, Sudan, Somalia and elsewhere were influenced by global dynamics in the form of Wahhabi and Takfiri teachings and shadowy networks such as *al-Qa'ida* and the so-called Afghan Arabs. But these African groups were also shaped by domestic political concerns. Moreover, Islamist projects in Egypt and Sudan in particular had a significant influence on the wider Arab world beyond Africa. Analysts should therefore proceed from the assumption that Africa's warscapes are simultaneously local, national, regional and global, albeit to varying degrees. Although the levels-of-explanation problem cannot be resolved at the abstract level alone, it would be useful if more historically grounded studies would try and clarify which levels are doing most explanatory work and how they interrelate.

Major Features of the African Terrain

With these insights in mind, how might we summarize the most important characteristics of Africa's recent armed conflicts? This section addresses this question by sketching the political context, the central actors, and some of the methods frequently employed by the belligerents. Of course, these do not apply equally to all of Africa's wars, but this brief survey aims to illuminate the main features of the political terrain on which these conflicts were played out. Subsequent chapters in the book examine particular cases in more detail, while the conclusion to this chapter offers some general explanations for why Africa's wars have unfolded in this way.

As discussed in chapter 1, even basic questions about the number of armed conflicts in Africa have failed to generate a consensus. Part of the reason for this is the different methodologies employed by researchers. But there is also the more fundamental problem that the basic categories of 'war' and 'peace' are not always easy to tell apart. As David Keen warned, 'We should not let the words "war" and "peace" seduce us into believing that neither has elements (or seeds) of the other.'[55] Of course, warfare is usually defined as involving organized violence that produces casualties. But warfare routinely involves much peaceful activity interspersed with what Clausewitz famously described as 'pulsations of violence'. Indeed, military service was said to be about enduring long periods of boredom punctuated by spasms of utter terror.[56]

From the other end of the war–peace spectrum, Peters and Richards observed that 'armed conflict is at times no more than an intensification of structural violence present in 'peaceful' society.'[57] Chapter 1 considered how the relevant data-sets adopted different casualty thresholds to determine what counts as 'armed conflict', 'major armed conflict' or 'war'. And in defining these terms it also appears to matter how people are killed. Violent deaths resulting from organized criminal activity, for instance, are rarely counted. Nor are victims of riots involving civilian mobs. Nor are most victims of state repression who have not formed an organized insurgency. If these types of organized violence were included, our graphs of war and peace might look quite different. South Africa's 'miraculous' transition from apartheid during the late 1980s and early 1990s involved thousands of violent deaths each year. Similarly, Nigeria would constantly be placed in the 'war' category if violent deaths through state brutality or organized riots were counted. Between 2000 and 2007, for example, the Nigerian police force alone is estimated to have killed more than 8,000 civilians, and in the period between 1999 and 2006 well over 11,000 people died in ethnic, political and religious violence in the north of the country (see also chapter 7).[58] In a similar vein, lots of African countries continued to experience high numbers of violent deaths even after 'peace' was ostensibly attained through the signing of agreements ending the various wars. In the two extreme cases of Angola's protracted conflict and Rwanda's 1994 genocide, it is important to recall that the majority of the victims were killed after the respective peace agreements ending the civil wars had been concluded. These issues are thus particularly important when addressing the question of war endings and are discussed in more detail in chapter 9.

A second important feature of Africa's post-Cold War conflicts was the multiplicity of actors involved. In crude terms, these can be divided into armed and unarmed groups. Those who found themselves in war zones without guns (or without some form of armed protection) were generally either local civilians caught up in armed conflicts or personnel working for international organizations and humanitarian and/or development NGOs.

Of the armed groups, there were those who carry guns legitimately, such as the representatives of states and various types of peacekeepers from international organizations such as the UN and regional arrangements (see chapter

10). There were also many varieties of less legitimate armed non-state actors, among them insurgents, militias, paramilitaries, self-defence groups, mercenaries, private military contractors and criminal gangs. Many of these actors have included children within their ranks, perhaps most notoriously Laurent Kabila's *kadogos* (little ones) or Charles Taylor's small boy units.

There are many reasons why people resorted to using guns in Africa's conflict zones. It is also important to remember that these motives often changed over time as circumstances altered. For one thing, small arms and light weapons were relatively abundant, easy to use and cheap. Moreover, wielding a gun could bring benefits as a means to seek revenge for previous humiliation, to generate instant obedience and extort resources, or perhaps to gain respect. As one child combatant in Liberia's civil war put it, 'When I get a gun I can be free.'[59] Some individuals turned to arms to try and address political grievances when other avenues were closed down, while for others guns offered the only way to defend themselves and their families. Wielding a weapon thus sometimes formed an important part of a survival strategy in situations where often the worst position to occupy was that of an unarmed civilian caught between rapacious rebels and unpaid and unprofessional government troops. In Zaire/DRC, for example, it was common to hear the phrase *civil azali bilanga ya militaire*: 'the civilian is the [corn] field of the military.' Many others were simply coerced into fighting.

Two other important general points are worth noting about the actors in Africa's war zones. First, it was often difficult to distinguish between combatants and non-combatants, especially when the fighting involved non-state actors and where children were participants. Second, even if one could identify the combatants, it was not always easy to discern whose side they were on. Sometimes, this was because of rapidly shifting alliance politics in conflicts involving numerous armed factions. On other occasions it was because the combatants did not always follow orders from their superiors and changed sides based on their own cost–benefit calculations of the situation at hand. The archetypal example of this sort of behaviour was Sierra Leone's 'sobels' – soldiers/rebels – the nickname given to soldiers who fought for the government during the day but who discarded their uniforms at night so that they could pretend to be rebels in order to extort local civilians. These same soldiers also engaged in regular acts of collaboration with their erstwhile rebel opponents. In what was known locally as the 'sell game', barter and exchange between ostensible enemies was quite common and sometimes even included exchanges of weapons and ammunition.[60]

Of all the actors in Africa's war zones, it was governments and insurgencies which proved the most significant during the post-Cold War period. As discussed in part II of this book, African states embroiled in armed conflicts can be divided into three broad types. First, there were states characterized by weak and incompetent institutions, which consequently suffered from an inability to control their own territory and populations. Whether this weakness stemmed from the decline of superpower patronage after the Cold War ended or whether it was down to an inability to generate sufficient domestic sources of revenues to train competent security forces, governments in these states proved unable to protect their citizens or their border zones from rebel incursions. Some of these can be dubbed 'archipelago states' because their rulers concentrated on controlling only those regions that provided significant economic resources, or what French colonists referred to as *Afrique utile* (areas that produced revenues sufficient to pay for administration) (see also chapter 4).[61] Samuel Doe's Liberia or Joseph Momoh's Sierra Leone would fit comfortably into this mould.

Then there were states where national security institutions were deliberately kept weak and factionalized by paranoid rulers – what Alex de Waal dubbed 'fragmentation as policy'.[62] Perhaps the quintessential case of this policy was Zaire, where President Mobutu effectively handed out to local strongmen licences to pillage and loot. He did this in order to keep the country sufficiently destabilized to avoid a threat to his power coming from within the military itself. In Somalia, President Mohamed Siad Barre's decision to arm various clan-based militias in order to try and retain his grip on power had a similar effect on the authority of the national army and the fate of the Somali state. While leaders of such states generally developed some form of trusted presidential guard, the rest of their armed forces were highly unlikely to engage in the sustained, efficient and dedicated defence of the regime. This was clearly demonstrated in Mobutu's case, as Zaire's army all but collapsed when Laurent Kabila and his (misnamed) Alliance of Democratic Forces for the Liberation of the Congo marched on Kinshasa in 1996–7.

Although some of the literature discussing the concept of 'new wars' suggests that they occur in the context of weak and disintegrating state structures, there are also cases of African armed conflicts where the regime in question was a force to be reckoned with when it came to wielding instruments of violence, if not necessarily with great efficiency or across all of its nominal territory. In these cases, regimes used state institutions to oppress segments of their populations either for the purposes of extortion or to weaken political opponents. In the most intense period of bloodletting in the whole post-Cold War period to date, between April and July 1994, institutions of the Rwandan state were used to exterminate perhaps as many as 1 million Tutsis and moderate Hutus (see chapter 6). In such cases, the government's official armed forces were normally supplemented by proxies of various kinds. If these various paramilitary groups could not be harnessed to the regime's agenda through appeals to nationalism, ethnic identity or other forms of ideological persuasion, promises of land, status or loot in return for their violent services often worked just as well. Of all the African cases where this scenario applies, it is probably President Omar al-Bashir's regime in Sudan (1989–present) that has had the most extensive practice at using proxy militias to wage its wars in the south, west and east of the country.

After states, insurgents were the most important armed actors in Africa's recent war zones. Insurgents assumed many different forms depending on the nature of their enemies and their relationship to the local population in areas where they operated.[63] While some, like the RUF rebels in Sierra Leone, were pitted against weak states with ragtag armies, others, such as Jonas Savimbi's UNITA rebels in Angola, were forced to fight long, protracted campaigns against well-funded governments with large militaries. Similarly, while some insurgents tried to build support among local populations (e.g. the SPLA and POLISARIO), others treated civilians as little more than resources to be pillaged whenever they saw fit (e.g. the LRA and FDLR). And, as noted above, many of Africa's insurgents went transnational, using territory outside their target state to mobilize and sustain their activities.[64]

As Christopher Clapham pointed out, if we analyse Africa's armed actors according to the functions they perform it is sometimes difficult to draw clear distinctions between governments and insurgents, because some insurgencies assumed the characteristics of states in important respects: their participants usually had physical control of a territory and population; they were often recipients of international aid, especially that distributed through NGOs; and some of them had varying but sometimes formal, diplomatic relations with external states. In these circumstances, Clapham noted that 'the dividing line between 'states' and 'non-states' ha[d] become so blurred as to be virtually imperceptible.'[65]

During Liberia's civil war, for instance, when Amos Sawyer become head of the Interim Government of National Unity (IGNU) in late 1990, most of the country and its resources was controlled by Charles Taylor's National Patriotic Front rebels. In this situation, being head of the Liberian state came with virtually no practical power and with the sizable headache of assuming responsibility for paying off Liberia's national debts, which were owed to various international financial institutions. Between 1990 and 1994, for instance, Taylor's income was estimated to be at least $75 million a year, while Sawyer was saddled with a $3 billion debt and an income of approximately $20 million per year, most of which came from fees paid on the international fleet of Liberian-registered ships.[66] This situation generated a popular joke in Monrovia that the IGNU really stood for the Imported Government of No Use.[67]

The widespread prevalence of such cases led Clapham to conclude that the post-Cold War order in Africa was not 'crisply divided into entities which do and do not count as "states"'. Instead, it consisted 'of a mass of power structures which, regardless of formal designation, enjoy greater or lesser degrees of statehood.'[68] It is in this context that Cox's focus on state–society complexes is particularly useful because, as even this brief discussion illustrates, non-state actors sometimes possessed more of the attributes of empirical statehood than the internationally recognized governments they were fighting.

Once war and society are understood as existing in a symbiotic relation-ship, it becomes clear that the type of actors and societies involved will influ-ence the type of wars that develop. So how did Africa's belligerents conduct their conflicts? The short answer is that Africa's wars, like those elsewhere, tended to reflect the objectives being pursued by the actors conducting them as well as the incentive structures open to them. And, as David Keen has persuasively argued, three aims were particularly evident beyond traditional notions of victory: limiting the exposure of one's own forces to violence, accumulating resources, and suppressing political opposition.[69]

The first point to note is that, during war, as with periods of peace, all parties need to accrue resources. Without resources – especially loyal follow-ers, provisions and weapons – waging war is impossible (see chapter 4). When resources flowed in relative abundance from a foreign superpower or another external patron such as a Gaddafi, Bashir or a diaspora network, this was not too time consuming, although it did create headaches over how to manage the distribution of those resources in ways that did not weaken group cohe-sion and effectiveness.[70] When external patronage dried up or resources were scarce, however, it was particularly important not to waste them. Although it is often forgotten, the quickest way to lose resources or degrade one's armed forces is to engage in sustained combat with a competent opponent. Consequently, and quite sensibly from a military point of view, with the notable exception of the war fought between Ethiopia and Eritrea (1998–2000), several African conflicts did not witness many large or decisive battles because the belligerents usually tried hard to avoid fighting reasonably com-petent opposition: why fight enemy soldiers when you might be able to cut deals with them and extort local civilians instead? In Sudan, for instance, during periods where the frontlines were relatively well established, govern-ment and SPLA soldiers were rarely keen to fight each other but instead would fire ritual warning shots when patrols came close to one another. One observer wryly remarked, 'No wonder this war has taken so long. It is like a boxing match on a football pitch.'[71]

Most of Africa's conflicts were therefore characterized by the use of guer-rilla tactics and counter-insurgency operations, with relatively few large-scale engagements. Arguably the most common form of extended battle consisted of the sieges of particular towns and/or garrisons that occupied strategically valuable locales, such as Abyei or Bukavu, or which overlooked important supply routes and sources of minerals, such as Kisangani and Goma in the DRC or the diamond-rich areas of Sierra Leone and Liberia. The single most important settlement, largely because of the sovereignty benefits that might come with it, was often the capital city of the state in question, and certainly significant battles were waged over some of these, including Freetown, Kigali, Kinshasa, Luanda, Mogadishu and Monrovia. Other wars, however, never made it to the capital and were confined largely to the periphery. This had traditionally been the case in Sudan, which is why the JEM's blitzkrieg of May

2008, which reached the outskirts of Khartoum, was particularly shocking for the ruling regime.

The importance of resources meant that all belligerents (governments and non-state actors alike) had to develop effective strategies to accumulate and keep them. Away from the battlefield, one of these strategies was 'selling' their cause through appealing propaganda in the hope of attracting political support and funds from domestic or external allies or diaspora communities.[72] A more direct approach was to employ coercion to plunder and extort.[73]

Of all the forms of coercion employed by African governments and insurgents, it was the use of atrocities against civilians that usually attracted the greatest attention from outsiders, particularly Western media outlets. Indeed, the barbaric nature of atrocities committed against civilians is a central leitmotif running through many journalistic accounts of Africa's wars. Any list of atrocities is potentially very long, but a useful starting point is the seventeen types of violations identified by the Truth and Reconciliation Commission of Sierra Leone in its study of that country's civil war (1991–2002): abduction, amputation, arbitrary detention, assault/beating, destruction of property, drugging, extortion, forced cannibalism, forced displacement, forced labour, forced recruitment, killing, looting, physical torture, rape, sexual abuse and sexual slavery.[74] While in Sierra Leone's case the majority of these actions were perpetrated by RUF rebels, government soldiers also frequently committed them as well.

There are several common explanations for why civilians were deliberately targeted in Africa's wars. The first relates to the broad definition of 'the enemy' used in many African conflicts. When the enemy was defined broadly to include civilians and non-combatants on the opposing side (or even anybody not on 'your side'), it helped belligerents to legitimize violence perpetrated against ordinary people. Moreover, it was always easier to attack civilians than other armed groups. In the most extreme cases, defining the enemy to include all 'Tutsis', or 'Fur', or '*abids*', or 'non-believers', etc., helped to legitimize a wide variety of atrocities where the aim was the extermination or displacement of a particular group of people. In such circumstances, the depiction of women as the bearers of the next generation of 'enemies' or the prize assets of enemy males was used to justify all sorts of sexual violence and torture. In cases where the principal aim was expulsion rather than extermination, atrocities tended to be used against the few in order to spread fear among the many.

A second explanation involved a variety of practical considerations used to justify the targeting of civilians. Chief among these were arguments that the civilians were really insurgents or they were supporting the rebel/government forces. With reference to Mao Tse-tung's classic guerrilla warfare analogy, it was sometimes necessary to target civilians in order to drain the water in which the guerrilla fishes were swimming.

A third set of explanations related to the symbolic and political functions of what de Waal has called 'conspicuous atrocity'.[75] Here, the point was not just to commit atrocities but to do so conspicuously because of the fear and hence obedience it might generate. This helps explain why some acts were recorded and disseminated to amplify the perpetrator's power or to sow fear among the wider populace. In Liberia, for example, Charles Taylor's threats of a 'carnival of blood' helped him gain significant military advantage, and Prince Johnson's dissemination of the videotape of him and his colleagues torturing and killing President Samuel Doe undoubtedly enhanced his prestige as a warlord.[76] This type of atrocity also sometimes involved inflicting certain injuries upon captives but letting some of them go free, so that they might tell others of their ordeal and hence encourage people to run away before the perpetrators arrived at the settlement in question, or, if they remained, quickly give into their demands. The use of public rape and sexual violence, particularly in ways that inverted traditional social hierarchies and customs, was often part of such strategies. In addition, where armed factions relied on coercion to gather new members, getting new recruits to participate in such atrocities could play a role in cementing their loyalty to the group for fear of facing retribution by outsiders.

The relatively widespread use of these methods of warfare caused many local civilians to flee their homes in fear of what might happen if they stayed. As a result, Africa's wars triggered huge levels of displacement. This had terrible effects, because it is widely thought to be the single most important factor in whether a person succumbs to disease or the effects of malnutrition. Figure 2.1 shows the unprecedented levels of displacement witnessed in

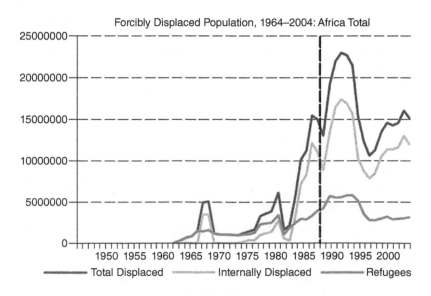

Source: Marshall, *Conflict Trends in Africa*, p. 9.

Figure 2.1 *The forcibly displaced population in sub-Saharan Africa, 1964–2004*

Africa during the 1990s in particular. Among the major epicentres of displacement were the conflicts in Sudan, the DRC, Uganda and Somalia. In the best-case scenario, the displaced might find sanctuary. Unfortunately, the more common destination was a displacement camp, often administered by foreign governments or international agencies. Precisely because such camps attracted foreigners with a relative abundance of resources, such as peacekeepers or humanitarian workers, they also attracted belligerents looking to refuel their war efforts and recruit new supporters, or simply for a place to organize (see chapter 11). Indeed, insurgencies such as the SPLA in Sudan, POLISARIO in Western Sahara, and the soldiers and militias of Rwanda's genocidal regime became adept at utilizing such camps for strategic purposes.[77]

Conclusion

This chapter has shown that a focus on state–society complexes operating across different levels of analysis provides a useful way of thinking about Africa's warscapes and the political terrain on which they were played out. It argued that there are several major reasons why things turned out this way. Chief among them was the way in which regimes in many of the continent's weak states prioritized their survival over pursuing genuinely national development and were quite willing to use violence to deal with any serious challengers. The regular use of violence and its connection to political power and economic advancement also served to saturate large swathes of the continent in militaristic ideas.[78] Ironically, the fact that the leaders of these regimes were often most worried about internal threats to their status meant that they rarely built effective, professional and well-equipped armed forces for fear that such troops might turn against them. Instead, their personal security was pursued by creating large palaces and some sort of private presidential guard. One consequence was that this regularly left more peripheral areas of the country unable to fend off even small rebellions and exposed the civilian population to unruly and unpaid soldiers.

A second key issue was the search for resources. In a geopolitical context where patronage from the Cold War superpowers quickly dried up, regimes and rebels alike needed to find other sources of revenue. One option utilized by both governments and insurgent leaders was to let their armed forces pay themselves by plundering the civilian population. Another was to focus their energies on the economically valuable areas of the country and farm out the other areas to either local strongmen or no one at all. In areas where civilians faced the prospect of regular encounters with armed rebels or government soldiers, it was not surprising that many of them chose to run away, even if it meant leaving their home and source of livelihood. Fortunately, for the combatants in Africa's wars, there was often a variety of international actors, from peacekeepers to humanitarian workers, most of whom brought useful resources with them. And, as the years wore on, rebels and government troops across the continent realized that there were often few severe penalties for plundering these 'external' resources.

External actors were also emblematic of the third main explanation for Africa's terrain of struggle: the intensifying interconnections available to belligerents through all sorts of cross-border networks, institutions and processes. Tapping into the global economy, diaspora networks or regional allies thus became the modus operandi for regimes and rebels alike. Whether this was to purchase weapons, attract political support or acquire some of the essential gadgets of twenty-first-century conflict, such as a Thuraya satellite phone or a Toyota Hilux land cruiser, Africa's conflicts were transnationalized. Importantly, however, they retained their local roots and idiosyncrasies. Understanding the key ingredients which went into these unique war recipes is the challenge that occupies part II of this book.

Ingredients

CHAPTER THREE

Neopatrimonialism

Since the 1980s, the concept of neopatrimonialism has frequently been used to explain the forms of political domination apparent within African states.[1] Critics, however, argued that the concept was being used in an unclear and ambiguous manner which tended to rob it of any potential analytical utility.[2] This chapter defends the idea that a refined understanding of neopatrimonialism is a vital concept for understanding the roots of many African conflicts.[3] In particular, it analyses the extent to which a link can be identified between neopatrimonial systems of governance and armed conflict in post-Cold War Africa.

Overall, I argue that neopatrimonial systems of governance do not automatically lead to armed conflict because they can vary considerably, taking more or less severe forms, and because some rulers have been adept at managing factionalized politics and effectively stifling the opportunities for rebellion. Nevertheless, the factionalization of society that neopatrimonialism inevitably produces leaves them at a significant risk of instability. This system of governance should therefore be understood as an important underlying factor that enhances the risk of armed conflict but does not necessarily mean warfare is inevitable. The risks were especially acute when neopatrimonial systems experienced a crisis which the ruling authorities were unable to contain. Such crises tended to occur when external resources (financial or political) dried up, when outrageous behaviour tested the limits of the system's legitimacy, or when other factors developed that made armed rebellion feasible for marginalized segments of the population. As William Reno concluded, the 'critical juncture' appeared when rulers were 'no longer able to assert their dominance over local strongmen in their patronage network'. At that point, armed groups were utilized 'for their own commercial and political benefit without the ruler's authorization'.[4]

To explore these issues, the chapter proceeds in three main parts. It begins by outlining the central characteristics of neopatrimonial systems of governance. These can be understood as state–society complexes where the machinery of the modern bureaucratic state is infused with traditional ideas about patronage and clientelism. Understanding how power operates in neopatrimonial systems helps us understand the local roots of many of Africa's wars. The second section discusses two pathways through which neopatrimonial regimes were linked to armed conflict in post-Cold War Africa: periods of economic and political crisis and the challenges thrown up by democratization. The final section explores how neopatrimonial structures in Sierra Leone eventually collapsed under a variety of political and economic crises, resulting in a decade-long and bloody civil war.

Neopatrimonialism: A Brief Aetiology

Neopatrimonial regimes are hybrid, uncertain, unstable and usually authoritarian systems of governance. They are a hybrid mix of legal-rational bureaucracy and personalized systems of power involving clientalism and patronage.[5] They produce a significant degree of uncertainty over which of these two systems will dictate the decision-making process in any given situation. These regimes encourage the factionalization of society and tend to exhibit authoritarian tendencies inasmuch as the institutions of state are regularly used to sustain patrons and supporters and weaken political opponents. Political order in neopatrimonial systems is therefore inherently unstable because it rests on threats of retribution against opponents rather than general satisfaction with the status quo.[6] None of these characteristics are absolutes; they are matters of degree along a spectrum. As one analyst put it, although Houphouet-Boigny's neopatrimonialism in Côte d'Ivoire clearly had its drawbacks, it was 'infinitely preferable' to Idi Amin's version in Uganda.[7] Within neopatrimonial regimes the most senior elites are engaged in a constant balancing act to ensure stability and thereby preserve their status. Periods of crisis threaten this often delicate balance.

The number of neopatrimonial regimes in post-Cold War Africa is a source of some debate. Some analysts argued that 'neo-patrimonialism is virtually the only workable mode of governance in tropical Africa' and 'is the *core* feature of politics in Africa'.[8] Similarly, writing in the late 1990s, Chabal and Daloz argued that it was plausible to claim that every state in black Africa except South Africa suffered from at least some form of neopatrimonialism because they lacked a professional and uncorrupted civil service – one where kinship ties or communal loyalty to ruling elites did not count for more than qualifications or professional competence.[9] Other analysts have discussed cases where the patrimonial logic did not dominate government, including the *dergue* in Ethiopia, the military executives which at various times ran Niger, Mali and Ghana, and Botswana and Gambia, both of which were offered as examples of pluralist politics where the presidents frequently acted as if there were some real constitutional constraints on their power.[10]

For the purposes of this chapter, I assume that neopatrimonial rule was a widespread though not necessarily universal phenomenon and that it was particularly pronounced in many of the African countries which experienced armed conflict after 1990.

With these points in mind, it is important to flesh out the ideas of hybridity, uncertainty and instability in a bit more detail. In contrast to traditional patrimonial systems, where the personal whims of the ruler dictated state policy regardless of formal bureaucratic rules and procedures, *neopatrimonial* systems are commonly understood as a hybrid mix of personalized and bureaucratic logics of governance. As Clapham argued, neopatrimonialism was 'a form of organisation in which relationships of a broadly patrimonial type pervade a political and administrative system which is formally constructed on rational-legal lines. Officials hold positions in bureaucratic organisations with powers which are formally defined, but exercise those powers . . . as a form . . . of private property.'[11] In other words, these were hybrid systems, but it was the ruler's personal interests that called the shots inasmuch as formal bureaucratic procedures would rarely be allowed to stand in the way of the wishes of the president and senior political elites. Nicolas van de Walle made a similar point when he suggested that 'African political systems became *neopatrimonial*' when 'an external façade of modern rational-legal administration' co-existed 'with an internal patrimonial logic of dyadic exchange, prebendalism, and the private appropriation of public resources by state elites'.[12] He also made the important observation that the system of modern rational-legal administration at the national level was not hermetically sealed off from international forces. Rather, what he called 'the international development business' – which included international financial institutions and various transnational corporations as well as development and humanitarian NGOs – also played an important part in setting the system's rules.

However, as Erdmann and Engel have argued, the idea that the rational-legal administration was simply a 'façade' behind which personal rule dominates arguably overstates the dominance of personal interests, or at least in many cases hides a more complicated reality. For them, it was not always the case that when personalized and bureaucratic systems of governance met the former automatically prevailed over the latter; rather the outcome often depended on the issue in question, particularly the extent to which it was perceived as being connected to issues of regime security and survival. Consequently, they suggested that neopatrimonial systems accepted the distinction between the public and private realms, at least formally, and public reference could be made to this distinction.[13] In sum, the two spheres of patrimonial and rational-legal relations not only coexist but 'permeate each other'. Erdmann and Engel therefore defined neopatrimonialism as 'a type of political domination which is characterised by *insecurity* about the behaviour and role of state institutions (and agents)'. This insecurity structures the reproduction of the system inasmuch as actions of state institutions or by state agents are not calculable; formal state institutions cannot fulfil their universalistic purpose for public welfare, which is instead decided by particularistic interests and orientations; and political informality has reached such proportions that one can even speak of institutionalized informality.

The upshot of their analysis was that, while Africa's post-Cold War political leaders regularly deviated from their bureaucratic roles, there were also situations in which political elites – even quite senior ones – did follow rational-legal procedures. Of course, this was most likely to occur when the formal rules coincided with elite interests. Thus, as Goran Hyden put it, 'political leaders in Africa have had a very instrumental view of constitutions and formal institutions, treating them seriously only when it has suited them.'[14] While this was certainly true on many occasions, there were also times when elites were not able to ignore completely rational-legal constraints. A good case in point was the Nigerian Senate's May 2006 decision to reject a bill which would have permitted President Olusegun Obasanjo to secure himself a third presidential term.

At a more general level, it is also notable that, in twenty-first-century Africa, 'the formal rules of the game are beginning to matter in ways that they previously have not.'[15] Between 1990 and 2005, for example, eighteen African presidents reached the two-term limit imposed on their presidency by their state's constitution. Of these, nine left office and nine tried to change the constitution in order to extend their terms, of whom three failed and six succeeded.[16] While the fact that six presidents succeeded in bending the rational-legal system to fit their own preferences suggests that some states still resemble personal fiefdoms, it is also notable that

> Each of these leaders was probably strong enough to have voided his country's constitution and declared himself president for life, as many previous African leaders once did. Yet each of these more recent presidents felt the need to spend considerable political and financial capital trying to secure the votes to change the constitution – a feeling that in itself shows how heavily the formal rules have come to weigh.[17]

There is thus reasonably compelling evidence to suggest that rulers of neopatrimonial regimes faced increasing challenges to their ability simply to dictate political outcomes. Yet it is also true that these challenges were not nearly so pronounced in the early 1990s as they were by the twenty-first century.

Returning to the theme of uncertainty, important practical and analytical questions still remain: Why and when will political leaders deviate from their legal-rational roles? How far will they deviate? And, to what extent is it possible to predict and avert such behaviour? It is because the behaviour of Africa's state elites could not be predicted with a great degree of accuracy that uncertainty should be considered a central characteristic of neopatrimonial systems.

But even uncertainty has its limits. First, more senior political elites were more likely to overrule the official bureaucratic procedures. Hence, while presidents got their way far more often than not, officials lower down the pecking order might not be able to break the bureaucratic rules quite so easily or so frequently. Second, in cases of national (or, more accurately, regime) security, bureaucratic procedures were more likely to be cast aside in the interests of regime survival.

Moreover, uncertainty had its uses for certain well-placed actors. Indeed, Chabal and Daloz coined the phrase 'the political instrumentalization of disorder' to describe 'the process by which political actors in Africa seek to maximize their returns on the state of confusion, uncertainty, and sometimes even chaos, which characterizes most African polities.' This 'condition' thus offered significant 'opportunities for those who know how to play the system'.[18] Specifically, it allowed them to respond to the demands for protection, assistance and aid made by their constituents in exchange for the recognition of the political prominence and social status which, as patrons, they craved. The instrumentalization of the prevailing political (dis)order thus served as a disincentive to develop a more properly institutionalized rational-legal state. This, in turn, often had repercussions for the regime's ability to suppress rebellion.

The final two elements in my understanding of neopatrimonial systems relate to authoritarianism and political instability. For some analysts, 'neopatrimonialism corresponds with authoritarian politics'.[19] This is relevant for analysing armed conflicts because recent quantitative analysis suggests that 'civil wars tend to occur within more authoritarian states'.[20] Others, however, take a slightly less draconian line, arguing that 'there is nothing in patrimonialism that leads directly to any one regime type, and there is nothing inherent in patrimonialism to prevent the creation of a democracy by leaders determined to do so.'[21] While I believe neopatrimonial rule is likely to encourage authoritarian tendencies, there is, as noted above, an important question of degree but also a substantive difference. On the latter, Paul Richards has made a persuasive argument, derived from his studies of Sierra Leone, that the central 'bad' point of neopatrimonial rule is the 'chronic tendency towards factionalization between those who "enjoy" and those who feel excluded'.[22] In this sense, neopatrimonialism does not automatically equate to dictatorship, but it does divide societies and render the subsequent divisions increasingly important in political, economic and social terms.

The essence of this politics of division was captured most eloquently by the Nigerian novelist Chinua Achebe, who used his country as a backdrop to describe the essential dynamics of post-independence politics in the following manner:

> A man who has just come in from the rain and dried his body and put on dry clothes is more reluctant to go out again than another who has been indoors all the time. The trouble with our new nation was that none of us had been indoors long enough to be able to say 'to hell with it'. We had all been in the rain together until yesterday. Then a handful of us – the smart, and the lucky and hardly ever the best – had scrambled for the one shelter our former rulers left, and had taken it over and barricaded themselves in. And from within they sought to persuade the rest through numerous loudspeakers, that the first phase of the struggle had been won and that the next phase – the expansion of our house – was even more important and called for new and original tactics; it required all argument to cease and the whole people to speak with one voice and that any more dissent and argument outside the door of the shelter would subvert and bring down the whole house.[23]

Over forty years later, Richard Dowden correctly observed: 'Most Africans have been in the rain ever since. In most African countries the elite grabbed the postcolonial state for themselves and boarded it up against the people. They embraced all the oppressive colonial laws and changed very little except the size of their bank accounts.'[24]

Those at the top end of neopatrimonial regimes thus faced a constant political balancing act to manage the divide between those inside the house and those still stuck in the rain. This was usually done via various strategies of elite co-optation or accommodation.[25] As Kenneth Omeje has described it,

> Elite co-optation is one method of conflict regulation and settlement that many neo-patrimonial states in Africa use effectively to weaken opposition and rebuild a form of consensus aimed at more or less preserving and perpetuating the status quo. By elite co-optation African political regimes aim to placate, disorganize, silence or weaken salient pressure groups by luring vocal and influential members of the groups into the ruling circle with offers of strategic appointments, government contracts and other tangible benefits designed to incorporate them into the state patronage network. In turn, the co-opted activists are expected to mellow their antagonism against the state and possibly also appeal to their members to follow suit.[26]

When carried out successfully, this strategy caused the size of the incumbent party and its supporters to inflate. In such circumstances, it was difficult for individuals to oppose the ruling party effectively from the outside. Not only would incumbents tend to deploy the institutions of state to their own advantage to discredit and weaken opponents, but in countries without a tradition of electoral democracy it was often difficult to get people to reject their current leaders. As one commentator wryly noted, 'Opposition candidates in Africa are frequently told, "I will vote for you when you are President." '[27] In addition, opposition leaders were often treated with great suspicion, as one rather humorous example illustrates. In 1991 Neil Kinnock, leader of the British Labour Party, then in opposition, was touring southern Africa when bad weather forced his plane to land in Zimbabwe at a small airstrip in the bush. When he proudly announced he was leader of the opposition in Britain, the local authorities arrested him, thinking they had caught an important terrorist.[28]

The main point here is that the logic of neopatrimonialism was not simply forced upon completely unwilling societies by a tiny elite; rather this mode of governance had a degree of legitimacy which reflected certain widely held assumptions about the purpose of political power and leadership. As Robert Bates has observed, the lack of adherence to rational-legal rules in neopatrimonial regimes was not only supported by those at the top of the political food chain; it also had supporters nearer the bottom end. Here, 'constituents viewed politicians as their agents whose job it was to bring material benefits to the local community – jobs, loans, or cash.'[29] After all, in neopatrimonial systems, the 'truly destitute are those without patrons'.[30] From the perspective of the politicians at the top, their primary purpose was to 'distribute benefits in a way designed to return [themselves] to office, while preserving as large a portion as possible for their own consumption'.[31] As one Zambian minister opined, 'If I don't appoint people from my own region, who else will?'[32] This sentiment also spilled over into situations of armed conflict where, drawing on evidence from West Africa's wars, Reno concluded that the primary goal of insurgents was 'to force their way into the social system from which they are excluded, not to overthrow it'.[33]

Changes in Africa's political leaders thus tended to occur when either the incumbent died or the baton was passed to a handpicked successor. To challenge a ruling party – even at the polls – was thus usually to invite a considerable level of personal risk with little chance of winning. In Hyden's words, 'being part of the political opposition' was generally considered 'a losing strategy'.[34] And because the state's resources were likely to be deployed almost entirely to bolster the incumbent, would-be challengers were often forced to rely on personal finances or foreign support; the latter in particular would fuel local suspicion about who was really calling the shots. Moreover, in the early 1990s major Western donors declared a new-found respect for multi-party democracy. More and more governments thus found it useful to declare that they had held and won general elections against some form of opposition. However, as Posner and Young correctly note, 'Permitting a challenger to run . . . is not the same thing as putting oneself at real risk of losing power.'[35] Most elections thus tended to return the ruling party to power.

To summarize, neopatrimonial regimes can be thought of as hybrid blends of bureaucratic and informal politics characterized by a significant degree of uncertainty and factionalization. Although this type of political order is inherently unstable, with the right strategies and tactics it can be managed effectively for considerable periods, as demonstrated by Mobutu's rule in Zaire (1965–97), Denis Sassou-Nguesso's rule in Congo-Brazzaville (1979–92) or Omar Bongo's rule in Gabon (1969–2009). It is at its most unstable in times of crisis, especially when faced with a segment of the population that is both marginalized and organized. It is in these circumstances that the likelihood of armed conflict increases.

Neopatrimonial Pathways to Violence

How might neopatrimonial systems of governance raise the risk of armed conflict? This section explores two possible pathways to violence, associated with periods of economic and political crisis and the challenges posed by democratization, respectively. It is followed by a short case study of how neopatrimonial rule was implicated in the war in Sierra Leone (1991–2002).

Times of crisis

As discussed above, it was hardly surprising that the most common approach to achieving economic or political advancement within neopatrimonial states was to seek entry into 'the house'/incumbent party. However, when the door was kept firmly closed or the house became so decrepit that it was in danger of collapsing completely, neopatrimonial regimes were likely to face a political or economic crisis, respectively. Sometimes the incumbent regimes managed them effectively; on other occasions they did not.

One pathway to armed conflict followed the onset of a serious economic crisis which weakened the regime's ability to satisfy its supporters. While African leaders were often guilty of spending relatively vast sums of money on personal or 'white elephant' projects such as stadiums, palaces or lavish conferences, arguably the more serious problem for neopatrimonial rulers was that the unavoidable balancing act of elite co-optation encouraged them to adopt policies which increased the likelihood that their state would suffer an economic crisis. As van de Walle has documented in considerable detail, between 1979 and 1999 'economic policy decisions in Africa can be understood as resulting from the combination of the state's neopatrimonial tendencies, its low capacities [especially trained administrative personnel], and its ideological biases, and the negative synergies among these three factors that evolved over time following independence.'[36]

Robert Bates made a similar point when he noted that, in the late twentieth century, many African governments became 'control regimes' which pursued policies that promoted a closed economy, distorted key prices in the macroeconomy, and heavily regulated industries and markets, all to further the short-term interests of the incumbent elites.[37] The results were disastrous, especially for many of Africa's farmers. They intensified divisions between urban elites and the rural masses and between different regions within the state. In some cases, these divisions would later provide fertile soil for would-be insurgents to recruit supporters. The choices made by these control regimes also triggered a cycle of decline: as public revenues dwindled so public sector salaries eroded, and with them the quality of public services. It wasn't long before teachers, nurses, police and other civil servants abandoned their posts or turned to corruption or private trade in search of income. The most immediate problem for political order, however, came when the state's soldiers began to pay themselves.

Sometimes, this self-induced trauma was exacerbated by pressures from external actors, especially what van de Walle labelled the 'international development business' (see above and chapter 11). In this scenario, an economic crisis could be triggered if external partners or donors suspended crucial sources of revenue. In Liberia, for example, Charles Taylor's rebellion in late 1989 was precipitated by the US government's decision that the incumbent regime led by Samuel Doe was too corrupt and uninterested in reform to warrant further support. In this situation, the social glue that held the ruling coalition together started to dissolve and, as fewer and fewer resources trickled down to the ordinary population, the ruling coalition's legitimacy eroded, thereby increasing the likelihood of violent revolt from below.[38] Bratton and van de Walle summed up the situation nicely: 'shrinking economic opportunities and exclusionary rewards are a volatile recipe for social unrest.'[39]

But it is important to note that, although an economic crisis might trigger a conflict and/or regime change, it did not necessarily signal wholesale rejection of the idea of neopatrimonialism by the new elites or the population at large. As Chabal and Daloz observed, 'it is the decline in the resources available for patronage rather than dissatisfaction with the patrimonial order *per se* which has undermined the legitimacy of political elites on the continent.'[40] In other words, although the personalities at the top may change – from Doe to Taylor, Mobutu to Kabila, Stevens to Momoh, Moi to Kibaki, Obasanjo to Yar'Adua, etc. – politics within these states remained 'grounded in a logic of clientelistic reciprocity'. This constituted 'very strong evidence that a certain notion of leadership remain[ed] fundamental in Africa'.[41]

It was precisely this zero-sum notion of leadership that encouraged political crises, because segments of the population were left angry and marginalized. Anger could stem from multiple sources, including a sense of relative deprivation or a ruler's willingness to engage in excessive behaviour which went well beyond traditionally acceptable (social and/or political) limits and hence undermined their own legitimacy.[42] Frustration could also build when people were denied the ability to influence political processes that affected them. In this sense, the tendency of most neopatrimonial regimes to suffocate legitimate political opposition, either through the use of direct coercion or by controlling other institutions such as the judiciary and/or the media, was not helpful.

Take the case of Meles Zenawi's Ethiopian People's Revolutionary Democratic Front (EPRDF) government. For many years this was widely touted by Western governments as a model for Africa's renaissance, exemplified by the fact that Meles was one of only two sitting African heads of state invited to form part of Tony Blair's Commission for Africa during 2004 and 2005.[43] Yet, just two months after the Commission released its report, Ethiopia's national elections were mired in controversy, and nearly two hundred people who protested against the results were killed by government security forces in the streets of Addis Ababa. Across the country an additional 30,000 people were arrested or detained, and the so-called 111 high-level detainees were charged with many offences, including treason and genocide. The parliamentary commission of inquiry which investigated this episode concluded that the actions of the security forces had been 'legal and necessary'.[44] Writing later that year, Christopher Clapham noted how the local population was left with few legitimate avenues to challenge the ruling government peacefully. 'People who opposed the government for whatever reason', he observed, 'have had no options beyond passive obedience, covert subversion under a guise of acceptance, or outright revolt.' This was primarily because the EPRDF had 'shown no inclination at all to accept any compromise or power-sharing solution, even though this has been proposed by the opposition.'[45] While the EPRDF regime was never seriously in danger of being toppled militarily, insurgencies emerged in several parts of the country, most notably perhaps in the form of the Oromo Liberation Front (OLF) and the Ogaden National Liberation Front (ONLF) (see also chapter 5).

This trend was not only visible in Ethiopia. Arguably the two most important academic studies of African insurgencies (published a decade apart) both reached similar conclusions about the origins of the continent's guerrilla movements. For Clapham, they derived 'basically from blocked political aspirations, and in some cases also from reactive desperation'.[46] Similarly, the editors of the more recent volume concluded that African guerrillas were best thought of 'as manifestations of a rage against the "machinery" of the dysfunctional neopatrimonial state'.[47] In essence, they argued, these insurgencies stemmed from common experiences rooted in the excesses of corruption, violence, poverty and marginalization that occurred within the continent's most dysfunctional neopatrimonial states.[48] Within this overall context, regimes which created large pools of disaffected youth and left them with few 'means of achieving status or material improvement' were thought to be particularly susceptible to violent rebellion.[49] These qualitative studies lend additional support to the quantitative evidence, noted above, which suggested civil wars tend to occur in more authoritarian states.

Of course, if neopatrimonial regimes could manage political opponents effectively and keep potential insurgents in check, they could endure for decades. To do this, rulers needed to ensure that sufficient resources trickled down to their clients to keep the majority satisfied. In this sense, the legitimacy of elites in neopatrimonial systems was tied to 'their ability to nourish the clientele on which their power rests'. In practice, this usually meant using the state's resources for patrimonial purposes.[50] The more their legitimacy eroded, the more dependent they became upon maintaining enough coercive power to scupper any rebellions.

As the post-Cold War historical record demonstrates, however, many African regimes were not very good at preventing rebellions or stopping them once they had started. Part of the explanation lay in the fact that it didn't always take many disgruntled people with guns to form a significant insurgency. The Revolutionary United Front (RUF) of Sierra Leone, for example, started life with fewer than forty fighters, while Charles Taylor's infamous National Patriotic Front of Liberia (NPFL) could only muster approximately a hundred soldiers when it invaded Liberia in 1989.[51] A similar story was evident with Joseph Kony's longstanding Lord's Resistance Army, which is thought to have revolved around a core of 300 to 400 stalwarts who shepherded several thousand rank-and-file recruits.[52]

More recent insurgencies have also coalesced around a small core of committed fighters. The Liberians United for Reconciliation and Democracy (LURD), for instance, began its attacks on Charles Taylor's regime with only seventy fighters.[53] In Sudan, the Darfur Liberation Front (DLF) started its campaign with about 300 troops before it morphed into the subsequently much larger Sudan Liberation Army (SLA).[54] In Algeria, the Salafist Group for Preaching and Combat (GSPC) was thought to have originated with approximately 700 fighters.[55] About 800 were evident in the early days of the Patriotic Movement of Côte d'Ivoire (MPCI).[56] And, although it has engaged in more criminalized activity, the Movement for the Emancipation of the Niger Delta (MEND) took on the Nigerian state with fewer than 300 fighters (see chapter 4).[57] Even Africa's largest wars have been driven by relatively small warring parties. In the DRC, for example, the two main non-state armed groups in the east of the country, the *Congrès national pour la défense du peuple* (CNDP) and the *Forces Démocratiques de Libération du Rwanda* (FDLR), are estimated to control only between 4,000 and 7,000 and 7,000 combatants, respectively.[58]

What these figures reveal is that many major political crises derive from small and hence vulnerable rebel movements. As Jeffrey Herbst has argued, it would therefore have been prudent to deal with them before they became mature insurgencies.[59] The problem was that paranoid African rulers often kept most of their armed forces weak and divided on purpose – usually as part of a broader response to insecurity which entailed 'the intentional destruction of state institutions in favour of basing political authority on the ability to control markets'.[60] This approach may have reduced the risks of palace coups but it rarely produced effective armies. Consequently, it was not always easy for neopatrimonial authorities to defeat even small rebellions, including those listed above. The parlous state of the armed forces also allowed rebels to exploit the governing regime by encouraging defections within its army or by simply routing ineffective troops. Probably the best example of the latter scenario was the campaign launched by Laurent Kabila's Rwandan- and Ugandan-backed Alliance of Democratic Forces for the Liberation of Congo–Zaire (AFDL) in 1996 against Mobutu Sese Seko's government in Zaire. Mobutu's army was so weak that 'the AFDL mostly saw it running away; the only fighting during the campaign was done by foreigners' (namely mercenaries, the army of the former Rwandan government and its *Interahamwe* militias, as well as some UNITA rebels from Angola).[61]

Before moving on, it is important to note two further general observations. First, the existence of marginalized groups – even large ones – did not automatically produce an insurgency. For a rebellion to develop, those groups with grievances needed to organize and retain followers, keep them supplied with weapons, and avoid early military defeat. Second, it was rarely the truly destitute who started Africa's insurgencies. Using data collected by the Afrobarometer survey on seven southern African states – Botswana, Lesotho, Malawi, Namibia, South Africa, Zambia and Zimbabwe – Anthony Leysens concluded that 61.6 per cent of the populations of these states were marginal-ized in socio-economic terms; 30 per cent existed in a precarious relationship to the mode of production; and 8.4 per cent were integrated into the formal economy.[62] When each group was analysed in terms of its potential for resis-tance, Leysens found that not only was the protest potential of the marginal-ized majority lower than that of the economically integrated but they were also more tolerant of authoritarian forms of government. Consequently, he concluded that 'societies where large parts of the population are poor and marginalised are not necessarily more prone to political instability in the form of protest actions (violent or nonviolent).'[63] In short, it is possible for regimes to face severe political and economic crises and avoid the outbreak of civil war.

The threat of democratization

A second pathway to violence begins when neopatrimonial regimes attempt to democratize. As discussed in chapter 1, the Political Instability Task Force (PITF) examined 141 episodes of instability worldwide during the period 1955–2003 in order to 'identify states that will or will not experience political instability two years hence with over 80% accuracy'.[64] Sub-Saharan Africa was the most unstable region during this period, accounting for forty-nine epi-sodes of instability, or 34.8 per cent of the global total. After assessing 'accu-mulated data for more than 1,000 variables', the Task Force concluded that 'relatively simple models can identify the factors associated with a broad range of political violence and instability events around the world.'[65] Specifically, 'partial democracies with factionalism' were 'an exceptionally unstable type of regime' and most at risk of severe political instability.[66] As the Task Force concluded,

> by far the worst situation in terms of risks of instability were for a political landscape that combined deeply polarized or factionalized competition with open contestation. The combination of a winner-take-all, parochial approach to politics with opportunities to compete for control of central state authority represents a powder keg for political crisis.[67]

These findings were confirmed in a separate study by other PITF members, which concluded that 'anocracies' – countries whose governments are neither fully democratic nor fully autocratic – 'have been much more vulnerable to new outbreaks of armed societal conflict; they have been about six times more likely than democracies and two and one-half times as likely as autocracies to experience new outbreaks of societal wars.'[68]

The Task Force team defined 'factionalism' as occurring 'when political competition is dominated by ethnic or other parochial groups that regularly compete for political influence in order to promote particularist agendas and favor group members to the detriment of common, secular, or cross-cutting agendas.'[69] Although they do not use the term explicitly, their understanding of partial democracies/anocracies combined with factionalism bears more than a passing resemblance to my definition of neopatrimonial systems. The Task Force did not suggest that partial democracy and factionalist politics are the only significant factors producing severe instability, but they did note that the kinds of patterns of political authority that characterize neopatrimonial regimes are 'the critical factor'.[70]

On sub-Saharan Africa specifically, the PITF identified five other ingredients which played a significant role 'in shifting the relative odds of instability':[71]

- trade openness: states 'with lower trade openness . . . had roughly two to three times higher odds of near-term instability than countries with higher openness to trade';
- state-led (economic or political) discrimination;
- colonial heritage: 'countries that were not formerly French colonies [have] odds of instability roughly four to thirteen times greater than former French possessions';
- leaders' years in office: 'new leaders (less than five years in office) and "entrenched" leaders (those more than fourteen years in office) . . . faced higher odds of instability than their peers who had been in office from 5–14 years';
- a state's religious composition: 'Countries that had a dominant religious majority (over two-thirds of the population identified with the main religious group) were *more* likely to experience instability than countries in which the population was more evenly divided among different religious groups.'

The Task Force's overall conclusion was startling: 'in our data *every African country that mixed partial democracy with factionalism suffered instability.*'[72]

In sum, the most likely time for a country to experience severe political instability is when it begins to make the transition from an autocracy to a partial democracy. This was precisely what happened across many parts of the African continent as the Cold War came to an end.[73] Expressed in numerical terms, while, in 1988, 90 per cent of sub-Saharan African states had autocratic governments, by the early twenty-first century that figure had dropped dramatically.[74] Interestingly, the Task Force noted that a rush to establish electoral competition without ensuring 'a system of checks and balances' to constrain 'elected chief executives' was a recipe for generating instability.[75] These are wise words, and the issues they raise are discussed more thoroughly in part III of this book.

The Case of Sierra Leone

The war in Sierra Leone (1991–2002) provides a good example of these pathways in action. Since at least its independence in 1961, the country's politics had been based upon corrupt patrimonial networks that operated across both the formal and the informal economy.[76] William Reno used the phrase 'shadow state' to explain the relationship between corruption and politics in Sierra Leone whereby the power of successive rulers was based upon their ability to control both formal and informal markets rather than upon some concept of popular legitimacy.[77] After 1968 the system of patronage revolved around Siaka Stevens and his All Peoples Congress (APC). For all intents and purposes, politics in Sierra Leone turned into 'an affair for and by APC members and supporters . . . that made access to resources impossible for non-members; it made membership of the party a *sine qua non* to get by; exclusion literally meant death by attrition.'[78]

During this process of privatizing power and wealth, Afro-Lebanese businessmen such as Jamil Sahid Mohammed played a crucial intermediary role between the global economy and patrimonial accumulation within the country.[79] Since these Lebanese dealers had few local social networks from which they could challenge Stevens's rule, they were allocated the bulk of diamond mining licences in preference to African dealers. They also had access to international diamond markets and credit networks, particularly in the Middle East, that helped make collaborative ventures with Stevens a success. During the 1970s and 1980s, however, the state's institutions withered as Stevens became increasingly dependent upon Lebanese management of the economy to provide his supporters with resources.

By the time Stevens's handpicked successor, Joseph Momoh, assumed power in 1985 the country was in crisis.[80] Stevens's patrimonial networks had pocketed increasing portions of the country's primary assets, especially diamonds. By 1987, for instance, taxable revenue generated by alluvial diamond mining was a mere $100,000 compared with over $200 million in 1968.[81] With dwindling state coffers, it wasn't long before the civil service – which by the mid-1980s employed an estimated 100,000 staff – became increasingly demoralized in the face of falling wages and a lack of resources. By 1985, civil servants received only 40 per cent of 1975 salary levels, if they were paid at all.[82] Public expenditure declined from 31 per cent of GDP in 1980–1 to 16 per cent by 1987–8, with development expenditures falling from 4.9 per cent to 2.2 per cent over the same period. The education system – once heralded as making Sierra Leone the 'Athens' of West Africa – was also devastated: teachers increasingly refused to teach and students dropped out of school in large numbers. Later, these drop-outs became easy prey for the rebels' anti-establishment rhetoric.[83] In practice, the armed forces came to represent virtually the only visible state institution – and they were neither professional nor effective.[84] By 1989–90 some 2.8 million people (68 per cent of the population) lived in absolute poverty, most of them in the country's rural areas. This number grew with the influx of refugees (equivalent to 5 per cent of the population) from the war in neighbouring Liberia.[85] Indeed, in Sierra Leone's case the political crisis that triggered the war came as a direct result of external forces, most notably the support given to the RUF rebels by Libya's Colonel

Gaddafi and Liberia's Charles Taylor. In this sense, the crisis spread as more and more individuals and groups within Sierra Leone took advantage of the rebellion for their own purposes.[86]

Facing the twin challenges of a decrepit set of state institutions and a snowballing insurgency, Momoh's regime struggled to keep the wheels of patronage turning, and in April 1992 he was overthrown by Captain Valentine Strasser. However, Strasser quickly found himself facing those same pressures. Meanwhile, the RUF rebels grew stronger, collaborated with a variety of disenchanted army units and forcibly deprived the state of access to its most lucrative resources, diamonds. But it was not only the rebels who benefited from this state of affairs: the RUF incursions also provided the cover for a variety of alienated and excluded groups (including youth, private miners and government soldiers) to participate in trading networks that had previously been dominated by Freetown elites and state officials and to exploit both local civilian and material resources in these areas.[87]

By 1995 the rebels had advanced to within striking distance of the capital, Freetown. Even so, Strasser was unable to divert all state resources to the war effort because his external creditors expected his regime to continue its debt repayments. This made it difficult to build, train, equip and pay an army capable of defeating the RUF. Consequently, in late 1994, Strasser had hired the private military company Gurkha Security Guards Ltd to gain control of resource-rich areas of the country. However, after falling victim to a rebel ambush in which several of its leading figures were killed, the company left Sierra Leone. It was replaced with the South African-based Executive Outcomes, which was much more successful in gaining control of the diamond fields.[88] While this strategy brought Strasser control of some economically important areas, it produced a situation where the commercial success of certain elements within the army and various foreign firms came to depend upon a state of war against the RUF. What Reno dubbed the 'threat of peace' led one hardliner, Julius Maada Bio, to launch a successful coup in January 1996.[89] Bio quickly succumbed to external pressure to allow the elections that saw Ahmed Tejan Kabbah assume the presidency. However, in May 1997, Kabbah too was toppled by yet another coup, led by Major Johnny Paul Koroma.

As even this brief account makes clear, Sierra Leone had suffered from decades of neopatrimonial rule without an open rebellion. It was only during the economic and political crises of the late 1980s that the RUF emerged on the scene. Although there is not a complete consensus on the reasons behind the RUF's rise, analysts generally agree that an important part of its membership came from the country's lumpen youth, who were mobilized by a small group of people angry at their exclusion from an opaque and corrupt patrimonial system that did not provide for their needs.[90] They were supported economically, politically and militarily by external parties, including the authorities in Libya and Burkina Faso and, perhaps most importantly, Taylor's rebel group in Liberia, the NPFL.

Even with the dire state of the country, the RUF leaders were not particularly successful in attracting large numbers of voluntary recruits; this was because of their confused political message (which had not been helped by Sankoh organizing the murder of the movement's best intellectuals)[91] and the terrible atrocities they perpetrated against civilians. In order to grow its numbers the RUF thus quickly resorted to coercive methods. It was able to continue this process for a considerable period in large part because of the terrible state of Sierra Leone's armed forces. Yet, even as it grew more coercive, the RUF still attempted to rationalize to its new 'abductees' why they had been 'recruited'. As one RUF lecture put it,

> There was no fairness and transparency in the system in Sierra Leone. Despite mineral riches, there was no development of roads, schools and health centres in rural areas. No one in government was listening. Thus the time for talking had passed. Violence was now the only option. Young people had been abducted for guerrilla training to regain their birthright.[92]

And sometimes it struck a chord. As one young abducted rebel fighter put it, 'I'm revolutionary to the bone. I came to know how things were transpiring in this country. It's only a game of dirty politics!'[93] While the RUF's demands for a slice of the national cake were understandable, the methods it employed in pursuit of these demands were unjustifiable.[94] It thus quickly alienated the vast majority of Sierra Leoneans through its attacks on civilians and its failure to promote a genuine programme of societal transformation.[95] The RUF's moral bankrupcy was reflected in its repeated use of conspicuous atrocity. While all sides in the conflict were guilty of abuses, the Truth and Reconciliation Commission (TRC) of Sierra Leone concluded that the RUF committed by far the highest proportion of atrocities.[96] Specifically, these rebels were thought to have been responsible for nearly 60 per cent of all violations recorded by the TRC during the war (see figure 3.1).[97]

Nevertheless, as President Kabbah correctly noted, 'while we [may] unreservedly condemn the junta and its RUF allies, we must not forget to ask ourselves why it happened.'[98] Part of the answer was that, since Siaka Stevens's rule, successive leaders of Sierra Leone had not only given people reason to sympathize with an insurgency but, in order to preserve their patrimonial networks, had dismantled the primary means to combat the one that emerged: an effective and accountable army.[99]

Conclusion

In a piece reflecting on the controversial elections in Ethiopia in 2005, Christopher Clapham argued that 'The place to start trying to understand any political crisis is always with the government in power.'[100] The evidence provided in this chapter suggests he is correct, especially when the government in power ran a neopatrimonial system. Although neopatrimonial rulers

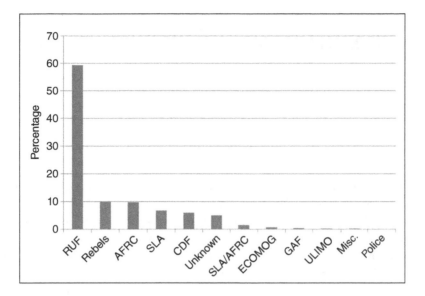

Source: Conibere et al., Appendix 1, p. 23.

Figure 3.1 *Sierra Leone: proportion of violations by perpetrator group*

who possessed astute leadership skills and a surfeit of resources could avoid large-scale armed conflict for long periods of time, the inherent factionalism and the subsequent tendency to rely on coercion produced fundamentally unstable political orders. In this sense, neopatrimonial governance was an important ingredient in many of Africa's armed conflicts. The usual trigger factors which caused the system to break down were an economic or political crisis or the 'threat' of genuine democratization. With the West's triumph in the Cold War, the threat of democratization appeared more regularly across the continent. In addition, it was ironic that the strategies deliberately pursued by neopatrimonial regimes often increased the risks of generating economic or political crises and made it harder to deal with insurgencies when they formed.

Sierra Leone was just one tragic example of these dynamics at work. In arguably the most careful study of the conflict, David Keen concluded that, by the end of the Cold War, the country's 'long history of underdevelopment culminating in some two decades of single-party APC rule and endemic corruption had generated considerable support for some kind of radical "shake up".'[101] When a small group of the marginalized had finally had enough, external support for their rebellion, combined with widespread disenchantment among the populace and the security services, ignited and sustained what one analyst dubbed 'a dirty war in West Africa'.[102] Unfortunately, it was far from being the only one.

CHAPTER FOUR

Resources

Africa's wars are often referred to as resource wars, fought not over compet-ing political ideologies but by greedy individuals in order to accumulate wealth by extracting the continent's 'natural' resources such as oil, gems, minerals and timber. This is not unique to Africa. Over the last sixty years, the UN Environment Programme (UNEP) estimated that at least 40 per cent of all intra-state conflicts worldwide have been linked to natural resources. Worryingly, UNEP concluded that these conflicts were twice as likely to relapse into violence in the first five years after a settlement.[1] Some analysts suggested the drying up of superpower patronage after the Cold War exacerbated this trend by encouraging Africa's belligerents to become self-financing.[2] Others argued that the end of the Cold War changed little: Africa's rebellions were always best explained 'by the atypical circumstances that generate profitable opportunities'.[3] This 'greed thesis' argued that rebels were motivated principally by the prospects for looting and exploiting resources rather than by rectifying injustice. From this perspective, rebellion was essen-tially a form of criminal activity, only it was less common because of the greater risks and start-up costs involved.[4] Lots of African rebels seemed to fit the bill. Sierra Leone's Revolutionary United Front (RUF), for example, was comprised of lumpen youth, mostly 'unemployed and unemployable' males 'prone to criminal behaviour, petty theft, drugs, drunkenness and gross indis-cipline'.[5] Rwanda's genocidal militias were said to consist of many 'small-time criminals' and 'young thugs who worked for the highest bidder'.[6] Similarly, the *janjawiid* in Darfur were characterized as 'outlaw-type bands' and 'bandit militia' comprised mainly of unemployed youths whose main motivation was a desire to acquire resources.[7]

In post-Cold War Africa's political landscape the greed thesis seemed simple, intuitively appealing, and seductive to policymakers. It was simple because war was defined as having a clear economic rationale – or, as David Keen put it, 'the continuation of economics by other means'.[8] The thesis was appealing because resources did seem to play a crucial role in many African wars. Indeed, some analyses concluded that there was 'an economic core . . . common to all of them'.[9] The greed thesis was also appealing to policymakers not least because it held out the promise that conflicts might be managed from the outside by imposing sanctions regimes which could cut off rebel resources and hence their ability to wage war. And, despite all their known problems, imposing sanctions was much easier than getting bogged down in the messy business of finding political solutions and perhaps even having to engage militarily.

While this perspective contains an important grain of truth it is also misleading, particularly in the popular caricature of these arguments that suggests there is something about 'resources' which explains warfare. Among its most important limitations are its preoccupation with the rebel side of the civil war equation at a time when most violence has been initiated by state elites and when there is sometimes a porous state/rebel divide; its strange tendency to de-politicize conflicts, reflected in its complete silence on one of the most important resources in Africa – sovereignty (see chapter 5); its lack of discussion of the transnational corporations which facilitate the buying and selling of the commodities in question; its simplistic, static and deeply cynical understanding of the motives behind why people join armed groups; its reliance on inappropriate proxies (especially in its quantitative form); and its confusing and misleading approach to thinking about resources.

The last point is particularly important for this chapter. Resources are not phenomena that exist apart from society which somehow exert a gravitational force over human behaviour. Rather, it is society that generates resources – i.e. those things which enable actors to achieve their objectives. Resources are thus intimately tied to both the fulfilment of material needs and the social construction of value. Put another way, resources enable but they do not cause. When they are understood as enablers, it becomes clear that wars cannot be fought without resources. It therefore makes little analytical sense to talk of resource wars because it makes little sense to talk about non-resource wars. Resources such as people, money and weapons are necessary to sustain a regime and launch a rebellion, whatever their objectives and whatever motivates their participants.

It is therefore also unhelpful to distinguish 'natural' as opposed to some type of 'unnatural' resources, because phenomena only become resources when they are perceived as useful in pursuit of somebody's agenda. Consequently, the trap of 'natural resource reductionism' needs to be avoided because it ignores the inherent political and social dimensions of armed conflict.[10] The fact that many of Africa's belligerents were self-financing does not mean the conflicts were about resources *per se*. When some resources generated profits beyond what was necessary to sustain an actor's military campaign, it provided armed groups with an incentive to continue fighting and avoid peace. But this is not the same as saying resources cause wars. At most, economic motivations were present along with several other factors, but pure 'looting rebellions' did not exist. If they did, more of Africa's military leaders would surely 'cash out after they have made millions, invest those monies in a hedge fund and retire to more pleasant surroundings'. Instead, Jonas Savimbi, Charles Taylor and other war leaders continued 'to engage in the extraordinarily dangerous and perhaps unprofitable strategy of trying to capture the capital'.[11] Contrary to the greed perspective, case study evidence provides overwhelming support for the argument that it is political systems, not resources *per se*, that are the crucial factor in elevating the risk of armed conflict. As discussed below, greater emphasis should thus be given to examining the apparatuses of resource governance.

This chapter addresses these issues in three sections. It starts by analysing the most popular general hypotheses about the relationship between resources and armed conflict. The basic argument is that, because resources are socially constructed, more attention should focus on the political economy of the particular contexts which increase the likelihood of warfare. The chapter then discusses the two types of commodities that were at the forefront of debates about Africa's wars (oil and diamonds), in large part because of their importance to the global economy beyond Africa. The final section examines the recent resurgence of interest in demographic issues and environmental change, particularly changes linked with climate, water and land.

Resources in Armed Conflict

Natural resources are often said to lie at the root of many African conflicts. One example is the NGO Global Witness and its focus on 'conflict resources', defined as 'natural resources whose systematic exploitation and trade in a context of conflict contribute to, benefit from, or result in the commission of serious violations of human rights, violations of international humanitarian law or violations amounting to crimes under international law'.[12]

This type of thinking has generated numerous attempts to classify the relationship between natural resources and armed conflict. The UNEP, for example, identified a trilogy of links.[13] First, struggles to control resources contributed to the outbreak of conflict when the wealth derived from them was not apportioned fairly; when there was competition for scarce resources including land, forests and water; and when states were dependent on the export of a narrow set of primary commodities. Second, natural resources contributed to financing and sustaining conflicts, usually by making insurgencies economically feasible and by encouraging parties to secure the assets that enabled them to continue their struggle. Third, continued access to profitable resources undermined the prospects for peacemaking. A similar but more nuanced list was generated by Macartan Humphreys, who identified five links between natural resources and warfare:

- *rent seeking*: the political impact of the availability of large natural resource rents to ruling elites (popularly known as the resource curse);
- *grievances*: primarily associated with the illegitimate distribution of natural resource wealth and socioeconomic impacts of extractive operations;

- *economic instability*: generated by the distortions associated with high dependence on natural resources;
- *conflict financing*: how natural resource wealth affects the means for belligerents to continue fighting;
- *peace spoiling*: when natural resource wealth provides disincentives for peace.[14]

Whereas the first three were associated with the outbreak of armed conflict, the final two focused on the role of resources in fuelling war.

As these examples suggest, contemporary thinking about the causes or outbreak of armed conflicts has been dominated by two broad and seemingly contradictory hypotheses: (1) a scarcity of important resources increases the risk of war; and (2) an abundance of valuable resources increases the risk of war.

The *resource scarcity* perspective has a long pedigree and global reach. Indeed, the dominant interpretation of the long sweep of human civilization offered across the social sciences, humanities and natural sciences suggests that competition for scarce resources – particularly somatic and reproductive resources – is the ultimate cause of fighting between groups of humans.[15] The contemporary variant is that groups will fight to secure access to the natural resources necessary for their survival: the more scarce the resource, the more bitter the fight. Among examples in Africa are shrinking range/grazing pasture, desertification of productive agricultural land, or declining water resources. Cases which would appear to confirm this thesis can certainly be found in Africa, particularly when focusing on relatively localized episodes of violence. Cattle-herding communities which straddle the Kenya–Uganda border, for example, have often engaged in organized violence when there have been dramatic changes in available resources. When mixed with modern firearms, their traditional forms of raiding have often left scores of people dead – certainly enough to warrant inclusion as a 'minor armed conflict' in Uppsala terminology.[16] Another example hit the headlines in late 2009 when a so-called fish war broke out around the village of Dongo in the DRC's Equateur province.[17] Fighting began when a militia from the Enyele community attacked members of the Monzaya, apparently over access to fishing ponds and nearby farm land. The violence left nearly fifty people dead and caused more than 20,000 to flee their homes. Even with the subsequent arrival of government troops and UN peacekeepers the situation escalated, causing the displacement of an estimated 145,000 people. On closer inspection, however, this episode had as much to do with political intrigues within and between the communities as with access to fish.[18]

In certain contexts an *abundance of resources*, particularly 'lootable' resources, is said to be a curse rather than an opportunity for development. Specifically, revenues generated from these resources influence the likelihood of armed conflict breaking out, the character and dynamics of conflicts, and conflict duration. Resources are commonly thought to extend conflicts because profit provides a powerful disincentive for peace. In relation to conflict dynamics, an abundance of resources is said to turn political rebellions into criminal rackets, to intensify fighting around resource-rich areas and, particularly if mass atrocities are committed, possibly to generate sanctions regimes in the buyers' markets.

In relation to the outbreak of violence, several mechanisms are commonly identified. Extreme versions of abundance arguments verge on the deterministic by suggesting there is something inherent in certain types of resources that produces conflict. For example, the editor of *Foreign Policy* magazine, one of the best-selling publications on international affairs worldwide, recently declared that 'poor but resource-rich countries tend to be underdeveloped not despite their hydrocarbon and mineral riches but *because of their resource wealth*.'[19] A more nuanced position argues that 'lucrative natural resources *can have* detrimental effects on the socioeconomic and political stability of a country, creating permissive causes of violence and armed conflict.'[20] Another variant suggests that certain types of resources are likely to stimulate particular types of conflict dynamics.[21] Separatist conflicts, for instance, are said to be more likely in resource-rich regions.[22]

Apart from these common variants, Michael Ross has identified two additional ways in which resource abundance relates to the onset of wars. In the first scenario, resource wealth helped trigger conflicts by encouraging interventions from neighbouring powers, thus placing the emphasis firmly back on political decisions. In Africa, Ross discussed two cases where external powers supported nascent rebel groups against incumbent governments, in part to gain access to natural resource wealth: Charles Taylor's support for the RUF rebels in Sierra Leone and the support provided by Ugandan and Rwandan forces to rebel movements in the DRC.[23]

The second mechanism was when rebel groups and/or governments sold what Ross called 'booty futures' – the right to exploit mineral resources that the prospective seller has not yet captured. Once again, this emphasizes the crucial importance of relationships between actors rather than the existence of resources *per se*. Ross observed that booty futures were significant ingredients in the conflicts in the Republic of Congo, the DRC, Angola, Sierra Leone and possibly Liberia. Although rebels in these conflicts initially possessed few lucrative resources, they had a chance of securing them in combat. Insurgents traded the prospect of access to these future mineral rights to foreign firms and neighbouring governments and used the proceeds to pay soldiers and buy arms, and thus gain the capacity to capture the promised resource. In April 1997, for example, Laurent Kabila was able to sign a deal worth $885 million with American Mining Fields when it became clear that his AFDL forces were going to topple Mobutu's regime. Similarly, in the Republic of Congo, Ross recounts how a former president, Denis Sassou-Nguesso, received $150 million from the French oil company, Elf-Aquitaine, to help him defeat the incumbent president, Pascal Lissouba, either by force or through a national election; the payment was clearly meant to ensure Elf's access to Congolese oil in a future Sassou government. The election never took place. Instead, Sassou and Lissouba fought a four-month war [during 1997] that destroyed much of Brazzaville and cost 10,000 lives, eventually leaving Sassou in charge.[24]

Although out of power at the time, Sassou was no ordinary rebel since, despite being voted out of office in 1992, he maintained good relations with several neighbouring regimes and international institutions, and senior figures within Congo's armed forces remained loyal to him rather than Lissouba. Indeed, the residue of his sovereign connections reflects the fact that it is usually much easier for governments than for rebels to sell booty futures. During Sierra Leone's war, the government saved itself from defeat twice by selling off the right to exploit diamond fields that it did not yet control. Similarly, in the early 1990s the Angolan government sold off future exploitation rights to two oil fields under its control but also diamond areas, some of which were controlled at the time by UNITA rebels.[25]

While the scarcity/abundance approaches have generated some interesting insights, particularly Ross's work on external intervention and booty futures, the general hypotheses are unhelpful for several reasons. First, it is too deterministic to posit an automatic link between scarce/abundant resources and the likelihood of armed conflict. This underplays the more important effects of governance structures and the social relations of particular actors. It also means these perspectives have difficulty accounting for changes in the effects of 'dangerous' resources over time. For instance, it is widely acknowledged that the likelihood of civil wars in countries that produce oil, gas and diamonds increased significantly from the early 1970s to the late 1990s.[26] Yet nothing inherent in those commodities changed during this period. Rather, changing political conditions altered their social value and effects.

The conflicts in Zaire/DRC provide an excellent example of these political dynamics at work. Although eastern DRC has always possessed huge amounts of minerals and gems, the presence of these items did not cause the recent conflicts there. Rather, what eventually became known as Africa's world war started because of a mix of cross-border security issues in the aftermath of the 1994 Rwandan genocide and governance issues in Zaire, where anti-Mobutu groups saw an opportunity finally to topple the wily old dictator with the help of the regimes in Rwanda and Uganda. Of course, the political economy of the country's resources soon became a crucial factor in shaping the dynamics of the conflict, but resources do not explain its beginning or the underlying motives of its participants.[27]

The second key point to recall about the Congo wars is that these resources did not extract and sell themselves – this was done by particular actors. Analysts therefore need to understand the identities of those actors, how they operated and, crucially, what political relationships and agendas influenced them. The most detailed early answers to these questions were set out in two reports to the UN Security Council by panels of experts, which concluded that the central mechanism in the 'illegal exploitation' of DRC's resources was the 'elite network'. These networks operated in three areas of the DRC: government-controlled, Rwanda-controlled and Uganda-controlled.[28] They consisted of a small core of political and military elites and business persons who cooperated to generate revenue. Such enterprises were made possible by their control over the military and other security forces in their area which they used to threaten and intimidate and to monopolize production, commerce and fiscal functions. In the Ugandan and Rwandan areas they also maintained the façade of rebel administrations. The financial benefits were derived through a variety of criminal activities conducted by business companies or joint ventures formed explicitly for this purpose. The UN panels concluded that the networks required the participation of eleven African transit states and seventeen end-user countries in Asia, Europe, the Middle East and North America. In addition, the networks sought out the support of organized or transnational criminal groups. In the government-controlled area, Congolese and Zimbabwean political, military and business elites generated at least $5 billion of assets, mainly revenues from minerals. In the Rwanda-controlled area the elite network was managed centrally from the army's Congo Desk. This explicitly tied the revenues from diamonds and coltan into a state security project which generated well over $300 million for the Rwandan military. Unlike the centrally managed Rwandan operation, the Ugandan network was decentralized, less hierarchical and run largely for the personal benefit of high-ranking UPDF officers, private businessmen and selected rebel leaders/administrators. It too generated most of its revenues from coltan and diamonds. The concept of elite networks reminds us that resources are always part of a political project. It is these political agendas, not the resources themselves, which generate conflict.

A second problem with the scarcity/abundance approaches is their tendency to focus on a narrow subset of countries. A more comprehensive look at resource endowments which includes rich, stable states as well as poor, unstable countries suggests that the effect of resources is non-monotonic – that is, it initially increases risk, but at a high level natural resources start to reduce the risk of war.[29] Again, this suggests resources themselves do not generate uniform effects but depend on the political circumstances.

A third limitation is that mineral wealth can explain only a small percentage of contemporary armed conflicts. For example, as Christopher Cramer observed, of the twenty-two states worldwide that experienced 'complex humanitarian emergencies' between 1992 and 1994, only seven could be called mineral-dominant economies.[30] Only three out of the nine African emergencies during this period occurred in mineral-dominant economies (Angola, Algeria, and Liberia – the last being a borderline mineral-dominant economy, with only 45 per cent of its total exports being mineral/fuel exports in 1980).[31]

A fourth problem stems from the fact that scarcity and abundance are both relative terms. Consequently, this approach suffers from a levels-of-analysis problem – that is, what might be scarce at a global level may be abundant at the local level and vice versa. For example, while 'coltan' (columbite-tantalite) production is relatively rare globally, approximately 10 per cent of the world's reserves are in central Africa and the DRC was probably the world's second largest source of tantalum in the 2000s. As a consequence it is not always very clear whether it is local abundance or global scarcity doing the explanatory work.

A fifth problem, associated particularly with the scarcity thesis, is that scarcity itself is often a product of armed conflict rather than its cause. For example, most famines in Africa were the direct or indirect product of war. In addition, the scarcity thesis ignores numerous general counter-arguments, including that resource scarcity can result in socio-economic innovation to diversify an economy; that international trade and market mechanisms can to some extent counterbalance localized scarcities or motivate innovations and shift resources; that states in resource-poor areas are more dependent than resource rich-countries on diversified financial inputs, so the government is more likely to be accountable and representative towards society; and that it is in the interest of the elite in resource-poor states to develop and harness human capital, rather than protect scarce or non-existent resource rents.[32]

A final problem with this mode of thinking, and in many ways the most fundamental, is that resources are, by definition, not natural; they are socially constructed. As Philippe Le Billon neatly put it, resources are not, they become: 'Whether or not *nature* is transformed into a resource is related to human desires, needs, and practices.' Specifically, nature's transformation 'into tradable commodities is a deeply political process; involving the definition of property rights, the organisation of labour, and the allocation of profits.' In other words, it requires not just nature's 'gift' but the construction of a 'political economy of resources' – that is, 'the creation of markets and associated commodity chains, predicated upon the social construction of desirable resources'.[33] Take the case of diamonds, Africa's archetypal conflict resource. They have no industrial use except for cutting and their abrasive properties: their high value stems from their symbolic importance in societal rituals concerning engagement, marriage, beauty and fashion and the international markets which have developed around them. Moreover, shifts in world production processes regularly change the natural elements which humans consider most valuable. With the increasing importance of micro-processors used in mobile phone and computer technologies, previously abandoned tin mines become valuable once again as routes to extract coltan – a crucial component of such goods. Similarly, as prices of cassiterite started rising on the world markets, especially in 2007–9, miners in the North Kivu region of the DRC focused their attention on extracting it rather than coltan.[34]

These points suggest that analysts need to think both about the political contexts in which particular resources are created and which ones might increase the likelihood of armed conflict. The two principal contenders in this approach are contexts of relative deprivation and conditions of 'bad' governance and political instability.

Gudrun Østby and her colleagues have made a strong case for focusing on resources in contexts of relative deprivation, arguing that even comparatively weak relative deprivation figures (e.g. two-thirds the national average) mixed with extractable commodities make a region significantly more susceptible to armed conflict.[35] They build upon Ted Gurr's classic argument that deprived individuals are more likely to take up arms against their governments. Gurr defined relative deprivation as the discrepancy between what people think they deserve (value expectations) and what they actually think they can get (value capabilities). From this perspective, people become frustrated if they do not enjoy what they think they are rightfully entitled to. If such frustration is felt for prolonged periods or intensely enough it generates anger which may be expressed violently. In Gurr's words, 'The potential for collective violence varies strongly with the intensity and scope of relative deprivation among members of a collectivity.'[36] Among their examples, Østby et al. discuss the case of Chad, where the relatively resource-rich southern regions wanted greater autonomy in order to secure a greater share of revenues from oil discoveries in their regions. As figure 4.1 illustrates, the civil war in Chad in 1997 broke out in several regions that had oil deposits and yet were socially worse off than the national mean.

The other main approach suggests that the domestic political structures are crucial in determining how resources are put to use. Since the presence of natural resources rarely triggers war in stable political environments, it must be the combination of resources and unstable governance which represents the most explosive mix. This approach has stimulated at least two variants, which might be categorized as focusing on *exploitative* governance structures and *unstable* governance structures, respectively.

A prominent example of the first variant is Colin Kahl's state exploitation thesis. Based on his analysis of the relationship between demographic and environmental issues and armed conflict in Kenya during the early 1990s, Kahl argued that state elites and their supporters exploit rising resource scarcities and channel societal grievances to advance their own political agendas.[37] He concluded that there were two key intervening variables in this process. The first was the inclusivity of political institutions – i.e. whether key social groups were empowered to participate in and influence the decision-making by state elites. Kahl concluded that more inclusive institutions reduce the likelihood that state elites will exploit demographic and environmental stress. The second key factor was what he called 'groupness' – the extent to which individuals rely on distinct identity groups for their physical, economic and psychic security. A high degree of groupness was said to increase

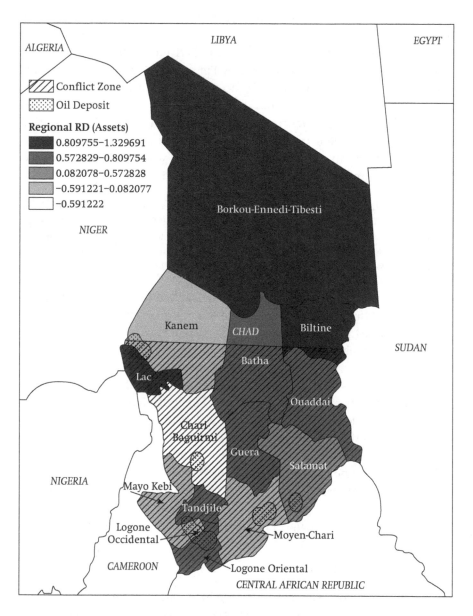

Source: Østby, Nordås and Rød, 'Regional inequalities', p. 319.

Figure 4.1 *Relative asset deprivation, natural resources, and conflict onset in Chad, 1997*
The regional RD figures refer to the relative deprivation level of the region based on the model developed by Østby et al. to measure regional assets such as socio-economic indicators, levels of education, presence of natural resources, etc.

the likelihood of state exploitation by facilitating the formation of conflict groups.

A good example of the second variant is the critique of the resource curse thesis in Congo-Brazzaville conducted by Pierre Englebert and James Ron.[38] Like Kahl, they too highlight the crucial importance of the 'interaction between primary commodities and domestic politics' in understanding the likelihood and course of war. Unlike Kahl's stress on powerful exploitative elites, Englebert and Ron argue that it is political instability, not authoritarianism and elite manipulation, which when mixed with resource abundance creates the most combustible cocktail.[39] In their words,

> If a country has a stable political system, authoritarian or otherwise, it is unlikely to experience civil war, regardless of resource availability and distribution. . . . No matter how tempting natural resources might be and how they may exacerbate ongoing instability and armed conflict, they are unlikely to stimulate civil war on their own unless the political context is already unstable.[40]

Their analysis concluded that Congo-Brazzaville had been dependent on oil for decades but that Denis Sassou-Ngeusso was able to avoid civil war between 1979 and 1992 by running a stable, single-party neopatrimonial regime (see chapter 3). The problem came in the early 1990s, when he came under international, primarily Western, pressure to democratize. Elections were held in 1992, but Sassou's subsequent defeat precipitated several rounds of 'brutal militia fighting' over the next seven years which displaced one-third of the country's population, left tens of thousands of people dead and injured, and saw thousands suffer sexual assaults. Sassou regained control of the capital city in 1997, and, ironically, the conflict was brought to at least a temporary end in 1999 when he was able to engineer what Englebert and Ron called a 'patrimonial peace', wherein he bought off most of his elite opponents by offering them jobs in the public sector. This left many Congolese poor, disenfranchised and with a corrupt set of rulers, but it did stop the civil war.

The Usual Suspects

The following section refines my analysis by disaggregating the broad category of 'resources' into particular types of commodities and their relationship to armed conflict. At the forefront of debates about warfare in Africa have been oil and diamonds, but there was also a recent resurgence of interest in demography and environmental change, especially issues related to water, climate and land.

Diamonds

In recent decades, Africa's 'blood diamonds' were widely considered a powerful source of conflict. The UN Security Council, for example, established sanctions on the export of diamonds from rebel-held parts of Angola from 1998, as well as Sierra Leone from 2000. There were also significant efforts to reform the international diamond industry by developing various forms of certification to prove the origins of particular stones.[41]

In reality, the relationship between warfare and diamonds is complicated. First, there is important quantitative evidence from large-N studies which concludes that the presence of alluvial diamonds in particular can increase the risk of civil war, especially in political contexts characterized by tensions over governance structures.[42] Alluvial diamonds are riskier because they are open to artisanal mining, whereas primary or Kimberlite deposits require high levels of industrialization for extraction; particularly in weak states, governments struggle to control artisanal mining; and the stones are small and weigh very little and are thus easy to steal and transport.

On the other hand, more qualitative analysis suggests that, although there are an estimated twenty conflicts worldwide between 1946 and 2005 which could plausibly be related to diamonds, in the period after 1990 there are only two African cases where diamonds were 'strongly related to conflict': Sierra Leone (1991–2001) and Angola (1993–2002) (see table 4.1).[43] Even in these two cases, however, there is no persuasive evidence that diamonds

Table 4.1 Diamond-related armed conflicts in Africa, 1990–2005

Location	Government (Side A)	Rebel (Side B)	Duration	War-related deaths	Major rebel funding sources
Sierra Leone	Sierra Leone, ECOWAS, UK	RUF, AFRC	1991–2001	75,000	Diamonds ($25–$75 million p.a.)
Angola	Angola	UNITA	1991–2002	700,000	Diamonds ($200–$600 million p.a.)
DRC	Zaire	AFDL, Rwanda	1996–7	230,000	Proxy
DRC	DRC, Zimbabwe, Angola, Namibia	RCD, MLC, Rwanda, Uganda	1998–2003	2.5 million	Gold, coltan, coffee, diamonds
Liberia	Liberia	NPFL	1989–96	200,000	Iron, timber, rubber, diamonds
Liberia	Liberia	MODEL, LURD	2000–3	2,000	Proxy
CAR	CAR, Libya	Military faction	2001–2	500	Proxy
Côte d'Ivoire	Côte d'Ivoire	MPCI, MJP, MPIGO, FN	2002–5	850	Cocoa, timber, diamonds
Angola	Angola, Cuba	UNITA, South Africa	1975–91	500,000	Proxy
Guinea	Guinea	Military faction, RFDG	2000–1	1,100	N/A

Source: Adapted from Le Billon, 'Diamond wars?', p. 353.

caused the conflict. Where diamonds were relevant they seemed to play two roles: first, as a source of revenue for parties already in conflict; and, second, to the extent that revenues from their extraction were unfairly distributed, they generated grievances which fuelled justifications for rebellion.[44]

In Sierra Leone diamond mining had gone on for decades in more or less the same fashion without generating a civil war. Nor is there any good evidence to claim that the RUF rebels emerged as a vehicle to accumulate diamonds.[45] It is also not true that once started the conflict was fought over diamonds. As the country's Truth and Reconciliation Commission (TRC) concluded, even this is 'only partly true', because the war 'would have taken place even without the existence of diamonds in the country'. At most, diamonds were one among many elements 'that fuelled the conflict'.[46] The TRC placed the ultimate responsibility for the conflict squarely on the shoulders of successive corrupt and anti-democratic regimes, an analysis which supports the emphasis placed on neopatrimonialism provided in chapter 3 of this book. As Christopher Cramer observed, successive post-independence governments in Sierra Leone adopted policies which destroyed other non-mineral economic activities, 'thereby increasing the relative value of natural resources and shunting these resources closer to the heart of Sierra Leone's politics.'[47]

Angola is another case where the presence of diamonds during wartime does not explain why there was conflict. At the most basic level, diamonds were first discovered in Angola in 1912, but the war did not start until the 1960s. Moreover, diamonds did not play any significant role until a new phase of the war erupted in October 1992 – after disputed elections and the battle of Luanda. By this stage the drying up of various external sources of Cold War finance had imposed new strategic imperatives on the conflict parties. The government's economic lifeline lay with oil (see below). On the other hand, the key to the continued war effort for the UNITA rebels was the diamond fields, the main deposits of which were in the central highlands populated by the Ovimbundu. It was therefore crucial that UNITA was able to utilize Ovimbundu support in order to protect and institutionalize a shadow economy built around the illicit export of diamonds.[48] Between 1992 and 1998 alone, UNITA is estimated to have acquired cumulative revenue of about $2–3.5 billion. Nevertheless, it is important to distinguish means and ends. Although UNITA relied upon diamond revenues, its primary purpose was not to generate profit but to continue Savimbi's campaign for power. UNITA remained a political organization which attempted to distort the diamond trade to its benefit by (1) engaging in direct production and labour control; (2) selling licences to diamond buyers to operate in areas under its control; and (3) taxing independent mining operations that it tolerated in its territory.[49] In sum, it was Angola's war which encroached upon the existing diamond trade and made the lives of those who worked within it much more difficult and dangerous. It is also important to remember that the war ended swiftly in April 2002, less than two months after Savimbi was killed in an operation which took months of planning. Angola's diamond trade continues.

Oil

In quantitative large-N studies analysing the causes of armed conflicts, nothing has generated a greater degree of consensus than the idea that oil is dangerous and that oil exporters are at an elevated risk of civil war.[50] This occurs through several mechanisms.[51] First, oil-rich regions are said to foster insurgencies either by enabling insurgents to raise money to buy weapons or by generating grievances about the way the oil is extracted and/or the profits allocated. Consider, for example, how most Nigerians must feel about the fact that, between 1970 and 1999, the country's oil industry generated $231 billion in rents but during the same period its GDP per capita actually fell from $264 to $250.[52] Second, extractable oil makes control of the government more attractive because of the large revenues at stake. In the Gulf of Guinea oil-producing states, for example, one estimate suggested that on average the oil sector generated 68 per cent of government receipts.[53] Third, the fluctuating price of oil on the global markets means that it can render governments unstable through a process linked to trade shocks. The first two points are particularly salient in light of the argument that oil-rich regimes are also likely to become more authoritarian, as they have 'little need to take seriously the task of widening the tax base'.[54]

Once again, however, it is unhelpful to think of oil causing Africa's wars. Brief illustrations from two of Africa's biggest oil producers, Angola and Nigeria, should make the point. As noted above, Angola's war was regularly labelled one of Africa's key commodity conflicts. Historically, Angola has been what Christopher Cramer called 'the ultimate primary commodity economy' – based first on slaves, then on coffee, then on diamonds and, over the last few decades, on oil.[55] It is also clear that oil revenues shaped Angola's conflict in important ways. But they did not cause the war. Instead, war, profit and power existed in a complex and shifting relationship. Like diamonds, oil had little to do with the start of the conflict in the 1960s. And, even after the war began, people did not make rational cost–benefit calculations about whether to join a particular side – for most people their participation was down to coercion. Nor did oil revenues completely erase political agendas – even with oil monies the goal of the key leaders was military and political victory, as evidenced by the significant time and effort that went into the campaign to kill Savimbi.

After the Cold War ended, it was certainly fortunate for the MPLA that more and more off-shore oil was discovered, for it could not otherwise have afforded its army and armaments. Even so, as Ross observed, it was forced to sell off various booty futures and hire private firms to bolster its military campaign. The oil business was also quickly corrupted – an entirely unsurprising development given its integration into the MPLA's centralized, illiberal and anti-democratic structures. This, in turn, stunted the ability of Angolan firms to run the country's oil industry effectively. Instead, it was only multinational firms – especially Chevron, Petrofina, Texaco and Elf – that were competent enough to extract the oil. In sum, it seems reasonable to conclude that 'high levels of commodity dependence did not initially cause civil war; instead, increasing reliance upon natural resources by both the state and UNITA has been a consequence of protracted conflict as other sectors of the economy were progressively destroyed.'[56] Or, as Cramer put it, 'war and economic mismanagement . . . have created oil dependency rather than the other way around.'[57] It was political relationships that were the heart of Angola's war, and they remained its nervous system even when both sides turned to oil and diamonds to toughen their epidermis.

Politics was also the core ingredient in the Niger Delta conflict. Home to roughly 28 million people, the Delta covers 70,000 square kilometres, much of it a complex network of wetlands, rivers and mangrove swamps that houses a massive oil infrastructure consisting of 606 fields, 5,284 wells, 7,000 kilometers of pipelines, ten export terminals, 275 flow stations, ten gas plants, four refineries and a massive liquefied natural gas sector.[58] It is one of the richest oil grounds in the world, holding roughly 90 per cent of Nigeria's oil and gas reserves, yet its people live well below the country's mean level of development. This is partly because oil extraction has decimated the Delta's environment – the World Wildlife Fund estimated some 6,000 oil spills between 1970 and 2006.[59] The beneficiaries have been a tiny majority of political elites, with estimates suggesting that 85 per cent of oil revenues have gone to 1 per cent of the population, and some $50 billion of the total $270 billion accruing to the Nigerian central government between 1960 and the early 2000s has simply 'disappeared'.[60]

Decades of largely peaceful protest spearheaded in the early 1990s by Ken Saro-Wiwa and the Movement for the Survival of the Ogoni People (MOSOP) failed to change these underlying political dynamics. The central government's response was to deploy thousands of notoriously corrupt and ill-disciplined security forces and effectively to de-centralize its brand of corrupt governance by passing on a greater percentage of oil revenues to the regional governors in the Delta, making them 'political godfathers' in their own right.[61] In the 1990s the central government also turned 'community development' in the Delta over to the transnational oil companies, which continued to destroy local fishing and agriculture and provided few local jobs in return.[62] In November 1995, Saro-Wiwa and the 'Ogoni nine' were executed by the government, prompting more minority groups to take up the Ogoni's struggle, including the Adoni, the Itsekiri and the Ijaw. It also catalyzed more violent forms of resistance. By 2007, for instance, over 36 per cent of Delta inhabitants revealed a 'willingness or propensity to take up arms against the state' – more than enough to produce the estimated 25,000 militants.[63]

The most coherent and well organized of the militant groups was the Movement for the Emancipation of the Niger Delta (MEND), which emerged in late 2005 and began attacking pipelines and installations and kidnapping oil workers. Michael Watts described its appearance as 'the almost inevitable end-point of a process of marginalisation, alienation and political mobilisation'.[64] As one local commentator put it, 'Behind the mask of MEND is a political subject forced to pick up an AK47 to restore his rights.'[65] The Movement's stated goals included reducing Nigeria's oil output by 30 per cent, which it accomplished within a year. By March 2009, national production had fallen to 1.6 million barrels of oil per day, down from 2.6 million in 2006.[66] MEND also called for the demilitarization of the Delta, for Shell to pay $1.5 billion in compensation for its destruction of the environment, and for negotiations mediated by a neutral third party over how to distribute the revenues from oil wealth.

Oil is thus clearly an important ingredient in the conflict equation, but it is wrong to think of it as the principal cause of the war. The crucial underlying factor was the corrupt political relationships which made up what Watts called Nigeria's 'oil complex' – the murky alliances between local political, military and business elites, the transnational firms that represent the global oil industry, and a variety of foreign governments which turned a blind eye to the whole sordid process.[67] At the heart of the complex was the desire to maintain control of the institutions of state power and the vested interests that came with the control of (most of) Nigeria's oil. It was the impulse to change this terrible system that spawned the Delta's various resistance movements; it was the government's failure to listen which turned them into today's petro-insurgents.

Demography

Population change occupies a central place in Africa's history. It is, as John Iliffe put it, 'the thread that ties African history together at all its different periods and levels'.[68] During the second half of the twentieth century, he suggested that demography 'may have become . . . the chief historical motor of change in Africa'.[69] It is therefore plausible that demographic dynamics might be a key ingredient in Africa's war recipes. Unfortunately, 'until recently, no field of study existed that focused on the demographic aspects of war.'[70] As a result, the emerging conclusions about the relationship(s) between demography and warfare in Africa remain tentative.

Of course, this did not stop some writers making bold assertions. Harking back to much older Malthusian ideas, Robert Kaplan argued that West Africa's series of bloody civil wars during the 1990s resulted from a mix of overpopulation and environmental factors.[71] Africa's population was certainly growing – since 1900 the continent experienced a sustained and dramatic increase – although in recent decades the trend has been slowed significantly by the impact of HIV/AIDS.[72] But Kaplan offered a crude and misleading depiction of the relationship between population and war.

In the quantitative literature on the subject, demography does appear significant, although not in the way suggested by Kaplan. The three relevant but not particularly revealing conclusions are:[73] (1) states with more people are more likely to suffer civil wars;[74] (2) states with higher population density are more likely to experience civil war; and (3) there 'has been little support for the notion that excessive population growth is a risk factor for civil war'. On this last point there is a divide between large-N studies and more qualitative case studies, with the latter identifying high population growth as a significant ingredient in the outbreak of a variety of African conflicts, including those in Kenya,[75] Côte d'Ivoire,[76] Nigeria,[77] Senegal[78] and Uganda.[79] These types of studies also made the powerful point that the attempts to theorize 'a single demography of conflict' should probably be rejected in favour of an approach based on the recognition of different 'demographies of conflicts'.[80]

Two other issues have been identified as having significant bearing on the relationship between demography and war. The first is the combination of rising levels of urbanization and low levels of GDP per capita.[81] However, this finding has been strongly contested.[82] The second is a coincidence of 'youth bulges' – the number of young people in a population – and low economic growth (producing under- and unemployment).[83] This conclusion has generated particular cause for concern in Africa, given the very different demographic structure of the continent's weak states compared with the advanced industrial democracies within the European Union (see figure 4.2).

In sum, there is no solid evidence that demographic changes were a principal cause of a contemporary African war, although they do appear to be a significant underlying condition in some cases. New evidence may emerge as this embryonic field of study develops, but the slow rate of demographic alterations makes it difficult to see how they could ever trigger violence in the absence of other more important factors. Once again, therefore, the effects of demography can be said to depend upon political context.

Climate

Climate and ecosystems clearly have a huge impact on human society. The developing orthodoxy in studies examining the politics of climate change is that it 'will enhance the fragility of many African states' by feeding 'increased volatility in the region in the next few decades'.[84] But what of climate's relationship to armed conflict in the past? Some analysts have argued that environmental changes have played a major role in the outbreak of armed conflict in post-Cold War Africa. Marshall Burke and his colleagues, for example, concluded that, between 1980 and 2002, sub-Saharan Africa showed a strong correlation between annual temperature variations and the incidence of civil

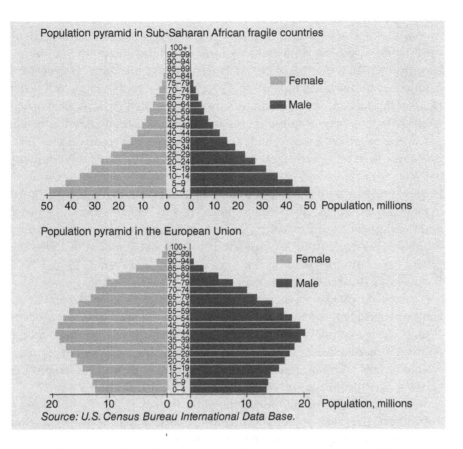

Figure 4.2 *Population structures in Africa's 'fragile' countries and the European Union*

Source: European Development Report, *Overcoming Fragility*, p. 3.

war.[85] Others agreed that the weather was crucial but that interannual variability in rainfall was a much more significant determinant of African conflicts than land degradation and freshwater resources (see below).[86] For others, the most dangerous factor was 'high levels of soil degradation'.[87] On the other hand, some analysts contested all such findings on the basis that the shaky foundations of much knowledge about African environments, as well as the speed, extent, drivers and political consequences of environmental change, render all conclusions distinctly unclear and contested.[88]

In this context, the war in Darfur has been the most widely debated test case, not least because in recent decades Sudan has experienced an environmental crisis. The region has significant droughts occurring every three to five years and its local ecosystems have been collapsing under the interrelated impacts of land degradation, deforestation and climate change.[89] According to the UNEP, while armed conflict has degraded Sudan's environment, environmental issues such as competition over oil and gas reserves, Nile waters and timber, as well as land (especially rangeland and rain-fed agricultural land), have been contributory causes of conflict, including in Darfur. Specifically, UNEP emphasized that twenty-nine of the forty violent local conflicts in Darfur since independence in 1956 involved grazing and water rights.[90] In addition, Sudan's massive, conflict-generated population displacement (affecting over 5 million people) caused significant environmental damage, especially in areas around the larger displacement camps. Desertification rates have increased significantly since the 1930s, with the boundary between semi-desert and desert moving southwards by an estimated 50 to 200 km, bringing with it reductions in food production and a greater threat of drought and floods. At the same time, pressures on resources in general and the rangelands in particular were intensified by the country's rocketing number of livestock (from 28.6 million in 1961 to 134.6 million in 2004). The picture in relation to deforestation was also grim: between 1973 and 2006 Darfur lost a third of its forest cover.

But how did this environmental crisis relate to the war in Darfur? Some analysts concluded that the war 'can accurately be labelled the first modern climate-change conflict'.[91] A typical argument was that the region's fragile political situation was 'exacerbated beyond the tipping point by climate-related factors'.[92] The key tipping point in this case was identified as conflicts between agriculturalists and pastoralists over 'land and water resources'[93] – or what one observer called 'the drying of Darfur'.[94]

An alternative view argues that, while climate change was a significant part of the structural context which made Darfur's war possible, it does not explain why war broke out. This was down to more contingent catalytic factors, including the central individual actors and their tribal, ethnic and religious loyalties; government policies; the breakdown of traditional dispute resolution mechanisms; the Naivasha peace process to end the so-called North–South conflict; the role of Chadian armed groups; and the influx of small arms and light weapons into the region.[95] As Alex de Waal put it, if there was a key culprit, it was the Sudanese government, not the weather.

In many respects the debate about climate change and the war in Darfur leads us back to the analytical distinction between underlying conditions and triggers. The complex brew of decades of social turmoil, oppressive governance and environmental crisis set the twenty-first-century stage on which various actors decided to prosecute the war. Environmental change was certainly not a necessary condition for Darfur's conflict, as even supporters of the climate conflict thesis acknowledge.[96] But the weather was part of the story. To use a theatrical metaphor, the weather was more like a stage prop which affected the atmosphere of the scene, but it did not have a speaking part or determine how the characters reacted. As a contextual factor, how humans respond to climate change is politically open-ended. In situations of poor governance and conflict it is likely to be a threat multiplier or an exacerbating factor.[97] But it is fatalistic to think that this is the only effect it might stimulate: in situations with stable and inclusive political institutions it might just as well encourage cooperation and constructive innovation. Overall, the Darfur case bears out Idean Salehyan's conclusion that 'The overly structural logic linking climate change to armed conflict ignores human agency, ingenuity, the potential for technological innovation, and the vital role of political institutions in managing conflict (or failing to do so).'[98]

Water

Parts of Africa suffer from severe water scarcity, and this is likely to intensify with global warming.[99] The dramatic shrinking of Lake Chad, for instance, has on occasion led to tensions between some fishing and pastoralist communities who live around it. At the regional level, the primary concern has revolved around the allocation of the Nile waters.[100] Examples such as these have kept alive one variant of the resource scarcity arguments, namely, the 'water wars' thesis – the idea that water scarcity will eventually stimulate armed conflict. Historically, however, the evidence for this thesis is negligible. As a leading environmental historian put it, water wars 'have not happened for several millennia, if ever'.[101] Indeed, given that more than 3,600 treaties have been signed regarding aspects of international waters, 145 of them since 2000, it is strange that water does not enjoy a more prominent status as what one analyst called 'humanity's greatest learning ground for building community'.[102] In sum, there is significant evidence that building institutions, at the local, national and supranational level, is an effective strategy to mitigate water scarcity as a trigger of warfare.

The principal note of caution is that, although 'the historical record suggests that with well-organized states, the probability of warfare arising from drought-induced water shortage is low; the risk rises in the presence of weak states within which those components of society most aggrieved by drought are less constrained in their responses.'[103] The number of weak states in Africa is thus a cause for concern. But, once again, this would suggest the key issue is governance in weak states, not water scarcity *per se*.

It would appear that the more fundamental explanation for the persistent strength of the water wars thesis is linked to human psychology, specifically the fact that evidence from the past seems unable to overcome completely people's fears about the future.[104] No amount of historical evidence that water scarcity has not been a major cause of war either yesterday or today will convince some people to reject the idea that it will be central to the wars of tomorrow. It is therefore quite likely that the debate about water wars will continue to intensify.

Land

Although not one of the resources singled out in the quantitative literature on the causes of civil war, land is clearly at the heart of many African conflicts and therefore highlights the centrality of the local level of analysis discussed in chapter 2. But it is not just any land. Tensions have focused on the most useful parts of the continent, what French colonists referred to as *Afrique utile*.[105] This land, as Aboidun Alao has argued, is 'undoubtedly the most important natural resource in Africa'.[106] Naturally, different groups consider different pieces of land *utile* for different reasons. As discussed in chapter 5, potential national homelands are considered crucial for some groups regardless of the mineral, oil or other commodities located there. For other groups, the land's utility will be directly related to its commercial value. As with other resources, the central point is that land has often been a critical enabler for somebody's political agenda.

Africa's land is crucial for several reasons. For one thing, because most other resources are found on or in it, control of the land is vital for many types of resource extraction. Second, much of the continent's economic activity remains based in agriculture, with all that this implies for the centrality of land. Third, Africa's land often has important spiritual value as a sacred place that should be kept for future generations.

On the more specific question of the relationship between land and armed conflict, analysts have proposed a variety of ways that land ownership, management and control have been linked to conflict: scarcity of useful land, conflicting laws governing land tenure, boundary disputes and conflicting claims over specific portions of land, arguments over 'landlord–tenant' arrangements, racial imbalance of land ownership, the clash of spiritual considerations with economic and political realities, complaints over government regulation policies, increasing population densities especially when a rapid influx of outsiders occurs, and land–labour relations.[107] The result is that, particularly in the continent's secessionist struggles and in relation to much more localized struggles, control of the certain pieces of territory was at the heart of conflict between and within groups from Zimbabwe and Zanzibar to Darfur and the DRC. As the African Union panel was regularly told by Darfuris, 'land was one of the root causes of the war . . . and it remains a key issue in future negotiations.'[108]

Conclusion

Thinking about Africa's wars as resulting from the scarcity or abundance of natural resources suffers from a variety of flaws and limitations. Not least, these approaches fail on their own terms: they cannot explain why 'an abundance or scarcity of valuable resources is not a necessary or sufficient factor of conflict.'[109] A more useful approach is to see resources as socially constructed enablers – as means not ends. While resources enable and empower particular actors, they do not cause events. Their political effects are thus theoretically open-ended, although they are related to their historical context and the dominant political agendas therein. As the evidence presented here suggests, this seems to hold true regardless of whether the focus is oil, diamonds, demography or environmental factors. Inserted into a context where corrupt autocrats have the advantage, resources will strengthen their hand and generate grievances among those denied access to their benefits. Inserted into a stable democratic system, they will enhance the opportunities for leaders to promote national prosperity. Analysts should therefore focus their efforts on understanding the historical and political context in question, particularly its dominant systems of governance.

Resources were clearly not central ingredients in the outbreak of Africa's wars, but they were sometimes important for understanding how certain conflicts endured and why they assumed the forms they did. In particular, since the social construction of resources was usually directly connected to developments in the global economy, this tended to make Africa's warscapes more transnational, regional and global. If the resources in question proved profitable, they also made conflicts more intractable and provided disincentives for belligerents to pursue peace (see part III). The next chapter investigates whether the same can be said for one of the most important of all resources – sovereignty.

CHAPTER FIVE

Sovereignty

This chapter examines the extent to which issues of sovereignty were a key ingredient in Africa's post-Cold War armed conflicts. The basic argument is that the benefits accruing from sovereignty and the continuing importance of self-determination played a significant role in the framing and pursuit of a variety of African conflicts. Although the literature on so-called natural resources – analysed in chapter 4 – has almost completely ignored sovereignty, it is actually one of Africa's most important resources and has been fought over on a regular basis. As Pierre Englebert observed, 'many of Africa's ongoing conflicts are not so much waged over the control of natural resources than over the control of the tools of sovereignty.'[1] Similarly, although self-determination could no longer be invoked as an automatic path to statehood and independence, the concept still resonated with marginalized minorities across the continent. Stated more precisely, my argument is that Africa witnessed relatively few wars waged with the express purpose of creating new states, but it has experienced a considerable number of conflicts fought with reference to the broader idea of self-determination – i.e. to make the existing states better places to live for their marginalized minorities.

The discussion of neopatrimonialism's exclusionary and unstable dynamics in chapter 3 emphasized how political life without access to the sovereign's patronage system was usually difficult. In extreme cases, excluded groups were left with little option but to use force, either to create a new state or to gain a serious say in the governance structures under which they lived. The latter option *might* – but need not – include significant reform of the state in relation to the decentralization of its institutions, provisions for minority rights, or autonomous regions. Evidence of both options could be seen in post-Cold War Africa.

Part of the difficulty in analysing these issues is that the meaning of self-determination in international law, and to a lesser extent in international politics, has changed considerably since the early phase of decolonization. Put bluntly, self-determination is not a right to statehood. Instead, it has become a much more limited procedural principle to ensure peoples can participate meaningfully in state governance. This helps explain why there have been relatively few genuinely separatist wars designed to break up Africa's existing states, but lots of conflicts fought about self-determination to make those states work better for the groups currently marginalized from power.

To address these issues, this chapter begins by summarizing the contemporary meanings of sovereignty, secession and self-determination. It then analyses four central examples of conflicts which revolved around the unfinished business of decolonization and the struggle to build new states, namely, Eritrea/Ethiopia, Somaliland/Somalia, Western Sahara/Morocco and Cabinda/Angola. In each case the imperial powers were African rather than European governments. The final section then discusses conflicts where the central aim was not to create a new state but to make the existing one a better place to live for at least some of its marginalized inhabitants. Although often wrapped up in the language of separatism, these conflicts were really about self-determination in its procedural sense – that is, gaining a greater say in the running of the state but leaving its international boundaries intact. Illustrations are used from the Casamance conflict in Senegal and the struggles of the Tuaregs in Mali and Niger. The two exceptional cases of Ethiopia and Sudan are also considered because of their unusually high number of conflicts with separatist dimensions.

Sovereignty, Secession and Self-Determination

Few grievances are as politically powerful as the feeling of being oppressed by foreigners. As the principal means to reject imperial rule, what role has the idea of self-determination played in Africa's armed conflicts? To understand the relevant dynamics it is necessary to clarify the meaning of three important and interrelated concepts: sovereignty, secession and self-determination.

Sovereignty is intimately bound up with the idea of statehood. In international law, the 1933 Montevideo Convention on the Rights and Duties of States concluded that, to be legally recognized as a state, an entity required a permanent population, a defined territory, a government, and a capacity to enter into relations with other states. Although additional attributes have been discussed since then, this core of prerequisites has held relatively stable.[2] More sociological definitions of statehood, however, have raised the bar much higher by including in their definitions a test of the government's ability to perform certain tasks. The most famous of these is Max Weber's argument that the acid test of an *effective* state was whether or not its national government could lay claim to a monopoly of legitimate force in the territory under its jurisdiction.[3] The problem with Weber's approach is that Africa contains numerous states which do not come close to meeting this requirement but which persist nonetheless. Indeed, for all Africa's weak states, the continent's international political map has hardly changed since the 1960s.

The answer to this puzzle lies in the fact that the legal and sociological definitions point to different elements of sovereignty, what are often referred to as its empirical and juridical dimensions.[4] Empirical sovereignty refers to the ability of governments to fulfil certain functions related to security and welfare and to exclude other states from their domestic affairs. It is essentially about how well governments can exercise control. Juridical sovereignty, on the other hand, refers to a status in international law where a state is recognized as sovereign by other sovereign states and relevant international legal entities and its government is recognized as the legitimate, *de jure* authority. Understood in this manner, numerous entities, including insurgencies, can possess various attributes of statehood.[5] But, to be recognized as a member of international society and gain UN membership, juridical sovereignty holds the key. As Africa's failing states attest, as long as juridical sovereignty is maintained, a government's inability to control its territory, population and affairs does not significantly endanger its statehood.

Secession is about the redrawing of *international* political borders. It occurs when a group of people acquire statehood by successfully breaking away from an existing state (or states) and becoming recognized as the sovereign authorities over their territory and population. Given the huge diversity of ethnic groups in Africa and the poor performance of many of the continent's states, the number of secessionist conflicts has been remarkably small (see table 5.1).

Table 5.1   Africa's secessionist conflicts, 1990–2009

Country	Region	Years of violence
Angola	Cabinda	1991, 1994, 1996–8, 2002, 2004, 2007, 2009
Comoros	Anjouan	1997
Ethiopia	Eritrea	1990–1, 1998–2000[b]
	Ogaden	1996, 1998–2002, 2004–9
	Afar	1990–1, 1996
	Oromia	1990–1, 1999–2009
Equatorial Guinea	Bioko	1993[a]
Mali	Tuaregs	1990, 1994, 2007–9
Morocco	Western Sahara	1990–2009[a]
Namibia	Caprivi Strip	1999[a]
Niger	Tuaregs	1992, 1994, 1997
Nigeria	Niger Delta	2004
Senegal	Casamance	1990, 1992–3, 1995, 1997–8, 2000–1, 2003
Somalia	Somaliland	1990–1
Sudan	Southern Sudan	1990–2004

[a] Secessionist struggle identified but no record of twenty-five battle-related deaths in one calendar year.
[b] To the extent that the war between Ethiopia and Eritrea (1998–2000) was about the demarcation of the border between them, this could be viewed as a continuation of Eritrea's separatist struggle.
Source: Uppsala Conflict Data Programme, at www.pcr.uu.se/gpdatabase/search.php.

The most convincing explanation for this state of affairs is Englebert's argument that it was very difficult for new peoples to acquire juridical sovereignty in contemporary world politics and that international recognition endows African state actors with the hugely important power of legal command.[6]

Although international boundaries are fundamental to sovereignty and secession, I am not suggesting that a large number of Africa's conflicts occur simply because of the arbitrary nature of the continent's political borders. This is a common argument, but it ignores the fact that *all* international political borders arbitrarily dissect identity groups – although usually not as blatantly as some African cases – and all of them rely, ultimately, on the coercive capabilities of actors with the power to make them stick. Borders can make life more difficult in various ways but on their own they rarely cause wars. As discussed in more detail below, my point is that, where these borders prevent legitimate cases of decolonization occurring, they are likely to increase the risk of armed conflict.

Self-determination is an altogether more complicated concept, not least because international society has imbued it with different meanings over time. It is also complicated by the prevalence of two powerful myths: that self-determination is about independence (i.e. it is broadly synonymous with secession) and that the UN Charter provides for self-determination in such terms. As Rosalyn Higgins has pointed out, neither view is accurate.[7] These myths probably emerged because, during the 1950s and 1960s, self-determination became bound up with the issue of decolonization and the idea that colonies had a right to choose independence, even though Article 73 of the UN Charter mentions only 'self-government', which is not the same thing. Self-determination gradually came to be accepted as a legal right in the context of decolonization, but it was never restricted to a choice for independence (the entity in question could join with another state or remain in a constitutional relationship with the former colonial power).[8] Self-determination also became associated with human rights norms: specifically, it became accepted that the right of self-determination was applicable 'to peoples subject to foreign or alien domination' as spelt out in the non-binding UN Declaration on Friendly Relations of 1970.[9] Higgins noted that the central point about self-determination was that it offered 'a proper range of options' for 'a dependent people and that they are given the opportunity to express their choice'. In sum, self-determination was about offering 'peoples' choice rather than simply independence.[10] Referendums became a common mechanism to exercise this choice.

Understood in this manner, a central challenge was how to decide which groups counted as 'peoples'. In sum, who was the 'self' in self-determination? Traditionally, international law had defined 'peoples' as all the people of a state, not as distinctive minority groups based on race, ethnicity or religion. This meant that minorities *per se* did not have a right of self-determination or secession.[11] Where minorities were in serious jeopardy, international law offered them protection through guarantees of human rights and the provision of minority rights. The logic underlying this approach was, as Higgins neatly put it, 'Virtually every minority has its own minority, and the fear and oppression gets pushed further down the pyramid. The lesson we must draw is that the right of self-determination is interlocked with the proper protection of minority rights – but that they are discrete rights, not to be confused with each other.'[12]

In the context of decolonization, however, the 'self' of self-determination came to be associated with colonized peoples. Hence international law considered decolonization an acceptable reason to recognize a new state. As decolonization continued, more and more governments that had achieved their independence became anxious to ensure that the norm of self-determination was 'harnessed to, and not the enemy of, territorial integrity'.[13] African governments agreed to this explicitly via the OAU's Cairo Declaration (1964), which confirmed their support for *uti possidetis*, the legal doctrine that colonial administrative boundaries would become international boundaries when the political unit in question achieved independence. States could agree to redraw their boundaries through mutual consent, but they were not required to alter their boundaries because of the norm of self-determination. Changing borders without host state consent was thus perceived as an act of colonialism. As Mali's president at the time, Modibo Keita, put it, 'We must take Africa as it is, and we must renounce any territorial claims, if we do not wish to introduce what we might call black imperialism.'[14] Once Africa's new postcolonial leaders had achieved their own independence they did not want peoples within 'their' state breaking away pieces of it.

Over time, therefore, international legal mechanisms firmly separated the concept of self-determination from secession (and thus from its association with a particular territory as well). The opinions of international courts reflect a similar trend whereby they declined to view self-determination as an enforceable right and instead saw it as a procedural principle.[15] Self-determination was thus reconceptualized from being a right for colonies to become independent to the principle that peoples had a right to be heard. Jan Klabbers summarized the process when he observed:

> Now that self-determination can no longer simply be construed as a right of colonies to independence, it has evolved into a right of peoples to take part in decisions affecting their future. . . . [Today,] self-determination is best understood as a procedural right; that is, entities have a right to see their position taken into account whenever their futures are being decided. That may not amount to a right to secede or even a right to autonomy or self-government, but it does amount to a right to be taken seriously.[16]

This discussion clarifies the legal fact that demands for self-determination can be accommodated within the existing state by developing decentralized governance structures and paying greater attention to minority and human rights of the people in question. Altering political borders is, as Arnold Hughes observed, 'an extreme political option'.[17]

The National Liberation Struggle Continues

Despite decades of decolonization and the end of the Cold War, Africa began the 1990s with at least five cases of unfinished decolonization.[18] These centred on apartheid South Africa's control of Namibia and its own non-white population; Ethiopia's incorporation of Eritrea; Morocco's obstruction of a referendum on self-determination for Western Sahara; Somaliland's struggle to become a recognized state for the second time; and Angola's efforts to quash separatist initiatives in the enclave of Cabinda. The Namibian struggle for independence was all but over by the time the Cold War ended and so need not detain us here. And while the unravelling of apartheid took a few more years it did not generate calls for a redrawing of South Africa's international borders – indeed, it was only the apartheid government's experiments with so-called national homelands that tried to redraw the country's international borders. In contrast, armed groups in Eritrea, Somaliland, Western Sahara and Cabinda all called for international political maps to be redrawn and were formed around the explicit idea of creating a new state. All of them continued at a greater or lesser degree of intensity throughout the entire post-Cold War period and thus comprise the focus of this section.

Eritrea

In May 1991, after a long and bloody war of liberation which lasted approximately three decades and killed some 60,000 of its fighters, the Provisional Government of Eritrea (PGE) was established. In a shrewd move it decided not to use its formidable military powers to create immediately an independent state of Eritrea. Instead it sought a lasting legal and political resolution to the conflict by acquiring the consent of its allies in the Transitional Government of Ethiopia and by announcing that it would create a multi-party system and hold an internationally sanctioned referendum on independence in 1993.[19] On 23–5 April of that year, over 99 per cent of voters said 'yes' to Eritrea's independence from Ethiopia. As it turned out, although this settled the matter of Eritrea's independence, it did not solve the problem of where the new state's borders would lie.

The legal basis for Eritrea's independence was rooted in the separate status it had under Italian colonial rule (it was established as an Italian colony in 1889 and fell under British administration in 1941). After much debate about what to do with Eritrea, in 1952 the UN approved the creation of the Ethiopian–Eritrean Federation. For Eritrean nationalists this was a severe blow: they immediately lost the UN as a forum to articulate their aspirations because only member states could directly express their views. Over the following decade Ethiopian authorities broke the terms of the federation and assimilated the territory within Ethiopia.[20] Addis Ababa suspended the Eritrean assembly and constitution, imposed Amharic as the sole language of the state and schools, discarded Eritrea's flag, and imposed the Ethiopian penal code. In 1960, Eritrean government was downgraded to an administrative unit within Ethiopia. In 1962, Ethiopia abolished the federal system altogether and declared Eritrea its fourteenth province. These developments triggered an armed struggle by the Eritrean Liberation Front in 1961, initially spearheaded by Muslim elites, as they had borne the initial brunt of Ethiopia's attempts at assimilation.[21] But it wasn't long before Ethiopia's increasingly heavy hand alienated many more Eritreans. Throughout the campaign, funds from the Eritrean diaspora played a vital role in sustaining the struggle.

Although their legal case was solid, Eritrean nationalists faced huge political obstacles, primarily because of Ethiopia's deft international diplomacy, which managed to distort accepted international norms in order to contain the Eritrean demand for national self-determination.[22] In particular, Ethiopian elites depicted their country as a vanguard of pan-Africanism and the continent's liberation struggle. They also played on the fact that in Africa colonized peoples were often defined in a limited sense as those under *European* rule. Ethiopia used this loophole, as well as invoking fears of continental 'Balkanization', to pursue ruthlessly its vision of a 'Greater Ethiopia' to incorporate additional territory, notably Eritrea and the Ogaden and Haud regions. Thus during the era of decolonization Ethiopia managed to expand its territory and assemble what Ruth Iyob called an 'empire state'.[23] Edmund Keller described Ethiopia as a 'bureaucratic empire' and its incorporation of Eritrea as an act of 'late colonialism'.[24] This was all too apparent to the Eritrean People's Liberation Front (EPLF), which was at pains to point out that Eritrea had 'been occupied by a neighbouring country.... Eritrea is not part of Ethiopia and we are not Ethiopians. *We are an African country colonised by another.*'[25] Even on the eve of victory the PGE was not convinced the wider world had received the message. It sent a memorandum to the UN in which it reiterated that 'The Eritrean case was a just struggle conducted against a coercive incorporation and not a case of secession.'[26]

Although Eritrea is the only case analysed here which successfully won juridical sovereignty, just a few years later it became clear that the demarcation of its border with Ethiopia remained unsettled. Sadly, it led to one of Africa's most destructive recent wars. After earlier disputes about trade and currency, as well as minor border clashes, on 6 May 1998 Eritrean troops launched an attack which took over the Ethiopian-administered settlement of Badme. Various attempts at mediation by the United States, the OAU and the UN proved unsuccessful, and by June 2000 the conflict had cost between 70,000 and 100,000 lives and displaced more than 1.2 million people.[27] Two peacekeeping missions, UNMEE and OLMEE, were mandated to monitor the ceasefire as well as the redeployment of the armed forces of both sides in line with the temporary security zone (TSZ) envisaged in the Cessation Agreement of June 2000. This was not easy: the exact location of the TSZ was not agreed until June 2001, and then only in principle rather than in practice.

In December 2000 the two governments signed the Algiers Agreement wherein the parties agreed to 'terminate hostilities' and 'refrain from the threat or use of force against the other' (Article 1.1); 'release and repatriate' all prisoners of war (Article 2.3); establish 'a neutral Boundary Commission . . . to delimit and demarcate' the disputed border between the two countries (Article 4); and establish 'a neutral Claims Commission' to address 'the negative socio-economic impact of the crisis on the civilian population' (Article 5).

When the Boundary Commission announced its decision on 13 April 2002, this was supposed to be 'final and binding' under Article 4.15 of the Algiers Agreement, and initially both countries accepted this decision. In practice, however, Ethiopia, in particular, prevented the implementation of the decision by refusing to allow UNMEE and Boundary Commission staff to cross from Eritrea into Ethiopia. They also questioned the Commission's neutrality and refused to work with UNMEE's force commander, General Cammaert. Part of the problem was that the Commission's April Decision did not specify the final disposition of the settlement of Badme, which had been at the centre of the dispute. In March 2003, in a set of 'Observations', the Boundary Commission awarded control of Badme to Eritrea, a ruling the Ethiopian government rejected as 'totally illegal, unjust, and irresponsible'.[28] The Commission responded that Ethiopia's actions were an illegitimate 'attempt to reopen the substance of the April Decision . . . and to undermine not only the April Decision but also the peace process as a whole'.[29] The UN Security Council also passed several resolutions (1430, 1466, 1507, 1531) calling for Ethiopia's full cooperation on this issue. It was not until November 2004 that the Ethiopian government accepted the Commission's ruling in principle, but called for a 'peace-building dialogue' in practice.[30]

Believing that the process of legal arbitration had upheld its claims, Eritrea became increasingly frustrated with the UN Security Council's inability to enforce Ethiopia's compliance with the Boundary Commission's ruling. Over time, it began to place greater restrictions upon UNMEE, declaring in late 2007 that the UN force was in effect maintaining Ethiopia's 'occupation' of Eritrean territory.[31] The plot thickened when, on 30 November 2007, the Boundary Commission dissolved itself, declaring that it had fulfilled its mandate even though it had not physically demarcated the border.[32] Instead, it demarcated the boundary with reference to coordinates on a map but did not ensure that these coordinates were represented physically by pillars on the ground. Eritrea viewed this 'virtual demarcation' as an incomplete but 'important step forward towards the demarcation on the ground'; Ethiopia argued that the Commission's demarcation coordinates were 'invalid because they are not the product of a demarcation process recognized by international law'.[33] In July 2008 this impasse forced the Security Council to withdraw UNMEE, and since then this contested border has remained tense and heavily militarized.

Somaliland

Unlike Eritrea, Somaliland failed to achieve juridical sovereignty but made huge strides on the empirical side of the equation, especially when compared with the rest of Somalia. On 26 June 1960, Somaliland gained its independence from Britain and was recognized by thirty-five states, including the United States. Five days later the area of Italian Somalia was given its independence. The legislatures from the two territories decided to unify with the southern city of Mogadishu as the capital. The main northern political party, the Somali National League, boycotted the subsequent referendum on unification. Three decades later, in May 1991, the Declaration of the Conference on Somaliland Communities declared the Republic of Somaliland independent for the second time. The trigger for this declaration was the brutal repression of Somalilanders carried out in the preceding years by Siad Barre's regime, which claimed to be responding to an insurgency led by the Somali National Movement (SNM) campaign. Barre's attacks are thought to have generated an estimated 20,000 casualties and 1 million refugees.

The legal basis for Somaliland's struggle for statehood rests on its separate colonial identity. The political evidence used to bolster this claim has assumed many forms, but chief among them is the fact that the state of Somalia functioned only for the thirty years between 1960 and 1990. Even then, many commentators have questioned whether it existed as a meaningful polity before its collapse. As one long-time observer put it, Somalia was only ever a 'toxic state' which gave its citizens oppression, not protection.[34] Since 1991 Somaliland had developed many aspects of empirical sovereignty: a constitution and political parties as well as internal conflicts (in 1992 and 1996). It had a defined territory (despite the odd border dispute), it had a population who identified themselves as Somalilanders, and it engaged in a range of international relations from diplomacy to civil aviation. It also elected a president who was not a member of the dominant (Isaaq) clan and formed a national government that provided security for its people, exercised significant control over its borders, managed public assets, levied taxes, issued currency and driving licences, and formulated development policies.[35] All this was done without the benefits of juridical sovereignty and funded primarily by remittances from the Somaliland diaspora. These were vital, but the country remained poor, with revenues of only about $20 to $30 million a year, far too little to meet the costs of public administration.[36] On the positive side, Mark Bradbury observed that this 'internally generated process of recovery' helped 'to forge a separate identity, a feeling of self-reliance and a belief amongst Somalilanders that "Somaliland is becoming a reality"'.[37]

In 2002, the Somaliland authorities formally invited the African Union to assess its suitability for membership of the continental organization. The AU Commission fact-finding mission that investigated this question three years later concluded that Somaliland's case was 'unique and self-justified in

African political history' and would not open the door to other secessionist claims on the continent.[38] The mission recommended that the AU 'should find a special method of dealing with this outstanding case' as soon as possible. In December 2005, Somaliland's President Rayale reiterated the view that his country was 'literally a nation in prison'.[39] Despite some dialogue between the Somaliland authorities and AU representatives, the application for membership did not move forward. In spite of its impressive empirical credentials and impeccable legal case, Somaliland still lacks juridical sovereignty. Although this case has not generated large levels of violence between the authorities in Hargeisa and armed groups in southern Somalia, it did produce sporadic clashes with the authorities in Puntland and raised a potentially fundamental problem for efforts to resurrect a single Somali state.

Sahrawi Arab Democratic Republic (Western Sahara)

In 1973 the POLISARIO was established as the vehicle for Western Sahara's national liberation struggle. Three years later, on 27 February 1976, the movement announced the creation of the Sahrawi Arab Democratic Republic (SADR). Although at the time SADR lacked both the empirical and juridical dimensions of sovereignty, over time it has come closer to acquiring juridical sovereignty than any other African entity bar Eritrea: while it has failed to achieve UN membership, it became a member of the OAU in 1982. Empirically, however, it has made very little headway, primarily because of the military stranglehold on its territory maintained by Morocco. As such, while it has not witnessed high levels of violence for some time, the conflict over Western Sahara remains far from resolution, leaving many of its people suspended in a political limbo.

SADR's claim to statehood rests on the fact it was not previously owned by either Morocco or Mauritania but was a colonial dependency of Spain whose people were therefore entitled to exercise self-determination.[40] Support for this position was evident within the OAU, which adopted a resolution at its Rabat Council of Ministers meeting in June 1972 calling for a self-determination referendum in Western Sahara. Western Sahara's case was given a huge legal boost on 16 October 1975, when the International Court of Justice issued an advisory opinion which concluded that it was not *terra nullius* at the time of Spain's colonization and nor was there any territorial sovereignty between it and Morocco or the 'Mauritanian entity'. Morocco's (ultimately unconvincing) juridical response resided in its concept of Greater Morocco, which harked back to the eleventh and twelfth centuries when it controlled Morocco, Western Sahara and Mauritania, as well as northwest Mali and most of western Algeria.[41] It appears that Rabat's major political concern, however, is not the loss of prestige but fear of the domino effect SADR's independence might have on Berber militancy in the Agadir valley and the notoriously rebellious northern Rif region.

What Morocco lacked in the legal realm it made up for in its ability to create facts on the ground. Empirically, therefore, Western Sahara soon found its path to statehood literally blocked by two key developments: the Green March and the building of the berm. In November 1975, King Hassan II of Morocco led 300,000 civilians into Western Sahara in the Green March. These joined Moroccan and Mauritanian troops who had been attacked by POLISARIO. A military coup in mid-1978 ended Mauritania's participation in this war, and on 14 August 1979 Morocco officially seized the Mauritanian area of Western Sahara. However, Morocco's inability to pacify the entire territory led to the second key development: the building of a great wall known as the berm. Even with support from Algeria, POLISARIO was unable to generate any real military leverage over Morocco. Instead, SADR relied more on its juridical claims to statehood. These were impressive, and in 1982 the Republic was accepted into the OAU, prompting Morocco's departure from the organization in 1984. However, SADR was excluded from both the Arab Maghreb Union – founded in 1989 and comprised of Mauritania, Morocco, Algeria, Tunisia and Libya – and, more importantly, the UN. The door to UN membership was left significantly ajar, however, when in August 1988 Morocco and POLISARIO accepted, in principle, the UN-brokered Settlement Plan. This included provision for a referendum on self-determination and led to the establishment of a UN peacekeeping operation, MINURSO, in 1991 to ensure the plan's full implementation.

Since 1991, numerous peace plans have been devised and debated – several orchestrated by the US diplomat James Baker until his resignation in June 2004[42] – but the referendum on Western Sahara's self-determination did not take place. The key technical sticking point revolved around how to identify the eligible voters and whether the eligibility criteria should be based on territorial or ethnic links (the so-called contested tribes issue).[43] Broadly speaking, POLISARIO wanted territory; Rabat wanted ethnicity. The key political sticking point, however, was the inability of the UN Security Council to marshal the political will necessary to see this case of decolonization through to its logical conclusion.[44]

SADR thus remained tantalizingly close to acquiring juridical sovereignty inasmuch as the UN had officially opened the door to its membership but proved unwilling to force a referendum on the issue. Today, SADR continues to occupy an ambiguous legal status in African and wider international society because it has lacked the material power to carry through its juridical entitlements.

Cabinda

Despite decades of struggle, Cabinda's separatist movement made very little headway in relation to either empirical or juridical sovereignty. The territory remained under the tight control of the Angolan government and there was no sign that this would change. What little pseudo-governmental apparatus the Cabindans built remained largely outside the territory. Often dubbed 'Angola's forgotten war', this conflict received little international attention with the exception of reporting by human rights groups.

Cabinda is a non-contiguous part of Angolan territory with an estimated population of between 300,000 and 600,000. Since oil was discovered off the coast of Cabinda in the 1960s the territory has provided a significant amount of Angola's oil revenues, estimated at about 50 per cent in the early 2000s.[45] The separatist movement, the Front for the Liberation of the Cabinda Enclave (FLEC), has used its estimated 2,000 fighters to wage a low-level guerrilla campaign since August 1963, first against the Portuguese and later against the Angolan government. It was dealt a severe blow in late 2002 when some 30,000 Angolan troops deployed to the region after they had defeated the UNITA rebels. With the destruction of several FLEC bases in Congo-Brazzaville and the DRC and losses within Cabinda itself, various Angolan government representatives were quick to proclaim FLEC's defeat.[46] While it became clear this was not the case, the government again declared the war officially over in August 2006, when it signed a Memorandum of Understanding with a senior figure who claimed to represent the two main FLEC factions. The memorandum included an amnesty, a demobilization and reintegration pro-gramme for former FLEC combatants, and government posts for some former FLEC officials. It was rejected by the FLEC-FAC (Cabindan Armed Forces) faction, however, which continued its violent struggle.

FLEC's claim to statehood is that Cabinda was never a part of Angola. Clearly Cabinda has no geographic border with Angola, but the key point is that it was a separate Portuguese colony and hence entitled to independence. The argument is that it became a Portuguese Protectorate with the signing of the Treaty of Simulambuco in 1885 at the Berlin Conference, becoming known as the Portuguese Congo from about 1900 onwards. In its 1996 Charter, the self-declared government of the Republic of Cabinda emphasizes two further points: first, that Cabinda was recognized as distinct from Angola in the 1933 Portuguese Constitution; and, second, that in 1964 the OAU recog-nized it as being a decolonized African country, distinct from Angola. In 1956 Portugal joined the administration of its Protectorate of Cabinda to that of its Colony of Angola. In 1975 Cabinda was incorporated into independent Angola. In January 2010 the conflict briefly hit the international headlines when FLEC fighters claimed responsibility for attacking the convoy transport-ing Togo's football team to an Africa Cup of Nations match.

Self-determination without Separatism

As discussed above, contemporary self-determination is basically about ensur-ing that groups have a meaningful say in how they are governed. It is not synonymous with political independence and separatism. This distinction is crucial for understanding a good number of Africa's recent armed conflicts. For one thing, it allows analysts to cut through much separatist rhetoric and see self-determination struggles for what they really are. For another, groups that cannot make a convincing legal argument that theirs is a case of legitimate decolonization would struggle to acquire juridical sovereignty even if they could develop many of its empirical trappings. As Pierre Englebert has argued, the major impulse in such struggles is usually 'to become the local dominant class' and gain greater access to the benefits of sovereignty rather than build a new state. Challenging the government is therefore a way of also challenging the local dominant group by persuading the former to downgrade the status of the latter in light of the armed struggle.[47] In the following section I show how this accurately reflects what has happened in two relevant cases centred on the Casamance conflict in Senegal and the struggles of various Tuareg groups in Mali and Niger. I then briefly discuss two states where the relationship between self-determination and separatism has become particularly complicated: Ethiopia and Sudan.

Casamance

The Casamance region of southwest Senegal south of Gambia is home to approximately 1.1 million people.[48] As in the rest of Senegal, the majority of its people are Muslims, but religious difference has not been a major political issue. Since 1982 the region has been the focal point of a struggle which has often been couched in explicitly separatist terms spearheaded by the Movement of Democratic Forces of Casamance (MFDC). Interestingly, when the MFDC was founded in 1947 it was *not* seen as a separatist movement. The struggle turned violent in the late 1980s as the MFDC began using its armed wing – the Attika, meaning 'warrior' in Diola – which had been formed in 1985. Although it never posed a strategic threat to the Senegalese authorities, the Attika attracted particular notoriety for its use of suicide attacks and 'a scorched-earth policy, including widespread and anarchic minelaying with no mapping' in 1997.[49] This had a devastating effect on local fishermen and farmers. The Movement also became associated with armed robbery and the illicit trade in timber, cashews and cannabis, and during 1998 got directly involved in fighting Senegalese troops in neighbouring Guinea-Bissau. In 2004 the MFDC's fighters were estimated to number between 2,000 and 4,000.[50] Estimates of the conflict's intensity suggested between 3,000 and 5,000 people had been killed.[51]

Following a large MFDC offensive in 1990 the government concluded a ceasefire with the rebels. This was to be the first of several (failed) ceasefires in the following years as the violence stopped and started, reaching a peak of intensity in late 1995. It was during the subsequent series of talks throughout the 1990s that the MFDC leadership began to split, primarily into northern and southern fronts, revealing rifts over the central purposes of the

Movement. The central issue was whether to pursue independence or better social and economic development for Casamance within Senegal. Gradually, the goal of greater development won out.

During the struggle two principal types of separatist claims were articulated. The first claimed the region had been attached to Portuguese Guinea before it came under French control in the 1860s. However, the MFDC's juridical argument was dealt a severe blow in 1993 after its leaders agreed to the appointment of a French expert to examine the historical merits of the case. The expert ruled that Casamance was never autonomous or a protectorate during the colonial era.[52] This left the MFDC unable to invoke convincingly the principle of decolonization separate from Senegal. It did not, however, alter the logic of Father Augustin Diamacoune Senghor, the Movement's leader, who carried on much as before. In contrast, external commentators described Senghor's basic position as little more than 'an ill-formed and unrealizable demand for independence'.[53] Independence had always been a pipe dream, but without a credible legal case it was simply 'out of the question'.[54] This meant that the Movement's leading intellectuals generally fell back on a second set of ethnic, cultural and economic arguments to justify separatism from the *nordistes* (the northern Senegalese).[55] The argument here was that the region's majority Diola people are more closely related to ethnic groups in Gambia and northwest Guinea-Bissau than the Wolof people who are dominant in Senegal. The MFDC's grievances were primarily economic and cultural, as Senegalese authorities essentially deprived the rising Casamance elites from participating in the benefits of state resources.

By the late 1990s it was evident that the MFDC was making little headway in relation to either empirical or juridical sovereignty. Englebert suggests that this is not surprising because it had ceased to be a genuinely separatist movement years earlier. Pointing to the Movement's splits, the fact that many of its senior leadership had only tenuous links to the region, and that so many of them were receptive to Senegalese offers of money in exchange for abandoning their separatist claims, he concluded that the MFDC was more a vehicle for 'the formation of a local dominant political class as it was about the assertion of cultural identity'. In sum, Englebert saw the MFDC as a way for its senior figures 'to achieve elite status and benefit from sovereignty'.[56] To these reasonable points it should also be added that, from the government's perspective, the long-running conflict became an increasing source of embarrassment for President Wade, especially when he became one of the principal architects of the New Partnership for Africa's Development and tried to mediate in other West African conflicts, such as that in Côte d'Ivoire. The relatively low level of damage the MFDC had inflicted on Senegal's economy and its cultural pluralism, combined with the potential dent to Wade's image, meant that the government was reasonably forthcoming with offers to resolve the problem.[57] These lay not in redrawing international boundaries but in giving MFDC elites greater access to the benefits of sovereignty within Senegal.

Tuaregs in Mali and Niger

A similar picture emerges from the struggles of Tuaregs in Mali and Niger. The Tuareg are a nomadic Berber people spread across several countries of northwest Africa. In both Mali and Niger they represent about 10 per cent of the population, and as minorities in those two countries they certainly have legitimate grievances. As Englebert put it, 'over the last century, theirs has been a history of decline, immiseration, and marginalization.'[58] Although some separatist appeals have appeared based around the notion of Azawad (the Tuareg name for their region), the principal motives behind the various Tuareg rebel groups were to acquire a greater share of revenues from mineral resources, more meaningful political participation, and protection against encroachment and environmental degradation of their lands.[59] The nomadic identity of the Tuareg also placed them in a rather unconventional position with regard to building a homeland.

In Mali, the rebellion started in 1990 and was characterized by low-intensity skirmishes. Some groups did call for the establishment of an independent Azawad, but the practical demands focused on regional autonomy. In this case at least, the state granted significant concessions in the form of decentralization, culminating in local elections in 682 communes in 1999.[60] Englebert interpreted these actions as an attempt by the Tuareg militants to win state recognition of their status as a local elite. Specifically, their goal was to replace the traditional chiefs, who they felt had been given privileges by the regime and marginalized the Tuareg. In sum, he argued, 'they fought the state to obtain concessions from it and become the locally dominant group.'[61]

The evidence since the late 1990s would seem to support Englebert's contention. The subsequent lull in fighting lasted until February 2006, when Tuareg rebels led by Colonel Fagaga deserted their posts in the military and called for the genuine implementation of the 1996 National Pact, which had not involved any commitment to separatism. Fagaga's group became known as the *Alliance Démocratique du 23 Mai 2006 pour le Changement* (ADC). By July 2006, Algeria had brokered the Algiers Accord between the ADC and the government. It granted special status to the Kidal region, created an interim regional council to oversee investment matters, set up military units recruited predominantly from the local Tuareg population, and transferred a number of the local military garrisons to local forces. This seemed to satisfy most of the rebels. But in late 2007 another Tuareg rebel group, the *Alliance Touareg Nord-Mali pour le Changement* (ATNMC), launched a fresh wave of attacks in the north, killing several soldiers and causing a number of civilian casualties. Despite further Algerian efforts to mediate an agreement, the fighting continued, and the government launched a more forceful response in early 2009.[62] It appears that the problem for the ATNMC and its leader, Ibrahima Ag Bahanga, was not that their state-building aspirations were blocked but that their particular ethnic group did not do well enough out of the previous round of deals.

In Niger a similar logic was evident, but the government proved less willing to compromise in comparison to the regime in Mali. Violence here also began in 1990 with a series of hit-and-run attacks, followed by severe government reprisals and repression of the Tuareg. Here the Tuareg called for a federal system granting ethnic groups a greater degree of autonomy in 'their' regions. Their demands were not outrageous or greedy: these people were poor and marginalized and wanted to be less poor and have a greater say in governing the region where they lived. They extracted some limited concessions at the Ouagadougou peace agreements in 1994 and 1995 in the form of more public jobs for Tuaregs and a bigger slice of the revenues from the region's mining industry.

In February 2007, however, a new Tuareg rebel organization, *Mouvement des Nigériens pour la Justice* (MNJ), attacked an army post in the Air Mountains. The MNJ demanded greater Tuareg representation in the Agadez regional government, more Tuareg in the senior ranks of the army, and a greater slice of revenues from mineral extraction in the region (15 per cent was promised to local communities in a 2006 law). President Tandja's government dismissed the MNJ as bandits and drug traffickers and refused to negotiate with them. The conflict escalated, and the MNJ said they would target workers of the French and Chinese mineral extraction companies operating in the region. In response, the government declared a state of alert in the Agadez region, banned all foreign journalists, deployed 4,000 troops and purchased Russian helicopters to support them.[63] Nearly 400 soldiers and rebels were reported killed between early 2007 and early 2009.[64]

After providing a convincing description of these conflicts, Englebert concluded his discussion by saying that, 'In both Mali and Niger, it is misleading to think of the rebellions as self-determination movements. Secessionist desires are muted.'[65] The problem with his formulation is that it implies self-determination and separatism are synonymous when they are not. The Tuareg struggles were not separatist, but they were rooted in the desire to achieve a greater degree of self-determination.

Sudan and Ethiopia

Two other cases merit brief discussion because they go against the grain of Africa's separatist deficit. They are the so-called north–south war in Sudan and the multiple conflicts in Ethiopia. The war in southern Sudan between the ruling National Congress Party (NCP) and the rebel Sudan People's Liberation Movement/Army (SPLM/A) has come to occupy an unusual position in relation to self-determination and sovereignty issues (see also chapter 7). For most of its duration, neither side's leadership was focused on redrawing the country's international borders. While Omar Bashir's NCP Islamists wanted to subject all Sudan's people to their version of an Islamic state, John Garang's vision of the SPLM as a vehicle to bring about a 'New Sudan' was also focused on the country's entire population, the intention being to reduce oppression against its marginalized populations rather than break the state in two.[66] On the SPLM side there were clearly differences of opinion, with many of the movement's rank and file supporting a secessionist agenda. However, others were reluctant to frame the conflict in secessionist terms because it did not play well worldwide, and especially in much of Africa, where other governments feared what precedent a new southern Sudanese state might set. On the empirical side of the equation, the reality on the ground in southern Sudan was that many of the available resources were delivered by external aid agencies, and the SPLM was not adept at creating functioning parallel institutions of government. To this day the south of the country remains an infrastructural and developmental backwater. As one observer put it, SPLM officials 'formulate policies and demand recognition but, for all intents and purposes, govern nothing and have nothing with which to govern.'[67]

On paper at least, things changed dramatically with the signing of the so-called Comprehensive Peace Agreement (CPA) in 2005. Among many other things, this provided for a referendum on southern secession after an interim period of six years, during which time both parties were supposed to work together within a Government of National Unity to 'make unity attractive'. The huge problems in the subsequent attempts to implement the CPA made it highly likely that the southerners would choose to break away from the north, thereby creating a new state. This they duly did in January 2011, when approximately 99 per cent of voters opted to secede from the north, which will almost certainly lead to the formation of a new state in July 2011. This type of secessionist settlement is the opposite of most African conflicts which, as the Casamance and Tuareg and perhaps the Western Sahara and Cabinda cases illustrate, may start with some separatist aspirations but usually end up only with self-determination options within the existing state. Despite not being a separate colony, the juridical dimension of sovereignty was open to the southern Sudanese because, officially at least, the secession took place with the consent of Sudan's government.

The other unusual African case is Ethiopia. As discussed above in the context of Eritrea's liberation struggle, Ethiopia's successful resistance of Italian colonization, its imperial tendencies towards some of its African neighbours, and its simultaneously leading role in the pan-African movement meant it occupied a special position within African international society. In large part because of this history, its domestic political structures are also unique within Africa with regard to questions of self-determination and secession. Specifically, in 1995 the country established a constitution which gave certain units within it the possibility of secession. As a result of this unusual incentive to pursue separatist agendas, Ethiopia has accounted for a significant portion of Africa's secessionist struggles.[68]

During the Cold War, the Ethiopian state became increasingly centralized, Amharic was imposed across the country as its language and Amhara assumed a disproportionate place in its senior bureaucracy. The result was that Afar, Eritreans, Ogadenis, Oromos and Tigray all fought to break the Ethiopian state. In 1991 Mengistu Haile Mariam's regime was replaced with a coalition led by the Tigray People's Liberation Front (TPLF). In part because the Tigray had long been considered 'the junior imperial partner to the Amhara', ending Amharic dominance and inserting themselves atop the new coalition was more important than challenging the Ethiopian state *per se*.[69] Upon assuming power the TPLF engaged in a rare experiment in ethnic federalism, granting minorities local autonomy. The centrepiece was the 1995 federal constitution, which created ethnically defined federated regions for the Afar, Amhara, Oromo, Somali and Tigray. It also stated that 'nations, nationalities, and peoples' within Ethiopia had the constitutional right to secede.

However, as the Tigray elite began to build and dominate its own neopatrimonial system in Ethiopia, so many barriers were placed upon the secession option that it became 'largely theoretical'.[70] As Christopher Clapham observed, the constitution trapped the regime between two stools. On the one hand, Ethiopian nationalists were concerned that it set Ethiopia on a similar path to the Soviet Union and was little more than a divide-and-rule strategy for the benefit of the Tigray. On the other hand, representatives of the country's marginalized minorities 'felt that the EPRDF had promised a level of autonomy that it had then totally failed to deliver.'[71] It wasn't long before some Ogadenis and Oromos in particular returned to insurgency. Although none of these insurgencies have posed a serious strategic challenge to Meles Zenawi's regime, they reflect the unique dynamics which Ethiopian federalism has spawned. One brief example should suffice.

Formed in 1984 as an off-shoot of the Western Somali Liberation Front, the Ogaden National Liberation Front (ONLF) increased in popularity in 1991 after the ousting of the incumbent regimes in both Ethiopia (Mengistu) and Somalia (Siad Barre). At this point its members became embroiled in the corrupt neopatrimonial dynamics which characterized the relationship between the Region 5/Somali Region and the EPRDF regime.[72] After registering as a political party and competing successfully in the region's elections, between 1991 and 1994 the ONLF led the regional government. In 1994 the ONLF-dominated Regional Assembly resolved to hold a referendum on independence for the Ogaden. This did not go down well with the federal government, and in response the EPRDF regime dismissed the ONLF-led cabinet – replacing it with the more pliable Ethiopian Somali Democratic League. In 1995 the federal government also moved the Region 5 capital north from

Godey to Jigjiga, where Ogadenis formed a minority. It was at this point that the ONLF began its armed struggle against the EPRDF regime, using guerrilla tactics against federal troops and officials stationed in the region. As well as support from the Ogadeni diaspora, the ONLF received funds and training from Sudan and, after 1998, Eritrea.[73] The ONLF has never posed a strategic military threat to the incumbent regime, in part because it has suffered debilitating leadership splits and in part because it does not have total support among the region's clans for its brand of ethnic and separatist politics. There are no reliable estimates of its military strength, but in 2007 it hit the international media headlines for an attack on a Chinese construction camp which was used to prospect hydrocarbons and was protected by Ethiopian forces. The attack reportedly killed seventy-four people, including nine Chinese.

The lack of publicly available independent information about the ONLF has left even its central objectives murky to outsiders. As one expert on the region concluded, 'It is not always clear whether an independent state of "Ogadenia", a Somali Region under Ogadeni rule, or a reunification with a future rebuilt Republic of Somalia constitutes its main agenda.'[74] On the other hand, the organization's website claims it is fighting for 'self-determination, peace, development and democracy'.[75] In July 2010 the ONLF foreign secretary stated that his organization's primary objective was to allow the Ogadeni people to choose their political future in a referendum, and that this might involve independence, union with a greater Somalia or regional autonomy within Ethiopia.[76] Given the importance of neopatrimonial bargaining in the politics of Region 5 and the menu of possible political futures, it is at least plausible that elements within the ONLF, like the Tuaregs and MFDC, are concerned primarily with using violence to acquire greater local political dominance rather than seeking to redraw Ethiopia's international boundaries.

Conclusion

As this chapter has shown, sovereignty and self-determination have been vital ingredients in some of Africa's longest-running armed conflicts. Not only has sovereign statehood been a resource worth fighting over, but international norms of sovereignty, degrees of international support for secession, and the changing legal meaning attached to self-determination have shaped how some African armed groups framed their struggles and pursued their goals. Although genuinely separatist struggles were relatively rare and confined to cases of unfinished decolonization, it was quite common for marginalized peoples in African states to take up arms to achieve a greater say in how they are governed. While separatist conflicts are about breaking states to build new ones, self-determination struggles are about making existing states work better for their peoples. These dynamics were widely recognized during the Cold War.[77] They did not stop being true after it ended.

CHAPTER SIX
Ethnicity

Although all armed conflicts involve identity politics, people's ethnic identities are commonly held to be of greater significance than their other identities. Journalists and scholars both regularly use 'ethnic' as shorthand to describe a particular kind of warfare and the explanation for it. It was also frequently claimed that 'ethnic wars' increased dramatically in the post-Cold War era. Stefan Wolff, for instance, concluded that 'proportionally speaking more ethnic conflicts began in the last decade of the twentieth century than in any other.'[1] Talking about wars in this manner implies that there is something about ethnicity which, under the right circumstances, begets organized violence. This approach is not unique to African conflicts, but ethnic explanations have been particularly common in this part of the world.

But what does it mean to say that a particular type of violence is an ethnic conflict? And how useful is this way of thinking about Africa's recent wars in particular? The idea that ethnic difference alone 'causes' war can be quickly dismissed. If this were true, the world's many different ethnic groups would be in a perpetual state of conflict, whereas the vast majority of the time they live peacefully side by side. This means that ethnic difference *per se* is not the crux of the problem. Nor is ethnic similarity a panacea: as the case of Somalia since the late 1980s demonstrates, the fact that inhabitants share the same ethnicity is no guarantee of internal harmony. Analysts might therefore focus on 'ethnicity plus', where the 'plus' is some additional mechanism, factor, development, attribute or tendency that might explain the outbreak of organized violence. Among the usual suspects are manipulative elites and some sort of economic or political crisis, such as a sharp crash in commodity prices or the assassination of an important public figure.

This chapter addresses these issues in three stages. It begins by summarizing what ethnic identities are and how they have materialized in contemporary Africa. It then examines the potential ways in which ethnic identities are related to armed conflict. Finally, the chapter analyses the extent to which the 1994 Rwandan genocide was an 'ethnic' conflict. Although Rwanda was unusual inasmuch as the Hutus and Tutsis shared the same language and religion and had high levels of intermarriage, it is a crucial case for several reasons. Not only was it Africa's most intense period of violent bloodletting between 1990 and 2009, but more than any other conflict it has been depicted as occurring because of the differences between 'Hutus' and 'Tutsis'. Yet, even in the eye of Rwanda's genocidal storm, the participants in this political drama did not always view ethnicity in rigid, primordial terms.

The basic argument of this chapter is that ethnicity does not cause armed conflict; rather so-called ethnic wars are usually the result of political power struggles between elites whose actions do not simply reflect static ethnic identities but instead shape identities and the political consequences that flow from them. In this sense I agree with the sentiment that ethnic difference does not have a strong relationship with the incidence of armed conflict.[2] Nevertheless, the construction of specific ethnic identities to support particular political agendas has frequently been an important ingredient of Africa's wars. With this in mind, Lee Ann Fujii's work on the 1994 Rwandan genocide provides a useful way to conceptualize these dynamics by viewing official or state-sponsored understandings of ethnicity as a script for violence, rather than a direct cause of it.[3] The officially endorsed ethnic 'scripts' in Rwanda illustrate the connection between regime strategies and organized violence. While scripts can be propagated which facilitate violence either across or within ethnic groups, individuals and groups will respond to them in different ways, sometimes following the official script in letter and/or spirit and on other occasions departing from it to a greater or lesser degree.

What are Ethnic Identities?

Ethnic identities can be understood as 'a kind of social radar, a perceptual device through which people come to see where they stand in relation to the human environment'.[4] Dating back to the Greek word for nation – *ethnos* – ethnicity usually refers to a group of people who perceive themselves as sharing certain 'ethnic' reference points such as 'common descent, history, fate and culture, which usually indicates some mix of language, physical appearance and the ritual regulation of life, especially religion.'[5] As Donald Horowitz famously suggested, ethnicity is 'the idea of common provenance, recruitment primarily through kinship, and a notion of a unique inventory of cultural traits'.[6] In the name of ethnicity, young people are often told who they are (and are not), what to associate with other ethnic groups, and what rituals and symbols are of consequence, including key dates, beliefs, events, appearance, places, dress, cuisine, etc.

Ethnic identities should also be understood as being simultaneously inter-subjective, factionalized and relational. Describing ethnicity as intersubjective highlights the fact that it is defined through social interactions and is therefore a property of a group and not solely a matter of personal choice. Although individuals may try and assert their own understanding of ethnicity in particular ways, the group concerned is often the final arbiter of what will stick, and in this sense can ascribe specific ethnic identities to unwilling individuals. In the modern era, institutions of the state have enjoyed arguably the greatest power to ascribe political identities to their population. As Mahmood Mamdani noted, 'If the law recognises you as a member of an ethnicity, and state institutions treat you as a member of that ethnicity, then you become an ethnic being legally and institutionally.'[7] Such a process of institutionalization was how ethnicity emerged as a key element in the discriminatory practices of many modern African states. Viewing ethnic identities as intersubjective also means that, in terms of scale, conceptions of ethnicity must transcend face-to-face interactions and hence revolve around some type of 'imagined community' in the sense used by Benedict Anderson.[8]

Describing ethnicity as factionalized reflects the fact that no ethnic group is completely homogeneous; there are always debates – and hence factional splits – over the authentic interpretation of the ethnicity in question. As Milton Esman observed, factions 'compete for the right to control [the group's] institutions and collective resources, to speak authoritatively on its behalf, and to represent it to outsiders.'[9] In Burundi, for example, the Hutu/Tutsi binary has only limited explanatory value for understanding the country's postcolonial conflicts. As well as conflict between Hutu and Tutsi, there were also crucially important intra-aristocracy cleavages between the old guard and the young modernized elite, intra-Tutsi rifts between the military and the political elite and, more recently, intra-Hutu disputes, as well as a plethora of regional and intra-ethnic differences across class, clan and personal lines.[10] Moreover, all of these contemporary dynamics were wrapped up in a more longstanding and malign process of mythmaking based around the history of genocidal violence in Burundi, which itself became a constitutive element of further violence.[11]

As a relational concept, the substantive content of a particular ethnic identity always develops in relation to an 'other'. 'Ethnicity', Esman wrote, 'has no meaning except in relational terms. There must always be an "other".' And, as I discuss in more detail below, he is also correct to point out that, 'Where there is no other, identities and conflicts focus on kinship groups, regional differences, or economic interests.'[12]

In post-Cold War Africa, the most prominent ethnic identities have their roots in the modern encounters between colonial and local forces. These encounters were generally mediated on the African side by local chiefs and village headmen – individuals Bruce Berman called 'local African strongmen' or 'enforcers' – and on the European side by colonial administrators, missionaries and professional anthropologists.[13] While colonial powers routinely exploited the locals, their arrival also injected new sources of wealth and power into the continent, thereby intensifying ongoing local struggles over custom, power and property. Thus while they attempted to protect themselves against colonialism's destructive effects, Africans also struggled to take advantage of the new opportunities it provided. Since the imperialist's organizing script revolved so heavily around ethnicity – partly because many European administrators believed Africans naturally lived in tribes and partly because they tried to freeze identities to make administration easier – colonialism encouraged Africans to think ethnically as well.

For Berman, some of the most important characteristics of these emerging ethnicities were their stress on common culture, language and descent; the importance accorded to customary law, with the central issues being defining communal membership, gender relations, access to land and control of labour and resources; their predominantly masculine and patriarchal character; and their 'invented histories and noble lies', which usually attempted to justify the exigencies of current political struggles.[14] As discussed in more detail in chapter 7, in some cases religious beliefs also played an important part in influencing group dynamics and individual behaviour.

Ethnicities and War

To what extent are so-called ethnic conflicts actually about ethnicity? A reasonable place to start is with the contemporary IR literature, which has generated a variety of general hypotheses about ethnicity and war. Those espousing a primordial conception of ethnicity have argued that hatreds between ethnic groups persist over generations until something triggers an eruption of mass violence against the despised group.[15] Those analysts who view ethnicity in more instrumental terms, however, have argued that violence occurs when power-hungry elites manipulate a variety of institutions to encourage widespread fear of some other ethnicity and create incentives for publics to take ostensibly defensive measures to ward off the source of the threat.[16] In a similar vein, constructivists have argued that it is symbolic politics and emotions that matter most, because each ethnic group is defined by a 'myth–symbol complex' that identifies which elements of shared culture and what interpretations of history bind the group together and distinguish it from others. Extreme violence results from group myths that justify hostility, fears of group extinction and chauvinist mobilization.[17]

At the quantitative end of the spectrum, a recent study which claimed to cover all politically relevant ethnic groups between 1946 and 2005 concluded that ethnic groups are more likely to rebel when (1) more representatives of that ethnic group are excluded from state power, especially if they experienced a loss of power in the recent past, (2) the group's capacity to mobilize is high, and (3) the group has experienced conflict in the past. In sum, the authors concluded that ethnicity *plus* marginalization, organization and a history of violence are 'an important part of the dynamics leading to the outbreak of civil wars'.[18]

At the more qualitative end of the spectrum, certain types of ethnic geography at the state level have been associated with an increased likelihood of war. A widely cited case in point is Michael Brown's argument that ethnic geography is often an underlying factor – i.e. necessary but not sufficient – for the outbreak of internal war. In particular, he noted that 'states with ethnic minorities are more prone to conflict than others, and certain kinds of ethnic demographics are more problematic than others.'[19] In sum, different types of ethnic geography are likely to produce different kinds of internal problems. A particular risk concerning territory is that, where minorities are not deeply intermingled but distributed along regional lines, countries are said to be 'more likely to face secessionist demands'.[20] Other analysts have agreed, noting that a combination of ethnic and territorial claims seems 'a particularly explosive mix for the occurrence of violent ethnic conflict'. This view suggests that, where ethnic identities 'are in part based on claims to the same stretch of territory, violent escalation of their disputes over rights and self-determination is more likely.'[21]

When it comes to the proximate causes or triggers for particular wars, Brown rails against the idea of ' "no-fault" history' and instead heaps most of the blame upon certain 'influential individuals' rather than broad ethnic categories.[22] This approach raises at least two issues. First, if certain forms of ethnic geography are necessary but insufficient factors in the outbreak of war, armed conflict cannot simply appear overnight but requires some sort of gestation period in which ethnic groups form, cohere and eventually develop the capabilities to wage war.[23] It also assumes that the political content of ethnicity – for example, what does it mean to be a supporter of Hutu power? – can change over time, allowing for more or less conflict-prone permutations. Second, Brown's focus on certain 'influential individuals' begs the question of how these people attract followers – that is, how do they mobilize state institutions or publics to support their agendas?

Although there is clearly no one-size-fits-all response to this question, it is quite plausible that sometimes elites are just doing what their followers want them to do, in which case popular mobilization should be relatively simple, and it would seem unfair to blame the elites alone for the policies pursued.[24] When there is a divergence between elite agendas and those of the masses, however, questions of mobilization are more complicated. In general it seems that, when elites engage in war-mongering, most 'ordinary' people try and remain neutral, which usually translates into passivity in the face of the existing authorities.[25]

But what explains why people actively support violent agendas rather than remaining passive? One of the more sophisticated attempts to analyse why people follow the extremists revolves around the power of emotions in human behaviour. Drawing on findings from neuroscience, Stuart Kaufman has argued that, when trying to understand why people act in certain ways, emotions such as fear, anger, hatred and love are more important than rational calculations. Since emotions set priorities – for example, fear might cause people to prioritize security over other values such as wealth, or love might cause them to risk their own lives to rescue a potential victim of genocide – we need to understand why people find certain symbols and ties particularly evocative. Politicians who can use symbols to evoke emotions are thus most likely to motivate their supporters to act.[26] However, since symbols are always open to varying degrees of interpretation, and because individuals and groups will react to those symbols in different ways, populations never behave in a homogeneous manner in situations of armed conflict. As Fujii put it, even during wartime, when pressures to conform are at their most intense, 'ethnic masses do not act as a single unit, but as a variety of groups and groupings that do not always follow ethnic lines.'[27]

Another popular way of thinking about the relationship between ethnicity and warfare at a general level derives from the work of economists Paul Collier and Anke Hoeffler. They suggest that, although the primary explanation for Africa's civil wars lies in the continent's economic structures (see chapter 4), in certain circumstances ethnic factors can increase the likelihood of warfare. While fractionalized societies are significantly safer than homogeneous societies, countries where 'ethnic dominance' exists – that is, where the largest ethnic group is between 45 per cent and 90 per cent of the population – face approximately double the risk of conflict of other societies. The good news for Africa, according to Collier and Hoeffler, is that only 40 per cent of states are characterized by 'ethnic dominance', whereas in other developing regions 57 per cent of countries are so characterized.[28] They thus concluded that Africa's 'social characteristics . . . generated atypically low risk' of civil war and saw 'the rising trend of African conflict' in the 1990s as due to 'the contingent effect of economic circumstances' rather than Africa's 'deep problems in its social structure'.[29] Some of the reasons why this economic explanation should not be accepted at face value were discussed in chapter 4.

With these general approaches in mind, I suggest that it is useful to move beyond thinking of ethnicity as simply a backdrop or underlying factor in the outbreak of armed conflict. Ethnicity is not a static feature of the political landscape but can be constructed and deployed strategically by actors in order to shape the contours of that landscape. In this sense the key question becomes: How can particular framings of ethnic identities open up pathways to violence? The answer is that two pathways stand out as particularly relevant here: inter-ethnic disputes and intra-ethnic disputes.[30]

The first pathway is where armed conflict takes the form of ethnic group X versus ethnic group Y. Using Kaufman's terminology, this is more likely to occur when a group's myth–symbol complex is defined by greater degrees of hostility towards an external 'other'. Whether these conflicts are fought over territory or control of a particular government, common variants of such inter-ethnic group violence include the security dilemma (where the logic of fear is paramount), status concerns (where the logic of injustice compels subordinate groups to rebel), hegemonic ambitions (where a logic of contempt towards the other drives the hegemonic group to maintain dominance through violent repression) and elite aspirations (where ethnicity is used by elites to manipulate followers to engage in violence against a perceived external enemy).[31] It is notable that comparative studies of genocide and mass killings tend to conclude that this type of violence is frequently a 'pathologically defensive reaction' usually carried out by governments.[32]

In this pathway, what Fujii has described as 'state-sponsored ethnicity' plays a crucial role. 'State-sponsored ethnicity' refers to the official construction of meanings about ethnicity evident in any given context. These constructions do not represent 'the sum total of ethnic meaning in all social and political life' but are better understood as 'one set of meanings among many that exist at the same time'. Because they are backed by the institutions of state power, these official meanings can come to dominate interpretations of events, especially for outsiders with little knowledge of local history and politics. In times of conflict and crisis, the meanings encapsulated by state-sponsored ethnicity act as what Fujii calls a 'script' for violence: 'a dramaturgical blueprint for an imagined world, one that is self-contained and populated by specific characters who say and do specific things at specific moments in time.' Based on her work on Rwanda's genocide, Fujii concludes that 'The creators of this script are usually threatened elites in the capital who come to see genocide as their best strategy for staying in power.'[33] As discussed in more detail below, the idea of a script allows us to understand heterogeneity of behaviour within ethnic groups: while some people may be only too happy to follow the official script, others might act out their roles with a degree of artistic licence, while still others may depart from the script entirely.

The war in Darfur, Sudan, provides a good example of state-sponsored ethnicity in action. In early 2003, a rebellion organized mainly by the Fur, Zaghawa and Masalit tribes in Darfur enjoyed considerable military success against the government's forces. In response, the government of Sudan pursued a counter-insurgency strategy based on funding and arming local militias within Darfur and telling them that they could keep whatever land and loot they acquired in the process.[34] The government opted for this approach partly because its own armed forces could not be trusted to get the job done; partly because it had used this strategy numerous times before, particularly in the south of Sudan; and partly because the use of militias provided an element of plausible deniability for instances of excessive violence. Success, however, was far from certain, not least because in many respects some of the Arab tribes that ultimately formed the core of the dreaded *janjawiid* – crucially, the landless Northern Rizeigat – were as marginalized, if not more so, than the tribes which had started the rebellion.[35] Initially, the government organized, funded and armed a number of local outlaws commonly known as *Hajjana*. Although not all the *Hajjana* were Arabs, both of its two most notorious members were.[36] As the rebellion grew, however, the government needed greater numbers of recruits for its counter-insurgency operations. To this end, Khartoum's political elite played on fears among Darfur's other tribes by depicting the rebellion as anti-Arab. In particular, it claimed that the Zaghawa were especially keen on pushing the Arabs out of Darfur.[37]

Khartoum's plan was helped by three factors: first, the rebels had not consulted with Arab tribal leaders before launching their campaign; second, rebel forces began to attack Arab settlements and loot camels; and, third, international actors largely turned a blind eye to attacks against Arab civilians.[38] In this sense, the Sudanese state managed to depict a rebellion that was essentially driven by political grievances as one that was driven by ethnic (Arab versus African) issues. In so doing, its state-sponsored brand of ethnicity increased the political significance of the distinction between 'Arab' and 'African' within Darfur. This had important effects for insiders and outsiders alike.

The second pathway involves violence stemming primarily from intra-ethnic conflict, or what might be classified as a purging of ethnic group X. In this scenario, armed conflict stems from a desire to 'purify' the ethnic group in question in the face of moderate attempts to degrade it – i.e. to defend threatened boundaries or retain/grab power.[39] Here, the 'ethnic card' is typically played as a result of political infighting within the incumbent ethnic group between ethnic extremists and moderates.[40] In this pathway, the axes of extremism–moderation vary but might include political differences, regional differences, economic differences, religious differences, etc.

In some armed conflicts, both pathways will be in evidence, often at the same time. In Burundi's civil war, for example, factionalism within Hutu and Tutsi political groups went hand in hand with the struggle between the two ethnicities. As Daley observed, this factionalism was 'an expression of ethnic extremism and of individual rivalry among key members; the latter becoming more significant in the allocation of ministerial portfolios'.[41] Both pathways also require a reasonable degree of political organization and the formation of armed groups (ranging from large and sophisticated militaries to small bands of thugs) as well as some catalyzing forces such as a crisis and Brown's 'influential individuals'. Once violence has erupted and been carried out in the name of ethnicity, so ethnic stereotypes are likely to proliferate and gain a greater degree of credence. While this will increase the numbers of people who think ethnically about their predicament, it would be wrong to assume that ethnic groups act in homogeneous ways or even that ethnic identities can explain the dynamics of the conflict in question.

The Case of Rwanda

What role did ethnic identities play in the 1994 Rwandan genocide? This is a crucial case not only because of the number of people killed in the name of ethnicity in such a short space of time but also because it has typically been depicted in ways that give ethnicity the central role in explaining both the outbreak of genocide and its dynamics. Nevertheless, Rwanda is clearly also an unusual case inasmuch as its different ethnic groups shared a number of important commonalities, such as language and religion, and there was a significant degree of intermarriage across the groups. It is also a case which illustrates, unlike many of Africa's weak states, how a strong set of state institutions could be turned on its own citizens.

While it would be impossible to understand the violence in Rwanda without making reference to the categories of 'Hutu' and 'Tutsi', ethnic differences alone cannot adequately explain what happened or why the violence started in earnest in April 1994. In reality, the genocide was the result of a complex mix of ingredients. As Peter Uvin has persuasively argued, these can broadly be divided into three core elements (the frustration caused by the longstanding condition of structural violence in Rwanda, the strategies of manipulation by elites under threat from economic and political processes, and the widespread existence of racist values in society) and four secondary factors (the prior history of violence in Rwanda and neighbouring Burundi, opportunism, the absence of external constraints, and the colonial legacy).[42] The crucial trigger was the (ultimately counterproductive) attempt to consolidate the waning power of a small group of powerful extremists within the Habyarimana regime known as the *akazu*.[43]

In short, the genocide was clearly the result of group dynamics, but it is not at all clear that the key identity ties within them were ethnic as opposed to regional or ideological. The main orchestrators were Colonel Théoneste Bagosora, his allies in the military, and a group of ideologues mainly from northwestern Rwanda. The genocide required sophisticated, detailed and sustained ideological and military preparations, including a version of ethnicity sponsored by both the Habyarimana regime and the coup plotters who overthrew it.[44] Thus, while Rwanda's civil war (1990–4) can be understood as an example of inter-ethnic armed conflict, the genocide arose primarily out of an intra-Hutu struggle. This section analyses how ethnicity was understood in Rwanda and then examines some of the blind spots of ethnic approaches to explaining the genocide.

Ethnicity in Rwanda

The closest term for ethnicity in the Kinyarwanda language is *ubwoko*, which means the type or kind of something. When referring to a person, however, the word used to refer to someone's clan, all of which were multiethnic and multiclass. In contrast, the terms 'Hutu' and 'Tutsi' originated as references to an individual's status in society. Over time, however, they solidified into labels referring to groups. As Alison Des Forges noted, 'The word "Tutsi," which apparently first described the status of an individual – a person rich in cattle – became the term that referred to the elite group as a whole and the word "Hutu" – meaning originally a subordinate or follower of a more powerful person – came to refer to the mass of the ordinary people.'[45]

The distinctions between Hutu/Tutsi and the socio-political gaps between them became more pronounced during the period of European control in the late nineteenth and early twentieth century. During the 1920s and 1930s, the Belgian colonial authorities decided to impose a Tutsi monopoly on public life by decreeing that only Tutsis could be officials. Hutus were removed from official positions and denied access to higher education. To facilitate such policies, the Belgian authorities tried to categorize every individual as Hutu, Tutsi or Twa ('pygmies'). One widely cited interpretation of how this categorization took place suggests that each Rwandan was subsequently asked to choose their group identity: roughly 15 per cent chose Tutsi while approximately 84 per cent chose Hutu.[46] An individual's designation was then registered in local government offices and written down on identity cards that all adult Rwandans were obliged to carry.

This process institutionalized the ethnic identities of individuals as Hutu, Tutsi or Twa. It also afforded privileges to Tutsis, some of whom began to believe the hype about their own superiority over the Hutus. Traditionally, however, a person's *ubwoko* was not set in stone but could be altered, either through a change of status or through concerted strategic action.[47] For example, in terms of status, an individual's level of wealth (in terms of cow ownership) could result in a change of *ubwoko*: possessing lots of cows made someone Tutsi; losing cows would relegate a Tutsi to a Hutu. Obtaining a new identity card would represent an example of changing *ubwoko* through strategic action. In both cases, a degree of consent was required from people within the local community to legitimate the identity change.

After decades spent engineering a situation of Tutsi dominance, in the final years of their rule the Belgian colonists changed their tactics and began supporting the Hutus. This precipitated the violent events known as the 'Hutu revolution' of 1959–61. During this time the tables were turned and power relations between Hutus and Tutsis were dramatically reconfigured. The percentage of Tutsis in the Rwandan population declined sharply, partly because many had been massacred or fled and partly because some found ways to redefine themselves as Hutu.[48] As a consequence, while Tutsis represented 17.5 per cent of the population in 1952, by 1991 they counted for only 8.4 per cent.[49]

In more recent times, Rwandans learnt about this more restrictive interpretation of ethnicity in a variety of ways and in different forums. Children found out about their ethnic identities at a young age and from various sources, including daily life outside the home and in school curricula, as well as through peer and teacher pressure.[50] Ethnicity was also defined according to people's interactions with the state: importantly, all Rwandans over sixteen years of age were required to carry identity cards stating their *ubwoko*, which now classified them rigidly as Hutu, Tutsi or Twa. There was also a quota system dating from independence in 1962, which capped enrolment in schools and issuance of government posts to 9 per cent for Tutsis to match the official percentage of Tutsis in the population.[51] Finally, two post-independence censuses (in 1978 and August 1991) also reinforced a fixed notion of ethnicity. Interestingly, however, people often misrepresented themselves to the census takers.[52] This is curious because for all the importance it attached to ethnicity, the state remained willing to rely on people's self-identification and hence left open space in which individuals could make strategic choices about their stated ethnicity.

Ethnicity and violence

As even this brief discussion suggests, Rwanda's ethnic identities were constructed categories with fuzzy if not entirely fluid boundaries. To what extent do these identities explain the violence? As Lee Ann Fujii has observed, ethnicity-based approaches have problems explaining some important issues, not least, the timing of the genocide; Hutu non-participation in the genocide; why local leaders had to force so many people to participate in the killings; why some Hutus helped Tutsis; and why some of the targeted were Hutus.[53]

The first point to note is that the genocide did not occur during some of the highpoints of ethnic tension, particularly the economic crisis of the late 1980s or the Rwandan Patriotic Front (RPF) invasions of the early 1990s.[54] Nor was genocide an automatic response even after President Habyarimana's assassination on 6 April 1994. Indeed, in the week after the assassination Colonel Bagosora and his supporters faced resistance from other Rwandans. At a local level, genocide was usually delayed until representatives of the interim government arrived to confirm what needed to be done. People thus appear to have been waiting for confirmation of the order to commit genocide.[55] This suggests that we need to understand the non-ethnic factors that facilitated mass mobilization, because ethnic tensions alone were clearly not enough to spark genocide. In this case, mass mobilization seems to have occurred because of the combined effects of propaganda, fear and anger, as well as greed – i.e. promises of property and other material rewards.

For the elites orchestrating the genocide, the primary objective was to gain and consolidate their control of state institutions in the face of what they saw as Habyarimana's sell-out to the RPF under the peace accord signed in Arusha in 1993. The key factors in the mobilization of ordinary people lower down the political hierarchy, however, seem to have been fear combined with a degree of anger about the 'Tutsi' role in the country's economic crisis and later the assassination of President Habyarimana,[56] as well as the opportunity to engage in acts of violence and looting with impunity. Ordinary people appear to have been afraid of two things in particular: first, what an RPF/Tutsi military victory might mean for them and their families; and, second, what the genocidaires might do to them if they refused to participate. On the first point, the so-called Bahima conspiracy depicted the RPF as a royalist army of pastoralist raiders intent on restoring feudalism across the entire Great Lakes region. The RPF, in cahoots with local Tutsis, was said to be actively planning to slaughter Hutus unless drastic preventative measures were taken to stop them.[57] These fears were lent further fuel in late 1993, when officers in neighbouring Burundi's Tutsi-led army assassinated the first democratically elected Hutu president, Melchior Ndadaye. This event generated a wave of killings and an exodus of approximately 300,000 Hutu refugees into Rwanda.[58] The arrival of a 600-strong RPF battalion in Kigali as part of the Arusha Accords also added to the volatile mix of fear and rumours.

Widespread fear thus provided a crucial backdrop for the genocide. In Fujii's words, the 'script for genocide' thus began 'with a scene of apocalyptic proportions – the threatened existence of the group deemed innocent and good. The level and immediacy of mortal danger steadily increases, culminating in heroic defense of the threatened group through annihilation of the group's greatest enemy.'[59] From anxieties about the economic future to worries about an RPF victory and the assassination of the president, fear was consistently invoked to justify genocide as a necessary defence against the enemy onslaught. Far from being unique to Rwanda, this is the usual modus operandi of perpetrators of mass atrocities.[60]

Regarding people's fears of how genocidaires might react if they refused to participate in the killing, Human Rights Watch researchers noted how burgomasters used both carrots and sticks to mobilize the population. Specifically, they

> directed or permitted communal police, militia, or simply other citizens to burn down houses and to threaten the lives of those who refused to join in the violence. . . . They also offered powerful incentives to draw the hesitant into killing. They or others solicited by them provided cash payments, food, drink and, in some cases, marijuana to assailants. They encouraged the looting of Tutsi property, even to the point of having the pillage supervised by communal police.[61]

It is important to note, however, that such material incentives did not persuade all Hutus to participate in the killing. Nor was it the case that the poorer elements of society were more willing to join the killers. For example, people in the prefecture of Butare, one of the poorest in the country, 'were the last to join the killing campaign'.[62]

The second and related problem for ethnic approaches is the high level of Hutu non-participation in the genocide. At the elite level, a crucial part of the explanation for this is that the mechanics of genocide were planned by a small group of northern extremists.[63] Approaches that rely upon ethnicity as a central explanatory variable cannot account for this crucial intra-ethnic fault line: the regional rivalries between competing centres of Hutu power – specifically, the northern *akazu* versus the centre-south. At the local level, the participation rate in the genocidal violence differed across the country: the genocide was, in Prunier's words, a 'hill-by-hill and a home-by-home thing'.[64] Although the exact number of genocidaires will probably never be known, they can be roughly divided into one of the following groups:

- the presidential guard: numbering approximately 600, they played a crucial role in eliminating the political opposition in the early stages of the genocide;[65]
- the regular army: comprised of some 7,000 troops in 1989, by 1992 it contained approximately 30,000 soldiers;[66]
- the gendarmes/police force: created in 1961 with 3,000 men (mainly from northern Rwanda), by the time of the genocide it had increased to 6,000;[67]
- the *interahamwe* and *impuzamugambi* militias: most estimates suggest these numbered approximately 30,000.[68] The former were generally associated with the ruling MRND party while the latter were organized by the CDR and largely comprised of its youth wing;
- criminals released from prison;
- other 'joiners':[69] probably the largest group but also the hardest to generate accurate numbers for. They included a wide range of people, among them many subsistence farmers, who participated in the killings.

Based on these figures, a minimal estimate would be that well over 60,000 people participated directly in the killing of non-combatants during the genocide. If they each killed one person per week for 100 days, this would produce a death toll of just under 860,000. The figure of 60,000 would represent only some 3 per cent of the male Hutu population aged over thirteen, meaning that approximately 97 per cent of Hutu males did not kill their fellow citizens.[70] This estimate led John Mueller to his overall conclusion that, 'insofar as it is taken to imply a war of all against all and neighbor against neighbor . . . ethnic war essentially does not exist.'[71]

However, a more detailed estimate by Scott Straus concluded that there were between 175,000 and 210,000 perpetrators (defined as any person who participated in an attack against a civilian in order to kill or to inflict serious injury on that civilian). Using Straus's figures, and defining active adults as eighteen to fifty-four years old, this number of perpetrators equates to 7 to 8 per cent of the active adult Hutu population at the time of the genocide and 14 to 17 per cent of the active adult male population.[72] Although the percentages of adult males involved are significantly higher than Mueller's estimate, it still strongly suggests that most Hutu males did not become killers.

While estimating the numbers and types of people directly involved in the slaughter is important for several reasons, we must remember the broader social context in which the genocide took place. The key point here is that it was made possible not just by the killers but by the actions and/or inactions of thousands of people who helped facilitate, organize and administer – the genocide's bureaucrats – as well as the many other bystanders who did nothing to help the victims.

Proponents of the 'ethnic hatreds' thesis would also find it difficult to explain why local leaders had to force so many people to become killers when hatred of 'Tutsis' was supposed to be a powerful enough motivator. In spite of the intense levels of fear, 'the vast majority of Hutus seem to have stood by' and not actively participated in the killings.[73] Testimonies gathered from both joiners and survivors also suggest that relations with their neighbours were usually reasonable before the violence began. Moreover, the joiners did not generally say that they killed because of a collective hatred of Tutsi.[74]

This suggests two conclusions. First, a person's ethnic identity played only a partial (and arguably minor) role in whether they participated in the violence; the more important factors were whether they belonged to one of the aforementioned groups and a variety of personal circumstances and motivations. As Des Forges observed, genocidaires killed for a variety of reasons: some were 'moved by virulent hatred, others by real fear, by ambition, by greed, by a desire to escape injury at the hands of those who demanded they participate, or by the wish to avoid fines for nonparticipation that they could not hope to pay.'[75]

Second, it suggests that mobilization required much more than just appeals to ethnic solidarity. Rather, people had to be mobilized by local leaders – usually the prefects and burgomasters. As Human Rights Watch noted:

> Prefects transmitted orders and supervised results, but it was burgomasters and their subordinates who really mobilized the people. Using their authority to summon citizens for communal projects, as they were used to doing for umuganda [organized, periodic communal work programmes], burgomasters delivered assailants to the massacre sites, where military personnel or former soldiers then usually took charge of the operation.[76]

Particularly in jurisdictions where none had previously existed, the burgomasters were aided by so-called security committees/councils composed of locally important people such as military, police, clergy or government officials.

In many cases, however, neither sticks nor carrots could incite people to participate in genocide. Sometimes, Hutus actively sought to rescue Tutsis and Hutus who had been targeted. Once again, ethnicity often had little to do with such outcomes. Instead, such behaviour was driven by emotional bonds of love and friendship. On occasion, Tutsis were able to bribe burgomasters and other local strongmen to let them live. Occupying the middle ground were the majority of Hutus who 'did not answer the call of the local cell leader but neither did they respond to the cries of Tutsi in distress. As one witness reported, "We closed the door and tried not to hear." '[77]

A fourth problem for ethnic approaches is that some of those slaughtered were Hutus.[78] Among the first people targeted for assassination by the genocide's ringleaders were Hutus, including the prime minister and other moderate politicians. This is a stark reminder of the intra-Hutu core of the conflict. Beyond the struggles within the political elite, it is also important to recall that some people 'who were legally Hutu were killed as Tutsi because they looked Tutsi'.[79] Even relatives of powerful local elites sometimes suffered in this way. For example, 'Hutu relatives of Col. Tharcisse Renzaho, the prefect of the city of Kigali, were killed at a barrier after having been mistaken for Tutsi.'[80] In the climate of fear and confusion, it was not surprising that local leaders and strongmen 'became final arbiters of ethnicity in their communities. Deciding who was or was not really Tutsi was the clearest expression of leaders' power. In this way, the performance of genocide was ultimately about power, not putative identity.'[81]

Conclusion

As it appeared during the 1990s, ethnicity in Rwanda was a thoroughly modern creation which was amenable to change under certain conditions. Arguably the central factor was the ways in which an ethnicity script was used as camouflage for the power plays of a small elite who sought to control the government. The ethnic categories forged by that elite were so powerful that they facilitated genocide on a huge scale and in open and communal forms. But this process also reveals that ethnicity 'had to be packaged for genocide, for its "natural" state was too ambiguous and fluid.'[82] At the local level, however, while they undoubtedly provided a crucial backdrop for the genocide, ethnic categories were sometimes less important in determining particular outcomes than other factors related to the local configurations of political power and personal relationships between the genocidaires and their prey. These conclusions reflect the power of Fujii's argument that the official discourse about ethnicity should be understood as a script for violence. In her words,

> Viewing state sponsored ethnicity as a script for violence, not a cause alters our expectations for how ethnicity operates during genocide. . . . Some actors will follow the text closely, such as when killers go after Tutsi and only Tutsi. Some will stray from the text as when killers target Hutu as well as Tutsi for killing. Some may abandon the script altogether as when killers help Tutsi instead of hurt them. The advantage of conceptualizing state-sponsored ethnicity this way is that it leads us to disaggregate the violence and to investigate the complexities and ambiguities embedded within the genocide.[83]

In sum, it seems clear that wars are never fought solely over ethnic difference. So-called ethnic conflicts are really political wars triggered by 'influential individuals' who attempt to harness political and economic forces to their own agendas, thereby strengthening their supporters and weakening their opponents. Broad ethnic categories have their place in understanding how societies function, but they are too ambiguous to be reliable guides for understanding how armed conflicts are triggered or how they unfold. As the next chapter argues, much of the same could be said about the concept of religion and Africa's wars.

CHAPTER SEVEN

Religion

Particularly in the early post-Cold War period, religion was frequently discussed as a resurgent force in world politics, generating a wide range of opinions from politicians, pundits and professors. Few were given as much airtime as the American professor Samuel Huntington, who propounded an influential but badly mistaken thesis that human history was in essence a recurring clash of immutable civilizations defined largely in terms of religion – 'possibly the most profound difference that can exist between people'.[1] Huntington claimed civilizations – but especially Islam – were responsible for a variety of fault-line conflicts in Africa (in Sudan, Nigeria, Ethiopia, Chad, Kenya and Tanzania) in which the 'most meaningful' identity for any human being is 'almost always . . . defined by religion'.[2] Although Huntington's thesis was little more than a patchwork of stereotypes with an admixture of highly selective historical examples, it attracted many supporters, who felt they were given an added boost after the 9/11 terrorist attacks on the United States.[3]

Huntington's work is part of a long tradition which sees religious beliefs, practices and organizations as particularly prone to violence because religion is absolutist, divisive and irrational.[4] Religion is said to be absolutist, since it is relatively easy for believers who think they know *the* truth to claim superiority over, and hence sanction violence against, non-believers who remain in ignorance; it is divisive because it encourages binary thinking such as us versus them, good versus evil, and hence can justify a total struggle against its enemies; and it is insufficiently rational inasmuch as, since religious beliefs cannot be proved or disproved, there is no rational basis on which disputes can be resolved. In contrast, other scholars have emphasized that religion is more often a resource for conflict resolution and peacemaking than conflict and violence.[5] Still others believe the whole distinction between religious and secular forms of violence is mythical.[6]

I conceptualize religion as a particular form of belief system, the key component of which relates to the faith in connections between the material world and an invisible, spiritual world. Understood in this manner, religious differences alone do not offer a compelling explanation for why armed conflicts begin. Different religious beliefs do not cause groups to fight but they can be interpreted to justify all sorts of behaviour, from altruistic acts of compassion to spiteful acts of hatred. As the Fourth Rightly Guided Caliph,

Ali ibn Abu Talib, put it with reference to Islam, 'The Qur'an is a script bound between two covers. It does not utter, but men speak of it.'[7]

Religion's openness to interpretation gives it a protean quality that can be used to legitimate violence as well as promote peace. Especially in times of conflict, it can be a potent motivator for action and mobilization in part because it is thought to offer an explanation for traumatic events, but also because religious identification is often a powerful basis for establishing secure identities.[8] While religious beliefs alone do not account for war, the processes through which religious organizations are formed, become involved in politics, and relate to particular conflict parties should form a central part of conflict analysis. Once this is recognized, the relationship between religious organizations and governance structures can help explain heightened risks of armed conflicts in *some* African cases. Thus religion, like the ethnic identities discussed in the preceding chapter, can become an officially endorsed 'script' for violence. Once again, the notion of scripts is useful for understanding the heterogeneity of behaviour within religious groups.

In postcolonial Africa, religious beliefs drawn from three main families – traditional, Islamic and Christian – have been an important part of life for many people. But these beliefs have rarely been a significant ingredient in the continent's wars. Of course, there are usually exceptions to every rule, and it is some of the potential exceptions that constitute the primary focus of this chapter.

To address these issues the chapter begins with a discussion of the literature which has searched for generalizable hypotheses about the relationship between religion and warfare in Africa. The second section then analyses seven of the key cases in this debate, namely, conflicts depicted as struggles between Islam and various opponents in northern Nigeria, Algeria and Sudan; intra-Islamic disputes in contemporary Somalia and Darfur; and conflicts which took place with reference to a mixture of Christian and traditional beliefs in northern Uganda and the role of the Catholic Church in Rwanda's genocide. Overall, with a few exceptions, religious beliefs and organizations were more influential in shaping the dynamics of combat than in triggering the outbreak of war. The exceptions occurred when particularly absolutist and divisive groups of political elites used religious organizations to promote their violent agendas.

Religion and Armed Conflict in Africa

In a widely discussed article in 1998, Stephen Ellis and Gerrie ter Haar argued that anyone attempting to understand African politics had to grapple with the influence exerted by religious ideas.[9] This section assesses the extent to which this applies in relation to Africa's recent armed conflicts.

First, it is important to clarify what I mean by religion. Definitions of religion are often notoriously vague, but they tend to share a number of family resemblances. In Emile Durkheim's words, 'all religions are comparable, all species of the same genus, they all share certain essential elements.'[10] Arguably the main resemblances are belief in an invisible supernatural being (or beings) which have the ability to affect life in the material world; a method of communication between humans and that being (or beings); some form of transcendent reality (e.g. heaven, hell, etc.); a distinction between the profane and the sacred; a worldview which interprets life on earth and articulates the believer's role(s) within it; and a community of adherents with similar beliefs.[11] In light of these points, I follow Ellis and ter Haar in defining religion as 'a belief in the existence of an invisible world, distinct but not separate from the visible one, that is home to spiritual beings with effective powers over the material world'.[12]

When thinking about the relationship between religion and armed conflict, it is also useful to draw several distinctions between different types of religious resources: *religious ideas* are what people believe; *religious practices* are what people actually do on the basis of such beliefs; *religious organization* involves the formation and functioning of religious communities; and *religious experiences* involve the subjective experience of inner change or transformation.[13]

Understood in this manner, how has religion been implicated in Africa's wars? This question has certainly aroused polarized opinions. Some analysts conclude that religion's role 'as a source of conflict . . . cannot be overemphasized'.[14] Others have argued that religion has been 'strangely absent . . . in most African wars'.[15] Neither view is accurate. Although differences in religious beliefs have only rarely been a primary ingredient in the outbreak of war, many of Africa's conflicts have had important religious dimensions. In Liberia's civil war, for example, beliefs about the power of the spirit world shaped the behaviour of a variety of the combatants. Although the main drivers of the conflict were the desire to 'gain wealth and prestige or to take revenge', power was necessary 'in order to achieve these goals'. And it was here that religious beliefs led some fighters to believe that they could acquire 'the strength of others through eating their vital organs or drinking their blood'.[16] Religious beliefs did not cause Liberia's war, but 'The ways in which people at all levels thought about power was rooted in religious ideology.'[17] One particularly bizarre example of such beliefs occurred at one of the NPFL checkpoints set up outside Monrovia. At the God Bless You Gate, fighters had a monkey which they believed had the power to recognize people from the Krahn ethnic group. Because the Krahn were famed monkey-hunters, the fighters believed the monkey could identify its predators and hence they would kill anybody the monkey touched.[18]

An alternative example of religion at work was the Mai-Mai soldiers in eastern Zaire who believed their connection with the spirit world gave them supernatural powers – hence their willingness to lead Laurent Kabila's AFDL forces into battle against President Mobutu's soldiers.[19] Literally meaning 'water-water', the name Mai-Mai comes from the belief that bullets could be turned into water as a result of a *dawa* potion being poured over their body to prevent weapons killing and maiming. As a result, Mai-Mai warriors often fought naked or dressed in leaves. Although Mobutu's troops were badly trained, poorly equipped and suffered from low morale, their fear of the Mai-Mai does seem to have contributed to their rapid retreat.

These brief examples suggest that religion has sometimes influenced the dynamics of particular conflicts. But has religion been a principal ingredient in the outbreak of Africa's wars? Two attempts to develop general hypotheses about this question concluded that religion was relevant to the incidence of armed conflict. Using quantitative methods, Collier and Hoeffler determined that a state's religious composition was related to the risk of instability, but not in the way Huntington's clash of civilizations predicted. Rather, they found that significant religious factionalization (many roughly equal religious groups) within states actually reduced the risk of armed conflict.[20] This resonates with the fact that Africa is by and large a deeply religious continent yet most of its wars are not about religion. Instead, the biggest risk factor was said to be situations of religious preponderance where a dominant religious majority existed (defined as over two-thirds of the population identifying with the main religious group).[21]

The other study, by Basedau and De Juan, based on a mix of quantitative and qualitative methods, agreed, but added the caveat that the 'most trouble-ridden constellation . . . is a polarized structure in which a religious majority faces a strong religious minority or in which two main groups, such as Christianity and Islam, are almost the same size.'[22] For these scholars, context was crucial, particularly the governance structures that existed in the area in question. Their study identified twenty-eight armed conflicts in twenty-four sub-Saharan African countries between 1990 and 2007 in which religious factors played a significant role.[23] They concluded that theological ideas were at least partial causes of armed conflict in eight cases, 'either because aggressive proselytization caused resistance or because theocratic elements of the state order . . . were disputed between conflict parties'. Their most clear-cut cases were in northern Nigeria, Sudan, Somalia and possibly northern Uganda.[24] In at least nine cases they decided that 'religious actors and institutions contributed to the escalation of conflict by (religious) legitimization or incitement of violence.'[25] Nonetheless, the authors acknowledged the preliminary state of their data and the fact that 'other classic risk factors seem to explain conflict prevalence after 1990 better than religious factors' and that, overall, 'religion is relatively rarely at the heart of conflict.'[26]

These final thoughts chime with Bjørn Møller's more historical study of religion and warfare in Africa. Møller argued that, with the partial exception of Sudan's so-called north–south conflict, there was no 'significant correlation between conflict propensity or terrorism and religion', either 'in the sense that religious diversity gives rise to any "clash of civilizations"' or 'in the sense that the predominance of any one religion (e.g. Islam) make a country more prone to conflict or terrorism'.[27] This view was shared by Ellis and ter Haar, who concluded that, with the partial exceptions of Sudan and Nigeria, 'there has been rather little violence on religious grounds in African conflicts.' 'Properly speaking', they argued, 'there are no religious wars in Africa south of the Sahara.'[28] This is also in line with one of the most widely cited studies of intercommunal conflict worldwide, which found religion to be 'at best a contributing factor in communal conflict and seldom the root cause'.[29]

As discussed below, when we combine these general findings with the conclusions reached by authors of detailed historical studies of the particular armed conflicts in question, it is hard not to infer that, in the vast majority of cases, religion was not a major ingredient in Africa's wars. This is certainly borne out in the conflicts in Algeria and Nigeria. In these cases, what appear at first sight to be clashes caused by different religious beliefs are actually more closely connected to the struggle among competing groups of elites for political power and prestige. Nevertheless, several exceptions remain, most notably the series of conflicts involving the Islamist junta in Sudan, the strange case of Joseph Kony's Lord's Resistance Army in northern Uganda, and the most recent wave of fighting in southern and central Somalia between various militant Islamist organizations.

Key Cases

In these attempts to develop general hypotheses about religion and warfare in Africa, several conflicts keep reappearing and can thus plausibly be taken as the crucial cases for debating this issue. The following section analyses seven cases based on an admittedly loose tripartite distinction between those which have commonly been depicted as fitting the mould of Islam versus others (northern Nigeria, Algeria and Sudan/SPLM); those involving intra-Islamic struggles (Somalia and Sudan/Darfur); and those which took place with reference to a mixture of Christian and traditional beliefs (northern Uganda and the role of the Catholic Church in Rwanda's genocide).

Northern Nigeria

Northern Nigeria provides many examples of organized violence which are routinely characterized as the result of conflict between Muslims and Christians. The conflict intensified and violence began to erupt regularly after 1999 in the wake of the decision by twelve northern states to impose *shari'a* law for their criminal codes. In most cases this decision was instigated by local politicians to bolster their popularity with predominantly Muslim populations. Along with the subsequent movement of non-Muslims out of these states, violent clashes started to break out over the following few years in a variety of towns, such as Kaduna, Kano, Gombe, Bauchi and Jos.

These riots (and subsequent reprisals) caused a large number of fatalities. Although the estimates vary wildly, it is clear that they would easily surpass the intensity levels necessary to be classified as a 'war' according to either the UCDP or PITF criteria (see chapter 1). They do not appear on these data-sets, presumably on the grounds that the clashes did not occur between organized conflict parties. Probably the most reliable estimates of the violence in Plateau State were from Human Rights Watch and the UN Committee on the Elimination of Racial Discrimination: the former suggested that 'more than 12,000' people had been killed since 1999, while the latter put the figure at 'over 13,500'.[30] A committee appointed by the Plateau State government estimated many more deaths: between September 2001 and May 2004, 53,787 people were said to have been killed in the violence (18,931 men, 17,397 women, and 17,459 children).[31] In the town of Jos alone, thousands of deaths were recorded. This predominantly Christian town of somewhere between 500,000 and 800,000 inhabitants just a few hours drive from Nigeria's capital city became the epicentre of the riots. Among the more widely reported episodes of mass killings were those in September 2001 (about 3,000 dead), November 2008 (over 700 fatalities, immediately followed by the arbitrary killing of more than 130 young Muslims by government soldiers) and March 2010 (over 500 dead), which were widely seen as reprisals for the more than 300 people killed in January 2010.[32]

On the surface, deadly riots such as those in Jos look like spontaneous outbursts of inter-religious hatred between Muslims and Christians. Certainly, in the eye of the violent storm, individuals were targeted because of their religious affiliation. A closer look, however, reveals that the root causes of the violence are linked more closely to other ingredients, such as the historical legacies of mining-related and colonial-related migration in the region; control over government jobs and institutions, which have been crucial in the allocation of states resources, especially those from oil revenues; fierce competition for jobs and access to institutions of higher education; and the deliberate manipulation of ethnic and religious identities by local politicians and other community leaders.[33] The last point is particularly important because it is difficult socio-economic conditions rather than religious differences that better account for the underlying grievances felt by the participants in the violence.

In this political tinderbox, however, the mobilization and manipulation of religious and ethnic identities could spark violence relatively easily. 'Even when religion is not the most basic cause of conflict', David Smock noted that 'it is frequently used to incite either or both sides to mob violence.'[34] Similarly, Human Rights Watch concluded that factors related to political governance played a more important role in the outbreak of violence than religious differences, especially discriminatory government policies which relegated many 'non-indigenes' to the status of second-class citizens. In their words,

> Non-indigenes are openly denied the right to compete for state and local government jobs or academic scholarships, while state-run universities subject non-indigenes to discriminatory admissions policies and higher fees. As poverty and unemployment have both become more widespread and severe in Nigeria, competition for scarce opportunities to secure government jobs, education, and political patronage has intensified dramatically. Religious, political, and ethnic disputes often serve as mere proxies for the severe economic pressures that lie beneath the surface.[35]

In Jos, specifically, much of the animosity seems to have originated between the Hausa-Fulani (who are mainly Muslim) and the other Jos Plateau communities – including the Berom, Anaguta and Afisare – who have increasingly become Christian. As more and more local people began voting along religious lines, the dominance of Christians – who make up over 90 per cent of the town's residents – made it very hard for Muslim candidates to win.[36] Indeed, it appears the appointment of a Muslim to a key position sparked the 2001 riots, but the conflict was able to escalate so quickly because the government ignored the warning signs and failed to engage in any serious attempts at reconciliation between the groups. It is thus reasonable to agree with Danfulani and Fwatshak that these violent riots 'rage on because of bad socio-economic conditions', but politicians 'use the religious card, under the cover of ethnicity'.[37]

In sum, it would appear that religious beliefs are at most one factor in Nigeria's volatile neopatrimonial mix and usually not the principal ingredient in the violent episodes. While in the midst of the riots certain individuals were clearly targeted because of their perceived religious affiliation, the group dynamics resulted from the official scripts for religious violence sanctioned by the local political authorities.

Algeria

Algeria's civil war (1990–8) has often been depicted as a religious conflict. It was precipitated by a series of violent riots which erupted across the country's principal urban centres during October 1988. Many hundreds of people were killed during these riots and the subsequent army crackdown. Within the next decade, over 100,000 people are thought to have been killed, with more than 500 fatalities a week during the most intense violence between 1993 and 1995.[38] The rioters targeted symbols of Front de Libération Nationale (FLN) power in frustration at the lack of benefit they had seen from twenty-five years of increasingly corrupt and authoritarian rule. The riots also shattered the myth propagated by the FLN's elites that their continued rule was justified because of their anti-colonial credentials gained during the liberation struggle against France.

In a subsequent attempt to legitimate its rule, the FLN permitted multi-party elections to take place in June 1990. These saw overwhelming support for the Front Islamique du Salut (FIS), and by 1991 the party was on the verge of victory when the Algerian military stepped in to prevent this outcome. Support for the FIS came from a wide variety of sources, including petty traders looking for a new government that would guarantee freedom of commerce; militant Muslims looking for a route to build an Islamic state; and unemployed and not very politicized youths who saw the FIS success in terms of revenge against the FLN for the way it had repressed the 1988 riots.[39] Importantly, voters who supported the FIS did not all condone a violent struggle against the regime. The subsequent state crackdown on the FIS, however, opened the door for various militant Islamist groups founded earlier to wage a violent *jihad* against the governing regime. Specifically, groups such as *Al Takfir wa-l Hirja* and the *Mouvement Islamique Armé* benefited from 'a fund of sympathy' from which they were able to raise funds and draw recruits.[40] But, at the same time, their call for *jihad* persuaded only a small segment of the 3 million FIS voters to take up the armed struggle.[41] While this disappointed the Islamist militants, it was the FIS elites who were arguably the biggest political losers. In 1991 they were 'at the gates of power', only to see their victory denied and then the mantle of resistance hijacked by the militant Islamists.[42]

In what sense did this constitute a religious civil war? The ruling regime was certainly under immediate threat from rebels who used the idea of *jihad* to mobilize support and justify sacrifice.[43] There were also clearly some deep religious cleavages present with Algerian society. But there were other important ingredients as well. Although not sufficient to explain the violence, the longstanding economic and social inequalities which had persisted during FLN rule were not completely unrelated to the conflict. More important, however, is Luis Martinez's argument that a widespread 'war-oriented *imaginaire*' (worldview) shared by government and rebel elites alike made violence an acceptable, even respectable, means of accumulating wealth, power and prestige.[44] The principal protagonists in the war had all seen how, historically, violence – more than any other medium – had succeeded in turning established social hierarchies upside down and increasing the symbolic and material resources of those who wielded it.

In this context, the *imaginaire* supported the emergence of a war economy – what Martinez called 'the profession of arms' – from which many people, even those at the lower end of the social hierarchy, made money.[45] This encouraged a change in the composition of the combatants. While initially the militants were led by a combination of 'Afghan Arabs' and FIS activists, by 1994 a younger, less educated generation took over and criminals became predominant. 'Emirs' – the leaders of the armed Islamic groups – gained social status and money, primarily from black-marketeering. This made it possible for the deprived segments of society to accumulate funds, but it also opened the door for the involvement of a variety of criminal elements.[46] Thus over time the conflict started to take on less of a religious appearance.

Martinez is careful not to suggest Algerians are inherently prone to resolve their differences through war. Nor does he suggest that this *imaginaire* was the only ingredient in the outbreak of civil war. But its deeply rooted place in Algerian history helps explain the repeated choices for war made by so many of the country's elites and aspiring elites.[47] For our purposes, the key point is that this had nothing to do with religion.

Sudan

Sudan's multiple conflicts since the 1980s are often framed as a clash of visions over the country's political future between a dominant northern Islamist identity, pushing to assimilate the rest of the country, and a dominant southern, often secularist identity, dedicated to resisting the Islamists (see also chapter 5).[48] Although it would be impossible to understand Sudan's conflicts without reference to religion, religious beliefs were only one ingredient among several in various war recipes, and they were less important than the political strategies pursued by the regime in power. 'Militant Islam', for instance, was central to only three of the ten root causes of Sudan's civil wars identified by one eminent scholar.[49]

Of most relevance here is the post-1970 version of this Islamist project associated with 'mullah-in-chief' Hassan al-Turabi.[50] This was a political ideology espoused by a riverain, northern Sudanese elite who sought to create a political order based on what they saw as God's revelation in order to justify their desire to maintain control over as much as the country as possible, especially the Nile Valley. As discussed below, they exported their project to the wider region in an attempt to destabilize its various opponents.[51] The fact that this ideology was the creation of particular political elites emphasizes the 'constant need to remember the distinction between being a Muslim and being an Islamist'.[52] Sudan's wars were not caused because most northerners were Muslims or by the fact that its population was religiously diverse. But the conflicts did have a lot to do with the attempt by Arab elites to forge a national identity and state institutions on the basis of a worldview which had religious principles at its core.

The country's most deadly conflict in the post-Cold War period was that between the governing regime and the SPLM/A. Two events were crucial in making religion a central issue in the conflict: the 'September Laws' (1983), which imposed *shari'a* across the country, and the Islamist coup in mid-1989, which brought a junta headed by Omar al-Bashir to power. According to the Sudanese scholar Francis Deng, these events made religion 'the central factor in the conflict'.[53] They also had the effect of producing 'more Christian converts . . . [in Sudan] than the entire colonial missionary enterprise did during the first half of the twentieth century'.[54]

In March 1991, al-Bashir's junta implemented a penal code based on their interpretation of *shari'a* which included *hudud* punishments. In January 1992 a *fatwa* was issued by *ulama* (scholars of Islamic doctrine and law) which defined the war against the SPLM as a *jihad*. This was followed by several local variants. The El Obeid *fatwa* of April 1992, for example, declared that 'an insurgent who was previously a Muslim is now an apostate; and a non-Muslim is a non-believer standing as a bulwark against the spread of Islam, and Islam has granted the freedom of killing both of them according to the following words of Allah.'[55] This not only led to the excommunication of Muslim members of the SPLA but precipitated the destruction of mosques in rebel areas, because rebellion against the state was now equated with a rebellion against Islam.[56] As well as cosmetic changes such as giving Islamic titles to government soldiers, the call to *jihad* was important because funds for the war effort could now be extracted from Sudan's *da'wa* (Muslim evangelical) agencies.

This war certainly seems to fit most ideas of a religious war. Indeed, one recent attempt to theorize the relationship between religion and civil war identified Sudan as an exemplary case of 'religious outbidding' – the idea that 'elites attempt to outbid each other to enhance their religious credentials and thereby gain the support they need to counter an immediate threat.'[57] For Monica Toft, Sudan's conflict was a case where 'religion moved from a peripheral issue to become the central issue.'[58] There is considerable merit in this argument inasmuch as the SPLM/A was explicitly designed to resist the Islamist assimilation agenda, and both sides used religion to mobilize people and resources. However, it is important to note that the SPLM/A was not resisting Islam *per se* but rather, at least after 1989, the particular Islamist vision for the future of Sudan espoused by al-Bashir's junta. Moreover, the way Christianity had come to many of the SPLA's soldiers was more a product of circumstance than conviction.

Take, for instance, the case of the *Jiec Amar* (Red Army): after the mass exodus of children who fled the war-induced famine in Bahr el Ghazal in the late 1980s, many thousands ended up in camps in Ethiopia, which often led to recruitment into the SPLA. While in Ethiopia, some 12,000 boys, who became known as the *Jiec Amar*, were educated in schools run jointly by the churches and the SPLA. Here, they were fed a diet of the SPLA's 'vision of the military liberation of their country, and a daily immersion . . . in the narratives and images of the Bible'.[59] Although Marxist rhetoric had been prominent within the SPLA during its early years, after the fall of its supporter, the Mengistu regime in Ethiopia, it became more open to the Christian ideas which were ardently held by many of its new recruits. Indeed, the *Jiec Amar*, among other converts, were not only involved in a struggle against Khartoum's attempt to force Islamic rules upon them, they were also involved in a struggle much closer to home to supplant the traditional spirit powers in their own communities with their newfound brand of Christianity. As Andrew Wheeler has shown, the rise of Christian beliefs across much of southern Sudan was primarily an attempt to deal with the horrors and disruptions brought by the war. In Wheeler's words, 'The impoverishment that has resulted, the desolation, the grievous loss and the isolation from all outside succour for many years, has resulted in a desperate need and hunger, both physical and spiritual. Body and soul in anguish cry out to God for help.'[60] The result was that, while those with an allegiance to Christianity comprised about 20 per cent of southerners in 1980, by the turn of the century the figure was between 60 and 70 per cent. Christianity apparently offered a better spiritual framework than local traditions to understand the war and withstand the intrusions of the outside world.[61]

Two other elements of Sudan's Islamist project are notable. First, it 'contributed to the global Islamic debate out of all proportion to its relative weight within the Muslim world.'[62] Second, and more importantly for our purposes, it quickly spread beyond Sudan's borders, helping to turn the Horn of Africa into what Alex de Waal described as 'one of the main theatres of conflict between jihadists and their enemies'.[63] Sudan's Islamists thus helped ferment conflicts elsewhere. In part, this was because of the activities Khartoum permitted the so-called Afghan Arabs – radicals cut off from their own societies and schooled in Salafi *jihadist* ideology in the anti-Soviet *jihad* – to orchestrate from bases in Sudan. But it was also because the Islamist project generated resistance within the region. The response of al-Bashir's regime was to support a variety of insurgent groups in neighbouring states, notably the Eritrean Islamic Jihad Movement (EIJM), *al-Itihaad al-Islaami* in Somalia/Ethiopia, various militant groups in Egypt and the Allied Democratic Forces (ADF) in Uganda, as well as providing a safe haven for the *al-Qa'ida* leadership during the early 1990s.

Drawing support from members of several Eritrean Salafi organizations, the EIJM was launched at a conference in Khartoum in 1988.[64] It was supported by the Sudanese government, which facilitated its headquarters in Sudan, and *al-Qa'ida*, which is thought to have trained 'several hundred' of EIJM's members.[65] According to one of its leaders, the movement's self-declared aims were 'to realise our position as servants of Allah, and to establish the Islamic State'.[66] Its principal enemies were what it saw as Eritrea's 'Christian regime' and 'hypocrites'. The EIJM began operating in Eritrea from 1989, and by the mid-1990s its estimated 500 fighters were carrying out raids and ambushes within the country.[67] By early 1994, Khartoum's hand in these attacks led Eritrean President Isseyas Afewerki to support the SPLA and the Beja Congress in retaliation. Although it was only a low-level insurgency, the EIJM continued to operate into the twenty-first century and in 2003 claimed responsibility for a hotel bombing and an ambush allegedly killing forty-six Eritrean soldiers.

Formed in 1991 as a by-product of Somalia's civil war, *al-Itihaad al-Islaami* was made up primarily of urban and semi-educated youths who looked to Islam for the answer to their predicament.[68] Along with various 'Afghans', the organization obtained support and training from Khartoum and 'quickly became an instrument of Sudanese foreign policy'.[69] As well as spreading out to the coastal cities in Somalia, *al-Itihaad* branched out into the Ogaden region of Ethiopia. It was also thought to be behind the 1996 assassination attempt

against the Ethiopian minister of transport and communications in Addis
Ababa. The organization was dealt a significant blow in August of that year
when it was forcibly ejected from its bases in the Somali towns of Luuq and
Buulo by an Ethiopian military intervention. After this, the group adopted a
much lower profile.

Khartoum is also said to have provided support for organizations, such as
Tanzim al-Jihad and *al-Gama'a al-Islamiyya*, that were behind the so-called Islamist
war in Egypt in the 1990s, which apparently produced at least 1,200 fatalities.[70] Sudanese officials and *al-Qa'ida* were said to have facilitated *al-Gama'a
al-Islamiyya's* attempted assassination of Egyptian President Husni Mubarak as
he attended an OAU summit in Addis Ababa in June 1995.[71]

In the Ugandan case, Khartoum sponsored the formation of the ADF in
1996. An Islamist organization with roots in the Tablik youth movement, the
ADF was responsible for various low-level guerrilla raids and bombings
(reportedly killing over sixty people in Kampala and Jinja).[72] For two years it
was seen to pose 'a serious threat in western Uganda', but by 1999 it was
facing defeat.[73] It is notable, however, that the ADF's Islamic credentials have
been questioned. One of its ex-fighters, for instance, argued that the Islamic
factor was simply 'a way to get support and recruits' and a means by which
the organization's leaders 'disguised their political motives'.[74]

This last point about political motives is important because, while
Khartoum's support for these militant organizations might appear to stem
from some sort of Islamic solidarity, it had at least as much to do with shifting political alliances across the region. For example, Khartoum's support for
non-Islamic insurgents such as the Lord's Resistance Army in Uganda shows
that it was willing to put aside religious conviction for political reasons. As
one analysis put it, 'On a regional scale . . . the LRA is fulfilling a political role
on the chessboard.'[75] Moreover, al-Bashir's junta, which came to power in
1989, did not always have hostile relationships with its neighbours and
entered into pragmatic alliances when required.

Finally on Sudan, it is important to recall that arguments over religious
beliefs were also one of the ingredients in the war in Darfur. Contrary to those
who claim the war had 'virtually nothing to do with religion',[76] the genesis
of the JEM rebels cannot be understood without recognizing the intra-Islamic
dispute over what should count as the authentic version of Islam and what
its relationship should be to the apparatus of the Sudanese state.[77] For other
rebel factions religion did not seem as important as other factors, but in one
sense their stated concerns about political and economic marginalization
were a direct result of the Islamist project emanating from al-Bashir's junta.

Somalia

Another case where intra-Islamic disputes came to play a significant role
was Somalia – Africa's collapsed state *par excellence*. Although the principal

ingredients which caused Somalia's protracted conflict had very little to do with religious differences, religion has assumed a more significant role in recent years. The catalyst for this change was the Ethiopian intervention in late 2006 that toppled the Union of Islamic Courts (UIC) regime that had assumed power in Mogadishu just a few months earlier. Superficially, the Ethiopian intervention might look like a Christian regime targeting a Muslim one. In reality, Ethiopia's primary concern was not the fact that the UIC was Muslim but that elements within them were calling for a violent *jihad* to build a Greater Somalia, which included taking over Ethiopia's Ogaden region. It should also be recalled that the regime of transitional president Abdullahi Yusuf which Ethiopia helped install in Mogadishu was also Muslim.

After its expulsion from Mogadishu the UIC splintered into rival factions. The divisions hardened considerably when one of the former leaders of the UIC, Sheikh Sharif, became president of Somalia's Transitional Federal Government (TFG) after the Ethiopian forces withdrew from Mogadishu in early 2009. At this point Sharif was derided by some Islamic militants as having sold out and as an Ethiopian and American stooge. Within a few months the political terrain in southern and central Somalia had fragmented in large part along religious lines. In this sense, the religious dimension became a more prominent feature of Somalia's conflict over time. This could be seen in the complex relationships between the four key armed groups after the Ethiopian campaign: *al-Shabaab*,[78] *Hizb al-Islam*, *Ahlu Sunnah Wal Jama* and the TFG.[79]

The first two groups were heirs to the stream of Saudi-sponsored Wahhabism which washed across Somalia in the 1980s but which was then moulded into a form of Salafi jihadism by *al-Ittihaad al-Islaami* (discussed above). The conflicts between them arose from two sources. First was the extent to which they were engaged in a nationalist as opposed to a pan-Islamic project. For *al-Shabaab* the ultimate goal appears to be a pan-Islamic caliphate – hence its growing ties to *al-Qa'ida*. It also reflected the significant impact foreign *jihadis* were having as a driver of Somalia's conflict. In contrast, the principal focus of *Hizb al-Islam* was creating a greater Somalia in the Horn of Africa. The other key source of tension was over the political utility of Somalia's clans. While *Hizb al-Islam* worked pragmatically with the clan structures, *al-Shabaab* saw Somalis' commitment to clans as proof that they were insufficiently committed to Islam.

From 2007 these groups took control of much of central and southern Somalia, but as well as fighting among themselves they stimulated resistance from locals who challenged their extreme interpretation of Islam and their draconian approach to local governance. By mid-2008 the most important of these groups was *Ahlu Sunnah Wal Jama*. Originally established in 1991, this group of Sufi scholars turned militia took up arms in response to *al-Shabaab's* attempts to ban Sufi religious practices, impose strict separation of the sexes, and mete out harsh punishments such as amputations and stonings. As one of the Sufi leaders of *Ahlu Sunnah Wal Jama* explained, 'Clan wars, political wars, we were always careful to stay out of those . . . But this time, it was religious.'[80] By the end of 2008 his group was receiving military support from Ethiopia and had formed an explicit alliance with the TFG forces against both *al-Shabaab* and *Hizb al-Islam*.

As the first decade of the twenty-first century drew to a close, in parts of Somalia at least, it appeared that how to interpret Islamic scripture and its relationship to governance structures was something worth fighting for.

Northern Uganda

The conflict waged by Joseph Kony's Lord's Resistance Army (LRA) against the Ugandan government and many civilians in northern Uganda and the surrounding region has often been depicted as having a significant religious dimension. Although he was never in command of more than several thousand fighters, for more than two decades Kony's LRA left a trail of destruction and displacement, becoming particularly infamous for its gruesome atrocities and its abduction and abuse of thousands of children. Once again, however, it is important to note that religious beliefs were just one ingredient among several in this particular war recipe.

The LRA's emergence can only be understood in the context of Acholi society and its predecessor, the Holy Spirit Movement, led first by Alice Lakwena and then, briefly, by her father, Severino Likoya Kiberu.[81] With regard to Acholi society, three factors help account for the formation of these movements.[82] In material terms, the two key issues were the continued widening of economic inequalities between north and south Uganda and the militarization of politics in the region. Both were processes started by British colonists but reinforced and sometimes intensified by subsequent independent governments. The region also endured another round of fighting in the late 1980s, when the Ugandan People's Democratic Army (UPDA) rebelled against Yoweri Museveni's new regime in Kampala. The third factor concerned the religious dimension of Acholi life, specifically the importance given to protective spirits, or *jogi*, which were used to explain afflictions that befell the Acholi, from Arab and European influence to tuberculosis. The mixture of these traditional beliefs with Christian and, to a lesser extent, Muslim ideas produced a widespread religious syncretism across the region.

In this difficult time for the Acholi people, Alice Lakwena's Holy Spirit Movement (HSM) emerged to offer 'hope for worldly as well as spiritual redemption in a dark hour of despair'.[83] It was thus unsurprising that Alice received considerable support from the Acholi, but simply being Acholi did not guarantee membership of the HSM. Membership required initiation, which was thought to endow recruits with powers such as the ability to turn stones into grenades or immunity from bullets.[84] In military terms the HSM's impact was limited. While Alice won a major battle near Kilak Corner in

November 1986, her forces were decisively defeated near Jinja in November 1987, although she escaped to Kenya. For a while afterwards her father, Severino Likoya Kiberu, tried to revive the movement's fortunes but failed. It was into this political space that the mantle of resistance passed to Joseph Kony.

A cousin of Alice, a school drop-out, an altar boy in the Catholic Church (according to some accounts) and later a member of the UPDA's black battalion, Kony rose to power claiming he was possessed by multiple spirits. By 1987 he commanded the HSM II, the goals of which seemed to be little more than vague ideas of 'overthrowing the government' and doing the bidding of the Holy Spirit.[85] Kony initially sought Alice's blessing, but after she refused he changed the name of his movement several times, finally settling on the LRA (in 1990), a deliberate reference to Museveni's National Resistance Army. As in the HSM, Kony's recruits also underwent initiation to separate them from ordinary Acholi and turn them into *malaika* (angels) – interestingly, Kony wore a Muslin *kanzu* during the ceremony.[86]

Between 1987 and 1994, religious ideas infused Kony's depiction of himself as a mouthpiece of God's apocalyptic vision for the Acholi, and he spoke regularly of his Ten Commandments (although these were primarily Christian-inspired, he later came up with some Muslim-inspired commandments, such as people farming pigs should be killed and those who worked on Fridays should have an arm amputated).[87] The thrust of Kony's message was that the only way out of this predicament was the complete rejuvenation of the Acholi people.

In 1991, the government's counter-insurgency campaign, Operation North, almost defeated the LRA but didn't finish them off – at which point a lifeline emerged in the form of support from the Sudanese government.[88] Although the LRA had always employed brutal tactics, a turning point occurred after the failure of the 1994 peace talks. From this point on Kony seemed to despise the Acholi people and their spiritual leaders, perhaps because they had failed his test of rejuvenation. This mentality may also have encouraged him to abduct children, as a way not only to bolster his forces but also to acquire a clean slate on which to create a new collective identity for the next Acholi generation.[89]

From even this brief summary it is evident that religious beliefs do not offer a convincing explanation for the LRA. Kony's army did emerge from a society saturated in religious beliefs, but it was also an economically marginalized and militarized region and the Acholi could point to a range of legitimate grievances against the central government. All these factors helped swell the ranks of the resistance movements in their early years. The LRA also owed a great deal to the formation and defeat of Alice's HSM. But unlike Alice, who intended to revitalize the Acholi's fortunes, Kony never intended the LRA as a vehicle for substantive political reform.[90] Instead, he claimed to be on a spiritual mission to 'rid the Acholi of witches' as part of their collective salvation and rejuvenation.[91] His warped agenda entailed killing many Acholi in order to save them. Unsurprisingly, it quickly alienated his army from Acholi society. Having survived Operation North, the LRA endured because of the combined effect of Sudanese support, an ineffective Ugandan military, and a central government which frequently failed to pursue non-military solutions and even hindered peace initiatives.[92] None of these factors had any religious basis.

Rwanda

In comparison to accounts of the LRA, the role of religion has not featured prominently in discussions of Rwanda's civil war and genocide – and rightly so, since religious beliefs were certainly not one of the principal ingredients behind the violence (see chapter 6). But the genocide does provide an interesting case of systematic violence against civilians being justified in religious terms within a country made up almost entirely of Christians. The key organization in this case was the Catholic Church.[93]

During Rwanda's genocide, it was common for the death squads to attend mass before going out to kill civilians, many of whom were murdered while seeking sanctuary in churches. In addition, in the years preceding the genocide, Hutu extremist propaganda outlets such as *Kangura* magazine regularly used Christian images to justify oppression of the Tutsi.[94] This has to be seen in the context of a Catholic Church which had a long history of gaining the confidence of successive ruling regimes in Rwanda.[95] After decades of supporting the establishment of a Tutsi ruling elite, from the late 1950s the Catholic Church began to offer more support to the downtrodden Hutu. Thus, after independence, a close alliance developed between the Catholic Church and state authorities, both of which became corrupt patrimonial organizations.[96] The Church was thus always a political institution, and in Rwanda it accommodated and sometimes endorsed the country's extremist ethnic politics as they intensified during the civil war.

In Timothy Longman's view, the end result was that the 'churches helped make genocide possible by making ethnic violence understandable and acceptable to the population. . . . Far from being passive bystanders, Christian churches provided essential support for the slaughter.'[97] For decades the Church had promoted deference to government authority. It did not denounce the massacres of civilians which occurred from 1990 to 1993, and when the genocide began it not only refused to endorse the principle of sanctuary for people trapped in churches but actually suggested that killing Tutsi was compatible with Church teachings.[98] This ultimately resulted in a situation where 'people in Rwanda could participate in the 1994 genocide believing that they were acting in a fashion consistent with Christian teachings.'[99]

While some members of churches took courageous stands, many others joined militias, and in Butare, Gikongoro and Kibuye prefectures pastors and priests appear to have been implicated directly in the killings. So it was that, 'For the Hutu population of Rwanda, being Christian meant supporting the government, and in 1994 supporting the government meant wiping out the Tutsi population.'[100] After the genocide the Church responded to accusations of its complicity by denying any institutional responsibility and blaming the church personnel involved for their individual moral failings. In a 1996 letter, the Vatican said, 'The church itself cannot be held responsible for the misdeeds of its members who have acted against evangelical law.'[101] Longman's account suggests otherwise.

Conclusion

In a continent as religious as Africa, it is hardly surprising to find that religious beliefs and organizations were present in many of its recent conflicts. Rather than putting an end to religion, war often made religious beliefs more intense, raised the stakes for people's religious affiliations, and shaped them in new ways. Depending where one looked, religious beliefs and organizations were a source of solidarity, comfort, explanation, assistance and peacemaking, as well as a means of justifying extreme acts of oppression and violence. It is this protean quality of religion that probably accounts for the divergent views on the relationship between religion and warfare evident in the relevant scholarly literature.

While it is possible for religious beliefs to remain, first and foremost, a personal matter between individuals and their God(s), when religious organizations and communities form, religion becomes a social and political matter. It is this process of group formation and dynamics which is most relevant to the study of Africa's armed conflicts. Once again, thinking about officially sponsored religious scripts for violence helps explain variation in behaviour among individuals with similar religious beliefs.

The evidence presented from some of the key cases in the post-Cold War debate suggests that Ellis and ter Haar's claim that there have been no religious wars in sub-Saharan Africa goes too far. Of course, everything hinges on what counts as a religious conflict, but if we reject monocausal explanations then a better question to ask is whether religion was ever a significant ingredient in Africa's war recipes. The answer to this question is 'sometimes'. There do appear to be exceptions to the general rule that most African conflicts were not about religion. Kony's LRA, for instance, is literally inexplicable without reference to the spirit world. Although al-Bashir's junta broke virtually every precept of Islam, by carrying out their political project in the name of God they gave the war a religious dimension and generated religious forms of resistance among southerners. Similarly, the latest round of violence in southern and central Somalia makes little sense without recognizing how different interpretations of Islam served as a mobilizing force for various conflict parties. The same might also be said about at least one rebel group in Darfur's conflict. In other key cases, such as Algeria and northern Nigeria, however, religion's role was less important than deeply ingrained political cultures and elite opportunism amidst a social context of severe poverty and inequality.

Responses

CHAPTER EIGHT

Organization-Building

The armed conflicts discussed in parts I and II of this book left significant swathes of Africa in such a state of crisis that on the cusp of the twenty-first century *The Economist* magazine seriously asked whether Africa was a hopeless continent.[1] Part III examines four types of international effort to immunize the continent from the devastating effects of these, and future, wars: organization-building, peacemaking, peacekeeping and aid. While, in practice, these responses were deeply intertwined, they are analysed in relative isolation only for heuristic purposes.

The first response strategy to Africa's wars involved strengthening the continent's conflict management organizations. It was based on the idea that keeping the peace required permanent organizations, not just ad hoc responses. The process of building such an organizational architecture across the continent entailed four elements: defining priorities, allocating resources (human and financial), and constructing both bureaucratic structures and mechanisms and a capacity to create and disseminate knowledge (and hopefully to act upon it). In the early 1990s, one of the central challenges was that Africa's regional organizations were generally not geared up to manage armed conflicts; they were underfunded, they lacked personnel, and most had been established to stimulate economic growth and sub-regional integration. Moreover, the attempt to refashion these organizations came at a time when armed conflicts engulfed much of the continent: African governments and their external funders were thus forced to try and build effective organizations while simultaneously attempting to stem a significant number of ongoing crises. As Mark Malan put it, African governments were 'trying to build a fire brigade while the neighbourhood burns'.[2] These attempts began under the auspices of the Organization of African Unity (OAU) and the so-called Regional Economic Communities (RECs). Since the start of the twenty-first century, however, they have coalesced in a new peace and security architecture which had the African Union's Peace and Security Council at its core.

To discuss these developments, the chapter begins with a brief overview of Africa's most important conflict management organizations from 1990 to the launch of the African Union (AU) in 2002. It then analyses the main elements of the African peace and security architecture, namely, the Assembly of Heads of State and Government, the Commission, the Peace and Security Council, the Continental Early Warning System, the African Standby Force and the Panel of the Wise. The basic argument is that, although significant progress was made in building this new architecture, its institutions struggled to overcome the significant challenges raised by the priority given to regime survival strategies by many of Africa's weak states.

African Conflict Management Organizations before the African Union

Between 1990 and 2002, the principal African organizations for conflict management were the OAU Mechanism for Conflict Prevention, Management and Resolution and various initiatives pursued by some of the continent's subregional arrangements. This section provides a brief overview of each.

The OAU Mechanism for Conflict Prevention, Management and Resolution

The immediate origins of the Mechanism for Conflict Prevention, Management and Resolution lie with proposals put forward by the OAU Secretary-General, Salim Ahmed Salim, in his 1992 report 'Resolving conflicts in Africa: proposals for action'. According to Said Djinnit, director of Salim's cabinet, during the subsequent negotiations at the OAU's Dakar summit in July 1992, 'a clear consensus emerged against the involvement of the OAU in peacekeeping.'[3] The public rationale for this stance was that its earlier attempt at peacekeeping in Chad (1980–2) had demonstrated that such operations were inherently difficult and that the OAU was ill-equipped for the task.[4] As discussed in chapter 10, the Nigerian-led enforcement operation in Liberia (1990–7) did not suggest things would get easier in the post-Cold War era.

The primary objective of the OAU Mechanism was thus defined as the anticipation and prevention of conflicts.[5] Rather optimistically, Africa's governments hoped that, by focusing on preventive diplomacy, they would dramatically reduce the need for subsequent peacekeeping missions on the continent. As a result, the OAU's limited vision in this area was to be able to support two 100-strong observer missions simultaneously.[6] To this end, the OAU Assembly announced the creation of the Mechanism at its June 1993 summit in Cairo, and it was inaugurated at the Tunis summit in June 1994. It included a new decision-making body called the Central Organ, which consisted of fifteen to seventeen member states elected annually from the continent's five sub-regions (on the basis of geographic representation) as well as the current and former OAU presidents.[7] A new Peace Fund was also established to finance peace and security initiatives.[8]

Events on the continent, however, especially the mass killings in Burundi and Rwanda (1993–4), caused the OAU to revisit its self-imposed ban on peace-

TABLE 8.1 Organization of African Unity peace operations, 1990–2002

Mission	Location	Duration	Size (approx. max.)	Main task
OAU Mission to Western Sahara	Western Sahara–Morocco	1991–unclear	Unclear	Fact-finding
OAU Military Observer Team (MOT)	Rwanda	1991	15	Observation
OAU Neutral Monitoring Group (NMOG 1)	Rwanda	1991–3	57	Observation
OAU Neutral Monitoring Group (NMOG 2)	Rwanda	1993	70	Observation
Observer Mission in Burundi (OMIB)	Burundi	1993–6	47	Observation
OAU Observer Mission in the Comoros (OMIC)	Comoros	1997–8	20	Observation
OAU Oberver Mission	DRC	1999–2000	43	Observation
OAU Liaison Mission in Ethiopia–Eritrea (OLMEE)	Ethiopia–Eritrea	2000–8	27	Observation
OAU Military Observer Mission in Comoros 2 (OMIC 2)	Comoros	2001–2	14	Observation
OAU Mission to Comoros 3	Comoros	2002	39	Observation

keeping. These episodes generated a series of internal debates organized by the OAU secretariat, which ultimately led the organization's 1995 summit to endorse the idea that 'ready contingents' should be earmarked within African armies for deployment on peacekeeping operations. As table 8.1 demonstrates, however, such contingents never materialized, and the Mechanism was left unable to field even one 100-strong observation mission, let alone a larger peacekeeping force. Nor was it able to recruit sufficient qualified staff: by mid-2001, only half of the envisioned forty-nine positions in the reconstituted Conflict Management Centre had been filled, and nearly half of these were only filled after 1999.[9] Nevertheless, compared with the OAU's conflict management activities during the Cold War, the new Mechanism did succeed in elevating the organization's profile. While some analysts lauded these initiatives as evidence of 'extraordinary activism',[10] others saw them as a rather meagre response to the wars sweeping across Africa during the 1990s.[11]

By the late 1990s, a growing number of African voices concluded that the OAU's old approach to conflict management involved little more than symbolic meetings, with little concrete action being taken on the ground. In particular, it was felt that the organization suffered from some important problems.[12] First, because conflict parties were members of the organization they could often act as their own judges. Second, the OAU's meetings lacked a clear set of appropriate rules and procedures. As a consequence, they were plagued by poor attendance, weak chairmanship, the unavailability of comprehensive data and often unclear itineraries. In addition, because documents were usually received only at the meetings, the opportunity to hold detailed discussion was almost zero. A third set of problems resulted from the conservative conception of sovereignty held by many members. This was generally attributed to fear of foreign domination, including by sub-regional hegemons within the continent.

In sum, therefore, although the OAU made some progress in its conflict management activities, these were extremely limited and able to handle only the most minor of military tasks, primarily observation.

Sub-Regional Conflict Management Mechanisms

With the OAU unable to undertake sizable peacekeeping operations and the Western world reluctant to conduct them on the African continent – especially after the Black Hawk Down episode in Mogadishu in October 1993 – it was the continent's sub-regional organizations which led the way. At the forefront was the Economic Community of West African States (ECOWAS), which revised its treaty in 1993 in large part to enable the organization to respond more effectively to security challenges. In light of its previous peace operations in Liberia, Sierra Leone and Guinea-Bissau, in 1999 ECOWAS established its Mechanism for Conflict Prevention, Management, Resolution, Peace and Security. This gave ECOWAS members the authority to devise a collective response in instances involving interstate conflict and intra-state conflict, as well as in cases of 'massive violation of human rights and the rule of law' or '[i]n the event of an overthrow or attempted overthrow of a democratically elected Government' (Article 25). A similar development took place in southern Africa in 1996, when the Southern African Development Community (SADC) created its Organ on Politics, Defence and Security. In practice, however, the Protocol on Politics, Defence and Security Co-operation was not adopted by SADC members until August 2001, nearly three years after different factions within the organization had conducted military enforcement operations in Lesotho (South Africa and Botswana) and the DRC (Zimbabwe, Angola and Namibia). The other organization to embrace a similar mechanism was the Economic Community of Central African States (ECCAS), which adopted its Protocol Relating to the Establishment of a Mutual Security Pact in Central Africa in February 2000 (entering into force in January 2004). These instruments opened up the internal affairs of SADC and ECCAS members to collective scrutiny and allowed for some type of military response.

Thus, before the AU was created, Africa's continental-level conflict management activities were restricted to the most limited end of the military spectrum, while the peace operations carried out in the name of several sub-regional organizations were generally ad hoc responses to specific crises. Part of the rationale behind dismantling the OAU and replacing it with a new union was precisely to establish a more coherent set of conflict management mechanisms with the capacity to conduct more than just small observer missions. The rest of this chapter discusses the major institutional components of what is commonly known as Africa's new peace and security architecture.

The AU Assembly of Heads of State and Government

The Assembly is the supreme organ of the African Union and defines the organization's overall objectives and policies. It consists of all fifty-three members, except those which are temporarily suspended for reasons such as non-payment of dues or because they are under political sanctions. Although the Assembly initially held ordinary summits once a year, since 2005 it has convened summits twice each year, usually in January and June. Assembly decisions are taken by consensus or, if this is not forthcoming, by a two-thirds majority. On procedural matters, however, decisions are based on a simple majority. Two-thirds of the total membership of the AU forms a quorum at any Assembly meeting.

In substantive terms, the institutional design and procedural rules of the Assembly share many of the characteristics of the old OAU.[13] Although the AU has retained its predecessor's general prohibition on intervention within the internal affairs of member states, there have been two increasingly important exceptions: its stance on unconstitutional changes of government and its new right of humanitarian intervention (codified in Article 4(h) of the AU's Constitutive Act, adopted in Lomé, Togo, in July 2001). Both these issues require some explanation.

Unconstitutional changes of government

In July 2000, the OAU Assembly institutionalized its rejection of what it called 'unconstitutional changes in government' on the continent.[14] This was a highly significant decision, given that postcolonial Africa had endured a large number of coups d'état: between 1956 and 2001, the forty-eight states of sub-Saharan Africa experienced eighty successful and 108 failed coups. West Africa was the centre of activity, accounting for 45.2 per cent of these figures, but the phenomenon was widespread, with thirty sub-Saharan states experiencing at least one successful coup during this period.[15]

Coups d'état became frequent in Africa in the latter half of the 1960s. Perhaps not surprisingly, given the OAU's limited resources and its founding commitment to non-intervention in the internal affairs of its members, the organization's traditional response had been official indifference. Coups thus disrupted the pattern of African diplomacy only marginally if they disrupted it at all. Interestingly, while coups were tolerated, Article III(5) of the OAU charter outlawed assassination of political leaders and 'subversive activities'.[16] The OAU continued with this approach even after the Cold War ended and in the face of intensified international calls for democratization. Indeed, according to Patrick McGowan, between 1990 and 2001 it had to deal with fifty coup attempts, of which thirteen were successful.[17]

The turning point in the OAU's approach came during the second half of the 1990s. The key cases appear to have been Major Pierre Buyoya's coup in Burundi in July 1996 and the series of coups during Sierra Leone's civil war, which culminated with the ousting of the democratically elected president, Ahmed Kabbah, in May 1997. In Buyoya's case the OAU imposed sanctions and a blockade. The reaction to Kabbah's ousting was more strident: the coup was widely condemned internationally, the OAU decided that other states had a duty not to cooperate with Johnny Paul Koroma's junta, and ECOMOG forces were used to help reinstall Kabbah's government.[18]

The task of building congruence between international standards on democracy and African politics was made easier for the OAU by the decision of both the Organization of American States and later the UN Security Council to authorize enforcement action against the military junta that took power in Haiti in 1991.[19] Although the Security Council emphasized the extraordinary nature of events in Haiti, it also condemned Buyoya's actions in Burundi and authorized similar enforcement measures against Koroma's junta in Sierra Leone. After initially issuing a presidential statement condemning the coup d'état, the Security Council placed Sierra Leone on its agenda in response to a letter from Nigeria's ambassador to the UN on behalf of the ECOWAS Committee of Four on Sierra Leone (Côte d'Ivoire, Ghana, Guinea and Nigeria). As chair of the OAU, Zimbabwe had echoed the committee's concerns in the Security Council. After several months of debate, the Security Council passed Resolution 1132, authorizing action against the junta, on 8 October 1997.

It was not until July 2000, however, that the OAU moved from adopting ad hoc responses to institutionalizing a permanent framework. Since then, the new AU has consistently condemned all coups. This raised two main issues: first, whether there was such a thing as a 'good coup' – i.e. when the military ousted a tyrannical regime and promised to set the stage for democratization. The coup in Mauritania in 2005, for example, was explicitly discussed in these terms.

A second issue concerned the Assembly's narrow definition of unconstitutional changes in government: it saw them as synonymous with coups despite the fact there are numerous unconstitutional means to change a government. For example, what would the AU do if an armed rebel group took power, if constitutions were rewritten by the incumbent regime to extend a president's term of office, if presidents illegally dismissed their parliaments, or if clearly fraudulent elections were held? In recognition of such concerns, by 2007 an internal debate had started over the extent to which the Union's focus 'must be enlarged to cover all forms of manipulations which either culminate in a coup d'état or in a democratically elected government re-forging the constitution without popular consent as genuinely expressed by the people, with a view to prolonging stay in office.'[20] The two main outcomes occurred in 2009: the AU created a new Committee on Sanctions, which would assess the different dimensions of the problem, monitor the implementation of any sanctions regimes and report back to the Peace and Security Council, and it adopted the Ezulwini framework document, which took a more appropriate wider view of unconstitutional changes of government.[21] Although the practical impact of these initiatives remains to be seen, it was notable that, at the AU summit in early 2010, the organization's new chairman, Malawi's President Bingu wa Mutharika, said that it was time to 'declare war on unconstitutional changes of government on African soil'.

An African right of humanitarian intervention?

In a radical departure from the OAU days, Article 4(h) of the AU Constitutive Act gave the Assembly the right to intervene in a member state 'in respect of grave circumstances: war crimes, genocide and crimes against humanity'. In the most thorough analysis available of why Article 4(h) was adopted, Carolyn Haggis argued that the specific text resulted from a rather odd confluence of Libya's lobbying for a stronger AU with powers to mobilize collectively against external aggression and the moral impetus to stop mass atrocities provided by the timely release of the OAU's report on the international failure to prevent Rwanda's 1994 genocide. Once the Libyans had placed the issue of intervention on the transition agenda, other African states – notably Egypt, South Africa and Nigeria – were responsible for finessing the wording to represent a limited right of African intervention in cases where mass atrocities were being committed rather than the Libyan preference for collective intervention to maintain order and stability within individual states.[22]

Unhappy at the final outcome, in February 2003 Libya led the charge to amend Article 4(h), requesting that it be changed to read as follows (the additional text is in italics):

> the right of the Union to intervene in a Member State pursuant to a decision of the Assembly in respect of grave circumstances, namely: war crimes, genocide and crimes against humanity *as well as a serious threat to legitimate order to restore peace and stability to the Member State of the Union upon the recommendation of the Peace and Security Council.*[23]

The amendment was officially adopted by the Assembly on 11 July 2003. No member state dissented or made reservations, but as of mid-2010 it had not yet entered into force, as only twenty-five AU members had deposited their instruments of ratification.[24]

Article 4(h) also raised some thorny political and legal implications. First, the idea that the AU Assembly can authorize the use of military force for humanitarian purposes without the host government's consent stands in direct contradiction of Article 53 of the UN Charter.[25] Perhaps in recognition of this problem, by 2005 the *Roadmap for the Operationalization of the African Standby Force* (discussed below) explicitly stated that 'the AU will seek UN Security Council authorisation of its enforcements actions. Similarly, the RECs/Regions will seek AU authorisation of their interventions.'[26]

Second, during the period under review here (1990–2009), Article 4(h) proved so politically toxic that the AU never once invoked it to override the wishes of a recognized sovereign government. As the international debates over the war in Darfur highlighted, despite clear evidence of 'grave circumstances' as the AU defines them, the Assembly was unwilling to countenance the use of military force without the consent of the government of Sudan. Indeed, a considerable amount of time during AU summits in 2005, 2006 and 2007 was spent debating whether to make Sudan's president chairman of the Assembly (in the event, this did not occur). Third, even if the Assembly was to invoke Article 4(h) in order to conduct a humanitarian intervention, without an effective African Standby Force the AU lacked the military capability to carry out such an operation, except against its smallest and weakest member states.[27] Despite these three important problems, the inclusion of Article 4(h) certainly changed the tenor of debates about conflict management on the continent.

The African Union Commission

The Commission provides the bureaucratic support – both preparatory and executive – which enables the AU to function. During the 1990s the OAU equivalent had been starved of resources and thus was unable to do much more than keep itself afloat. With the establishment of the AU, however, the Commission was bolstered in terms of both staff and resources and in the sense that the Assembly envisaged an enhanced role for the chairperson compared with that of the previous secretary-general of the OAU.[28] The Commission consists of eight portfolios or departments and is headed by a chairperson and deputy chairperson.[29] With regard to issues of peace and security, the two most relevant departments are Political Affairs (which has responsibility for human rights, democratic institutions, transparency and accountability, and the monitoring of elections) and the Peace and Security directorate. In practice, the latter took the leading role, not least because it received most external attention and because, with over fifty staff, it was the largest of the Commission's substantive departments.

The Commission's primary tasks involved steering the ongoing process of institutionalization, harnessing support from AU member states and donors, and promoting collaboration between the AU and the sub-regional organizations.[30] It was given a significant boost towards achieving these objectives when, in July 2003, an active former president, Alpha Oumar Konaré of Mali, was elected to act as chairperson. He played an important role in exercising leverage on behalf of the AU Commission. On 1 February 2008, Konaré was replaced by the former Gabonese foreign minister, Jean Ping, a longstanding and well-respected representative at the UN. The fact that Ping was not a former head of state raised concerns over whether his appointment signalled a downgrading of the Commission's status. On the basis of his first two years in office, however, Ping managed to retain the Commission's autonomous power; especially during Muammar Gaddafi's tenure as AU chairman (2009–10), this was no mean feat.

On the basis of the Union's first few years, some analysts went as far as to suggest that, 'as the custodian of AU documents, as well as the maker and interpreter of rules, procedures and regulations, [the Commission] acquired unlimited and overwhelming power.'[31] But this exaggerates the Commission's influence. As Mark Malan noted, especially as far as peacekeeping issues were concerned, it lacked 'the staff and the expertise to plan and conduct missions, and it certainly lacks the institutional capacity to absorb at the same time a confusing array of donor capacity-building assistance packages and schemes.'[32]

In relation to the Peace and Security Council (PSC) specifically (see below), the Commission personnel could certainly exercise some leverage, both through their role in drafting reports and recommendations, and in their ability to influence how the member states view particular issues.[33] This influence was arguably greatest in the Commission's dealings with the PSC at the ambassadorial and ministerial levels but was much more restricted when dealing with heads of government. As far as the latter group was concerned, it was arguably only Commissioner Konaré, himself a former head of state, who could regularly succeed in significantly altering their perspectives. Overall, however, the AU's member states clearly kept the Commission in general and the PSC's secretariat in particular in an emaciated condition.

The Peace and Security Council[34]

Officially launched in May 2004, the PSC is 'a collective security and early-warning arrangement to facilitate timely and efficient response to conflict and crisis situations in Africa'.[35] More specifically, its objectives were defined as promoting peace, security and stability in Africa; anticipating and preventing conflicts; promoting and implementing peacebuilding and post-conflict reconstruction activities; coordinating and harmonizing continental efforts in the prevention and combating of international terrorism in all its aspects; developing a common defence policy for the Union; and encouraging democratic practices, good governance and the rule of law, as well as protecting human rights and fundamental freedoms. In order to achieve these daunting objectives, the PSC was given eighteen 'powers', ranging from assisting in the provision of humanitarian assistance to military intervention.

The PSC was not part of the AU Constitutive Act but emerged out of an ad hoc process to reform the OAU Mechanism for Conflict Prevention, Management and Resolution. The initial substantive proposal had been for a council of seventeen states, ten of which would be permanent members. Although this position was supported by the continent's 'great powers' – South Africa, Nigeria, Algeria, Egypt and Libya – it was unacceptable to other states, notably Tanzania, which rejected the idea of permanent membership and any potential veto power conferred upon individual states.[36] The resulting compromise was that the draft *PSC Protocol* discussed by the Council of Ministers prior to the AU's Durban summit set out three options concerning the composition of the PSC: (1) fifteen members elected for a term of two years; (2) fifteen members of whom five would be permanent and ten elected for a term of two years; and (3) ten members elected for a term of two years, and an additional five members for a term of three years.[37] The third proposal was carried.

The PSC's membership is based on the principle of 'equitable regional representation and rotation' (Article 5), whereby the north, west, central, east and southern regions present candidates for election.[38] Article 5 also lists criteria on which to judge prospective candidates, including whether the state in question is in good standing (has paid its dues, respects constitutional governance and the rule of law, etc.) and whether it is willing and able to shoulder the responsibilities that membership would place upon it. Retiring members of the PSC are eligible for immediate re-election. Table 8.2 lists the thirty-five states elected to serve as PSC members between 2004 and 2012. It is notable that some of them showed little respect for constitutional governance, the rule of law and human rights, and several of them experienced violent conflicts during their period as PSC members. Nigeria is the only country to have sat consistently on the Council since 2004. This generated some grumblings because it undermined the PSC's explicit rejection of the idea of permanent members and the *Protocol*'s emphasis on specific criteria for membership.

The Council's procedural rules stipulate that its decisions 'shall generally be guided by the principle of consensus' (Article 8). If consensus cannot be reached, however, it 'shall adopt its decisions on procedural matters by a simple majority, while decisions on all other matters shall be made by a two-thirds majority vote of its Members voting.' Between 2004 and early 2010, all decisions within the PSC had been taken by consensus (details of the deliberations have not been made public). The PSC is officially in permanent session and able to assemble at any time. Most of its meetings have been held in Addis Ababa (where it is based), although it has also convened elsewhere, including Libreville (2005), New York (2007, 2008), Abuja (2007) and Sharm el-Sheikh

TABLE 8.2 Membership of the AU Peace and Security Council, 2004–12

Region	2004	2006	2007	2008	2010
North	**Algeria** (3)		**Algeria** (3)		Libya (3)
North	**Libya** (2)	**Egypt** (2)		Tunisia (2)	**Mauritania** (2)
West	Nigeria (3)	Nigeria (3)	Nigeria (3)		Nigeria (3)
West	**Togo** (2)	Burkina Faso (2)		Burkina Faso (2)	**Côte d'Ivoire** (2)
West	Ghana (2)	Ghana (2)		Benin (2)	Benin (2)
West	Senegal (2)	Senegal (2)		Mali (2)	Mali (2)
Central	**Gabon** (3)		Gabon (3)		**Equatorial Guinea** (3)
Central	Congo (2)	Congo (2)		**Chad** (2)	**Chad** (2)
Central	**Cameroon** (2)	**Cameroon** (2)		Burundi (2)	Burundi (2)
East	Ethiopia (3)		Ethiopia (3)		Kenya (3)
East	Kenya (2)	Rwanda (2)		Rwanda (2)	Rwanda (2)
East	**Sudan** (2)	Uganda (2)		Uganda (2)	Djibouti (2)
Southern	South Africa (3)		Angola (3)		Zimbabwe (3)
Southern	Lesotho (2)	Botswana (2)		Swaziland (2)	Namibia (2)
Southern	Mozambique (2)	Malawi (2)		Zambia (2)	South Africa (2)

Underlining indicates states experiencing a 'severe crisis' or 'war' according to the Heidelberg Conflict Barometer, 2004, 2006, 2007, 2008, 2009, at http://hiik.de/en/konfliktbarometer/index.html.

Bold indicates states declared 'not free' by Freedom House, *Freedom in the World 2004, 2006, 2007, 2008, 2010*, at www.freedomhouse.org. The survey measures freedom – the opportunity to act spontaneously in a variety of fields outside the control of the government and other centres of potential domination – according to two broad categories: political rights and civil liberties.

Figures in parentheses indicate the number of years for whch the country has been elected.

(2008). In August 2007, the PSC adopted a new set of working methods which suggested it should convene four types of session: public meetings (which the media may observe), private or closed meetings (involving only AU member states or AU organs), consultations (discussing briefings from the Commission and draft decisions) and 'Arria-type meetings', where Council members hold informal discussions with non-state entities outside the official meeting chamber.[39] By mid-2010, the PSC had held approximately 230 meetings, imposed sanctions against regimes in several African states (including Togo, Mauritania, Guinea, Guinea-Bissau, Madagascar, Niger and Eritrea) and authorized peace operations in Sudan, the Comoros (three times) and Somalia.[40]

In substantive terms, the PSC devoted relatively little attention either to the prevention of conflict or to structural issues that encourage 'bad governance'. Instead it tried to extinguish crises (usually armed conflicts or coups) after they erupted. Although it addressed a large number of such incidents, some conflicts did not make it onto the agenda – e.g. the insurgencies in the Niger Delta, the Ogaden region of Ethiopia, and northern Uganda or the continued tension between Ethiopia and Eritrea. Nor did tyrannical governments that managed to prevent coups and insurgencies, such as Robert Mugabe's ZANU-PF regime in Zimbabwe, occupy much space on the Council's agenda. In this sense, the PSC's willingness to debate the violent aftermath of Kenya's elections in December 2007 may indicate a softening of this approach.

The PSC also devoted little attention to the non-military dimensions of security, such as environmental degradation, organized crime and disease. Discussions within the Commission did raise the possibility of broadening the Council's remit in this regard, but this had not happened by early 2011.[41]

If it is to address any of these issues effectively, the PSC will need to be able to draw upon informed analysis and early warning of impending challenges. Within the new peace and security architecture, these tasks fall primarily to the Continental Early Warning System (CEWS).

The Continental Early Warning System

Early warning of violent conflicts did not become a significant issue for African organizations until the 1990s, particularly after the Rwandan genocide. At this stage the OAU Secretariat's Division for Conflict Management was created to collect, collate and disseminate information relating to current and potential conflicts and devise response options. And although the process of establishing a CEWS officially started at the OAU summit in Dakar in June 1992, nothing substantive occurred until June 1995, when the OAU Council of Ministers endorsed a proposal to establish such a system. This was given further endorsement by the OAU heads of state in the Yaounde Declaration of July 1996.[42] The main substantive outcome of these endorsements was the creation of a situation room in Addis Ababa two years later, the purpose of which was to gather information and alert the Secretary-General of 'looming crises'.[43] However, with few staff and financial resources, the situation room did not come close to resembling an early warning system.

With the establishment of the AU and the *PSC Protocol*, progress started to be made.[44] Starting in 2003, the AU Commission organized a series of workshops and consultations through which it developed with African and international consultants a roadmap for the implementation of the CEWS. Along the way, it received capacity-building support from, among other sources, the EU and UNDP, as well as the governments of Denmark, Germany and the United States. The German GTZ played a particularly significant role in this process.

The subsequent CEWS was to consist of two parts. At the continental level there would be a central observation and monitoring centre (the Situation Room) in Addis Ababa to collect and analyse data. The second component was the 'observation and monitoring units of the Regional Mechanisms', which would 'collect and process data at their level and transmit the same to the Situation Room'.[45]

As summarized by the head of the AU Commission's Conflict Management Division, the CEWS was intended to provide 'timely advice on potential conflicts and threats to peace and security in Africa to several key AU institutions, including the Chairperson of the Commission, the PSC and the Panel of the Wise.'[46] This was to be done using quantitative and qualitative methods of conflict analysis to detect the warning signs of violent conflicts, monitor their development, and formulate policy and response options. The CEWS did not focus on warning about natural disasters. In terms of sources, it drew information from a variety of outlets both inside and outside the continent, including international organizations, NGOs, the media, academia and think-tanks.[47] It also produced its own data through AU field missions and liaison offices as well as those generated by the continent's sub-regional organizations.[48]

One of the central challenges for the CEWS was defining its relationship with the various sub-regional early warning mechanisms already in existence, notably the IGAD Conflict Early Warning and Response mechanism (CEWARN) and the ECOWAS Warning and Response Network (ECOWARN).[49] The former was mandated 'to receive and share information concerning potential violent conflicts as well as their outbreak and escalation in the IGAD sub-region'.[50] Since June 2003, CEWARN has monitored and tracked cross-border pastoral and related conflicts in the two pilot areas of the Karamoja and Somali Clusters (these pilot areas were subsequently expanded). Interestingly, between 2003 and 2006 it recorded approximately 2,200 conflict-related deaths in the region.[51] The ECOWAS Peace and Security Observation System was established under the 1999 Mechanism and consists of an Observation and Monitoring Centre (OMC) – based at the ECOWAS Secretariat in Abuja – and four zonal offices which report back to the OMC.[52] SADC also created an early warning system, but it was integrated into the region's intelligence communities and based on classified information. It utilized the National Early Warning Centres in each SADC member state and a Regional Early Warning Centre based in Gaborone, Botswana.

By mid-2009 the CEWS had significantly refined its operating procedures and defined its three main tasks as data collection and analysis, early warning and engagement with decision-makers, and coordination and collaboration with other actors.[53] In institutional terms, the Situation Room was able to provide coverage twenty-four hours a day, seven days a week, and was producing a range of reporting mechanisms, including daily news summaries as well as more substantial updates on emerging issues. By this stage, however, the CEWS was not yet providing warnings directly to the PSC. Although it had some input into the reports that went before the PSC, its staff were unable to generate early discussions within the Council on the crisis surrounding the Kenyan elections in 2007 or the instability in Guinea-Bissau in late 2008. The delicate balancing act before the CEWS is that its mandate states that it should only provide information rather than engage in the process of making policy. Resources were also identified as a problem, particularly the need to recruit more and better trained analysts and to acquire the appropriate IT infrastructure.

The African Standby Force

If African governments cannot prevent armed conflicts, they will be required to manage their consequences. A crucial instrument in the envisaged response is the African Standby Force (ASF). Its immediate origins lie with a meeting of military experts and observers from forty-five African states in Harare from 21 to 23 October 1997.[54] Although various proposals were made, it was not until May 2003 that a framework was agreed for the ASF, based on five regional brigades of approximately 4,300 troops and some 500 light vehicles each.[55] Table 8.3 lists the membership of these regional brigades. The ASF is thus based on three interconnected levels: the continental level (notably the AU Commission's planning element), the sub-regional level (the five brigades) and the state level (the contributing countries).[56]

The original concept presented to the AU defence and security chiefs in 2003 was for a single on-call standby brigade level force that would be available to the AU on the model of the UN's Standby High Readiness Brigade (SHIRBRIG). In practice, however, the sub-regional level played the crucial intermediary role, which raised questions and complications, including those related to overlapping memberships and sub-regional decision-making structures.[57] In addition, earlier proposals included a sixth ASF brigade to be stationed in Addis Ababa and kept on high alert. This idea was rejected by the African chiefs of defence staff at their May 2003 meeting, apparently after particularly strong objections from South Africa.[58]

TABLE 8.3 African Standby Force regional membership

Central (FOMAC)	Southern (SADCBRIG)	Eastern (EASBRIG)	Northern (NASBRIG)	Western (ESF)
Angola		Sudan	Western Sahara	Mali
Democratic Republic of Congo		Ethiopia	Mauritania	Cape Verde
São Tomé and Príncipe	Malawi	Eritrea	Algeria	Senegal
Equatorial Guinea	Zambia	Djibouti	Tunisia	Gambia
Cameroon	Zimbabwe	Somalia	Libya	Guinea-Bissau
Central African Republic	Namibia	Kenya	Egypt	Guinea
Gabon	Swaziland	Uganda		Sierra Leone
Chad	Lesotho	Rwanda		Liberia
Congo (Brazzaville)	Botswana	Burundi		Côte d'Ivoire
	South Africa	Comoros		Ghana
	Mozambique			Togo
	Madagascar			Nigeria
	Mauritius			Benin
	Tanzania			Niger
				Burkina Faso

In its current configuration the force developed largely along the lines set out in the March 2005 *Roadmap*.[59] This envisaged the ASF responding to six crisis management scenarios (see table 8.4). The plan was for it to have the capacity to manage the entire spectrum of scenarios anywhere in Africa (or perhaps beyond) by 30 June 2010.[60] Unfortunately, none of the ASF brigades kept pace with the targets set out in the *Roadmap*, although the Western, Southern and Eastern regions made significantly more technical progress than the Northern and Central regions.[61] By mid-2009, for example, the AU had only achieved Scenario 4 as part of a broader UN peace operation – and technically, therefore, had not completed phase 1 of its development.[62] Indeed, some analysts argued that the current ASF structure may not be able to support Scenario 5 or 6 actions on anything but the smallest scale. As Jeffrey Marshall has argued, 'While the brigade structure will be effective once it is brought online, it simply will not be able to provide the capabilities required for Scenarios 4 and higher.'[63] By mid-2010 the plan had shifted to trying to achieve a rapid deployment capability for about 3,000 personnel from one of the regional brigades. The objective was that 'the deployment

TABLE 8.4 African Standby Force design scenarios

Scenario	Description	Deployment requirement (from mandate resolution)
1	AU/regional military advice to a political mission	30 days
2	AU/regional observer mission co-deployed with a UN mission	30 days
3	Stand-alone AU/regional observer mission	30 days
4	AU/regional peacekeeping force for Chapter VI and preventive deployment missions (and peacebuilding)	30 days
5	AU peacekeeping force for complex multidimensional peacekeeping missions, including those involving low-level spoilers	90 days, with the military component being able to deploy in 30 days
6	AU intervention, e.g. in genocide situations where the international community does not act promptly	14 days with robust military force[a]

[a] Here, 'robust' meant around 2,500 troops (1,000 within fourteen days, and a further 1,500 within the following fortnight) on the ground within thirty days (Cilliers, *The African Standby Force*, p. 10).

Source: AU, *Roadmap*, section A-1.

must be rapid (within 14 days of securing a mandate) and robust to contain the situation and protect itself. Furthermore, it must be self sufficient for at least 30 days.'[64]

Although the ASF clearly represented a radical departure from the old OAU days of conflict management, it continued to face a range of political and technical challenges. On the technical side, several issues stood out. First, any multinational force requires its different national components to be interoperable – that is, to combine and work together effectively. The problem is, 'the more multinational a force, the more difficult it is to train and operate.'[65] As a very multinational force, incorporating nearly twice as many states as NATO or the EU, the ASF needed to develop common doctrine, systems, tactics, techniques and procedures. Yet, since many African states continued to do these things differently, concerns were raised that 'ASF units will not collaborate properly and the chance for fratricide and other problems rises significantly.'[66] A second technical challenge concerned command and control structures. The problem here, as military experts pointed out, was that the ASF vision lacked an operational level of command – there is the AU Peace and Security Directorate and the ASF brigades, but nothing in between.[67] Strategic lift capabilities, or lack of them, posed a third challenge. To date, the AU remained dependent on donors such as NATO and EU states to provide airlift support.[68] Once in the field, the AU could only maintain its forces with effective logistics. Yet this too was commonly described as a 'hugely problematic' area.[69]

On the political side of the equation, an effective ASF required 'an extraordinarily high level of inter-state cooperation including difficult decisions regarding political processes and military details'.[70] While most African states officially consented to this cooperation, in practice it represented an incredibly daunting task which, to date, only NATO's Response Force seems to have met. In addition, African governments did not inject sufficient financial resources into the ASF. Consequently, analysts frequently concluded that 'the lack of adequate financial resources to meet the demands of peacekeeping in Africa remains the most obvious hurdle.'[71] A third political challenge was the need to ensure that the countries the AU selects to build capacity will actually deploy those assets when the Union calls. Here, as one military expert noted, 'Building capacity in countries that will not support continent-wide peace operations will only waste precious resources.'[72]

The Panel of the Wise

Article 11 of the *PSC Protocol* called for the establishment of the Panel of the Wise to support the work of the PSC and the AU Commission. It was to be comprised of people who have made 'outstanding' past contributions to peace, security and development. The panellists were to be elected for three-year terms by the AU Assembly, following proposals from the chairperson of the AU Commission. In large part because of arguments over the panel's composition, remit and funding, it was not until July 2007 that the first five members were named (from Africa's five sub-regions). The panel's modalities were not confirmed by the PSC until November 2007 and the panel was not inaugurated until the following month. It was also a little disconcerting that the first chairman, former Algerian president Ahmed Ben Bella, was ninety-one years old.

The main tasks of the Panel of the Wise lay in the areas of preventive diplomacy and peacemaking. More specifically, it was to facilitate communication channels between conflict parties and the PSC and AU Commission, carry out fact-finding missions where there is danger of armed conflict breaking out or escalating, engage in shuttle diplomacy between conflict parties and encourage dialogue between them, develop confidence-building measures, carry out reconciliation processes, assist mediation teams engaged in formal negotiations, and help other parties to implement peace agreements.[73] Since its inauguration, the PSC has identified five criteria which should guide the panellists in setting their agenda:

1   the degree to which a conflict situation already receives regional or international attention or not;

2   whether the PSC is already seized with a particular conflict situation and whether additional attention by the panel may add further to existing efforts;

3   whether a given situation has remained in conflict for a considerable amount of time or is in danger of descending into conflict despite multiple ongoing mediation and negotiation efforts;

4   whether a conflict situation has experienced a sudden and speedy decline;

5   whether a conflict situation has experienced difficulties in implementing a peace agreement and, therefore, faces the risk of reverting to conflict.[74]

In practice, the panel engaged with a variety of political crises, including those in Kenya and Zimbabwe. It also undertook some low-level activity in countries that were scheduled to hold elections. There is widespread consensus, however, that, without more serious staffing and resources, the panel will not be able to function as the dynamic and proactive advisory body envisaged in the *PSC Protocol*.[75]

Conclusion

As of early 2011, Africa's new peace and security architecture remained a work in progress. It is therefore impossible to draw definitive conclusions, but it is possible to identify the principal political challenges of the journey so far.

The first persistent challenge was the lack of funds African governments devoted to these conflict management initiatives. Recall that between 1993 and 2005 the OAU/AU Peace Fund received a total of approximately $68 million, of which roughly $45 million was provided by non-AU members.[76] Of the money supplied by the AU members, the vast majority came from just five states – Algeria, Egypt, Libya, Nigeria and South Africa – each of which contributes 15 per cent of the AU's regular budget. Since 2005, the largest donations have come from the EU's Peace Facility and bilateral deals with other governments, notably the US. This badly lopsided funding stream not only led to predictable shortfalls in terms of troops, police and finance, it also sent a significant political signal to Africa's civil servants that their careers may not be best advanced by serving in the AU's institutions. Without qualified and motivated employees with access to sufficient resources, no organization can prosper. The basic problem was that 'African states' ubiquitous failure to finance their own regional institutions . . . undermines both African leadership of the capacity-building process and donor faith in those institutions.'[77] As Malan concluded, until this is done, 'African ownership' will continue to be a 'politically correct' but 'practically flawed' idea.[78] As the so-called Prodi Report on AU peacekeeping operations concluded, 'In the final analysis, the AU will only be able to respond to crises effectively if there is sufficient political and financial commitment of its own members states and, more generally, of the international community.'[79]

The second persistent obstacle, which probably helps to explain the limited financial support invested by African governments, was the lack of substantive agreement on what these new institutions were supposed to do in response to particular crises. Despite many paper agreements, declarations and conventions, African international society remained badly divided over when and how foreign governments and the continent's organizations should get involved in other people's wars. This was reflected in heated debates over how Africans should respond to the conflicts in Sudan and Somalia in particular, but also the non-discussion of conflicts such as those in the Niger Delta and between Ethiopia and Eritrea. There is a degree of ambiguity as well over whether the willingness of African organizations to condemn coups should be interpreted as evidence of greater support for democratization or another way of protecting the continent's incumbent regimes. It was also fundamentally problematic to try and build effective early warning mechanisms when African governments were unwilling to allow the regional organizations freely to collect the relevant information. Yet regimes in many of the countries at most risk of instability were reluctant to support such activities out of a concern that they might lead to unwanted forms of external interference. This led some analysts to conclude that many African governments still viewed the new architecture in largely instrumental terms as a mechanism to extract assistance from foreigners and help preserve regime security.[80]

CHAPTER NINE

Peacemaking

The second international response to Africa's wars examined here was peace-making initiatives – that is, the process of engineering a negotiated settle-ment. For the purposes of this chapter, it does not encompass the longer-term process of peacebuilding through which such agreements are implemented (some important dimensions of which are discussed in chapter 10). Clearly not all African conflicts witnessed serious peacemaking initiatives; many were simply left to fester. Overall, however, peacemaking initiatives were a much more common feature of the post-Cold War era than was previously the case. This was part of a general global trend which saw a rise in the number and proportion of armed conflicts being brought to an end – if only temporarily in some cases – via negotiated settlements.[1] Between 1989 and 2004, for example, forty-six out of 119 armed conflicts listed by the Uppsala Conflict Data Programme witnessed peace agreements of some kind, many of them in Africa.[2]

In the two decades after the Cold War, peacemaking in Africa assumed various guises. In part, this variation reflected the lack of reliable mediation formulas. As one of the world's most experienced international mediators lamented, there was no 'road map on how [mediation] is to be conducted and there is still no official political doctrine upon which to rely.'[3] Nor was there any consensus on some fundamental questions about which parties to include in negotiations, which parties to welcome into transitional administrations, and how to engineer power-sharing within neopatrimonial regimes.[4] Perhaps most crucially of all, it was not always clear on whose terms peace should be built. Sometimes, as in Mozambique and Rwanda, the mediation process encouraged a liberalization of the country's political systems and social insti-tutions, with built-in requirements for multiparty democracy. On other occa-sions, as in Angola, the brand of democracy sponsored by external actors was based on winner-take-all elections. Sometimes, especially after the establish-ment of the International Criminal Court (ICC) in 2002, external parties emphasized various forms of retributive justice and war crimes trials in paral-lel with the mediation process. Hence, after 2004, conflict situations in Uganda, the DRC, the CAR and Sudan were referred to the ICC either by the host government or the UN Security Council. The Court also deliberated whether to open investigations into the post-election violence in Kenya

(2007–8). Most commonly, however, external mediators acted on the assumption that peace was most likely if all parties could plausibly claim they had won, or at least claim that they hadn't been defeated. In sum, peacemaking required some form of power-sharing, at least for a transitional period until the country could determine its more permanent governance structures.

The upsurge in mediation did not always bring about the desired results. Although relative successes were recorded in Burundi (2000), Liberia (2003), Sudan (2005) and Côte d'Ivoire (2007), there were also cases where mediation seemed to make already bad situations significantly worse, as in Angola (1992), Rwanda (1993), Sierra Leone (1999) and Darfur (2006). Worryingly, it was estimated that, if the implementation of the Bicesse Accords in Angola (1991) and the Arusha Accords in Rwanda (1993) had gone well, perhaps as many as 1.5 million people might not have died in the ensuing violence. In other words, the consequences of constructing the wrong kind of peace could be disastrous, reigniting violence, sometimes on a greater scale and intensity than before the peace process began. This led some critics to conclude that external parties should keep their noses out of other people's wars and instead 'give war a chance'.[5] Others thought 'external efforts to terminate internal warfare [in Africa] may be as much part of the problem as they are part of the solution.'[6] For others, the lesson for mediators to take away was not just to achieve 'peace per se but the right kind of peace'.[7]

This chapter addresses these issues by first providing an overview of the most common approach to external peacemaking, namely, the construction of power-sharing mechanisms. It then discusses some of the main obstacles to building the right kind of peace in Africa's war zones, specifically those resulting from the characteristics of the conflict environment and the nature of external, primarily Western-led attempts at peacemaking. The basic argument is that the power-sharing formula struggled to deal with parties which did not really want to share power. As a result, peacemaking should be conceptualized as an ongoing, usually painstakingly slow process of demilitarizing politics. This must entail building at least a minimal degree of trust between former adversaries, making a serious effort to reform the local security sector, and building justice systems which resonate with local and international standards.

Peacemaking as Power-Sharing

Writing in the late 1990s, Christopher Clapham argued that international peacemaking initiatives were increasingly influenced by a set of informal rules which assumed that almost all armed parties to the conflict should be accorded broadly equal standing and that the goal of the peacemaker was to seek a settlement acceptable to them all.[8] This deviated from what happened in the Cold War era, when governments were usually accorded a special status compared with other conflict parties. The other important difference was the stance of Western governments, which shifted from helping their allies win to ending those conflicts deemed to be sufficiently important as quickly as possible and at a minimal cost. These new rules of the mediation game created a situation where it often appeared that it was an armed faction's ability to cause havoc rather than the merits of its political agenda that determined whether it was granted a seat at the negotiation table – or whether, in some cases, it should be offered a place within the new government.

Clapham also identified three other important ingredients in this peace-making toolkit. First, belligerents were expected to respect a ceasefire – the sooner the better. Second, the terms of the peace agreement were to be built into the process of external mediation, usually via three mechanisms: agreement on a new constitutional structure; agreement that a transitional period would be shepherded by some form of broad-based government of national unity; and agreement that elections would decide the nature of the government after the transitional period had ended.[9] Third, external parties would act as custodians of the process, usually by offering some kind of international peacekeeping force.

Clapham argued that, in the case of Rwanda's civil war (1990–4), this peace-making recipe not only failed to avert genocide but actually helped create the conditions that made it possible. In particular, the Arusha Accords (1993) provided extremist groups with the ammunition they needed to label the moderate Hutu parties as traitors.[10] In part because of the lack of external security guarantees, the Accords also failed to stop preparations by all parties for a continuance of the civil war and the extremists' preparations for genocide (see chapter 6). The result was that many more Rwandans died after the peace process collapsed than in the years of civil war that preceded it.

Put crudely, the approach outlined by Clapham can be summarized as a power-sharing model of peacemaking. This often drew upon a popularized interpretation of Arend Lijphart's more precise notion of consociationalism – a system of governance based on elite cooperation which embodied three core ideas: significant group autonomy, proportionality as the basic standard of political representation, and minority veto powers.[11] Table 9.1 lists thirty-five peace agreements in Africa since 1990 which included power-sharing provisions, usually in relation to the political and/or military dimensions of governance.

The essence of the power-sharing idea is that '[i]ncorporation rather than exclusion is seen as the key to conflict resolution'.[12] It would therefore seem plausible that this approach should work well in cases where exclusion was part of the underlying reasons for war. These power-sharing agreements were supported for a variety of reasons. Sometimes, they were sold as the best way to manage conflict because it was assumed that, the more power-sharing was built into peace agreements, the less effort international custodians would need to invest to guarantee them.[13] At other times, they were championed as being better than the alternatives on offer, such as the winner-takes-all

TABLE 9.1 Examples of power-sharing agreements in Africa since 1990

Agreement location	Conflict location	Date signed
Bamako	Mali	11 April 1992
Rome	Mozambique	4 October 1992
Addis Ababa	Somalia	27 March 1993
Arusha	Rwanda	3 August 1993
Bujumbura	Burundi	12 July 1994
Lusaka	Angola	31 October 1994
Djibouti	Djibouti	26 December 1994
Abuja	Liberia	19 August 1995
Khartoum	Sudan	21 April 1997
Abuja	Guinea-Bissau	1 November 1998
Antananarivo	Comoros	23 April 1999
Lomé	Sierra Leone	7 July 1999
Pointe Noire/Brazzaville	Congo	16 November 1999, 29 December 1999
Arusha	Burundi	28 August 2000
Abuja	Sierra Leone	10 November 2000
Fomboni	Comoros	17 February 2001
Djibouti	Djibouti	12 May 2001
Luanda	Angola	4 April 2002
Sun City	DRC	19 April 2002
Arusha	Burundi	2 December 2002
Pretoria	DRC	16 December 2002
Linas-Marcoussis	Côte d'Ivoire	14 January 2003
Accra	Liberia	18 August 2003
Pretoria	Burundi	8 October 2003
Dar-es-Salaam	Burundi	16 November 2003
Ouagadougou	Chad	14 December 2003
Moroni	Comoros	20 December 2003
Nairobi	Somalia	29 January 2004
Naivasha	Sudan	9 January 2005
Abuja	Sudan	5 May 2006
Algiers	Mali	4 July 2006
Tripoli	Chad	24 December 2006
Ouagadougou	Côte d'Ivoire	4 March 2007
Sirte	Chad	25 October 2007
Bangui	CAR	21 June 2008

Source: author; Accord, *Peace Agreements in Africa Initiative*, at www.accord.org.za/
downloads/peaceagreements/PA_summary.pdf?phpMyAdmin=
ceeda2df659e6d3e35a63d69e93228f1; Mehler, 'Peace and power sharing', pp. 457–
61; UCDP, *Peace Agreements Dataset, 1989–2005*, at www2.pcr.uu.se/
research/UCDP/data_and_publications/datasets.htm.

elections which led to the resumption of war in Angola in 1992. Power-sharing 'pacts' were also sometimes justified as 'the only attainable short-term goal compatible with long-term democratization'.[14] Other commentators worried that, although the concept of power-sharing was sound, its 'central weakness' was that 'it runs into so many obstacles when put into practice.'[15]

The theory behind power-sharing agreements was that they encouraged moderate and cooperative behaviour because all parties could see the benefits of being able to participate in the governance of the territory concerned. In principle at least, they were also compatible with the West's newly found interest in promoting liberal democracy, although in practice they tended to support regimes founded upon (ethnic) group rights rather than individual rights. Thus mediators tasked with ending protracted conflicts in which no side was able to achieve a decisive military victory often saw power-sharing as a potential way out.[16] Although by no means perfect, efforts to end Burundi's long-running civil war were defended as one of the more effective practical examples of power-sharing in contemporary Africa.[17] Specifically, the Arusha Accords (August 2000) were said to have 'successfully brought to a close one of the longest civil wars in the Great Lakes region'.[18] Moreover, if 'the Burundi experiment holds any promise, this is in large part because of the carefully calibrated distribution of ethnic identities and party affiliations in the government, the National Assembly, the Senate, the communal councils, and, most importantly, the army.'[19]

Despite their popularity with international mediators, power-sharing agreements attracted three main lines of criticism: they rarely produced stable peace, they were simultaneously too inclusive and too exclusionary, and they rested on morally dubious assumptions that incentivized violence both within the war zone in question and beyond.

Ineffective?

Power-sharing was frequently criticized on the grounds that it failed to produce stable peace consistently. Andreas Mehler, for example, argued that 'It is doubtful whether the power-sharing ingredients of peace agreements are conducive to peace.'[20] This line of thinking drew, in part, on the idea that so-called civil wars which ended via negotiated settlements might relapse into violence within five years.[21] Certainly, a majority of the cases listed in table 9.1 experienced renewed armed conflict after the signing of a power-sharing accord.

The two major doubts about the effectiveness of power-sharing deals concerned their timing and their lack of transformative capacity. In relation to timing, part of the problem was that these agreements (indeed, any agreements) were unlikely to succeed unless they occurred during what William Zartman called 'ripe moments' – that is, when the conflict reached a stage where all significant parties felt they were stuck in a mutually hurting stale-

mate, had valid spokespeople, and could see a way out.[22] If they were con-
cocted at other times, the parties were likely to view agreements as little more
than a temporary lull in the fighting in which to rearm and reorganize until
they felt able to return to violent means of achieving their goals. In addition,
power-sharing negotiations allowed some political elites to engage in numerous rounds of talks when perhaps their participation was only for the sake
of material benefits – a charge frequently levelled against a wide range of
actors in both Somalia and the DRC. The tendency for agreements to be concluded at 'unripe' moments was usually put down to the idea that mediators
were sometimes more interested in getting an agreement signed than in
ensuring the durability of the peace that was supposed to follow.[23]

In terms of transformative capacity, the worry here was that agreements
struggled to change the incentives and hence the behaviour of conflict parties.
Specifically, power-sharing agreements usually assumed that former enemies
would become partners despite the fact that none of them had suffered military defeat. This was a big assumption. Writing of the power-sharing agreements in Liberia (1996) and Sierra Leone (1999), Liberia's former interim
president, Amos Sawyer, noted that the resulting governments were 'substan-
tially, if not totally, controlled by armed groups whose leaders could hardly
find in such arrangements sufficient incentive to blunt their greed and ambition.'[24] As discussed in chapter 3, it was particularly unclear how power-
sharing pacts could work well within neopatrimonial systems.

Cooperation was especially important within the military sector where
former enemies would need to be integrated into some sort of new, 'national'
security force.[25] In practice, however, this often proved to be a major stum-
bling block of peace processes. The problems were exemplified by the decade-
long (and so far unsuccessful) efforts to create an effective and integrated
national army in the DRC through the processes of *mixage* and *brassage*.[26]
Because power-sharing agreements tended to be elite pacts, this approach
also assumed that leaders at the top of their respective organizations were
able to morph into effective bureaucratic cogs in the larger institutional
machinery of the new regime, and hence its patronage networks. It also pre-
sumed that subordinates would continue to follow orders from those higher
up the official chain of command. In practice, both these assumptions frequently proved to be faulty. Without effective guarantees (probably requiring
some type of coercive instruments) and incentives, paper agreements were
unlikely to change the zero-sum attitudes towards political power held by
many African elites. Power-sharing agreements were thus likely to fail in situations where some actors felt they retained the possibility of achieving total
power, or at least of significantly altering the existing military balance
of power. This led critics to argue that a peace between warlords, if it endured
at all, was likely to be only temporary.[27]

One important variable in the power-sharing process was the presence of
effective external custodians who could try and provide guarantees – through

funds, diplomatic pressure or peacekeepers – to help keep the implementation of an agreement on track.[28] One good example was the significant South African effort put into shepherding Burundi's peace process through to fruition.[29] Unfortunately, Western states were often reluctant to put sufficient resources into African peace deals because of the continent's low strategic priority in their foreign policies (the partial exception was France's approach to some of its former colonies).

Using the Rwandan case once again, a good example was the relative neglect of the security provisions set out in the Arusha Accords (1993), which were put together with considerable international involvement. The implementation of the Accords was supposed to be assisted by the presence of a Neutral International Force (NIF), which, among other things, was mandated to:

- help provide security throughout the country, for humanitarian assistance, and for the expatriate community;
- monitor the ceasefire agreement, including the establishment and maintenance of a demilitarized zone around Kigali;
- investigate all reported infractions of the ceasefire agreement;
- help maintain public security by monitoring the activities of the gendarmerie and police; and
- assist with the demobilization and integration of the armed forces (expected to take seven to nine months and involve 50,000 government and RPF personnel).

In reality, however, the NIF was never established. In its place, the world's governments provided only a small and under-resourced UN peacekeeping mission, UNAMIR, which had only 2,500 troops, was largely confined to the capital city and its environs, and was ordered not to investigate the potential rearming of militia in Kigali as it became evident the Accords were unravelling.[30] This meant that, when the extremists carried out their coup in April 1994, there was nothing of military substance to stop the subsequent genocide.

Too inclusive and too exclusionary?[31]

Power-sharing agreements were also criticized for being simultaneously too inclusive and too exclusionary. They were too exclusionary in the sense that they offered ordinary citizens too little in terms of both participation in the process and a say in the final terms of the political settlement. The problem here was that power-sharing agreements were usually elite pacts negotiated between leaders of armed factions, without broad-based participation by the country's citizens. It was thus common for unarmed groups within civil society to be ignored altogether or to participate only at the margins of the peace process. Women's associations were the least likely of all to be taken seriously.[32] Civilian groups were thus said to lose out not only because of the war but because of the way in which peace was negotiated: from outside and from above.[33]

On the other hand, power-sharing agreements were also derided for their inclusivity when it came to armed factions. Critics argued this approach rewarded actors who resorted to violence and provided an incentive structure which encouraged rebel factions to splinter. Ian Spears dubbed this the 'power-sharing trap' where 'efforts to include and accommodate everybody in itself generated increasing factionalism and – intentionally or unintentionally – left some complaining that they had been excluded.'[34] Notable examples of such splintering during peace processes are the conflicts in Somalia after 1995 and in Darfur after late 2005.

Since post-Cold War Africa was awash with small arms and light weapons and, as discussed in chapter 3, it only took small bands of people to start an insurgency in weak states, it was relatively easy for armed gangs to gain a seat at the negotiation table. The flip side, of course, was that mediators could ignore potentially far more representative unarmed groups without any immediate and costly repercussions because these unarmed groups did not have the capacity to wreck the peace process. The upshot was that the power-sharing route to peacemaking generally left armed groups over-represented in any new dispensation.

Critics thus derided power-sharing agreements for providing a political pay-off to rebels that had failed to achieve victory on the battlefield. While some saw this as a realistic and pragmatic approach to mediation, others saw it as a form of appeasement.[35] The pay-off usually came in the form of inviting the rebels to enter the regime's neopatrimonial tent: while the leaders got jobs in the new government, the rank and file were supposed to accrue benefits through subsequent DDR or SSR programmes.

One particularly controversial and ultimately unsuccessful example was the Lomé Accord of July 1999, which was intended to end Sierra Leone's civil war (see also chapter 3). After the capital city, Freetown, had been ransacked in January 1999 by a combination of the RUF and West Side Boys rebels and disgruntled government forces operating under the label of the Armed Forces Revolutionary Council, much international pressure, especially from the US and the UK, was put on the democratically elected regime of President Kabbah to extend the hand of peace to the RUF. In addition to providing seven ministerial posts for members of the RUF and making their leader, Foday Sankoh, vice-president and putting him in charge of a new commission for mineral resources, the Accord granted amnesty to all parties for violations committed during the war. In several respects, the Lomé Accord was the worst of all possible worlds: it did not go down well with the local population; it was not taken seriously by the RUF and its external supporters; and it did not persuade powerful international actors to provide the necessary security guarantees to ensure its implementation.

Not surprisingly, the Accord quickly collapsed. According to David Keen, there were five entirely predictable reasons why this happened: the continued destabilizing influence of the Liberian president, Charles Taylor; obstructionism by the RUF leadership; the exclusion of the Sierra Leone armed forces from the agreement; the weakness of international support for the DDR process; and the weak international peacekeeping effort.[36] As it turned out, the war was finally brought to an end after a change in fortunes on the battlefield: this occurred with the operations conducted by Guinean troops, a revamped UN peacekeeping force, and after the British Army dealt a decisive military blow to the West Side Boys in September 2000. Faced with superior military power, the rebels crumbled, and there was thus no longer any need to pander to their demands, offer them automatic government posts or honour Lomé's amnesty provisions. Instead, the rebels were given a chance to morph into political parties and win the support of the people at the ballot box – something most of them failed to do.[37] In terms of the wider lessons of peacemaking, this episode lends significant weight to Tull and Mehler's conclusion that 'it is imperative to think beyond violence as the primary measure of political inclusion.'[38]

Incentivizing violence?

A third strand of criticism argued that the power-sharing approach was morally dubious because it incentivized rebellion elsewhere: providing rebels with a share of power even when they were unable to defeat an incumbent regime created an incentive structure that would encourage other rebel leaders to see taking up arms as an effective route into government. In Tull and Mehler's words, 'irrespective of their effectiveness in any given case, power-sharing agreements contribute to the reproduction of insurgent violence.'[39] This was primarily because these agreements levelled 'the political playing-field in favour of insurgents at the expense of state leaders'.[40] The problem was that, if these armed actors proved to be what Stephen Stedman called greedy spoilers – actors willing to use force to achieve their goals, which expanded or contracted based on calculations of risk and benefit – then providing them with inducements in the form of government jobs or rewards for disarmament was likely simply to whet their appetites.[41] Ironically, therefore, critics argued that, rather than doing no harm, this formula for conflict resolution may have undermined the prospects for conflict prevention more generally.[42]

Assessing this line of critique is difficult because it is hard to know what motivates rebel groups and their willing recruits to take up arms: what might look to one analyst like a cynical and greedy attempt to gain a slice of the political action might look to others like a desperate but legitimate attempt to achieve greater self-determination for a particular people. Moreover, people's motives change as circumstances alter, so even if we understand motives at any given point in time this may not remain true for long. The other point is that the current international norm of non-intervention already incentivizes violence, but of the kind that governments can wield against rebels. In this sense, both the traditional approaches which privilege the sovereign regime and the power-sharing approach which provides more scope for rebels incentivize violence, but they incentivize different types. Whether there is an appropriate middle ground remains up for debate.

Building the Right Kind of Peace: Key Challenges

Rather than focus on achieving an agreement to share power between the major belligerents, building the 'right kind of peace' involves the much more difficult and long-term task of constructing structures and mechanisms that do not institutionalize violence, corruption and impunity. In the short term this will almost certainly involve concluding an effective peace agreement, but this is merely the start of a long and complicated process which ultimately requires the demilitarization of the country's politics. With regard to the agreement itself, a central problem facing all mediators is that, in the absence of an overwhelming external security force, any agreement will have to accommodate the existing, often severe, power inequalities within the conflict zone in question. And, if those inequalities are challenged too drastically, some kind of backlash against the agreement is likely.[43] This is why some analysts have highlighted the potentially crucial importance of external custodians.[44]

But, as Terrence Lyons has pointed out, getting a peace agreement is only part of the battle, because agreements alone do not automatically create stable peace. Rather, they create new opportunities – what Lyons described as 'the starting point for another series of negotiations, bargaining, and institution-building rather than a blueprint that must be constructed'.[45] In this view, 'peace' is best conceptualized not as what occurs after the signing of an agreement but as an ongoing series of bargains between the key players which demilitarizes politics and institutions that sustained the war. Mediators and peacebuilders can encourage this process either through the marginalization of certain combatants (which will probably require some coercive 'sticks') or by the transformation of the belligerent parties so that they no longer see it as legitimate to use military force to achieve their objectives (which will probably require some 'carrots'). In the short term this will necessarily involve some way of accommodating the demands made by armed groups, but over the longer term it must involve serious efforts to reform the security sector and empower the unarmed majority so that their voices may also be heard.

The remainder of this section identifies two principal clusters of challenges to this process. The first relates to issues posed by the nature of Africa's recent conflict environments. The second revolves around issues related to the would-be peacemakers.

Challenges posed by African conflict environments

As chapter 2 discussed, Africa's wars usually involved multiple armed factions, and the multiplication of such groups was facilitated by pressures within both governments and their opponents. On the government side, troops frequently deserted or went rogue (e.g. AFRC in Sierra Leone and the FARDC in the DRC), while rebel leaders often struggled to control their subordinates from creating splinter factions (e.g. as happened to the NPFL in Liberia, the SPLM in Sudan and the SLA in Darfur). The resulting melange of fighters added to the complexity of conflict dynamics and presented would-be peacemakers with a formidable set of headaches. These were magnified when some or all of the belligerent parties resembled what Michael Doyle called 'incoherent factions', wherein individual members displayed little in the way of professionalism and often failed to follow orders in the official chain of command.[46] Doyle concluded that, where multiple incoherent factions remained hostile towards one another, the chances of implementing a peace deal were incredibly small.[47] A further complication was that some of these factions had little support from the local population they claimed to represent. In these circumstances, even when an agreement was signed between the leaders of such factions, their lack of popular representation reduced the likelihood that the mass of ordinary people would consider the agreement legitimate. In conflicts involving incoherent and unrepresentative factions it was also likely that these groups would view continued warfare as an important source of their livelihood; and, when war became a business, peace would inevitably mean unemployment or at least a drop in profits and brand recognition.

A second challenge stemmed from the political context in which these factions frequently operated. Alex de Waal captured the essence of this environment when he suggested that the contours of political life in Africa's conflict zones were organized according to a 'patrimonial marketplace' in which both governments and rebel groups tended to operate through kinship and patronage networks and often by licensing proxies to pursue their goals. In this marketplace, de Waal observed a series of auctions wherein political loyalty was traded among the different factions. Understood in this manner, armed revolts represented attempts by insurgents to gain a higher price for their loyalty; thus the war in Darfur could be seen as, in essence, a form of 'political bargaining using violence'. As discussed in chapter 5, this has some similarity with Englebert's understanding of pseudo-separatist movements such as the MFDC in Senegal.

The problem for would-be peacemakers was that they inevitably became part of that marketplace, but as players rather than referees. And, as players, they were usually disadvantaged because they were 'neither well attuned to the rules of the marketplace nor highly skilful in operating there'. To prevent the market from collapsing completely, de Waal distinguished between two options: buy-in and equilibrium. In the former scenario, 'the most powerful purchaser of loyalty (typically the national government) puts sufficient resources on the table to enable all elites to take a share.' In the latter, different centres of patronage are left 'controlling comparable levels of resources and able to match and deter one another'. As far as external peacemakers were concerned, de Waal concluded that agreements would work 'only if the formal negotiations over constitutional provisions and power-sharing take place in support of a patrimonial buy-in'. The problem this presented was that any such buy-in effectively gave the recognized parties a licence for corruption and might reduce the chances of bringing war criminals to justice. This approach also remained focused on those armed factions that currently wielded power and offered few prospects for empowering non-armed but potentially more representative groups. Finally, the bargain was 'only good for as long as the marketplace remains relatively stable'.[48]

A third complication for peacemakers was the fact that many of Africa's wars were messy and inconclusive. As a result, so were their endings. Situations where there were no clear winners – and, indeed, where winning in the traditional sense was not always the primary concern of the belligerents[49] – left peacemakers with a difficult set of challenges. For one thing, it left them facing governments that felt little need to offer concessions to insurgents and with rebel factions that were trying to win at the negotiating table what they had failed to win on the battlefield. Of course, most conflict parties tended to fight and talk simultaneously, but their talk often reflected the military balance of power at the time.[50]

This sort of problem was clearly evident in the wars in Sudan. The fact that a peace deal was concluded between the government of Sudan and the SPLM/A in January 2005 was at least partly due to the fact that the rebels had proved themselves capable of inflicting sustained military damage upon the government, especially in the south of the country. In contrast, part of the reason why the talks to end the war in Darfur repeatedly collapsed was because the rebels were unable to gain the upper hand militarily across the region for a sustained period of time.[51]

A fourth problem was the sheer scale of the tasks facing would-be peacemakers. In many cases the general level of underdevelopment, the collapse of effective state institutions and the destruction of infrastructure required nothing less than a huge injection of resources. This left peacemakers with a big problem as far as delivery was concerned: how could settlements stick if people continued to lack jobs as well as access to schools, hospitals and basic infrastructure? Once again, events in Sudan provide a sobering example. Although the so-called Comprehensive Peace Agreement (2005) was undoubtedly a significant diplomatic breakthrough, implementation of its many parts – including crucial strategic issues concerning the functioning of the Government of National Unity, the referendum on southern secession and wealth-sharing – assumed a level of basic administrative and social infrastructure that was lacking in most of southern Sudan. A similar story was evident eight years after the conclusion of Sierra Leone's civil war. In spite of the presence of a large UN peacekeeping operation, a follow-up peacebuilding mission and significant amounts of assistance from the UK, Sierra Leone continued to languish at the very bottom of the UN Development Programme's Human Development Index.[52] This led some observers to ask whether the ingredients of its original war recipe were starting to reappear under the noses of the UN and other peacebuilders.[53]

Yet as significant as these challenges were they were all arguably symptoms of a more fundamental problem: the militarization of politics.[54] Hence peacemakers need to figure out how to demilitarize the institutions which sustained the war, because the more demilitarized a society becomes the greater the chance of a successful transition from war to stable peace. If wartime institutions remain unreconstructed, peace agreements followed by elections may end wars – at least for a time – but they are unlikely to mark the transition to genuine democracy within which peace can become sustainable. For Terrence Lyons, the solution lay in three areas: building effective interim administrations – because transitioning territories still require government; transforming militarized organizations – regimes, insurgents and paramilitaries – into effective political parties;[55] and demobilizing combatants and engaging in security sector reform that can sustain democracy.[56] Although each conflict generates its own requirements, this is a sensible way to conceptualize the process and the primary issues.

Challenges relating to external mediators

A further set of challenges arose from the characteristics of the external mediation initiatives that tried to resolve Africa's wars. The first was attracting the right type of mediators – i.e. those that avoided what Lakhdar Brahimi and Salman Ahmed described as the 'seven deadly sins' of peacemaking.[57] Ignorance of the political dynamics and the causes of the conflict was the first sin. Unfortunately, they noted, 'ignorance-based decision-making . . . is the norm rather than the exception in post-conflict environments.' The second sin was arrogance. This often manifested in the failure to ask for help and the tendency to rely on the wrong people – often those locals who spoke the best English – when questions were asked. Arrogance was also apparent when mediators assumed that the current conflict was 'just like country X' – with X usually being one of their previous assignments. The third sin, partiality, was best avoided by mediators working hard to establish their credentials as honest brokers *before* they needed to deliver tough messages to the warring parties. Impotence, the fourth sin, usually stemmed from the mediators' inability to maintain strong relations with key external stakeholders, without which their leverage was likely to be minimal. Haste was the fifth sin. As Brahimi and Ahmed concluded, 'The best way to kill a potentially viable political solution is to float it prematurely.' Inflexibility was also a major problem, especially when it prevented peacemakers from coping with unforeseen developments. Surprises always occurred, but the mediators usually had some say in whether they created new opportunities or new obstacles to be overcome. The seventh sin of mediation was to make false promises. In particular, parties needed to be told that compromises would be essential. And, since political and technical problems would always arise, mediators must effectively manage expectations about the role of insiders and outsiders.

Judged against this list, most external peacemakers in Africa did not score particularly highly. Rarely were they real experts in the history and politics of the conflict zone in question. Sometimes they were relatively low-level officials in their country's government machine, and when diplomatic big-hitters did engage, they were often parachuted into the fray relatively late in the day, without sufficient institutional support, and with unrealistic dead-lines with which to operate. The brief appearances in the Darfur peace nego-tiations made by the US Deputy Secretary of State Robert Zoellick and the UK's Secretary for International Development Hilary Benn are perfect exam-ples of this type of parachute diplomacy.

A common outcome was that, for a variety of reasons, external peacemakers often lacked significant leverage over the conflict parties. First, some peace-makers were forced to operate without the united backing of the UN Security Council or other important players in the relevant region. Without a coherent approach to peacemaking in the Council or other relevant international organizations, diplomatic leverage was hard to generate. Second, for most of Africa's conflict parties, local political issues were of greater immediate importance than the decisions taken by the so-called international commu-nity. This position was reinforced by the widespread impression that external peacemakers usually lacked staying power. As one of General Paul Kagame's advisers observed in relation to the war in the DRC, 'The insistence on the signing of an agreement and not on its contents is definitely symptomatic of an impatient world that wants to run away from the problem rather than solve it.'[58] In such circumstances, locals were sometimes content to try and wait out the foreigners whom they suspected would not be around in signifi-cant numbers forever. At best, an agreement might ensue, but it was always highly unlikely to represent a realistic roadmap to stable peace. This was certainly the case with the Lusaka agreement of July 1999, which was sup-posed to pave the way for ending the DRC war. Not only did it ignore several of the key conflict parties, its contents amounted to what one respected observer called 'an international community wish list'.[59] Not surprisingly, the agreement failed to stop the war. As *The Economist* put it, 'The war is dead, long live the war.'[60]

The main explanation for these relatively feeble efforts was Africa's dimin-ished strategic importance after the Cold War. Compared to the relatively high political stakes associated with warding off communism, in the post-Cold War period Western governments were usually called on to 'do something' about Africa's wars only by specialist associations and charities within their own domestic populations. Without an obvious strategic rationale, Western governments were deeply reluctant to invest significant amounts of human and financial resources to resolve Africa's wars. The result was a form of low-intensity peacemaking where the resources were limited and initiatives often lacked political stamina. Indeed, some of them appeared designed more to satisfy the concerns of domestic audiences that something was being done rather than actually fixing the problems in the conflict zone. This stacked the odds against successful peacemaking from the start, because the clearest conclusion from the general literature on the subject was that 'mediating an intractable conflict requires a large commitment of time, energy, and other resources.'[61] In this context, international guarantees, if they came at all, were rarely credible on the ground.

In addition, it is important to recall that, when external mediators did appear in Africa's war zones, it was unwise to assume that promoting stable peace was always their first priority. As Crocker and his colleagues observed, this depended 'on the terms and implications of the settlement'. Sometimes, for example, external parties preferred not to see a friend or an ally make a significant concession during negotiations or judged that other bilateral interests with one of the conflict parties should take precedence over the need to reach a negotiated settlement.[62] And, with mediators such as Colonel Gaddafi, Omar Bongo and Idriss Déby, for example, these dangers were real.

A further challenge, strategic coordination, occurred in the relatively small proportion of African conflicts that attracted multiple external peacemaking initiatives simultaneously. These tended to be conflicts that generated activists and/or diaspora groups which made significant political noises in Western capitals. Although this was indicative of genuine interest in a conflict, 'having multiple high-level mediators and several international organizations with a large operational presence on the ground can create confusion about who is in charge of the political role.'[63] In particular, multiple mediators increased the likelihood of generating three significant problems: belligerents receiving mixed messages about the role of external actors; belligerents having an opportunity to go 'forum shopping', especially when discord over how to proceed was evident among the mediators; and mediators being able to pass the buck to the others when it came to apportioning responsibility for failure.[64]

Conclusion

In post-Cold War Africa, the assumption that the route to peacemaking lies through power-sharing was challenged on several counts, including that such agreements frequently failed to produce stable peace, paid inadequate attention to the mass of unarmed people trapped in Africa's conflict zones, and incentivized violence both in the conflict zone and beyond. But, while power-sharing clearly had its limitations, there was no simple or quick way to end Africa's wars. The task was made more difficult by both the characteristics of Africa's conflict environments and the type of peacemaking that was on offer. While the former frequently produced stubborn neopatrimonial regimes and a multitude of incoherent factions – some of which saw war as their best opportunity to make a living – the latter was heavily influenced by the West's lack of strategic interests on the continent. When mediation was attempted, it was often done on the cheap and without sustained political support at the highest levels. On the rare occasions there was a proliferation of mediators, strategic coordination between them was usually notable only for its absence.

In the short term, the key issue for peacemakers is to persuade the warring factions to stop using military force. It seems clear that this can be achieved only if external custodians have at their disposal both credible sticks and tasty carrots.[65] In the longer term, however, the route to stable peace lies in the demilitarization of politics and the marginalization of groups that seek power through violence. As chapters 3 and 5 discussed, this does not mean it is only the rebel side of the equation that needs attention: governments also need to be encouraged to work harder to provide marginalized groups with channels through which they can participate meaningfully in the country's politics. Following Lyons, peacemaking should be understood not as the search for an agreement but as an ongoing process of bargaining in which the long-term goal should be the demilitarization of the actors and institutions that sustained the war. The problem, of course, is how to stimulate and control such a process.

Although no one has all the answers, it is clear that for actors to lay down their arms permanently there needs to be a reasonable measure of trust and justice – both of which must lie at the core of future research agendas in this area. More effort must go into thinking how to build trust between individuals and groups at both the elite and the societal level.[66] With respect to justice, the trick will be learning how to combine indigenous and endogenous processes with external approaches.[67] Until the world's peacemakers get better at delivering both, the world's peacekeepers will be in for a tough time. And, as the next chapter shows, many of them had a very rough time dealing with Africa's wars.

CHAPTER TEN

Peacekeeping

Arguably the most visible international response to Africa's wars was the proliferation of peace operations, which between 1990 and 2009 numbered more than sixty – far more than on any other continent. This period was also the most tumultuous in the history of peacekeeping.[1] The operations themselves assumed various shapes and sizes, from tiny observer missions to huge enterprises involving tens of thousands of personnel. They were authorized and conducted by a wide variety of actors and international organizations and, as instruments of conflict management, they produced decidedly mixed results. This was in large part because the UN and other organizations had to learn while on the job how to keep the peace in messy civil wars. These organizations also had to develop the relevant tools and structures as they went along. Chapter 8 analysed the various attempts to build relevant African organizations, but it is often forgotten that at the start of the 1990s the UN's department for peacekeeping operations did not exist.

In this sense, the story of peacekeeping in Africa after the Cold War was in part a story of trying to professionalize peace operations. Since peace operations are a reflection of international society's assumptions and priorities about conflict management, tracing their evolution provides an important barometer of the extent and depth of international engagement with Africa's armed conflicts. The results are instructive. On the positive side, peace operations helped shepherd transitions from war to peace in places such as Namibia, Mozambique, Burundi, Sierra Leone and Liberia. On the other hand, peacekeepers failed to stop mass killings in Rwanda, Angola, Sudan, the DRC and elsewhere, and sometimes abused and exploited the local people they were supposed to help protect. Probably the central explanations for this mixed record were that some mission mandates were simply much tougher than others and some operations were given many more resources than others.

In order to discuss these issues, the chapter begins with an overview of Africa's peacekeeping landscape after the end of the Cold War by examining both African and external, primarily UN, initiatives. The second section then analyses seven of the most serious challenges that confronted peacekeepers on the African continent. The central conclusions are that peacekeepers were often used as a substitute for an effective political strategy focused on conflict resolution and that these missions were bound by the international legal requirement of seeking consent from host governments, even when those same regimes were a big part of the problem in several African conflicts, notably Rwanda, the DRC and Sudan.

Africa's Peacekeeping Landscape after the Cold War

By the end of 2009, Africa was home to ten military peace operations, involving more than 73,000 peacekeepers deployed in Côte d'Ivoire (UNOCI), Chad/CAR (MINURCAT and MICOPAX), the Democratic Republic of Congo (MONUC), Liberia (UNMIL), Somalia (AMISOM), Sudan (UNMIS, UNAMID), Burundi (AU Special Task Force) and Western Sahara (MINURSO). But Africa's peacekeeping landscape was not always this crowded. To explain how such a complex situation developed we need to analyse two intertwined sets of stories: first, conflict management efforts carried out by African states and international organizations; and, second, non-African, primarily UN and, later, EU initiatives. Although it is misleading to separate these two sets of initiatives completely – African governments were clearly involved in the UN's activities and external actors were usually involved in African initiatives – they did involve different sets of political dynamics which, at times, veered in very different directions.

In terms of sheer scale, the conflict management initiatives conducted by the UN and other non-African actors were considerably larger than those carried out by their African counterparts. Overall, between 1990 and 2009, a total of twenty-eight peace operations were conducted by African institutions. These missions involved the deployment of just over 74,000 uniformed personnel (the OAU missions accounted for approximately 300 of these; deployments by sub-regional organizations, principally ECOWAS and SADC, amounted to over 56,000 personnel; while over 18,000 were deployed as AU peacekeepers). By way of comparison, during the same period non-African organizations and actors, primarily the UN, conducted thirty-five peace operations on the African continent. These involved the deployment of approximately 200,000 uniformed personnel, of whom approximately 157,500 were UN peacekeepers while some 41,200 were deployed by other actors (of the latter group, 32,000 came from the US-led UNITAF operation in Somalia, 1992–3). In the twenty-first century, the UN's peace operations in Africa have accounted for some 70 per cent of its peacekeeping forces worldwide and cost the organization over $32 billion.

The African side of the story can be summarized as unfolding in two largely distinct phases: attempts at peacekeeping before the AU was established and attempts afterwards. During the first phase, military peace operations were generally conducted by some of Africa's sub-regional organizations, with the OAU deploying some small-scale observer missions. After 2002, peacekeeping on the continent was orchestrated primarily by the AU but with the occasional sub-regional operation. As discussed in chapter 8, while in 1993 the OAU established a Mechanism for Conflict Prevention, Management and Resolution, it did not conduct any significant military peace operations, although it did undertake a variety of small-scale observation and fact-finding missions, mainly in the Great Lakes region and the Comoros (see table 8.1, p. 151).[2]

In part because of the OAU's lack of peacekeeping capabilities, between 1990 and 2002 military peace operations were generally conducted by Africa's sub-regional organizations, most notably the ECOWAS and SADC (see table 10.1).[3] On the positive side, these organizations were at least attempting to fill the conflict management gap left during the 1990s when some of the UN's most powerful member states effectively turned their back on certain African wars, notably those in Liberia, Sierra Leone and Sudan.[4] In others, such as Burundi, the UN explicitly ignored local calls for a peacekeeping operation and instead sent only a fact-finding mission.[5] It is therefore reasonable to

TABLE 10.1 Peace operations conducted by African sub-regional organizations, 1990–2003

Mission	Location	Duration	Size (approx. max.)	Main task(s)
ECOMOG 1	Liberia	1990–9	15,000	Enforcement
ECOMOG 2	Sierra Leone	1997–2000	14,000	Enforcement
MISAB	CAR	1997–8	1,100	Peacebuilding
ECOMOG 3	Guinea-Bissau	1998–9	c.750	Peacebuilding/enforcement
Operation Boleas (SADC)	Lesotho	1998–9	3,850	Enforcement
Operation Sovereign Legitimacy (SADC)	DRC	1998–2002	15,500	Enforcement
CEN-SAD operation	CAR	2001–2	300	Peacebuilding
FOMUC (became MICOPAX)	CAR	2002–	380	Peacebuilding
IGAD Verification Monitoring Team	Sudan	2003–5	41	Observation
ECOFORCE (became ECOMICI)	Côte d'Ivoire	2003–4	c.1,500	Peacebuilding
ECOMIL	Liberia	2003–4	3,600	Peacebuilding

conclude that the UN's lack of engagement pushed Africa's regional organizations into operations for which they were not well designed and which they were not ready to execute.

On the negative side, these operations suffered from numerous problems. First of all, SADC's operations in particular were not examples of peacekeeping but were rather enforcement operations designed to help out friends in trouble, namely, President Laurent Kabila in the DRC and Prime Minister Pakalitha Mosisili in Lesotho. Second, some of these operations were conducted with dubious international legality. While those involving ECOWAS and SADC could be justified legally as collective defence operations under Article 51 of the UN Charter (i.e. helping to defend a state's *de jure* authorities from insurgents), they were generally sold to the world as peacekeeping operations, which should not slide into enforcement activities without explicit authorization from the UN Security Council, as stipulated in Article 53 of the UN Charter. Part of the uncertainty over this issue stemmed from the UN Security Council's less than clear response. As Jane Boulden observed, in response to such operations the Security Council 'demonstrated relatively little concern for ensuring the primacy of the Charter' and was 'remarkably unprotective of its own turf'.[6] A third problem was the lack of unity and consensus displayed within the regional organizations themselves. In Liberia, the DRC and Lesotho, for instance, both ECOWAS and SADC broke their own internal rules for deploying military operations, with small factions within each organization conducting the missions.[7]

A fourth set of problems revolved around practical issues, such as strategy, competence, deployment, management, logistics, and the provision of suitable materiel.[8] In Operation Boleas in Lesotho, for example, the intervening troops were initially surprised by the level of resistance they encountered. The resulting battle left much of the capital city, Maseru, in ruins, displaced thousands of people, and left over 100 people dead. ECOMOG troops proved similarly inept when, in September 1990, Liberia's President Samuel Doe was captured and subsequently killed while supposedly under the protection of ECOWAS peacekeepers. A fifth problem was the lack of professionalism and discipline displayed by some of these regional peacekeepers. Although most peace operations suffered some degree of misconduct by their personnel, ECOMOG troops reached new heights with their frequent summary executions of prisoners, as well as looting and sexual violence carried out against the local populations. Indeed, Liberian civilians came up with an alternative name for the West African force: Every Car Or Moving Object Gone.[9]

In the final analysis, perhaps the most damning indictment of these operations was that they were not particularly effective in managing the conflicts in question. The SADC states which conducted Operation Sovereign Legitimacy in the DRC, for example, protected President Kabila from foreign invasion but could not save him from one of his own bodyguards. Moreover, the presence of the troops from Angola, Zimbabwe and Namibia fuelled rather than dampened the wider war. They also engaged in a wide variety of activities to exploit the DRC's natural resources (discussed in chapter 4).[10] In Liberia, ECOMOG only delayed Charles Taylor's bid to become president and thus arguably simply helped prolong the civil war.[11] In Sierra Leone, ECOWAS was again internally divided and proved unable to defeat the Revolutionary United Front rebels. Instead, in July 1999 it helped facilitate the deeply flawed and misconceived Lomé peace agreement before Nigeria's new government withdrew many of its troops and passed the peacekeeping baton to the UN. In Guinea-Bissau, ECOMOG failed to alter the country's kleptocratic style of politics or the huge rifts between the political elites tied to the presidency and the armed forces.

Things began to change with the establishment of the new African Union. As demonstrated in chapter 8, the AU's Peace and Security Council became the hub of the continent's new peace and security architecture, carrying out seven operations and one hybrid mission with the UN (see table 10.2).

The story of non-African peacekeeping had a rather different trajectory (see table 10.3 for a comprehensive list of UN peacekeeping operations in Africa). The initial optimism that accompanied the end of the Cold War saw a raft of new UN operations begin between 1988 and 1992 in Angola, Namibia, Somalia and Mozambique. While the operations in Namibia and Mozambique went relatively well, those in Angola and especially Somalia went badly. After the so-called Black Hawk Down episode in Mogadishu in October 1993, the United States led a general retreat from UN peacekeeping, especially in Africa.[13]

TABLE 10.2 African Union peace operations, 2003–9[12]

Mission	Location	Duration	Size (approx. max.)	Main task(s)
AMIB	Burundi	2003–4	3,250	Peacebuilding
MIOC	Comoros	2004	41	Observation
AMIS	Sudan	2004–7	c.7,700	Peacekeeping/ civilian protection
AU Special Task Force for Burundi	Burundi	2006–9	c.750	VIP protection
AMISEC	Comoros	2006	1,260	Electoral monitoring
AMISOM	Somalia	2007–	4,300	Regime support
MAES	Comoros	2007–8	350	Electoral support
Operation Democracy in the Comoros	Comoros	2008	1,350 (+450 Comoros)	Enforcement
UNAMID (paid for by the UN)	Sudan	2008–	16,400 (13,500 African)	Peacebuilding/ civilian protection

TABLE 10.3 United Nations peacekeeping operations in Africa, 1990–2009

Mission	Location	Duration	Size (approx. max.)	Main task(s)
MINURSO	Western Sahara	1991–	237	Peacekeeping
UNAVEM 2	Angola	1991–5	c.475	Observation
UNOSOM 1	Somalia	1992–3	4,270	Peacekeeping
ONUMOZ	Mozambique	1992–4	c.8,125	Peacebuilding
UNOSOM 2	Somalia	1993–5	28,000	Peacebuilding/ enforcement
UNOMUR	Rwanda–Uganda	1993–4	81	Observation
UNOMIL	Liberia	1993–7	c.365	Observation
UNAMIR 1 and 2	Rwanda	1993–6	5,500	Peacebuilding
OMIB	Burundi	1993–6	47	Observation
UNASOG	Chad–Libya	1994	9	Observation
UNAVEM 3	Angola	1995–7	4,220	Peacebuilding
MONUA	Angola	1997–9	c.3,000	Peacebuilding
MINURCA	CAR	1998–2000	1,350	Peacebuilding
UNOMSIL	Sierra Leone	1998–9	352	Observation
UNAMSIL	Sierra Leone	1999–2005	17,670	Peacebuilding/ enforcement/ civilian protection
MONUC	DRC	1999–	c.18,600	Peacebuilding/ enforcement/ civilian protection
UNMEE	Ethiopia–Eritrea	2000–8	4,200	Peacekeeping
MINUCI	Côte d'Ivoire	2003–4	75	Observation
UNMIL	Liberia	2003–	c.16,100	Peacebuilding/ civilian protection
UNOCI	Côte d'Ivoire	2004–	c.9,200	Peacebuilding/ enforcement/ civilian protection
ONUB	Burundi	2004–6	c.6,100	Peacebuilding/ civilian protection
UNMIS	Sudan	2005–	c.10,100	Peacebuilding/ civilian protection
MINURCAT	CAR and Chad	2007–	3,000	Civilian protection/ humanitarian assistance
UNAMID	Sudan	2008–	16,400	Peacebuilding/ civilian protection

The most immediate and direct casualty of this attitude was the UN mission in Rwanda, UNAMIR, which was left severely under-resourced, with the consequence that the world effectively abandoned Rwanda's political moderates as well as its entire Tutsi population during the genocide of 1994.[14] Ironically, Washington publicly released its new, more restrictive set of principles for engaging in multilateral peace operations in May 1994, one month into Rwanda's genocide.[15]

As noted above, the UN's relative disengagement after the Black Hawk Down episode encouraged the idea that Africans should resolve the continent's problems for themselves – commonly referred to as the 'African solutions to African problems' approach. A specific variant of the regionalization approach to peacekeeping, the basic idea was that 'each region . . . should be responsible for its own peacemaking and peacekeeping, with some financial and technical support from the West but few, if any, military or police contingents from outside the region'.[16]

'African solutions' rhetoric found support from African leaders and Western governments, especially the US, the UK and France. The general thrust of the African position was captured by South African President Thabo Mbeki's arguments about how outsiders should respond to the war in Darfur, Sudan. 'It's critically important', Mbeki argued, 'that the African continent should deal with these conflict situations. . . . We have not asked for anybody outside of the African continent to deploy troops in Darfur. It's an African responsibility, and we can do it.'[17] Similarly, Western governments continued endorsing the 'African solutions' approach into the twenty-first century. As US Secretary of State Colin Powell made clear on a tour of four African states in spring 2001, 'Africans themselves must bear the lion's share of the responsibility for bringing stability to the continent' and should not 'sit around waiting for money to come [their] way'.[18] More recently still, the then British prime minister, Tony Blair, joined the chorus, stating that, although 'the West [should] fund it . . . peacekeeping [was] Africa's responsibility.'[19]

Several factors explain the resonance of the 'African solutions' idea.[20] First, it had deep historical roots in the anti-colonial struggle and reflected the powerful anti-imperial sentiment that Africans should be able to decide their own futures without being dictated to by outsiders. It thus drew on earlier pan-African themes such as the 'African personality', negritude, and the 'try Africa first' approach, which were important ideological rallying points in the late nineteenth and the twentieth century. In a positive sense, therefore, the 'African solutions' approach represented a normative defence of the pluralist conception of international society and a rejection of neocolonial enterprises.[21]

Second, its supporters emphasized that Chapter VIII of the UN Charter encourages African regional organizations to take the lead in the peaceful resolution of disputes in their own neighborhood. This is true, but it also bans them from undertaking enforcement activities without prior authorization from the Security Council.

As noted above, a third argument concluded that devising 'African solutions' was a necessary response to international disengagement from Africa after the Cold War. By the mid-1990s, the neglect of Africa had become so serious that the International Institute for Strategic Studies (IISS) concluded that, 'If there is a common thread running throughout Africa, it is fading international attention. The outstanding feature of Western policy in Africa is its absence.'[22] The obvious lesson to draw was that Africans could not afford to wait for the Western cavalry but would instead have to devise their own peacekeeping action plans.

A final argument noted that, even if international attention returned to Africa – as it did in the twenty-first century – Africans would be unwise to rely upon external donors whose priorities were notoriously fickle and who were generally less interested in resolving the continent's conflicts than in fighting their own 'war against terrorism' or securing access to African resources. Indeed, the former point was even acknowledged by Tony Blair's Commission for Africa, which concluded in 2005 that 'part of the rationale for promoting "African solutions" is that recent history has repeatedly demonstrated that African states and organisations are more likely to show the political will to respond to crises than non-African actors.'[23]

It was against this backdrop that UN peacekeeping began a resurgence of sorts in Africa in 1999 with the authorization of two missions, in Sierra Leone (UNAMSIL) and the DRC (MONUC). Initially, however, the UN's return to peacekeeping in Africa did not go well. While MONUC was unable to deploy in significant numbers until after President Laurent Kabila was assassinated in January 2001, UNAMSIL found itself suffering humiliation at the hands of RUF rebels until an intervention by British forces in May 2000 started to turn the tide of the war in favour of the UN and the legitimate government of President Ahmed Tejan Kabbah.[24] As demand for peace operations in Africa increased, so did concerns of overstretch at the UN. Western governments, however, began talking once again about 'saving Africa' – most notably in Tony Blair's 2001 speech to the Labour Party conference in the aftermath of the 9/11 terrorist attacks on the US. As a consequence, Western forces did make a few appearances in Africa, although usually not under UN command and control structures (see table 10.4). Despite these ad hoc operations, the US, the UK and France continued to deploy very few personnel to UN peace operations on the continent (see table 10.5 below).

By 2005, the trickle of new UN operations in Africa had become a virtual flood, with large expansions of UNAMSIL and MONUC as well as sizeable new operations deployed to Liberia, Côte d'Ivoire, Burundi and Sudan. By this stage, operations in Africa were accounting for over two-thirds of the UN's global peacekeeping commitments.[25] Yet it wasn't long before commentators suggested that UN peacekeeping, especially in Africa, had run into another crisis. By the late 2000s, peacekeeping was said to have entered an era of strategic uncertainty, not least because three crucial pillars on which it was

TABLE 10.4   Non-UN, non-African peace operations in Africa, 1990–2009

Mission	Location	Duration	Size (approx. max.)	Main task(s)
UNITAF	Somalia	1992–3	c.32,000	Enforcement/ humanitarian relief
CPAG	South Africa	1994	33	Security sector reform
Operation Turquoise (French-led)	Rwanda	1994	c.2,500	Enforcement/civilian protection
CPDTF	Sierra Leone	1998	7	Police training
Operation Artemis (EU)	DRC	2003	1,500	Enforcement/civilian protection
EUPOL Kinshasa (became EUPOL RD)	DRC	2005–7	c.30	Police training
EUSEC Congo	DRC	2005–9	40	Security sector reform
EU Support to AMIS 2	Sudan	2005–8	100	Technical support
EUFOR RD	DRC (CAR)	2006	c.1,250	Enforcement
EUPOL RD	DRC	2007–9	39	Security sector reform
EUFOR Chad/CAR	Chad and CAR	2008–9	3,700	Civilian protection

based had begun to erode: a shared political vision of peacekeeping at the UN Security Council, a willingness of financial contributors to pay the rising bill, and a willingness of troop contributors, critically from South Asia, to deploy their personnel on more complex and potentially dangerous missions.[26]

Major Challenges

No two peace operations are the same, and hence they all face a unique set of challenges. Nevertheless, some challenges appeared regularly across different missions in Africa, and this section analyses some of the most significant, employing illustrations from various UN and non-UN operations. Particular use is made of examples from the MONUC operation in the DRC, partly because it dealt with the continent's largest war and partly because for most of the twenty-first century it has been the biggest, most costly and, in many respects, most complicated peace operation conducted in Africa. As such it exemplifies many of the challenges faced by peacekeepers.

Difficult environments and complex conflicts

As George Downs and Stephen Stedman noted, peacekeeping is more difficult in some environments than others. In particular, they concluded that nine factors can make the strategic environment more challenging:

TABLE 10.5 French, UK and US uniformed personnel in UN peace operations in Africa, 2001–9 (31 December annually)

Mission	2001	2002	2003	2004	2005	2006	2007	2008	2009
MINURCAT	–	–	–	–	–	–	9-0-0	18-0-0	51-0-2
UNAMID	–	–	–	–	–	–	1-1-0	12-6-0	0-0-0
UNMIS	–	–	–	–	0-3-1	0-3-11	1-5-12	0-3-14	0-3-8
UNOCI	–	–	–	198-0-0	197-0-0	198-0-0	195-0-0	193-0-0	21-0-0
UNMIL	–	–	1-3-20	1-3-73	1-2-48	1-3-21	1-3-26	1-3-25	1-0-17
ONUB	–	–	–	0-0-0	0-0-0	–	–	–	–
UNAMSIL	1-22-0	0-21-0	0-32-1	0-21-0	–	–	–	–	–
MONUC	7-5-0	8-6-0	9-5-0	19-5-0	14-6-0	16-6-0	14-6-0	14-5-0	14-5-0
UNMEE	2-0-7	1-3-2	1-3-7	1-0-6	1-0-6	1-0-7	1-0-5	–	–
MINURSO	25-0-15	25-0-7	25-0-0	25-0-0	24-0-0	17-0-0	13-0-0	14-0-0	17-0-0
Country Totals (Fr–UK–US)	35-27-22	34-30-9	36-43-8	244-29-79	237-11-54	233-12-39	235-15-43	252-17-39	104-8-27
Combined P3 total	84	73	87	352	302	284	293	308	139
UN total (authorized)	27,431	30,631	47,731	59,871	54,646	49,576	80,380	86,161	87,698
P3 contribution	0.31%	0.24%	0.18%	0.59%	0.55%	0.57%	0.36%	0.36%	0.16%

1　a high number of warring parties;
2　the absence of a peace agreement signed by all major warring parties before intervention and with a minimum of coercion;
3　a high likelihood of 'spoilers';[27]
4　a collapsed state – i.e. a lack of functioning state institutions;
5　a high number of soldiers: cases with more than 50,000 soldiers are considered particularly difficult;
6　relatively easy access to disposable natural resources;
7　the presence of hostile neighbouring states or networks;
8　wars of secession (since these can frequently revert to all or nothing struggles);
9　the unwillingness of major or regional powers to engage in conflict management/peacemaking.[28]

To their list should be added the fact that operations deployed in remote areas with harsh physical terrain and a lack of basic infrastructure faced huge logistical challenges. Based on their analysis of over a dozen peacebuilding operations, Downs and Stedman concluded that the four most important factors were the existence of spoilers, neighbouring states hostile to the peace agreement concerned, the presence of disposable resources, and the presence of major power interest. While the first three reduced the chances of a successful operation, the last improved its chances. Indeed, without some sort of major power interest, Downs and Stedman advised international peacekeepers not to get involved.[29] Many of the peace operations deployed in Africa had to contend with most of the factors on this list.

In general, four common characteristics of African conflicts stand out as posing particular challenges for peacekeeping. First, as discussed in chapter 2, Africa's wars did not fit neatly within state borders. Thus, while the sinews of war in East, West and Central Africa regularly stretched across political boundaries, peace operations were generally deployed to particular countries or parts of countries. Peacekeepers were thus only ever able to deal with part of the problem confronting them. The UN's recognition of the cross-border nature of the conflicts across Sudan, Chad and the CAR and the deployment of related peace operations thus represented a welcome development.

A second complicating factor was the problematic nature of most of the peace agreements that peacekeepers were asked to support (see chapter 9). These agreements were often problematic in at least two senses: they did not address the complete range of incompatibilities driving the war and they were not fully comprehensive, inasmuch as they were signed by a limited number of the warring factions and usually ignored unarmed groups altogether. This left peacekeepers operating in zones where the reoccurrence of warfare was a constant threat. In some cases the war had not stopped at all, and peacekeepers were viewed by some parties as hostile elements attempting to impose an unjust peace. The AU mission in Sudan after the Darfur Peace

Agreement (May 2006) and the AU mission in Somalia after the Djibouti Agreement (August 2008) both suffered from this problem.

A third common problem was the large number of conflict parties. At various stages, peacekeepers in the DRC and Darfur, for example, were faced with approximately twenty armed rebel factions. Things were made even more difficult because many of these actors had unprofessional armed forces, sometimes comprised of little more than militias, thugs and criminals who rarely respected the laws of war or consistently followed chains of command. This raised the likelihood that armed groups would deliberately target civilians, either because they were considered enemies or because they possessed resources useful to the belligerents. A related challenge was that the conflict parties often formed bewildering and shifting alliances which made it difficult for peacekeepers to know who to support. The splintering of rebel factions in both the DRC and Darfur were cases in point. Moreover, armed groups whose members relied upon warfare to generate their livelihoods had a vested interest in maintaining conflict and hence often resented the presence of peacekeepers.

Coordination among multiple peacekeepers

No single organization was equipped to deal adequately with all of Africa's conflict-related problems. Although the UN was the most significant peacekeeping organization in post-Cold War Africa, it never had a monopoly on such activities. This proliferation of peacekeeping actors posed two principal challenges. At the strategic level it was often difficult to ensure coordination between these different actors over goals and methods.[30] While most actors agreed in the abstract sense that greater coordination was necessary for effective peacekeeping, none of them liked to be 'coordinated' if this meant following another institution's agenda. Such strategic coordination was especially important during the planning stages for potential missions but was often notable only for its absence. The AU's inability to pay for its own peace operations meant that its relationship with the UN and other donor states and institutions (notably the EU) became particularly complicated. Among other things, this generated a protracted debate over how to ensure African 'ownership' of operations that were paid for predominantly by Western states or the UN (as was the case with the AU missions in Sudan and Somalia).

At a more tactical level, the multiplicity of actors posed challenges related to interoperability, not least the fact that commanding multinational peacekeeping forces was made more difficult because personnel from different countries had been exposed to different doctrine and training and used distinct equipment. The main attempt to overcome this problem was the establishment of various peacekeeping training centres and the effort to build an African Standby Force, discussed in chapter 8.[31]

Not enough soldiers

Peace operations in Africa were also commonly forced to operate with insufficient numbers of troops. It has always been standard practice for politics at the UN Security Council to generate authorized deployment numbers at the low end of the recommended spectrum. (Indeed, the same is probably true for all international organizations.) This was usually done to save on costs and in order to increase the likelihood that member states would be seen to meet these targets. This was a problem that dogged many peacekeeping operations. In the case of MONUC in the DRC it occurred repeatedly. For example, although a UN report of March 1999 estimated MONUC would need more than 100,000 troops, it was granted fewer than 6,000.[32] Similarly, in October 2004, UN Security Council Resolution 1565 granted MONUC only 5,900 of the 13,100 additional troops it had requested, including denying the mission a brigade planned for the southeastern part of the country.[33] And again in 2006, the EUFOR RD force was deployed temporarily to the DRC in support of MONUC because the Security Council had declined the UN Secretary-General's request that MONUC be given an additional 2,590 troops to deal with security contingencies during the elections.[34]

An additional dimension to this problem was the length of time it usually took peacekeepers to arrive in the field. For example, although MONUC was established in 1999 it did not deploy in significant numbers until mid-2001, in part because of Kabila's intransigence and in part because the UN did not foresee the lack of progress on the ground. Among other notable examples were AMISOM taking nearly two years to reach *half* its authorized troop strength, UNAMID operating with some 10,000 uniformed personnel below its authorized strength *eighteen months* into its operations, and the fact that the 3,000 reinforcements authorized for MONUC in November 2008 took over a year to arrive.

Not enough Western soldiers

Particularly after the traumatic episodes in Somalia and Rwanda, most of the peacekeepers deployed in Africa came from the continent itself or from states in South Asia, especially Bangladesh, India and Pakistan. To take one recent example, when the latest crisis in northeastern DRC hit the international headlines in October 2008, MONUC was the largest peace operation in Africa, comprising just over 18,500 uniformed personnel. More than half of them came from India, Pakistan and Bangladesh. Most of the rest were from Uruguay, Nepal and five African states (South Africa, Morocco, Benin, Senegal and Tunisia). The permanent five members of the Security Council, in contrast, provided only 254 troops, or 1.37 per cent of the total, 234 of whom were from China. Indeed, since 2000, China was the only permanent member of the UN Security Council to increase significantly the number of peace-

TABLE 10.6 Chinese uniformed personnel in UN peace operations in Africa, 2001–9 (31 December annually)

Mission	2001	2002	2003	2004	2005	2006	2007	2008	2009
MINURCAT	–	–	–	–	–	–	0	0	0
UNAMID	–	–	–	–	–	–	3	321	324
UNMIS	–	–	–	–	35	469	468	474	467
UNOCI	–	–	–	3	7	7	7	7	7
UNMIL	–	–	77	597	595	593	581	569	582
ONUB	–	–	–	3	3	–	–	–	–
UNAMSIL	6	6	6	3	–	–	–	–	–
MONUC	10	10	230	230	230	230	234	234	234
UNMEE	7	5	6	7	7	9	7	–	–
MINURSO	16	16	19	19	18	14	13	12	10
Total	*39*	*37*	*338*	*862*	*895*	*1,322*	*1,313*	*1,617*	*1,633*

keepers it deployed in Africa (see table 10.6). The important point here, however, is not that these soldiers were incapable of fulfilling the tasks assigned to them – many of them were good peacekeepers. Rather, it is to emphasize that the developing world took on far more than its fair share of peacekeeping in Africa.

In contrast, as discussed above, Western states were reluctant to send their own soldiers on UN peacekeeping missions in Africa. Indeed, in the twenty-first century, France, the United Kingdom and the United States combined generally contributed fewer than 300 uniformed personnel to UN peacekeeping operations on the continent (generally accounting for less than 0.5 per cent of the total; see table 10.5). In order to deflect criticism for this poor showing, these states emphasized their financial contributions to UN operations, as well as the various training and assistance programmes they undertook to enable more African soldiers to carry out peacekeeping tasks.[35] Part of the rationale behind the call for more Western forces was their ability to conduct high-end military tasks and the fact that they generally brought with them important items of equipment, as well as logistical and air support. Furthermore, greater willingness of Western states to deploy their own soldiers rather than simply write cheques would have sent a powerful message about their political commitment to missions in Africa.

When France and the UK did send their troops to Africa to carry out peacekeeping tasks, they tended to do so outside UN command and control structures and for short periods of time (see table 10.4, p. 192). In the DRC, for instance, Western states conducted two military peace operations in support of MONUC's activities: Operation Artemis, which deployed around the embattled town of Bunia between June and September 2003, and EUFOR RD, which provided support to the electoral process between April and November 2006. The sporadic appearance of these troops signalled that the DRC's conflict was not important enough to risk putting Western soldiers under MONUC command. It also fed perceptions of the existence of two classes of peace operations: those where significant numbers of Western troops were present and those where they were not. As one analysis put it, the war in the DRC was 'too gruesome and devastating for the West to ignore, but too difficult and too low a priority to address seriously'.[36] In this regard, the willingness of European states to deploy over 3,000 troops to Chad and the CAR as the precursor to the UN's MINURCAT operation – and keep many of them deployed after the handover to the UN mission – was a welcome, albeit rather brief, departure from this general trend.

Not enough police

For much of the post-Cold War period, a growing number of peace operations were tasked with strengthening the rule of law and therefore required the deployment of civilian police rather than just soldiers. The greater demand for police was reflected in the UN Security Council's resolutions for its African operations: over 6,400 police were authorized for UNAMID; over 1,400 for MONUC; over 1,200 for UNMIL; just under 1,200 for UNOCI; and over 700 for UNMIS. By mid-2009, however, not all these targets had been met, with notable vacancies in the UN missions in Darfur (some 3,000 police short) and in the DRC (about 600 short). The AU struggled even more to deploy police officers in its missions. A major part of the problem was that good police officers were usually in even greater demand by the world's states than good soldiers. As a consequence, many countries lacked spare policing capacity, and those that had it were often reluctant to send many of their police officers abroad, especially into dangerous environments where legal and justice systems had been destroyed.

Complex mandates

Apart from relatively rare cases such as the operation in Western Sahara (MINURSO) and that between Ethiopia and Eritrea (UNMEE), peacekeepers in Africa were asked to undertake a long list of more complicated tasks than simply monitoring a ceasefire or demilitarized zone. Put bluntly, they were often asked to help build institutions of liberal democratic governance in some of the continent's poorest and conflict-ridden states. The usual lists of tasks ranged from electoral supervision, human rights monitoring, civilian protection, ensuring the delivery of humanitarian relief, providing security and order, strengthening the rule of law, and overseeing disarmament, demobilization and reintegration (DDR) and security sector reform

(SSR) programmes. These complex mandates did not always go down well with the troop-contributing countries. As the Indian representative to the UN put it in mid-2009, 'Peacekeeping mandates have become too broad and too all-encompassing.'[37]

The central challenges related to these daunting mandates revolved around four issues. First, peacekeepers were sometimes given contradictory instructions. For instance, MONUC was mandated to support President Joseph Kabila's government and protect the country's civilians, yet government soldiers (in the FARDC) were responsible for a significant proportion of the crimes committed against Congolese civilians. By 2009, MONUC was supposed to help the FARDC attack various rebel groups in the east of the country but then had to withdraw its support from key elements of the Congolese army when it was proved they were responsible for a large number of atrocity crimes committed against civilians.[38] On other occasions governments withdrew their consent for operations. In early 2006, for instance, the new government in Burundi demanded the drawdown of UN peacekeepers ahead of schedule. Another example came in early 2008, when Eritrea withdrew its consent for the UNMEE force because Asmara felt that the UN was not enforcing the ruling of the Eritrea–Ethiopia Boundary Commission. In 2009, the governments of Chad and the DRC both asked the UN peacekeeping operations to withdraw, in both instances before they had completed their mandated tasks. In other cases, host governments placed significant constraints on the activities of peacekeepers as a price for granting continued consent. This was a major challenge for the AMIS and UNAMID operations in Darfur, Sudan. Indeed, one analysis concluded that peacekeepers should not cross what it called 'the Darfur line' – that is, a peace operation should not be deployed where there is no real consent by the host state.[39] This challenge reflects the fundamental constraint placed on peace operations by the rules of the international system: they can operate legally only with host government consent.

The second challenge was the lack of clarity and ambiguity that often pervaded the texts handed down by the UN Security Council and other mandating authorities. As the head of the UN's Department of Peacekeeping Operations observed, not only were mission mandates 'more complex than ever' but 'there remains a lack of consensus on how certain mandate tasks should be fulfilled.'[40] Part of the problem was that peacekeepers were often told to 'assist' authorities and 'support' processes using 'all necessary measures' without being given further specific instructions or pre-deployment training on how to do this. Alternatively, a related problem stemmed from different national contingents within a peace operation interpreting these general instructions to mean different things in operational terms or ignoring certain orders from their UN force commanders altogether.

A particularly tragic example of national contingents disobeying orders occurred within UNAMIR during Rwanda's 1994 genocide. In an internal letter written during the genocide, the Canadian force commander General Dallaire told the senior officer of the Bangladeshi contingent that the mission's mandate allowed it to try to protect civilians in danger of massacre. 'Our orders from New York are quite explicit', Dallaire wrote: 'we are to conduct the evacuation of the expatriate community and to offer protection when feasible of Rwandese citizens. Within our peacekeeping rules of engagement we can use force to defend persons under UN protection and to prevent crimes against humanity. We must however balance the use of force with the requirement to protect our men.'[41] Nevertheless, members of the Bangladeshi contingent consistently ignored these orders, prompting Dallaire to issue the following complaint to UN headquarters in New York:

> The [Bangladeshi] contingent commander has consistently stated he is under national orders not to endanger his soldiers by evacuating Rwandese. They will evacuate expatriates but not local people. His junior officers have clearly stated that if they are stopped at a roadblock with local people in the convoy they will hand over these local people for inevitable killing rather than use their weapons in an attempt to save local people. This reticence to engage in dangerous operations and their stated reluctance to use their weapons in self-defence or in defence of crimes against humanity has led to widespread mistrust of this contingent among its peers in other units and amongst staff officers/UNMOs [military observers] at the headquarters when they are tasked to go with these men on dangerous missions.[42]

As it turned out, over the next few days members of the Bangladeshi contingent began to desert UNAMIR, taking UN vehicles with them, before UN Security Council Resolution 912 officially withdrew most of the mission, including their contingent.[43]

A third challenge occurred when conflict parties, usually rebel factions, viewed peacekeeping mandates as illegitimate. In the case of EUFOR Chad/CAR, for instance, some rebel groups viewed the presence of an EU force as illegitimate because of its close association with France, which had a long history of providing military support for President Déby's corrupt and authoritarian regime in the name of maintaining stability. To make matters worse for the EU peacekeepers, Déby's government banned them from operating inside the country's refugee and displacement camps, even though the primary purpose of their mission was the protection of civilians and the creation of conditions which would allow displaced people from both Chad and Sudan to return to their homes.[44]

A fourth set of challenges stemmed from the sheer difficulty of the tasks peacekeepers were asked to undertake, especially with limited resources and according to externally driven and usually unrealistic timetables. Among them were mandates to 'strengthen the rule of law' and reform the 'security sector'. DDR also posed huge headaches to peacekeepers over the years. It was hard enough to disarm former combatants when they were willing participants, but attempting to do it by force, as occurred in Somalia, was a recipe for disaster. Demobilization was also difficult to achieve, especially when there were few employment opportunities available to help 'reintegrate' these combatants into society. Sometimes the entire process was met with hostility by local civilians, who did not want to 'reintegrate' war criminals but instead wanted them punished. Consider the case of MONUC.

In the aftermath of Operation Artemis (2003) and the Bukavu crisis (2004), MONUC adopted a much more robust posture in eastern DRC. In 2005, it began a process of compulsory disarmament in Ituri province around the town of Bunia, disarming around 15,000 combatants by June. Some groups opposed forcible disarmament, and in February 2005 fighters from the Nationalist and Integrationist Front (FNI) attacked and killed nine Bangladeshi peacekeepers. In response, Nepalese, Pakistani and South African peacekeepers, supported by Indian attack helicopters, pursued the FNI, killed between fifty and sixty belligerents and disarmed more than 140, with only two MONUC soldiers injured.[45] Similarly, in October 2005, MONUC issued a disarmament ultimatum to the Hutu *Forces Démocratiques de Libération du Rwanda* (FDLR) – a militia associated with the genocidal regime that fled to Zaire in the aftermath of the 1994 Rwandan genocide and subsequently abused local civilians there. When the FDLR refused to cooperate, MONUC used helicopter gunships to destroy approximately fifteen camps. Although this weakened the FDLR and restricted its freedom of movement, it neither destroyed the militia nor forced them to disarm.[46] As a result, the FDLR continued to conduct its illicit activities, often in collaboration with the government's own armed forces, the FARDC.

The other major challenge was how to physically protect civilians.[47] Although many peace operations in Africa grappled with the problems of civilian protection throughout the 1990s, it was not until 1999 that all UN multidimensional peacekeeping operations in Africa included some explicit element of civilian protection in their mandates. Since 2003, the EU (notably Operation Artemis and EUFOR Chad/CAR) and the AU (notably AMIS) have also given some of their operations civilian protection tasks. But it is important to recall that these mandates always came with various caveats, usually that peacekeepers should only protect civilians 'under imminent threat of violence' and within their 'areas of deployment'. In addition, it was – quite rightly – left to force commanders on the ground to decide whether they had sufficient capabilities to carry out specific protection tasks.

Throughout the two decades after the Cold War, the majority of discussion and media attention centred on the many failures of peacekeeping operations, especially in Rwanda, Angola, Sierra Leone, Sudan and the DRC. Yet the news from Africa was not all bad. Even in truly dire circumstances the presence of peacekeepers usually made the overall situation better, not worse. For example, after Ugandan troops had withdrawn from Ituri in the DRC in spring 2003, some 700 Uruguayan peacekeepers managed to protect approximately 15,000 civilians in Bunia airport and MONUC's sector head-quarters.[48] Similarly, in 2005 the Pakistani brigade in South Kivu helped provide civilians with safe passage through the Kahuzi-Biega park and organized village defence communities to alert peacekeepers of imminent attacks, reportedly by banging pots and blowing whistles.[49] And even amidst the carnage of Rwanda's genocide, the beleaguered UNAMIR peacekeepers were estimated at one time to have protected approximately 30,000 people.[50] The basic problem was that there was only so much even well-resourced peace-keepers could do. As one analysis correctly observed, peacekeeping operations could not 'protect everyone from everything', nor could they 'operate without some semblance of a "peace to keep" or halt determined belligerents wholly backed by a state.'[51]

Misconduct

A seventh problem was that some peacekeepers abused the locals they were sent to help. In extreme cases this involved peacekeepers murdering locals – as in the case of Canadian peacekeepers in Somalia in the early 1990s. The more common problems involved the local perception that peacekeepers were unaccountable and immune from the law, corruption, and the sexual exploitation and abuse (SEA) of local civilians. These issues were important because such misconduct could 'put an entire operation at risk, severely hampering its ability to effect positive change in the host country.'[52]

It was corruption and SEA which grabbed the media headlines. Corruption came in a variety of forms, but among the most prominent examples in recent years were UN peacekeepers in the DRC illicitly dealing in gold and other conflict trade goods, including arms, and AU peacekeepers in Somalia engaging in arms trafficking.[53] In the DRC case, the allegations against Indian peacekeepers in particular apparently prompted Kabila's government to tell the UN Secretary-General that they should not be deployed to some parts of the country. This warning came in November 2008, just after the Indian government had offered to provide half (1,500) of the temporary reinforcements authorized for MONUC by the UN Security Council.[54]

In relation to SEA, there were numerous scandals involving peacekeepers raping and sexually abusing local women and children, as well as engaging in human trafficking. Although such abuses occurred in peace operations all around the world, MONUC personnel were accused of more abuses than any other UN operation. In 2004 the UN Office of Internal Oversight Services conducted an investigation into the situation around Bunia in eastern DRC, which concluded that the SEA of locals by peacekeepers was a regular occurrence and that MONUC management had turned a blind eye to the problem.[55] The positive news was that these scandals prompted a major UN investigation into the issue, led by Jordan's Prince Zeid, and the subsequent setting out of the so-called zero tolerance approach.[56]

Conclusion

Peacekeepers did not change the nature of African wars. Nor did they fundamentally alter the political dynamics in what de Waal called the 'patrimonial marketplace' (discussed in chapter 9). But they did help alleviate some of its worst symptoms, and they did this in spite of being given unrealistic deadlines and being starved of adequate resources and personnel. To be clear, Africa did not suffer from a lack of peacekeepers in absolute terms – with the exception of the Balkans, the continent received more peacekeepers than any other region during the 1990s and 2000s. The problem was that there were far too few peacekeepers relative to the complexity and magnitude of the tasks at hand.

Peacekeepers also suffered from the fact that their missions were not always tied to a viable conflict resolution strategy. Two particular weaknesses were the inability of most peacekeeping operations to tackle the local-level dynamics which lay at the heart of many of Africa's wars and their overly optimistic faith in the ability of power-sharing agreements and elections to usher in an era of stable peace. In one of the more thoughtful critiques of the MONUC operation, Séverine Autesserre observed how the mission's leaders relied too heavily on elections when they were 'a poor peacebuilding mechanism' and ended up framing 'local conflict resolution as an irrelevant, inappropriate, and illegitimate task for international actors', when in actual fact it was crucial to implementing peace agreements.[57] These conclusions could reasonably be levelled at many other operations as well.

It was also apparent that no single organization could handle the full spectrum of conflict management challenges facing the continent. The issue of (the lack of) strategic coordination thus cast a persistent shadow over the international landscape. During the 1990s the key relationships were between Africa's regional organizations and the UN. In the twenty-first century, however, the locus shifted to the crucial UN–AU–EU nexus, as the latter two organizations began to play larger roles in peacekeeping on the continent. Throughout both decades the notion of 'African solutions to African problems' was a prominent but not always helpful fixture in international debates.

In more positive terms, the two decades after the Cold War witnessed an unprecedented improvement in the professionalization of the world's peacekeepers and (as detailed in chapter 8) the institutionalization of Africa's conflict management structures. Although some big problems remained, the UN missions established in the early twenty-first century, such as UNMIL, ONUB, UNOCI, MINURCAT and MONUC, reflected a qualitatively different order of professionalization than those established in the early 1990s, such as UNAVEM, UNAMIR and UNOSOM. Similarly, although the AU tried to run before it could walk in the field of peacekeeping, it also made considerable progress, especially when considering the low baseline and the lack of interest displayed in peacekeeping by many of its members.

Finally, it is important to remember that even 'robust' peace operations with mandates to use force were not designed for war-fighting. Their purpose was not to achieve victory over particular enemies but impartially to uphold the principles and rules written into their mandate and the peace agreement concerned. When belligerents were genuinely committed to the peace process, peacekeepers helped make it stick.[58] When belligerents remained belligerent, peacekeepers could do little but help alleviate some of the symptoms of war. When forced into such situations, peacekeepers predictably drew hostility from all sides: governments complained they didn't disarm rebels; rebels complained they ignored government abuses; and civilians complained that they didn't protect them. In sum, the overriding conclusion from peacekeeping in post-Cold War Africa is that, when groups wanted to fight, under-resourced peacekeepers were rarely able to stop them.

CHAPTER ELEVEN

Aid

The final international response to Africa's wars discussed here was the provision of aid. Sometimes this came as part of an overall political strategy to end the conflict; often it did not. It arrived in two principal varieties: humanitarian relief, which claimed to focus on the alleviation of human suffering caused by war and displacement; and development assistance, which claimed to promote sustainable prosperity as a longer-term antidote to the risk of armed conflict breaking out. Both varieties of aid faced the same fundamental challenge: the dirty politics which characterized Africa's war zones. For relief agencies, the central conundrum was how to ensure that assistance made it to the genuine victims of the conflict when the belligerents had little respect for humanitarian principles, and how it could be used to encourage an end to the political problems that had generated the crisis in the first place. For development actors, the challenge was how to help a state develop when the regime in question did not want genuinely national development or particularly liberal governance structures.

As funding for both sets of activities increased but the wars and underdevelopment persisted, critics frequently argued that these instruments were not delivering the promised results. In addition, humanitarian organizations were accused of facilitating population transfers, of fuelling war economies, and of being opaque, selfish and ineffective. For their part, development actors were criticized for imposing upon Africa's weak states neoliberal policies which exacerbated instability rather than consolidated peace and, especially after the 9/11 terrorist attacks on the United States, for supporting the Western security agenda to contain threats (and populations) within the global South.

This chapter examines both forms of aid – humanitarian and developmental – in turn. The basic argument is that neither instrument was able to overcome the challenges posed by regime (and rebel) strategies which chose to ignore the laws of war. As such, humanitarian assistance and development policies in Africa's conflict zones were rarely part of effective conflict resolution strategies.

Humanitarian Assistance in Africa's Wars

In post-Cold War Africa, most humanitarian assistance (emergency food aid, water provision, medical care, shelter, etc.) was provided by what Alex de

Waal called the 'humanitarian international – the transnational elite of relief workers, aid-dispensing civil servants, academics, journalists and others, and the institutions they work for'.[1] In financial terms, the 1990s was a boom period for these actors. Between 1990 and 2000, official humanitarian aid increased from approximately $ 2.1 billion to $ 5.9 billion.[2] This was largely down to the policies of a small group of governments which by the late 1990s accounted for around 90 per cent of this figure (the US being the largest, along with Canada, Germany, Japan, the Netherlands, Norway, Sweden, Switzerland and the UK).[3] These official sources were supplemented by a significant amount of charitable donations given to an increasing variety of NGOs. Indeed, it was notable that during the 1990s governments began disbursing greater proportions of their humanitarian relief via NGOs. In some cases, organizations received so much of their funding from governments that it became reasonable to ask whether they remained truly *non*-governmental organizations.[4] Even with such subcontracting, however, a significant degree of centralization remained, with six or seven major families of NGOs managing approximately $ 2.5 to $ 3 billion, equivalent to roughly 45 to 55 per cent of global humanitarian assistance in 2001.[5]

Despite this relatively small circle of actors, the humanitarian international was certainly not a homogeneous entity. As Thomas Weiss observed, although these actors agreed that alleviating suffering was the principal objective of the humanitarian enterprise, they disagreed over how best to do this in practice.[6] To highlight their differences, Weiss developed a spectrum of humanitarian action along which he identified four ideal types of humanitarian engagement (see figure 11.1).

At one end were the 'classicists'. Led by the ICRC, they believed humanitarianism could and should be insulated from politics. The other three ideal types were variants of what Weiss called 'political humanitarians', such as Médecins

	Classicists ←→ Minimalists ←→ Maximalists ←→ Solidarists		
Engagement with political authorities	Eschew public confrontations	←——————————→	Advocate controversial public policy
Neutrality	Avoid taking sides	←——————————→	Take the side of selected victims
Impartiality	Deliver aid using proportionality and non-discrimination	←——————————→	Skew the balance of resource allocation
Consent	Pursue as sine qua non	←——————————→	Override sovereignty as necessary

Source: Weiss, 'Principles', p. 4.

Figure 11.1 *The political spectrum of humanitarians and their attitudes toward traditional operating principles*

Sans Frontières (MSF) and Oxfam. They all believed that politics and humanitarianism 'could not and should not be disassociated' and that humanitarian
action should form part of some international public policy to resolve or
manage conflict and promote long-term development. The underlying
assumption of this view was aptly summarized by the president of MSF-France
in the following manner:

> humanitarian action is primarily addressed to those whose right to exist clashes with
> the indifference or overt hostility of others. It is intended to reach those who are being
> robbed of life by violence and extreme privation. Consequently, if humanitarian action
> is to be consistent, it will inevitably clash with the established order. Its subversive
> dimension becomes apparent when it moves beyond an analysis of material needs and
> exposes the processes of discrimination that produce victims and prevent efficient
> protection and assistance programs from being established.[7]

In Weiss's schema, the groups who shared this broad orientation diverged
into the 'minimalists', whose aim was to engage in political action, but only
if it would 'do no harm'; the 'maximalists', who had a more ambitious agenda
of employing humanitarian action as part of a comprehensive strategy to
transform conflict; and the 'solidarists', who explicitly chose sides and abandoned any pretense of neutrality and impartiality. Although Weiss believed
that the classicists' aspiration of apolitical humanitarianism was a chimera,
he noted that the political humanitarians also faced a range of practical challenges which meant their own efforts did not always result in better policies
or results. 'Under the right circumstances', he concluded,

> the maximalist approach could be viewed as an opportunity to address the roots of
> violence rather than place emergency Band-Aids, however well funded and effective, on
> wounds. Nonetheless, some of the more grandiose claims of maximalists should lead to
> extreme skepticism: there literally is no space for conflict resolution or development
> activities when deep insecurity prevails. In the darkest moments of civil war, only
> emergency relief efforts are plausible, and even these are often under siege.[8]

All these different perspectives were evident in the many attempts to provide
humanitarian assistance in Africa's war zones. Along the way, the humanitarian international faced a variety of challenges.

One fundamental challenge was that (legally) delivering aid in a war zone
required the consent of the host government. As a consequence, the provision
of humanitarian relief was usually conducted on terms which supported the
incumbent regime and its political strategies. In some cases it did this literally, as in Operation Lifeline Sudan, where not only did the government
retain an effective veto over where aid could be delivered but in the early
1990s several besieged government garrison towns (including Juba, Terakeka
and Kapoeta) were saved by resources they received from relief airlifts.[9] Aid
agencies also bought into the government of Sudan's concept of 'peace vil-
lages', even though these were barely concealed attempts to control displaced

southern Sudanese and Nuba people and force them to work on farms owned by northerners.[10] In other cases it was the rebels who could dictate the terms, as when the Liberian warlord Charles Taylor demanded that a tax of 15 per cent was to be paid (in cash or in kind) on all aid entering territory under his control.[11] In another widely publicized case, it was the genocidal apparatus of Rwanda's interim government encamped in eastern Zaire which controlled how relief supplies were used in the camps. Here, as Fiona Terry demonstrated, 'humanitarian aid, intended for the victims, strengthened the power of the very people who had caused the tragedy.' Overall, 'the Rwandan refugee camps and the humanitarian aid therein guaranteed the survival of the genocidal force.'[12]

A second key challenge was how to control the uses to which humanitarian assistance was put. The problem here was that relief supplies could be used by actors to pursue a variety of goals which did not necessarily involve alleviating the suffering of the conflict's most needy victims. As David Keen illustrated, the three principal sets of actors in this equation were external governments, the belligerent parties, and the aid organizations themselves. For the so-called donor governments, Keen noted how humanitarian assistance served a variety of functions: it helped in the pursuit of strategic foreign policy goals by strengthening friends and weakening opponents; its provision encouraged and even legitimized political inaction (see below); and it helped limit large population flows seeping too far beyond the conflict zone.[13]

Among the conflict parties and local players, humanitarian relief also served a variety of functions beyond alleviating suffering: it was used to protect resident populations, sometimes at the expense of the displaced, and it was incorporated into the economic and military agendas of these groups.[14] In the economic sphere, the appropriation of aid and the ability to charge fees for protecting relief and relief workers were particularly common practices in Africa. In Somalia, for example, various NGOs resorted to hiring armed guards to protect their facilities, personnel and aid convoys. MSF estimated that, between October and December 1991 alone, the organization paid Somali strongman Osman Ato some $60,000 (Terry estimates MSF paid a total of $400,000).[15] Similarly, the ICRC was paying about 500 to 600 Somali gunmen $4 a day each for protection services, and this was in a situation where some 30,000 foreign peacekeeping troops were present in the country. Nevertheless, by 1994 the ICRC decided for security reasons to move all expatriate delegates to Nairobi.[16] In the military realm, aid was regularly consumed by fighters and their dependents, sold for arms, and used as a means to attract new recruits. Armed rebel groups were also quick to see the benefits of operating out of displacement/refugee camps. As Terry observed, these 'humanitarian sanctuaries' provided armed factions with three major advantages: since refugees have a protected status under international law, guerrillas benefited by mixing among them; sanctuaries attracted resources independent of the faction's patrons; and they provided mechanisms through which a guerrilla movement could control the civilian population and legitimize its leadership.[17]

With reference to the aid organizations themselves, Keen suggested that aspects of their organizational culture meant that their priorities did not always align with the provision of assistance to the most vulnerable. Here, along with the problems of using camps as the primary mechanisms for the delivery of aid, Keen identified the tendency for relief agencies to remain silent about abuses in order to maintain their access to certain areas; their inclination to chase funding, which often meant focusing on high-profile, media-accessible crises; and their propensity to suck bureaucratic capacity out of state institutions in crisis zones.[18] On occasion, NGOs were accused of corruption and hence depriving victims of resources. In the multi-donor evaluation of the Rwandan crisis, for instance, the team was unable even to locate one-third of the 170 NGOs registered, and $120 million of funds went unaccounted for.[19]

Of these pathologies, it was the debate about the pros and cons of camps as a means of delivering effective assistance that captured most international attention. On the one hand, camps were *relatively* easy for the aid agencies to organize and monitor, and they were encouraged by nearby states because they could separate resident and displaced populations, attract international resources, and facilitate early repatriation. But, on the other hand, they presented a host of problems for the victims and opportunities for the belligerents. Not only could centralizing people in camps raise the risk of infection and curtail the ability of the displaced to pursue economic strategies and other sources of livelihood, but it also provided armed groups with a concentrated pool of recruits and a ready-made series of mechanisms to organize the appropriation of relief supplies.[20]

In this context of competing agendas – none of which were entirely focused on providing assistance to the most needy – relief agencies usually faced the basic challenge of actually securing access to the real victims. In most of Africa's war zones, large swathes of territory existed where relief workers had no or limited access to suffering populations. In Angola, for example, even in the final stages of the war humanitarian organizations could operate only inside the 'security perimeters' drawn between 5 and 30 km around government-controlled towns, which left 80 to 90 per cent of the country beyond their reach.[21] In every case, access had to be negotiated with the host government, which, for the reasons noted above, often set tight parameters on where and when aid could be delivered. Even after deals were struck to gain access to rebel-held areas, aid agencies found themselves exposed to similar types of manipulation.

Operation Lifeline Sudan was the first example of this new concept of 'negotiated access'. As part of the deal, the SPLA's humanitarian wing – the Sudan Relief and Rehabilitation Association (SRRA) – was given a role in evaluating needs as well as in organizing and distributing aid. Not surprisingly, it inflated the numbers of people requiring aid, misappropriated resources before distribution took place, and helped compel civilians to transport rations they had been issued to SPLA warehouses. The SSRA was also alleged to have collaborated in simulating attacks to force relief workers to evacuate an area so that their supplies could be pillaged by SPLA troops.[22] Of course, relief agencies could have spoken out about what was happening under their noses, but many preferred not to reveal the sources of abuse in order to maintain their presence in certain areas. It was as if Operation Lifeline Sudan and the others like it became an end in themselves rather than a mechanism to address the causes behind the crisis.

Relief organizations were also faced with the challenge of how to deliver resources into a war zone without fuelling the conflict.[23] While an influx of humanitarian assistance – or indeed any resources – into a conflict zone could not fail to have some effect on the war economy, the pertinent questions were how much effect and upon what? The issue of paying protection money and levies has already been noted above, but another mechanism through which relief agencies were said to fuel conflict was through goods being stolen by combatants. In Liberia in 1994, for example, aid organizations had more than $5 million worth of materials stolen. In clashes in Monrovia two years later the figure rose to $20 million.[24] Yet criticism which depicted aid as a primary driver of Africa's war economies is not borne out by the evidence. As David Shearer observed, not only did the intensity of relief efforts commonly wax and wane with no discernible strategic impact on conflicts but, compared to the economic values generated by minerals, timber or oil, the impact of aid was puny.[25] There was probably a direct connection between the fact that such critiques often focused on the role of aid in the conflicts in the Horn of Africa (including Sudan, Ethiopia and Somalia), where mineral wealth and other forms of resources were minimal. Consequently, Fiona Terry offered a more sophisticated way of thinking about the impact of humanitarian aid when she concluded that its importance 'to the war economy is likely to be proportional to the resource base of the warring parties'.[26]

Another major challenge facing relief workers was to ensure that their activities did not become a substitute for political action taken by powerful governments to address the underlying problems. This was what David Rieff called the 'humanitarian alibi' – 'the misuse of the humanitarian idea and humanitarian workers by governments eager to do as little as possible in economically unpromising regions like sub-Saharan Africa.'[27] Of course, this risk of abuse was no reason to stop providing assistance, but it was grounds to think carefully about whether or not to engage in humanitarian assistance if it was not part of a coherent conflict management strategy. Here, organizations on the classical end of Weiss's spectrum, such as the ICRC, were much less likely to take a decision to disengage than those at the solidarist end, such as MSF. The logic behind this concern was that studies of famine and 'complex emergencies' were in general agreement that people usually become victims because 'they lack political clout within the institutions of their own society'.[28] Consequently, responding to what were essentially political crises with food, blankets and medicines instead of political strategies was a recipe for failure. Yet, as de Waal argued, 'Western governments and donating publics [were too often] deluded into believing the fairy tale that their aid can solve profound political problems, when it cannot.'[29] Commenting on the record of the 1990s, Shearer observed that this is precisely what usually occurred: 'major donors have substituted humanitarian aid for political action', with the result 'that civil wars are managed by dealing with their symptoms, not their causes.'[30] Terry reached a similar conclusion, arguing that, ironically, 'humanitarian action in the post-Cold War period has been transformed from a tool with which governments pursue foreign policy objectives to a tool with which to avoid foreign policy engagement.'[31]

The final challenge for the humanitarian international discussed here was actually to solve the problems it was supposed to address. In one sense this was mission impossible, since, by definition, relief agencies were 'only equipped to address the symptoms, and not the causes, of conflict'.[32] But, viewed another way, it did not matter that the agencies couldn't actually save the victims because, in the world of humanitarian aid, unlike the corporate world, it was not the satisfaction of the client that determined the financial viability of the humanitarian international; it was the satisfaction of the donors. And, in spite of all the problems, the donors appeared satisfied enough not to fundamentally alter the system.[33] This led Alex de Waal to make what was arguably the most damning verdict of the entire enterprise when he concluded, 'Contemporary international humanitarianism works, but not for the famine-vulnerable people in Africa.'[34] At times, as the next section discusses, the same could be said for the international developmentalism.

International Development in Africa's Wars

While humanitarian assistance sought to alleviate the worst immediate symptoms of armed conflict, international development policies were part of a longer-term project which included reducing the risks of war. As with international humanitarianism, by the end of the Cold War international development was no longer a set of activities conducted by governments and international organizations but had become a process involving a wider set of actors both above and below the national level, among them regional authorities, transnational firms, NGOs and philanthropists.[35] Some analysts referred to this collection of entities as an international development business.[36] Although officially their primary concern was poverty alleviation, many advocates of development thought it was also a vital part of any long-term conflict prevention strategy, because it could reduce the risk of war recurrence in so-called post-conflict environments and the risk of war onset more generally. The logic was simple: since civil war was 'overwhelmingly a phenomenon of low-income countries', Africa's civil wars must have occurred in large part because the continent was poor.[37] And if poverty increased the risk of war, then development could provide an antidote.

In several respects, this was true. Within the relevant quantitative litera-ture it was widely accepted 'that high-income nations are less likely to experi-ence civil wars than low-income nations.'[38] The literature specifically on Africa also concluded that the glut of civil wars between 1965 and 1999 was 'because its economies have performed so poorly both absolutely and relative to other regions.'[39] This meant it was particularly worrying that in sub-Saharan Africa 92 million *more* people were living on less than $1.25 a day in 2005 than in 1990 (391 million compared with 299 million).[40] The second area of broad consensus was that reversals in levels of prosperity were dangerous.

By and large, statistics on African states compiled by the World Bank bear out these conclusions. First, as table 11.1 demonstrates, 60 per cent of the twenty African states with the lowest GNI per capita in 1990 suffered from a state-based armed conflict or severe political instability during the 1990s. In the 2000s the figure rose to approximately 70 per cent. In contrast, during the 1990s only about 30 per cent of the twenty African states with the highest GNI experienced such conflicts (see table 11.2). For the 2000s, the figure was about 20 per cent. Notably, Algeria was the only state with a GNI per capita over $1,000 which suffered a state-based armed conflict between 1990 and 2009.

With regard to reversals, World Bank data on fifty-two African states shows that thirty-four had lower GNI per capita in 2000 than they did in 1980 (table 11.3). Of these, about 65 per cent experienced either a state-based armed conflict or an episode of severe political instability between 1990 and 2009. In comparison, of the eighteen African states that saw their GNI per capita increase between 1980 and 2000, about 39 per cent suffered in that way.

These figures suggest that development policies did matter for issues of warfare and instability. But *how* did they matter? Here, the quantitative litera-ture is not helpful, and analysts need a more qualitative understanding of particular historical cases. Unlike most African conflicts, the relationship between development activities and Rwanda's civil war and genocide has generated some scholarly debate which is worth reviewing here.

When the civil war began in 1990, Rwanda had the eighteenth lowest GNI per capita on the continent. Between 1980 and 1990 its GNI per capita rose steadily, from $250 to $370, but its Human Development Index score dropped from 0.361 in 1985 to 0.325 in 1990. Thus, while Rwanda was certainly one of the world's poorest countries, there was mixed news in relation to whether it experienced a clear reduction in prosperity levels in the decade preceding the genocide. It is also an important case because, before the civil war erupted, international development actors were heavily invested in Rwanda.

TABLE 11.1 Armed conflict and instability in the twenty African states with the lowest GNI per capita, 1990 and 2000 (US$)

State	GNI per capita 1990	State-based armed conflict (UCDP) 1990s	PITF political instability episode 1990s	State	GNI per capita 2000	State-based armed conflict (UCDP) 2000s	PITF political instability episode 2000s
Somalia	130	Yes	Yes	Somalia	No data	Yes	Yes
Mozambique	170	Yes	Yes	DRC	90	Yes	Yes
Ethiopia	180	Yes	Yes	Burundi	110	Yes	Yes
Tanzania	180	No	No	Ethiopia	110	Yes	Yes
Sierra Leone	200	Yes	Yes	Liberia	130	Yes	Yes
Malawi	200	No	No	Sierra Leone	130	Yes	Yes
Burundi	220	Yes	Yes	Eritrea	180	Yes	No
Zaire	230	Yes	Yes	Guinea	180	Yes	Yes
Guinea	230	No	No	Niger	180	Yes	Yes
Madagascar	240	No	No	Malawi	170	No	No
Nigeria	270	Yes	No	Chad	200	Yes	Yes
Mali	270	Yes	Yes	Mozambique	210	No	No
Chad	280	Yes	Yes	Mali	230	Yes	No
Niger	310	Yes	Yes	Rwanda	240	Yes	Yes
Gambia	310	No	Yes	Burkina Faso	250	No	No
Burkina Faso	330	No	No	Madagascar	250	No	Yes
Uganda	340	Yes	Yes	Nigeria	270	Yes	Yes
Equatorial Guinea	350	No	No	Tanzania	270	No	No
Rwanda	370	Yes	Yes	CAR	280	Yes	Yes
Kenya	370	No	Yes	Uganda	280	Yes	Yes
		12/20	13/20			15/20	14/20

Sources: World Bank, *World Development Indicators Database*, at http://data.worldbank.org/; UCDP at www.ucdp.uu.se; PITF at www.systemicpeace. org/inscr/PITF%20Consolidated%20Case%20List.pdf; Goldstone et al., 'A global forecasting model' (2010), pp. 205–6.

TABLE 11.2 Armed conflict and instability in the twenty African states with the highest GNI per capita, 1990 and 2000 (US$)

State	GNI per capita 1990	State-based armed conflict (UCDP) 1990s	PITF political instability episode 1990s	State	GNI per capita 2000	State-based armed conflict (UCDP) 2000s	PITF political instability episode 2000s
Libya	(1987) 6,170	No	No	Seychelles	7,310	No	No
Seychelles	5,050	No	No	Libya	No data	No	No
Gabon	4,900	No	No	Mauritius	3,730	No	No
South Africa	2,890	No	Yes	Gabon	3,190	No	No
Botswana	2,750	No	No	South Africa	3,060	No	No
Algeria	2,440	Yes	Yes	Botswana	3,040	No	No
Mauritius	2,320	No	No	Namibia	2,280	No	No
Namibia	1,800	No	No	Tunisia	2,080	No	No
Tunisia	1,430	No	No	Algeria	1,580	Yes	Yes
Swaziland	1,180	No	No	Egypt	1,490	No	No
Morocco	1,030	No	No	Swaziland	1,390	No	No
Congo	980	Yes	Yes	Cape Verde	1,320	No	No
Zimbabwe	920	No	No	Morocco	1,180	No	No
Cape Verde	880	No	No	Djibouti	880	Yes	No
Cameroon	870	Yes	No	Côte d'Ivoire	680	Yes	Yes
Egypt	810	No	Yes	Equatorial Guinea	680	No	No
Angola	800	Yes	Yes	Congo	600	Yes	No
Côte d'Ivoire	800	No	No	Cameroon	580	No	No
Senegal	720	Yes	Yes	Lesotho	550	No	No
Lesotho	610	Yes	Yes	Senegal	490	Yes	No
		6/20	7/20			5/20	2/20

Sources: World Bank, World Development Indicators Database, at http://data.worldbank.org/; UCDP at www.ucdp.uu.se; PITF at www.systemicpeace. org/inscr/PITF%20Consolidated%20Case%20List.pdf; Goldstone et al., 'A global forecasting model' (2010), pp. 205–6.

TABLE 11.3 Armed conflict and instability in African states experiencing negative GNI per capita growth, 1980–2000 (US$)

	GNI per capita 1980	GNI per capita 2000	Reduction in GNI ($)	Reduction in GNI (%)	State-based armed conflict (UCDP) (1990–2009)	PITF political instability episode (1990–2009)
DRC	630	90	540	85.7	Yes	Yes
Liberia	530	130	400	75.5	Yes	Yes
Sierra Leone	380	130	250	65.8	Yes	Yes
Nigeria	780	270	510	65.4	Yes	Yes
Niger	430	180	250	58.1	Yes	Yes
Zimbabwe	960	450	510	53.1	No	No
Zambia	630	310	320	50.8	No	Yes
Burundi	220	110	110	50	Yes	Yes
Angola	(1987) 840	440	400	47.6	Yes	Yes
São Tomé and Príncipe	(1988) 530	290	240	45.2	No	No
Madagascar	450	250	200	44.4	No	Yes
Côte d'Ivoire	1,140	680	460	40.4	Yes	Yes
Togo	450	290	160	35.6	No	No
Gabon	4,820	3,190	1,630	33.8	No	No
Congo	880	600	280	31.8	Yes	Yes
Ethiopia	(1983) 150	110	40	26.7	Yes	Yes
Sudan	470	350	120	25.5	Yes	Yes
Mozambique	(1981) 280	210	70	25	Yes	Yes
Algeria	2,080	1,580	500	24	Yes	Yes

TABLE 11.3 *Continued*

	GNI per capita 1980	GNI per capita 2000	Reduction in GNI ($)	Reduction in GNI (%)	State-based armed conflict (UCDP) (1990–2009)	PITF political instability episode (1990–2009)
Mauritania	460	350	110	23.9	No	Yes
Ghana	430	330	100	23.3	No	No
Kenya	440	350	90	20.5	No	Yes
CAR	340	280	60	17.6	Yes	Yes
Chad	240	200	40	16.7	Yes	Yes
Mali	270	230	40	14.8	Yes	Yes
Burkina Faso	290	250	40	13.8	No	No
Gambia	380	340	40	10.5	No	Yes
Malawi	190	170	20	10.5	No	No
Senegal	530	490	40	7.5	Yes	Yes
Cameroon	620	580	40	6.5	Yes	No
Benin	410	390	20	4.9	No	No
Rwanda	250	240	10	4	Yes	Yes
Somalia	100	n/a	n/a	No data	Yes	Yes
Libya	10,460	(1987) 6,170	4,290	No data	No	No
					20/34	24/34

Sources: World Bank, *World Development Indicators Database*, at http://data.worldbank.org/; UCDP at www.ucdp.uu.se; Goldstone et al., 'A global forecasting model' (2010), pp. 205–6.

By the late 1980s there were approximately 200 donors in the country: some twenty bilateral ones, thirty multilateral ones and about 150 NGOs.[41] By 1991, they were dispensing over $600 million in aid to Rwanda.[42] According to one expert commentator, the country had become a 'development dictatorship'.[43] The large international presence means it is indisputable that international development policies are part of the story of the genesis of the civil war and genocide. What is less certain is the nature of that part.

Some analysts argued that the main effect of the structural adjustment programmes was to erode the institutions of the Rwandan state, destroy economic activity, fuel unemployment and famine, and thus contribute to a political atmosphere in which genocide became possible.[44] Others have emphasized that such a view fundamentally misunderstands the central role of state power in conducting the genocide. Rwanda was not a weak state but a strong one which was turned on a segment of its own people. From this perspective, the challenge is to understand the ways (material and discursive) in which external agents of development supported 'a repressive and ultimately genocidal state apparatus'.[45] As Peter Uvin put it, the international development business provided a significant amount of the fuel that allowed 'the government machinery to exist, to expand, to control, to implement'.[46] From this perspective, genocidal violence in Rwanda was rooted in the longstanding dynamics of exclusion, marginalization, inequality, frustration and racism, and, for a variety of reasons, international development policies had helped enflame rather than dampen these dynamics.[47]

The first point for the prosecution is that the Rwandan state was clearly behind the vast majority of human rights abuses and massacres that occurred during the early 1990s, and this was known to international development workers.[48] The international financial institutions (IFIs), however, continued to assume the government was a benevolent actor committed to national development, albeit in difficult circumstances. In Uvin's words, the aid industry 'closed its eyes to the racist currents in society'.[49] Before 1990 the World Bank in particular developed close ties with the Rwandan government, largely because during the 1980s the country experienced a severe economic and social crisis made even worse by the 1986–7 falls in world coffee prices. The World Bank's own figures suggested foreign assistance accounted for over 70 per cent of public investment between 1982 and 1987, and the figure rose afterwards.[50] The Bank subsequently approved a structural adjustment credit (SAC) in June 1991, while the IMF accorded Rwanda a $41 million credit line to finance a three-year economic reform programme. Five World Bank supervision missions oversaw Rwanda's SAC between June 1991 and October 1993. In October 1993 the second tranche ($35 million) was refused because of managerial concerns about the SAC's implementation.[51] This second tranche was eventually cancelled in December 1994.

The basic problem seems to have been that, where the World Bank saw a benevolent state struggling to promote national development in adverse conditions, other observers saw an increasingly extreme regime deploying the machinery of state to retain its grip on power and destroy its political opponents in the face of an economic crisis and growing demands for political liberalization.[52] In the context of the civil war, and because of a lack of reliable information about the workings of the Rwandan state, the Bank had no way of preventing its funds being spent on military equipment. Indeed, according to its own estimates, it was aware that the government's defence and administration spending rose from 45 per cent to 64 per cent of the budget between 1985 and 1992.[53] The dilemma facing the Bank was thus whether to continue supplying funds in the hope that at least some found their way to the health and education sectors or suspend the loan package entirely until the civil war had ended. Part of the problem was that, before the Arusha peace process, the Bank's only official channel of communication was the Habyarimana regime.[54]

From even this brief sketch, it is clear that issues of structural adjustment and development cannot be divorced from political issues of conflict (and in this case genocide). The frightening conclusion is that, whatever their intentions, development actors were caught up in the longstanding processes of exclusion, marginalization, inequality, frustration and racism that helped produce civil war and genocide in Rwanda. In Uvin's words, 'the way *development* was defined, managed and implemented was a crucial element in the creation and evolution of many of the processes that led to genocide.'[55] This is clearly an extreme case, but it is not isolated: development actors were part of many conflict recipes across the continent.

After the Cold War, the principal instruments in these interactions were development assistance and debt relief. Debt relief was less directly connected to the politics of war than other forms of development assistance, so can be dealt with relatively briefly. According to UNCTAD, between 1970 and 2002, African countries borrowed $540 billion and repaid about $550 billion in principal and interest.[56] This heavy repayment burden was said to be severely stunting the continent's ability to develop. Hence, indirectly, debt relief became part of the project to reduce the risk of severe instability in Africa. Of course, relieving debt alone did not reduce poverty, although it could facilitate it. Nor did it alter terms of trade or other imbalances in the global economy which might also account for high poverty levels in Africa. Nevertheless, debt relief became an important part of Western governments' rhetoric about aiding Africa, not least because it accounted for the lion's share of assistance that the G8 gave to the continent.[57]

Interestingly, the G8 adopted debt relief only after being nudged and cajoled into doing so by a coalition of civic associations from across the globe, perhaps most notably the Jubilee 2000 Coalition, which formed in 1997 to push for the cancellation of all unpayable and 'odious' debts in all countries. International creditor institutions had first attempted to reschedule debt repayments over longer periods of time during the late 1980s, when it became clear that many debtors were in danger of defaulting. When this didn't work, they started to design mechanisms that would actually reduce the level of debt, including terms agreed by the G7 in Toronto (1988), Trinidad (1990) and Naples (1994).

In light of these initiatives, in 1996 the World Bank and IMF created the Heavily Indebted Poor Countries (HIPC) initiative. To be eligible, states had to have a low GNI per capita (c. < $1,000), have what the World Bank and IMF considered unsustainable levels of debt, have a World Bank and IMF programme, and follow a (potentially six-year) programme of reforms based on IMF criteria. If eligible countries completed the HIPC programme, they would get a reduction of their debts down to what the IFIs considered a sustainable level. Thus the HIPC did not involve cancelling all debts but was an attempt to reduce debt to a sustainable level. In 1999, however, the HIPC initiative was reformed, and in 2005, following the G8's focus on Africa at its Gleneagles summit, a new scheme was established called the Multilateral Debt Relief Initiative. This allowed countries that had reached the HIPC 'completion point' to receive cancellation of most of their debts (up to certain cut-off dates) to the IMF, African Development Fund and the World Bank. Debts accrued to other lenders (e.g. banks and private companies) were not part of these schemes. Progress on reaching the HIPC 'completion point' was slow, taking at least six years in most cases, which meant that the historic target of the millennium was missed. By 2006, however, twenty-two African states had completed the HIPC programme.[58] The biggest African beneficiaries were Tanzania and Uganda, which saw between $3.5 billion and $4 billion of their debts cancelled. Interestingly, Kampala persistently broke the terms of its various credit agreements by spending large amounts of money on its intervention in the DRC war.[59]

The missing giant in this equation was Nigeria, which did not qualify for HIPC status. By 2005, Nigeria had accumulated total external debts of about $36 billion, of which over $30 billion was owed to the Paris Club. This translated into annual repayments of about $1.8 billion, nearly two-thirds of which went to four countries (Britain, France, Germany and Japan). After President Obasanjo assumed office and first indicated his willingness to consider a deal on debt relief, it took nearly seven years of wrangling – both between Nigeria and its creditors and among the creditors themselves – to produce a result.[60] In mid-2006 Nigeria completed a deal related to its Paris Club debt worth around $30 billion ($18 billion was cancelled and the remaining $12 billion was paid back upfront in two tranches). The Nigerian government duly satisfied its creditors that it had undertaken sufficient reform and managed to pay off the required portion of its debt upfront, largely because of the international context of high oil prices in 2005–6. Whether the deal will result in a better life for most Nigerians remains to be seen, but it made it harder for Nigeria's political elite to blame foreigners for their country's developmental problems.

While debt relief schemes were clearly a significant structural factor, the majority of attention during the post-Cold War period fell on the more traditional instrument of development assistance – i.e. using aid to boost long-term investment and growth and to reduce poverty. The rationale for such aid was that the world's poorest countries could not develop without it. Indeed, by the turn of the millennium it had become popular to talk of states being caught in 'poverty traps' – defined by Jeffrey Sachs as a 'condition, seemingly paradoxical, in which a poor country is simply too poor to achieve sustained economic growth'.[61] These countries were said to have no hope without external aid. In contrast to this view, the case of Somaliland since 1991 is instructive, because it demonstrates that a political community trapped in one of the world's poorest and conflict-ridden countries could achieve significant levels of development without the benefits of juridical sovereignty and the financial rewards that come with it.[62]

The story of international aid policies in Africa during this period is broadly one of a shift from various forms of conditionality to various forms of selectivity. Conditionality strategies were based on the idea that development loans and assistance would come with various conditions attached – i.e. aid would be given if potential recipients promised to do certain 'good' things, such as reform their economy. The most important example was the structural adjustment programmes implemented by the World Bank and IMF.[63] Between 1980 and 1989, some thirty-six countries in sub-Saharan Africa took out a total of 241 loans from the IFIs.[64] By the end of the Cold War, there were growing calls for various 'political conditionalities' to be implemented alongside the prescribed economic medicine, including greater concern for human rights, democracy – conceived in liberal terms – and 'good governance' (see also chapter 9).[65] As Christopher Clapham noted, the resulting adjustment packages were promoted by a broad alliance of actors:

> international financial institutions, seeking to bring about the capitalist transformation of African economies; Western governments, flexing their diplomatic muscles in the aftermath of the Cold War; Western public opinions, outraged at the brutality and corruption of at least a significant number of African regimes; and finally, at least vicariously, the African publics who were vociferously demonstrating their own discontent with the existing order.[66]

In relation to armed conflict, the central debate in the 1990s revolved around whether neoliberal adjustment packages should be pushed through in the immediate aftermath of war. Interestingly, reflecting specifically on the African experience during the mid-1990s, UN Secretary-General Kofi Annan warned that neoliberal adjustments could be highly detrimental to states struggling to make the transition from war to peace. 'Conflict prevention including post-conflict peace-building', Annan argued,

> may require an urgent infusion of funds to support a fragile State during a delicate political transition. It is particularly necessary to avoid situations in which conditionalities

are imposed that are antithetical to a peace process, or in which international financial institutions and the donor community cut off funds from a weak Government making, in good faith, a popularly supported effort to pursue reconciliation or implement peace agreements. Where economic reform is needed it is necessary to consider how best to provide for a 'peace-friendly' structural adjustment programme while easing the conditionality that normally accompanies loans from the [IFIs].[67]

Annan's concerns were part of a broader set of critiques about the problems of the liberal peacebuilding agenda. Here, the central argument was that, in the aftermath of armed conflict, international attempts to turn war-torn states into market democracies too quickly and on the cheap could have seriously destabilizing effects which significantly increased the risk of war recurrence.[68]

Selectivity strategies, on the other hand, were about offering aid to reward 'good' performance. Here, donors waited until *after* potential beneficiaries had altered their policies and then selected recipients on the basis of performance. A good example of this approach was the US government's Millennium Challenge Account (MCA). Announced in March 2002, this was the first major new US bilateral aid initiative in over forty years, whereby funds were to be allocated only to countries that 'rule justly, invest in their people, and encourage economic freedom'.[69] Selective approaches such as the MCA were increasingly camouflaged by the language of 'partnership' and 'local ownership'. But they were basically rather transparent ways of making sure donors put their money where they wanted rather than simply focusing on the poorest countries. The biggest headaches thus came for actors who claimed to allocate aid on the basis of needs but had to justify why they were assisting the continent's better performers rather than its poorest countries.[70] The other main problem was one of international coordination, inasmuch as the world's donors were not all selective in the same manner.[71]

Reflecting on the lessons of several decades of development assistance, analysts agreed that aid was neither a magic bullet nor a fool's errand; used wisely it could reduce poverty and stimulate economic growth, but usually only in 'good' policy environments.[72] This left donors with the conundrum of how to alleviate poverty in Africa's many 'bad' policy environments – situations of warfare being one of those environments, but also states with authoritarian and/or corrupt regimes. It meant that, for aid to achieve poverty reduction, donors had to 'take much more careful account of the local political dynamics that undermine development in the poorest countries'.[73]

Unfortunately, this rarely happened in post-Cold War Africa. For one thing, most aid still went into states with 'bad' policy environments. In their study of the practices of thirty-one bilateral and seventeen multilateral development agencies between 1972 and 2004, Easterly and Pfutze demonstrated that a preponderance of aid went to corrupt and authoritarian countries and to countries other than those with the lowest incomes. Based on Freedom House's categories[74] of unfree, partly free and free, they concluded:

Unfree countries have retained about a third of aid, while around 80 percent of aid goes to countries either partly free or unfree. These proportions have not changed much over time, despite democratization throughout the world and much donor rhetoric about promoting democracy. The only substantial movement can be found in the early 1990s, when the share going to unfree countries first dropped to about 20 percent, then increased to almost 50 percent, and then slowly fell back to its historic level of about 30 percent. This pattern occurs because countries essentially hand out aid to the same countries year after year, but the countries themselves have shifted their status from unfree to free and back to unfree. To put it another way, donor agencies appear to be unresponsive to political changes in recipient countries. Only in the last couple of years before 2004 is there a change in the share going to unfree countries that is explained by a change in donor behavior – and this change is in the wrong direction.[75]

Perhaps more than any other indicator, these trends showed that donor governments persistently ignored the considerable evidence that aid did not work in 'bad' policy environments. This suggests that factors other than poverty alleviation were driving the allocation of aid budgets in most Western governments.

The second persistent problem was the tendency of Western governments to argue that alleviating poverty in Africa required lots more aid. This was exemplified by Tony Blair's Commission for Africa (2004–5), which called for international society, especially the G8, to provide Africa with a massive increase in aid, debt relief, trade and investment – an additional $75 billion of resources by 2010 – as the primary means of stimulating economic development. What was required, the Commission argued, was 'a big push on many fronts at once'.[76] The problem with the 'big aid' approach was that it completely ignored both the history of aid allocations (noted above) and political incentives for elites in Africa's neopatrimonial states. As Richard Dowden observed, 'Africa has had around a trillion dollars in aid in the last 50 years, roughly $5,000 for every African living today if distributed evenly at today's prices. If aid were the solution to Africa's problems, it would be a rich continent by now.'[77] Another estimate noted that aid to Africa increased

by an astounding annual average of 5 percent in real terms between 1970 and 1995 . . . At their peak, the Marshall Plan resources accounted for some 2.5 percent of the GDP of countries like France and Germany. By 1996, excluding South Africa and Nigeria, the average African country received the equivalent of 12.3 percent of its GDP in ODA, an international transfer . . . unprecedented in historical terms.[78]

In sum, Africa's principal problem was not a lack of aid but a lack of genuine political reform. And yet, despite continually pointing out that governance was the key to Africa's development equation, Blair's Commission failed to outline a strategy for how to reform the continent's neopatrimonial states. Unfortunately, they completely ignored the work of analysts such as William Reno, who had shown how, in several West African countries, attempts to transplant neoliberal policies into neopatrimonial states produced some rather counter-productive, unintended and distinctly illiberal effects. As well as providing a lifeline for various corrupt patronage systems, the emphasis on privatization, deregulation and integration into the global economy actually encouraged leaders of Africa's neopatrimonial states to dismantle them further.[79] Instead of addressing such problems head on, donors turned instead to schemes based on selectively rewarding Africa's good performers.

The main framework in which this was done was the OECD's Paris Declaration on Aid Effectiveness (2005).[80] This reiterated that aid was likely to be effective only if it was based on the principles of country ownership, alignment, harmonization and mutual accountability.[81] The basic idea was that recipient states should propose programmes for donors to fund and that donors should harmonize their policies to reduce transaction costs. In other words, it advocated a selective approach favouring the most capable governments which had put forward approved programmes. It also suggested that aid should increasingly come in the form of budget support through the recipient state's own public finance and budgetary systems rather than through externally managed discrete projects (discussed below). Aid should thus be used to support well-meaning but struggling governments stuck in what Sachs had called the 'poverty trap'. The problem was that most of Africa's stagnant low-income countries were not so virtuous; they were usually rather authoritarian and had no track record of struggling to achieve genuinely national development.[82]

The other important and often divisive issue was budget support as a means of aid delivery. For the UK, one of the strongest advocates of budget support, this approach had several attractions.[83] First, it was based on the notion of partnerships between donor and recipient rather than donor-imposed conditions. Second, it was an efficient form of lending because it reduced transactions costs. Third, when administered selectively it was viewed as supporting those states which had adopted 'good governance' reforms.[84]

Of course, when aid was deposited directly into the coffers of the recipient government, local financial accountability was crucial. As Joel Barkan correctly observed, budget support amounted to 'an expression of trust' on the part of the donor government that the recipient regime would live up to its stated objectives with regard to poverty reduction and financial accountability.[85] Thus, when recipient governments held up their end of the bargain, budget support could be an efficient and effective means of aid delivery and building local capacity. However, it was also susceptible to a number of limitations and problems. First, although promising macro-economic conditions are an important part of ensuring poverty alleviation, they are not sufficient on their own and thus could not guarantee poverty reduction. Second, especially when aid represented a significant proportion of the recipient's GDP, such support could perpetuate aid dependency by reducing incentives for the recipient regime to generate other sources of revenue such as through local taxation. The third and arguably most fundamental problem occurred when the recipient regime betrayed donor trust by reneging on its promises. When this occurred, budget support programmes were left hostage to the local political context.[86]

It was through these mechanisms that budget support helped sustain bad governance in several states. In Uganda, for example, British budget support helped facilitate President Museveni's gradual roll-back of democracy when, in 2005, he repealed the ban on a third elected term in office for the president. That same year Britain was put in a similarly awkward position when Meles Zenawi's regime in Ethiopia killed approximately 200 people and imprisoned thousands more in the aftermath of the country's fraudulent elections. It was particularly bad timing for Britain because Meles was at the time a member of Blair's Commission for Africa and pontificating about the importance of good governance.

Conclusion

Although both the humanitarian international and the international development business grew considerably after the Cold War, even on their own terms neither of them provided an effective response to the problems of war and underdevelopment in Africa. With regard to development, several points are worth making. First, in absolute terms, the fact that only one African state with a GNI per capita over $1,000 suffered a state–based armed conflict after the Cold War might mean there is merit in pushing states above this threshold *regardless of the country's political system*. Second, the fact that economic reversals also appeared significant suggests development policies should be designed to enhance the resilience of Africa's local economies from unexpected shocks. However, and third, as the Rwandan case illustrates, whatever policies are pursued, this must be done with a great sensitivity to the local political context and the survival strategies of the incumbent regime.

The Rwandan genocide and its deadly fallout in Zaire/the DRC also held ominous lessons for the humanitarian international. But there were plenty more troublesome cases where relief agencies struggled to overcome the challenges thrown up by the incumbent regimes in Africa's war zones. Their job was also made more difficult by a variety of rebels and external governments and by their own organizational cultures. In this complicated context, de Waal's three rules for representing humanitarian action remain as pertinent today as they were in the mid-1990s when he wrote them:

> The first is: do not obscure power relations. In other words, be frank that relief agencies are service contractors to Western donors, are pursuing their own institutional interests and implicitly supporting the host authorities. The second is, do not claim to have long-term solutions. Do not speak about 'justice' or 'long-term development', and still less make any claims that current humanitarian activity is helping to achieve these goals. The third is, do not seek the media limelight. A high media profile risks the severe danger that humanitarian action will be misrepresented, for example it will be inflated, distorted or used as an alibi by donors.[87]

Conclusion

This book had two principal aims: to understand why Africa experienced so many armed conflicts after the Cold War and to examine the main international attempts to end them.

On the first question, analysis quickly runs into the perennial philosophical headache of how to combine general ideas about the underlying conditions that increase the likelihood of warfare with more specific trigger factors that spark particular wars. The answer lies in using insights from quantitative and qualitative research. Conceptual frameworks which aim to explain warfare in general and the more sophisticated quantitative approaches are good at providing clues about how best to narrow down the list of ingredients which played important roles across a variety of Africa's armed conflicts. On their own, however, general frameworks risk downplaying or ignoring local nuances and idiosyncrasies, while quantitative studies are built on unreliable foundations and are open to widely different interpretations of the data. Consequently, a sophisticated understanding of one of Africa's particular war recipes requires the analyst to move beyond the abstract level to more historical and sociological forms of study.

Part II of this book attempted to do this by examining five of the most widely debated ingredients that were said to have played significant roles in many of Africa's war recipes: governance, resources, sovereignty, ethnicity and religion. Based on my survey of these ingredients between 1990 and 2009, I submit that, at the abstract level, students interested in understanding why Africa's wars break out could do far worse than focus their attention, at least initially, upon the dynamics within the continent's neopatrimonial regimes, the political struggles related to issues of sovereignty and self-determination, and the manipulation of ethnic identities by political elites (see chapters 3, 5 and 6). The discussions in chapters 4 and 7 suggest that analysts should be more sceptical about viewing so-called natural resources and religion as principal ingredients in the outbreak of Africa's wars. Nevertheless, both of these affected the dynamics of at least some armed conflicts in important ways. They are therefore a more pertinent source of study for those interested in why particular armed conflicts endure and assume certain forms over time.

If there is a thread that links Africa's conflict dynamics, I suggest that it is to be found in the nature of the continent's state–society complexes, especially the dynamics associated with the politics of regime survival in weak states. In terms of the levels-of-analysis framework offered in chapter 2, it is my sense that the political strategies pursued by regimes to maintain their privileged status provided the critical link between important local-level dynamics and the various regional and globalizing networks, structures and processes. When their status and legitimacy was directly threatened, the tendency for regimes to respond by instrumentalizing disorder and using violence to try and restore their authority only exacerbated the risks of war. Once armed conflict began, it was these same dynamics which often prevented rebels being comprehensively defeated and which encouraged plunder and the manipulation of extreme ethnic and/or religious bigotry to marshal support. Either way, it was usually ordinary civilians who bore the brunt of the violence.

Discriminatory and oppressive systems of governance which lacked effective means of resolving conflicts without resorting to violence were thus an important ingredient in every one of Africa's wars. Reading the more historical and sociological studies of many of these conflicts, one cannot help but be struck by the importance of political structures. Whether it was the problems faced by regimes in weak states which were unable to assemble armed forces capable of fending off even small rebellions, or the challenges raised by powerful but oppressive state institutions which unleashed genocidal campaigns on their own people, governance was a central ingredient in Africa's war recipes. Understanding who rules, according to what (formal and informal) rules, and the rules by which rulers are changed should be at the heart of conflict analysis. In that sense, I strongly endorse Christopher Clapham's point that 'The place to start trying to understand any political crisis is always with the government in power.'[1]

As the structures which frame political incentives and opportunities and determine how resources should be allocated, systems of governance are crucial to understanding and responding to war because they are fundamentally about conflict management. Indeed, one leading theorist in the field of conflict resolution summed up the situation by saying 'Governance is conflict management.'[2] This is why international actors must reflect upon how their policies can help to demilitarize governance structures in Africa's war-torn and weak states.[3] It will also mean revisiting the fundamental question of how much effort should be invested in retaining Africa's current international borders rather than supporting political communities that currently lack juridical sovereignty but may actually work far better for their people.[4]

As the analysis in part III of this book illustrated, regime political strategies also had huge repercussions for the major international attempts to end Africa's wars, namely, the effort to construct a new African peace and security architecture (APSA), as well as a variety of peacemaking, peacekeeping and assistance initiatives.

While the attempts to build the new APSA made some notable progress, particularly after the creation of the AU's Peace and Security Council in 2004, it clearly did not have a transformational effect on the political dynamics of organized violence on the continent. Put simply, these new institutions and instruments did not fundamentally alter the nature of politics in Africa's weak states or the international politics of statehood. Nor did they put a stop to the excesses of neopatrimonialism or the manipulation of ethnicity, and to a lesser extent religion, by power-hungry elites. They did, however, push a more restrictive definition of the means by which it was legitimate to gain entry into the club of African sovereigns. Since the late 1990s the OAU/AU has taken a more consistent stance against coups as a mechanism to gain membership of the African society of states. And in the last couple of years the AU has explored how it might operationalize a broader definition of what it calls 'unconstitutional changes of government' to include electoral fraud and the manipulation of state constitutions to increase the length of presidential terms. To the extent that these initiatives delegitimize violence as a tool of politics, they were a welcome step in the right direction. But, as the crises in Darfur, Somalia and elsewhere demonstrate, they also helped to obscure the continued lack of substantive political consensus within the AU over how to apply its new principles and instruments in response to specific events.

When it came to the various international peacemaking initiatives discussed in chapter 9, most of them proved unable to transform local neopatrimonial dynamics. As a consequence, most mediation efforts ended up having to embrace patronage politics to the extent necessary to ensure that the system did not revert to war and that those candidates at the top of the patrimonial pyramid did not engage in excessive levels of corruption and oppression. In the majority of cases, it was local rather than external actors who retained the greatest ability to shape outcomes on the ground. In comparison to local political elites, most external actors lacked staying power, sufficient leverage and sometimes political acumen. Nor were they usually willing to invest the amount of time, effort and resources that it would take to acquire such things. The rather depressing conclusion that follows is that, if powerful local groups really want to wage war, external forces will have a tough time trying to stop them. If correct, this means that most of the keys required to unlock the secret of building stable peace on the continent are held by local actors who are concerned primarily with local issues. In such circumstances, conflict resolution will not succeed unless these local issues are effectively addressed and local actors are persuaded, incentivized or coerced into adopting less violent forms of politics.

In sum, the top-down peacemaking of elite bargains will not offer any quick fixes to Africa's wars. Although it will take longer and be even more difficult, peacemaking efforts should be reconceptualized as an ongoing process of bargaining designed to demilitarize politics and the institutions that sustained the war. The long-term aim of this process is to delegitimize the idea that violence offers the surest route to status, wealth and political power. A good place to start is with the security sector, or what Robert Bates called 'the specialists in violence'.[5]

In such challenging political contexts, the numerous peacekeeping operations analysed in chapter 10 were only ever likely to address some of the worst symptoms of armed conflict. Indeed, most operations were so badly resourced that they could not cope with the symptoms of war, let alone address the underlying conditions. Over the course of the post-Cold War period, the world's peacekeeping organizations did become more professional, and greater numbers of peacekeepers were deployed to Africa's war zones. But they were given an increasingly daunting set of tasks and remained plagued by a perennial gap between means and ends. Closing this gap should be the fundamental starting point for any future reform initiatives.

A similar story was evident in the international attempts to provide humanitarian assistance and establish development projects in Africa's conflict zones. Both the humanitarian international and the development industry examined in chapter 11 grew larger and more professionalized between 1990 and 2009. But neither of these instruments proved capable of transforming political dynamics within neopatrimonial regimes, persuading the belligerents of the merits of abiding by humanitarian principles or pursuing genuinely national development policies. Indeed, for much of this period, too many people succumbed to disease and malnutrition and development indicators in too many African states went backwards. Although a state's level of wealth is clearly not synonymous with its prospects for peace, it would be a worthwhile experiment to see whether pushing African states above a GNI per capita over $1,000 really can help immunize them from armed conflict.

Taken together, the preceding insights add up to a hugely daunting agenda that will require considerable time, money and, most of all, political effort. Nevertheless, as one African proverb has it: peace may be costly but it is worth the expense.

Appendices

Abbreviations for the Appendices

AC	Action Congress (Nigeria)
ADC–IB	May 23 Democratic Alliance for Change–Ibrahim Bahanga faction (Mali)
ADF	Alliance of Democratic Forces (Uganda)
AFDL	Alliance of Democratic Forces for the Liberation of Congo–Zaire
AFRC	Armed Forces Revolutionary Council (Sierra Leone)
AIS	Islamic Salvation Army (Algeria)
ANC	African National Congress (South Africa)
ANPP	All Nigeria People's Party
AQIM	Al-Qa'ida in the Islamic Maghreb
ARDUF	Afar Revolutionary Democratic Unity Front (Ethiopia)
ARLA	Revolutionary Army for the Liberation of Azaouad (Mali)
ARPCT	Alliance for the Restoration of Peace and Counter-Terrorism (Somalia)
ARS	Alliance for the Reliberation of Somalia
ATNMC	North Mali Tuareg Alliance for Change
AWB	Afrikaner Resistance Movement (South Africa)
AZAPO	Azanian People's Organization (South Africa)
CNDD	National Council for the Defence of Democracy (Burundi)
CNDD–FDD	National Council for the Defence of Democracy–Forces for the Defence of Democracy (Burundi)
CNDP	National Congress for the Defence of the People (DRC)
CNR	National Council for Recovery (Chad)
CODETA	Cape Organization for a Democratic Taxi Association (South Africa)
CPJP	Convention of Patriots for Justice and Peace (CAR)
CRA	Coordinated Armed Resistance (Niger)
CSNPD	Committee of National Revival for Peace and Democracy (Chad)

EIJM–AS	Eritrean Islamic Jihad Movement–Abu Suhail faction
EPLF	Eritrean People's Liberation Front
EPRDF	Ethiopian People's Revolutionary Democratic Front
FAPC	People's Armed Forces of Congo (DRC)
FARF	Armed Forces of the Federal Republic (Chad)
FARF	Federalist Republican Forces (DRC)
FARS	Revolutionary Armed Forces of the Sahara (Niger)
FDLR	Democratic Liberation Forces of Rwanda
FDR	Democratic Front for Renewal (Niger)
FIAA	Islamic Arab Front of Azawad (Mali)
FIS	Islamic Salvation Front (Algeria)
FLAA	Aïr and Azawad Liberation Front (Niger)
FLEC–FAC	Front for the Liberation of the Enclave of Cabinda– Armed Forces of Cabinda (Angola)
FN	New Forces (Côte d'Ivoire)
FN–IC	New Forces–Ibrahim Coulibaly faction (Côte d'Ivoire)
FNI	Front for National Integration (DRC)
FPLA	Popular Liberation Front of Azawad (Mali)
FPR	Rwandan Patriotic Front
FROLINA	National Liberation Front (Burundi)
FRPI	Patriotic Force of Resistance in Ituri (DRC)
FRUD	Front for the Restoration of Unity and Democracy
FUCD	Rally for Democracy and Liberty (Chad)
GIA	Armed Islamic Group (Algeria)
GSPC	Salafist Group for Preaching and Combat (Algeria)
IFP	Inkatha Freedom Party (South Africa)
INPFL	Independent National Patriotic Front of Liberia
JEM	Justice and Equality Movement (Sudan)
JVA	Jubba Valley Alliance (Somalia)
LPC	Liberia Peace Council
LRA	Lord's Resistance Army (Uganda)
LURD	Liberians United for Reconciliation and Democracy
MAGRIVI	Farmers Mutual Society of Virunga (DRC)
MDD	Movement for Democracy and Development (Chad)
MDJT	Movement for Democracy and Justice in Chad
MFDC	Movement of the Democratic Forces of the Casamance
MIA	Islamic Armed Movement (Algeria)
MILOCI	Movement for the Liberation of Western Ivory Coast
MJP	Movement for Justice and Peace (Côte d'Ivoire)
MLC	Movement for the Liberation of Congo (DRC)
MNJ	Niger Movement for Justice
MODEL	Movement for Democracy in Liberia
MPA	Anjouan People's Movement
MPA	Popular Movement for the Liberation of Azawad (Mali)

MPA–SOC	Anjouan People's Movement–Said Omar Chamassi faction
MPCI	Patriotic Movement of Côte d'Ivoire
MPGK	Patriotic Movement of the Ghanda Koye (Mali)
MPIGO	Ivorian Movement for the Greater West
MPS	Patriotic Salvation Movement (Chad)
NDA	National Democratic Alliance (Sudan)
NDPVF	Niger Delta People's Volunteer Force (Nigeria)
NDV	Niger Delta Vigilantes (Nigeria)
NPFL	National Patriotic Front of Liberia
NRF	National Redemption Front (Sudan)
OLF	Oromo Liberation Front (Ethiopia)
ONLF	Ogaden National Liberation Front (Ethiopia)
Palipehutu–FNL	Party for the Liberation of the Hutu People–Forces for National Liberation (Burundi)
Palipehutu–FNL–LP	Party for the Liberation of the Hutu People–Forces for National Liberation–Lovers of Peace faction (Burundi)
PALIR	Armed People for the Liberation of Rwanda
PARECO	Coalition of Congolese Patriotic Resistance (DRC)
PDF	Popular Defence Force (Sudan)
PDP	People's Democratic Party (Nigeria)
PUSIC	Party for Unity and Safeguarding of the Integrity of Congo (DRC)
RAFD	Rally of Democratic Forces (Chad)
RCD	Congolese Rally for Democracy (DRC)
RCD–K–ML	Congolese Rally for Democracy-Kisangani-Liberation Movement (DRC)
RCD–ML	Congolese Rally for Democracy-Liberation Movement (DRC)
RCD–N	Congolese Rally for Democracy-National (DRC)
RENAMO	Mozambican National Resistance
RFDG	Rally of Democratic Forces of Guinea
RRA	Rahanweyn Resistance Army (Somalia)
RUF	Revolutionary United Front (Sierra Leone)
SDM	Somali Democratic Movement
SLDF	Sabaot Land Defence Force (Kenya)
SLM/A	Sudan Liberation Movement/Army
SLM/A–MM	Sudan Liberation Movement/Army–Minni Minawi faction
SNA	Somali National Alliance
SNF	Somali National Front
SNF–ADRA	Somali National Front-Ali Dheere and Rer Ahmad subclans

SNF–HRHHY	Somali National Front–Hawarsame Rer Hasan and Habar Ya'qub subclans
SNF–MSAB	Somali National Front–Mohamed Sheikh Ali Buraleh faction
SNM	Somalia National Movement
SPLM/A	Sudan People's Liberation Movement/Army
SPM	Somali Patriotic Movement
SRRC	Somali Reconciliation and Restoration Council
SSDF	Somali Salvation Democratic Front
SSDF	Southern Sudan Defence Force
SSNM	Southern Somalia National Movement
UFDD	Union Force for Democracy and Development (Chad)
UFDR	Union of Democratic Forces for Unity (CAR)
UFR	Union of Forces for the Resistance (Chad)
UFRA	Union of Forces of the Armed Resistance (Niger)
UIC	Union of Islamic Courts (Somalia)
ULIMO	United Liberation Movement of Liberia for Democracy
UNITA	National Union for Total Independence of Angola
UNPP	United Nigeria People's Party
UNRF II	Uganda National Rescue Front II
UPA	Union of Angolan Peoples
UPC	Union of Congolese Patriots (DRC)
USC/SNA	United Somali Congress/Somalia National Alliance
USC/SSA	United Somali Congress/Somali Salvation Alliance
USC/SSA–OMF	United Somali Congress/Somali Salvation Alliance–Omar Mohamed Mohamud 'Finish' faction
WNBF	West Nile Bank Front (Uganda)

APPENDIX A   State-based armed conflicts in Africa, 1990–2009

Conflict	Years of violence	Active dyads/years
Algeria	1991–2009	Govt vs AIS 1992–7 Govt vs AQIM 1999–2009 Govt vs FIS (AIS) 1992–7 Govt vs FIS (MIA) 1992–7 Govt vs GIA 1993–2003 Govt vs GSPC 1999–2009 Govt vs MIA 1992–7 Govt vs Takfir wa'l Hijra 1991
Angola	1990–5, 1998–2002	Govt vs UNITA 1990–5, 1998–2002
Angola (Cabinda)	1991, 1994, 1996–8, 2002, 2004, 2007, 2009	Govt vs FLEC–FAC 1994, 1996–8, 2002, 2004, 2007, 2009 Govt vs FLEC–Renewed 1991, 1994, 1997, 2002

APPENDIX A   *Continued*

Conflict	Years of violence	Active dyads/years
Burundi	1991–2, 1994–2006, 2008	Govt vs CNDD 1994–8 Govt vs CNDD–FDD 1998–2003 Govt vs Frolina 1997 Govt vs Palipehutu 1991–2 Govt vs Palipehutu–FNL 1997–2006, 2008
Cameroon–Nigeria	1996	Govt vs Govt 1996
Central African Republic	2001–2, 2006, 2009	Govt vs CPJP 2009 Govt vs forces of Francois Bozize 2002 Govt vs military faction (André Kolingba) 2001 Govt vs UFDR 2006
Chad	1990–4, 1997–2002, 2005–9	Govt vs Alliance National 2008 Govt vs CNR 1992–4 Govt vs CSNPD 1992–4 Govt vs FARF 1997–8 Govt vs Chad National Front 1992–4 Govt vs FUCD 2005–6 Govt vs Islamic Legion 1990 Govt vs MDD 1991–3, 1997 Govt vs MDJT 1999–2002 Govt vs Maldoum Bada Abbas faction 1991 Govt vs MPS 1990 Govt vs RAFD 2006 Govt vs UFDD 2006–7 Govt vs UFR 2009
Comoros (Anjouan)	1997	Govt vs MPA/Republic of Anjouan 1997
Congo	1993–4, 1997–9, 2002	Govt vs Cobras 1997 Govt vs Cocoyes 1997–9 Govt vs Ninjas 1993–4, 1998–9 Govt vs Ntsiloulous 1998–9, 2002
Côte d'Ivoire	2002–4	Govt vs FN 2004 Govt vs MJP 2002–3 Govt vs MPCI 2002 Govt vs MPIGO 2002–3
Democratic Republic of Congo–Zaire	1996–2001, 2006–8	Govt vs AFDL 1996–7 Govt vs CNDP 2006–8 Govt vs MLC 1998–2001 Govt vs RCD 1998–2001 Govt vs RCD–ML 1999–2000
Democratic Republic of Congo (Kingdom of Kongo)	2007–8	Govt vs Bundu dia Kongo 2007–8
Djibouti	1991–4, 1999	Govt vs FRUD 1991–4 Govt vs FRUD–Ahmed Dini faction 1999

Continued

APPENDIX A *Continued*

Conflict	Years of violence	Active dyads/years
Djibouti–Eritrea	2008	Govt vs Govt 2008
Eritrea	1997, 1999, 2003	Govt vs EIJM–AS 1997, 1999, 2003
Eritrea–Ethiopia	1998–2000	Govt vs Govt 1998–2000
Ethiopia	1990–1	Govt vs EPRDF 1990–1
Ethiopia (Afar)	1996	Govt vs ARDUF 1996
Ethiopia (Eritrea)	1990–1	Govt vs EPLF 1990–1
Ethiopia (Ogaden)	1994–6, 1999, 2000–2, 2004–9	Govt vs Al-Itahad al-Islami 1995–6, 1999 Govt vs ONLF 1994, 1996, 1999, 2000–2, 2004–9
Ethiopia (Oromiya)	1990–2, 1994–5, 1998–2009	Govt vs OLF 1990–2, 1994–5, 1998–2009
Guinea	2000–1	Govt vs RFDG 2000–1
Guinea-Bissau	1998–9	Govt vs military junta 1998–9
Lesotho	1998	Govt vs military faction 1998
Liberia	1990, 2000–3	Govt vs INPFL 1990 Govt vs LURD 2000–3 Govt vs MODEL 2003 Govt vs NPFL 1990
Mali (Azawad)	1990, 1994, 2007–9	Govt vs ADC–IB 2007–9 Govt vs ATNMC 2007–9 Govt vs FIAA 1994 Govt vs MPA 1990
Mozambique	1990–2	Govt vs RENAMO 1990–2
Niger	1991–2, 1997, 2007–8	Govt vs FLAA 1991–2 Govt vs MNJ 2007–8 Govt vs UFRA 1997
Niger (Air and Azawad)	1994	Govt vs CRA 1994
Niger (Eastern Niger)	1995, 1997	Govt vs FARS 1997 Govt vs FDR 1995
Nigeria	2009	Govt vs Boko Haram 2009
Nigeria (Niger Delta)	2004	Govt vs NDPVF 2004
Nigeria (Northern Nigeria)	2004	Govt vs Ahlul Sunnah Jamaa 2004
Rwanda	1990–4, 1997–2002, 2009	Govt vs FDLR 1997–2002, 2009 Govt vs FPR 1990–4 Govt vs PALIR 1997–2002, 2009
Senegal (Casamance)	1990, 1992–3, 1995, 1997–8, 2000–1, 2003	Govt vs MFDC 1990, 1992–3, 1995, 1997–8, 2000–1, 2003

APPENDIX A *Continued*

Conflict	Years of violence	Active dyads/years
Sierra Leone	1991–2000	Govt vs AFRC 1997–9 Govt vs Kamajors 1997–8 Govt vs RUF 1991–2000 Govt vs West Side Boys 2000
Somalia	1990–6, 2001–2, 2006–9	Govt vs al-Shabaab 2008–9 Govt vs ARS–UIC 2006–8 Govt vs Harakat Ras Kamboni 2008 Govt vs Hizbul Islam 2009 Govt vs SNM 1990–1 Govt vs SPM 1990–1 Govt vs SRRC 2001–2 Govt vs USC 1990–1 Govt vs USC faction 1991–6 Govt vs USC/SNA 1991–6
Sudan	1990–2009	Govt vs JEM 2003–4, 2007–9 Govt vs NDA 1996–2001 Govt vs NRF 2006 Govt vs SLM/A 2003–6, 2008–9 Govt vs SLM/A–MM 2006 Govt vs SLM/A–Unity 2007–8 Govt vs SPLM/A 1990–2004
Uganda	1990–2, 1994–2009	Govt vs ADF 1996–2002, 2007 Govt vs LRA 1990–1, 1994–8, 2000–9 Govt vs UNRF II 1997 Govt vs UPA 1990–2 Govt vs WNBF 1996

Source: UCDP, at www.pcr.uu.se/gpdatabase/search.php.

APPENDIX B Non-state armed conflicts in Africa, 1990–2009

Country	Years of violence	Active dyads/years	Fatalities (best estimate)
Algeria	1995, 1997–8	GIA El Ahd vs GIA El Khadra 1998 GIA El Forkane vs GIA El Khadra 1998 AIS vs GIA 1995, 1997–8	62 56 326
Burundi	1997, 2000, 2003–4, 2007	CNDD vs Palipehutu–FNL 1997 CNDD–FDD vs Palipehutu–FNL 2003–4 FDLR vs Palipehutu 2000 Palipehutu–FNL vs Palipehutu–FNL (LP) 2007	224 97 100 50
Cameroon	1991–4, 1998	Bafanji vs Balikumbat 1998 Banya vs Foulbe, Hausa 1991 Choa Arabs vs Kotoko 1992–4	51 50 106
CAR	1996	Baya vs Yakoma 1996	40

Continued

APPENDIX B *Continued*

Country	Years of violence	Active dyads/years	Fatalities (best estimate)
Chad	2000, 2006–7	Darsalim vs Kibede 2006	140
		Khozam vs Oulad Rachid 2000	72
		Zaghawa vs Tama 2007	126
Comoros	1998	MPA/Republic of Anjouan vs MPA–SOC 1998	40
Côte d'Ivoire	2000, 2002–5	Dioula vs Krou 2000, 2002–5	476
		FN vs FN–IC 2004	134
		FN vs MILOCI 2005	28
Democratic Republic of Congo	1993, 1995– 2004, 2007–8	ADFL vs FDLR 1997	120
		AFDL vs Mayi Mayi 1997	34
		Banyarwanda vs Hunde Nyanga 1993	3,051
		Alur vs Lendu 2002–3	140
		Bangadi militia vs LRA 2008	27
		Bena Kapuya vs Bena Nsimba 2007	25
		CNDP vs PARECO 2008	64
		FAPC vs FNI 2004	51
		FDLR vs RCD 1998	47
		FNI vs PUSIC 2003	67
		FNI vs Union of Congolese Patriots 2003	729
		FNI, FRPI vs Union of Congolese Patriots 2003	71
		Hema vs Lendu 1999–2003	4,267
		Hunde vs Hutu 1993, 1995–6	738
		Mayi Mayi CNDD–FDD vs RCD 2000	97
		Mayi Mayi CNDD–FDD, FDLR vs RCD 1999–2001	120
		Mayi Mayi vs RCD–ML 1999	60
		MLC vs RCD–K–ML 2001	40
		RCD vs FARF 2002	221
		RCD vs Mayi Mayi 1998–2000, 2002–3	683
		RCD vs RDC(PM) 2002	221
		RCD–K–ML vs Union of Congolese Patriots 2002	216
		RCD–ML vs RCD–K–ML 2000	35
		RCD–K–ML vs RCD–N 2003	45
		RCD–K–ML vs MLC, RCD–N 2002	158
Djibouti	1991	Afar, Oromo vs Issa 1991	40
Ethiopia	1991–2, 1998, 2000–9	Afar tribe vs Issa tribe 2002	75
		Afar tribe vs Kereyou tribe 2002–3	69
		Al-Shabaab vs ONLF 2007	40
		Amaro clan vs Guji clan 2006	30
		Amhara vs Oromo 1991, 2000–1	233
		Anuak vs Highlanders 2004	114
		Anuak tribe vs Dinka tribe (Ethiopia) 2002	41
		Anuak tribe vs Nuer (Ethiopia) 2002–3	137
		Arbore vs Borana 1992	317
		Bi'idyahan clan vs Ismail clan 2003	280
		Borana vs Degodia 1998	156

APPENDIX B *Continued*

Country	Years of violence	Active dyads/years	Fatalities (best estimate)
		Borana vs Garre subclan 2001	60
		Borana clan vs Gabra clan 1992	201
		Borana, Guji vs Geri 2000	72
		Borana vs Geri 2009	31
		Borana clan vs Guji clan 2006	101
		Borana clan vs Konso 2008	46
		Burji clan vs Guji clan 2006	37
		Dawa clan vs Gura clan 2003	55
		Derashe vs Konso 2008	33
		Derashe vs Zeyle 2001	40
		Dizi tribe vs Surma tribe 2002	35
		Gabra clan vs Guji clan 2005	43
		Gedo vs Guji 1998	700
		Gumuz vs Oromo 2008	145
		Issa vs Oromo 2000	40
		Majerteen subclan vs Ogaden clan 2004	54
		Marehan subclan vs Majerteen subclan 2006	100
		Me'en vs Suri 2001	34
		Merille vs Turkana 2005, 2009	72
		Murle vs Nuer (Ethiopia) 2006	59
		Nyangatom, Toposa vs Turkana 2006	58
		Ogaden clan vs Sheikhal clan 2002	435
		Oromo tribes vs Somali clans 2003, 2005	135
		Reer Liban vs Reer Samatar 1992	100
Ghana	1992, 1994, 1995, 2000–2, 2008	Abudu clan vs Andani clan 2002	36
		Kusasi vs Mamprusi 2000–1, 2008	119
		Gonja vs Nawuri Konkomba 1992	63
		Konkomba vs Nanumba 1995	109
		Dagomba, Gonja, Nanumba vs Konkomba 1994	2,000
Guinea	2000	Torma vs Torma Manian 2000	31
Kenya	1992–2001, 2005–6, 2008	Ajuran vs Garre subclan 2000	78
		Borana vs Gabra 2005	68
		Borana vs Samburu 2001	30
		Dassanetch vs Turkana 1997, 2000, 2005	206
		Dongiro vs Turkana 2006	48
		Garre subclan vs Murule subclan 2005, 2008	92
		Jie Karimojong vs Matheniko Karimojong, Turkana 1999	40
		Jie Karimojong vs Turkana 2008	40
		Kalenjin vs Kikuyu Kisii 1994	30
		Kalenjin vs Kikuyu 1992–3, 1998, 2008	274
		Kalenjin vs Luhya 1992	45
		Kalenjin vs Luo, Kisii 1992	40
		Kalenjin vs Kisii 2008	81
		Kikuyu vs Maasai 1993	39

Continued

APPENDIX B *Continued*

Country	Years of violence	Active dyads/years	Fatalities (best estimate)
		Kisii vs Maasai 1997	57
		Luo vs Kikuyu 2008	42
		Marakwet vs Pokot 2001	44
		Mooreland vs SLDF 2008	32
		Nandi vs Pokot 1998	35
		Nyangatom vs Turkana 1993, 2006	234
		Orma, Wardei vs Pokomo 2001	66
		Pokot, Samburu vs Turkana 1996	51
		Pokot vs Turkana 1995, 1999, 2006, 2008	262
		SLDF vs Mooreland 2008	32
		Toposa vs Turkana 2008	25
Liberia	1990–2, 1994–6	INPFL vs NPFL 1990	43
		LPC vs NPFL 1995	50
		NPFL vs ULIMO 1991–2	370
		NPFL vs ULIMO–Roosevelt Johnson faction 1996	2,000
		ULIMO–Roosevelt Johnson faction vs ULIMO–Alhaji Kromah faction 1994	303
Madagascar	2002, 2009	Didier Ratsiraka vs Marc Ravalomanana 2002	79
		Andry Rajoelina vs Marc Ravalomanana 2009	82
Mali	1994, 1997, 1999	Arabs vs Kounta 1999	59
		FIAA vs Azawad People's Movement 1994	30
		Puelh vs Touareg 1997	34
Mozambique	1991	Naparama vs Renamo 1991	63
Nigeria	1991–4, 1996– 2006, 2008–9	AC vs PDP 2008	33
		AD vs PDP 2003	35
		Adoni vs Ogoni 1993	962
		Afor vs Fulani 2009	33
		Almajiri vs Kalakato 1993	50
		Aguleri vs Umuleri 1999	320
		Anagutas, Afisare, Birom vs Fulani Hausa 2001	165
		Anagutas Birom vs Fulani, Hausa 2002	99
		ANPP vs PDP 2003–4, 2008	859
		Azara vs Tiv 2001	27
		Bachama vs Fulani, Hausa 2004	132
		Bini vs Urhobo 1998	50
		Christians vs Muslims 1991–2, 2000, 2006	560
		Efik vs Ibibio 2000	90
		Eleme vs Okrika 1999	25
		Fulani vs Karimbjo 1996	80
		Fulani vs Mambila 2002	50
		Fulani vs Tarok 2004	1,223
		Fulani vs Wurukum 1999	100
		Fulani vs Yugur 2003	40
		Gamai vs Pan 2006	25
		Hausa vs Igbo 2000, 2002	620
		Hausa vs Igbo, Yoruba 2001	200
		Hause vs Kataf 1992	46

APPENDIX B   *Continued*

Country	Years of violence	Active dyads/years	Fatalities (best estimate)
		Hausa vs Ninzam 1999	100
		Hausa vs Tarok 2002	35
		Hausa vs Yoruba 1998, 1999, 2002	253
		Ife vs Modakeke 1997–8, 2000	239
		Igbo vs Tiv 1998	32
		Ijaw vs Ilaje 1999	70
		Ijaw, Urhobo vs Itsekiri 1999	45
		Ijaw vs Itsekiri 1997, 1999, 2003	584
		Ijaw vs Urhobo 1998	30
		Izzi vs Ukele 2005	100
		Junkun vs Tiv 1991–2	130
		Kwala vs Tiv 2000	50
		NDPVF vs NDV 2004	63
		Oditkas vs Ogoni 1992	60
		Ogoni vs Okoloma 1994	30
		Ogoni vs Okrika 1993	90
		PDP supporters vs UNPP supporters 2003	31
Senegal	2006	MFDC Front Nord–Magne Diémé faction vs MFDC–Salif Sadio faction 2006	124
Somalia	1990–2006, 2008–9	Abgal clan vs Galgalo subclan of Habar Gidir (Hawiye) 1990	50
		Aulihan subclan of Ogaden clan (Darod) vs Mohamed Zubeir subclan of Ogaden clan (Darod) 2000	41
		Abdalle subclan of Habar Awal clan (Isaaq) vs Aidagalla subclan of Habar Garhadjis clan (Isaaq) 1996	34
		Abdalleh-Agon-Yar subclan of Abgal clan (Hawiye) vs Eli-Agon-Yar subclan of Abgal clan (Hawiye) 2000	26
		Abdulleh-Galmaha subclan of Abgal clan (Hawiye) vs Kabaloh subclan of Abgal clan (Hawiye) 2001	33
		Ayr subclan of Habar Gidir clan (Hawiye) vs Sa'ad subclan of Habar Gidir clan (Hawiye) 2001	50
		Abdalle-Aroneh subclan of Abgal clan (Hawiye) vs Eli-Omar subclan of Abgal clan (Hawiye) 1999	31
		Habar Jaalo clan (Isaaq) vs Habar Yunis subclan of Habar Garhadjis clan (Isaaq) 1992	500
		Abdirizak Bihi vs Ahmed Sheikh Buraleh 2001	33
		Hussein Ali Ahmed vs Muse Sudi Yalahow 1999	113
		Abdurahman Ahmed Ali 'Tur' vs Mohamed Ibrahim Egal 1994–5	465
		Galje'el clan (Hawiye) vs Xawadle subclan (Hawiye) 2000	62

Continued

APPENDIX B   *Continued*

Country	Years of violence	Active dyads/years	Fatalities (best estimate)
		Issa Muse subclan of the Habr Awal clan (Isaaq) vs Habar Yunis subclan of Habar Garhadjis clan (Isaaq) 1992	2,000
		Afi subclan vs Abtisame subclan 2004	26
		Agon-Yar subclan vs Warsangeli subclan 2002	87
		Ali-Gaf subclan vs Mahadade subclan 2002	33
		ARPCT vs ARS/UIC 2006	562
		Dabare subclan vs Luway subclan 2004	47
		Da'ud subclan vs Warsangeli subclan 2004	132
		Dir clan vs Marehan subclan 2004	121
		Dir clan vs Sa'ad subclan 2002–3	115
		Dizi vs Suri 1991, 1993, 2002	187
		Duduble subclan vs Suleiman subclan 2004	47
		Abdullahi Yusuf vs Jama Ali Jama 2002	52
		Galje'el clan vs Jejele subclan 2005	36
		Gaadsan subclan vs Ma'alin Weyne subclan 2008	40
		Garre subclan of Digil clan (Digil-Mirifle) vs Jiddo subclan of Digil clan (Digil-Mirifle) 2000, 2002	57
		Garre subclan vs Marehan 2005	99
		Habar Gidir clan (Hawiye) vs Xawaadle subclan (Hawiye) 1994	38
		Habar Gidir clan (Hawiye) vs Marehan subclan of Sede clan (Darod) 1993	30
		Huber subclan vs Yantar subclan 2005	35
		Jareer subclan vs Jiddo subclan 2002	28
		JVA vs JVA faction 2003	25
		JVA vs SSDF (Somalia) 2004	37
		Marehan subclan vs Fiqi Mohamed subclan 2003	104
		Marehan subclan vs Majerteen subclan 1997–9	516
		Mohamed Muse subclan vs Warsangeli subclan 2003	58
		Ogaden clan vs Sheikhal clan 1999	70
		Puntland vs Somaliland 2004	34
		RRA vs RRA–Madobe and Habsade faction 2002–3, 2005	294
		RRA vs USC/SNA 1995–9	427
		SDM pro-Aideed vs SDM pro-Mahdi 1992	70
		SNA vs SNF 1993	39
		SNF vs USC/SNA 1992, 1995	91
		Sa'ad subclan vs Suleiman subclan 2004–6	307
		SNF–ADRA vs SNF–HRHHY 2004	69
		SNF–MSAB vs SNF 1999	51
		SPM vs SPM/SNA 1993–4	214

APPENDIX B   *Continued*

Country	Years of violence	Active dyads/years	Fatalities (best estimate)
		SPM vs USC/SNA 1992	300
		USC/SNA vs SSNM 2003	28
		USC/SSA–F vs USC/SSA 2001–3	168
		USC/SNA USC/SNA–Osman Atto faction 1995–7	431
		USC/SNA vs USC–Peace Movement 1995	46
		SSDF vs USC/SNA 1993	200
		Abgal clan (Hawiye) vs Xawaadle subclan (Hawiye) 2008	31
		ASWJ vs al-Shabaab 2008–9	612
		Al-Ittihad al-Islami vs SSDF 1992	625
		Digil Salvation Army vs USC/SNA 1999	35
		Al–Shabaab vs Hizbul Islam 2009	121
South Africa	1990–6	ANC–Greens vs ANC–Reds 1993	30
		ANC vs AZAPO 1990	29
		Cape Amalgamated Taxi Association vs CODETA 1996	71
		ANC vs IFP 1990–6	1,575
		IFP vs United Democratic Front 1990	78
		Mangweni clan vs Mgodini clan 1993	26
		ANC vs United Democratic Movement 1998	29
		National Union of Mineworkers vs United Workers' Union of South Africa 1996	30
		Langa, Guguletu and Nyanga Taxi Association vs Western Cape Black Taxi Association 1991	31
Sudan	1990–2009	Awlad Omran clan vs Awlad al-Zuid clan 1993	108
		Awlad al-Zuid clan vs Zaghawa 2001	70
		Aliab (Dinka) vs Mundari 2009	52
		Aqar (Dinka) vs Aqok (Dinka) 2006	60
		Bari vs Mundari 2009	41
		Bor Dinka vs Mundari 2009	42
		Didinga vs Toposa 2007	54
		Dinker vs Nuer 1997	35
		Ereigat Abbala Arabs vs Zaghawa 2002	37
		Habaniya vs Falata 2007–9	333
		Habaniya vs Rizeigat Baggara 2006, 2009	394
		Hotiya Baggara vs Newiba, Mahariba and Mahamid 2005	251
		Janjawiid vs JEM 2003	186
		Janjawiid vs SLM/A 2005	30
		Janjawiid (Bin Kulaib) vs Janjawiid (Moro) 2005	44
		Jikany Nuer vs Luo Nuer 1993	1,001
		Lou Nuer vs Hol Dinka 2008–9	268
		Lou Nuer vs Jikany Nuer 2009	71
		LRA vs SPLM/A 1995–6, 1998, 2004	388

Continued

APPENDIX B   *Continued*

Country	Years of violence	Active dyads/years	Fatalities (best estimate)
		Luac Jang (Dinka) vs Awan (Dinka) 2009	30
		Masalit vs Rizeigat Abbala 1998–9	400
		Missiriya vs Rizeigat Baggara 2008–9	311
		Murle vs Bor Dinka 2007	106
		Murle vs Lou Nuer 2006, 2009	912
		Ngok Dinka vs Shilluk 2009	121
		Pari vs Toposa 1990	35
		Rizeigat Abbala vs Zaghawa 1996	166
		Rizeigat Baggara vs Ma'aliyah 2002, 2004	123
		SLM/A vs SLM/A (MM) 2005–6	102
		SPLM/A vs SPLM/A–Abd al-Aziz al-Hululi faction 1993	55
		SPLM/A vs SPLM/A–William Nyuon faction 1992–3	154
		SPLM/A vs SSDF 1991–4, 1997, 2002	4,428
		SPLM/A vs South Sudan United Army 2000	390
		SPLM/A vs Uganda National Rescue Front II 1997	210
		SPLM/A vs West Nile Bank Front 1995–7	213
		SSDF vs Popular Defence Force 2002	38
		SSDF vs South Sudan United Army 1998–9	515
		Terjam vs Rizeigat Abbala 2007	382
		Toposa vs Didinga 2007	54
		Toposa vs Turkana 1992	200
		Zaghawa vs Ma'aliyah 2008	41
Togo	1991	Moba vs Tchokossi 1991	31
Uganda	1998–2001, 2003, 2005, 2007	Arrow Boys vs LRA 2003	71
		Bokora Karimojong vs Jie Karimojong 2000, 2003, 2007	346
		Bokora Karimojong vs Matheniko Karimojong 1999	352
		Bokora Karimojong vs Matheniko Karimojong, Turkana 2000	60
		Bokora Karimojong vs Pian Karimojong 2003, 2005	64
		Dodoth vs Jie Karimojong 2000, 2005	198
		Dodoth vs Turkana 2000	70
		Dodoth vs Turkana, Toposa 2000	43
		Iteso vs Karimojong 2001	32
		Jie Karimojong vs Matheniko Karimojong 2005	26
		Karimojong vs Pokot 1998, 2000	194
		Matheniko vs Pokot 1999	36
		Pian Karimojong vs Pokot 2003	93
		Pokot vs Sabiny 2003	30

Sources: UCDP, at www.pcr.uu.se/gpdatabase/search.php; Eck, Kreutz and Sundberg, 'Introducing'.

APPENDIX C Campaigns of one-sided violence in Africa, 1990–2009

Country	Years of violence	Active dyads/years	Fatalities (best estimate)
Algeria	1993, 1997–2002, 2004, 2006, 2009	AQIM vs civilians 2004, 2006, 2009 GIA vs civilians 1993, 1997–2002	147 1,109
Angola	1990, 1993–5, 1998–2002, 2003	Govt vs civilians 2003 UNITA vs civilians 1990, 1993–5, 1998–2002	59 2,436
Burundi	1995–2005	Govt vs civilians 1995–2000, 2002–3 CNDD–FDD vs civilians 2001–3 Hutu rebels vs civilians 1995–2000 Palipehutu–FNL vs civilians 2002, 2004–5	3,963 229 2,066 356
Cameroon	1994	Govt vs civilians 1994	55
Central African Republic	2001, 2006–7	Govt vs civilians 2001, 2006–7	158
Chad	1990–5, 1997–8	Govt vs civilians 1990–5, 1997–8 FARF vs civilians 1997	722 30
Congo	1997–9, 2002	Govt vs civilians 1997–9 Cobras vs civilians 1997 Ntsiloulous vs civilians 1998, 2002	895 42 116
Côte d'Ivoire	2000, 2002–4	Govt vs civilians 2000, 2002–4 MPCI vs civilians 2002–3 MPIGO vs civilians 2003	401 153 65
Democratic Republic of the Congo/ Zaire	1990–2009	Govt vs civilians 1990–3, 1995–2000, 2002, 2004, 2006–9 AFDL vs civilians 1996–7 CNDP vs civilians 2007–8 FAPC vs civilians 2004 FAPC/FNI vs civilians 2003 FNI vs civilians 2002–5 FNI/FRPI vs civilians 2003 FNI/FRPI/RCD-K-ML vs civilians 2003 FRPI vs civilians 2002 FRPI/RCD-K-ML vs civilians 2002 MAGRIVI Interahamwe vs civilians 1996 Mal Mayi chinja chinja vs civilians 2004–5 Mayi Mayi Ngilima vs civilians 1996 Mayi Mayi vs civilians 1994,1999,2002 MLC, RCD-N vs civilians 2002 MLC, RCD-N vs civilians 2002 Nigilima Mayi Mayi vs civilians 1996 PARECO vs civilians 2008	8,966 7,255 157 28 33 2,235 325 160 164 1,000 315 167 50 359 117 50 50 38

Continued

APPENDIX C *Continued*

Country	Years of violence	Active dyads/years	Fatalities (best estimate)
		RCD vs civilians 1998–2003	5,197
		RCD mutineers vs civilians 2004	101
		RCD/CP vs civilians 2004	90
		RCD-ML vs civilians 2001	45
Ethiopia	1990–1, 1993, 2002–4, 2006–7	Govt vs civilians 1990–1, 1993, 2002–4, 2006–7	1,180
		ONLF vs civilians 2007	82
Guinea	2007, 2009	Govt vs civilians 2007, 2009	205
Kenya	2007–8	Govt vs civilians 2008	64
		Mungiki vs civilians 2007–8	69
		SLDF vs civilians 2007–8	56
Liberia	1990–4, 1996	Govt vs civilians 1990	976
		Armed Forces of Liberia vs civilians 1994	51
		INPFL vs civilians 1990	77
		LPC vs civilians 1994	390
		NPFL vs civilians 1990–3	2,010
		ULIMO vs civilians 1993	167
		ULIMO–Roosevelt Johnson faction vs civilians 1996	25
		ULIMO–Alhaji Kromah faction vs civilians 1994, 1996	91
Mali	1990–2, 1994	Govt vs civilians 1990–2, 1994	627
		FIAA vs civilians 1994	96
		MPGK vs civilians 1994	66
Morocco	2003	Salafia Jihadia vs civilians 2003	45
Mozambique	1990–2	RENAMO vs civilians 1990–2	1,028
Niger	1990, 1995, 1998	Govt vs civilians 1990, 1995, 1998	378
Nigeria	1990, 2001–5	Govt vs civilians 1990, 2001–4	362
		Bakassi Boys vs civilians 2005	32
Rwanda	1990, 1992–2000, 2004–9	Govt vs civilians 1990, 1993–7, 2009	509,715
		FDLR vs civilians 1996–2000, 2004, 2006–9	4,945
		FPR vs civilians 1990, 1992–4	960
		Interahamwe, ex-Rwandan armed forces vs civilians 1994	77
		Rastas vs civilians 2005–7	168
Senegal	1992–3, 1995, 1997–8, 2002	Govt vs civilians 1998	40
		MFDC vs civilians 1992–3, 1995, 1997–8	221
		MFDC–Northern Front vs civilians 2002	25
Sierra Leone	1991, 1994–2000	Govt vs civilians 1997	89
		RUF vs civilians 1991, 1994–6, 1998–2000	1,357

APPENDIX C *Continued*

Country	Years of violence	Active dyads/years	Fatalities (best estimate)
Somalia	1991–2, 1999, 2007	Govt vs civilians 2007 RRA vs civilians 1999 SPM/SNA OJ vs civilians 1992 USC vs civilians 1991	25 37 90 50
South Africa	1990, 1992–5	Govt vs civilians 1990 ANC vs civilians 1992 AWB vs civilians 1994 IFP vs civilians 1992–5 Pan-African Congress vs civilians 1993	32 36 26 301 27
Sudan	1990–2008	Govt vs civilians 1990–2008 Janjawiid vs civilians 2001–8 JEM vs civilians 2003 SLM/A–MM vs civilians 2006 SLM/A vs civilians 2005 SPLM/A vs civilians 1992–3, 1995–8, 2002, 2004 SSDF vs civilians 1991–3	8,865 3,321 69 72 63 1,057 2,307
Tanzania	2001	Govt vs civilians 2001	35
Uganda	1990–1, 1995–2009	Govt vs civilians 1990–1 ADF vs civilians 1997–2000 LRA vs civilians 1990–1, 1995–8, 2000–9 UNRF II vs civilians 1997 UPA vs civilians 1990	139 693 6,755 57 40
Zimbabwe	2008	Govt vs civilians 2008	165

Source: UCDP www.pcr.uu.se/gpdatabase/search.php.

Notes

Introduction

1 UNDP, *Human Development Report 2003*, p. 2.
2 This figure is based on Paul Collier's estimate that the national and regional cost of each 'typical' civil war in a low-income country is approximately $64 billion. See http://users.ox.ac.uk/~econpco/research/conflict.htm.
3 Peters and Richards, 'Understanding', p. 445.
4 On which, see Lubkemann, *Culture in Chaos*.
5 Lasswell, *Politics*.
6 On the war and society approach, see Howard, *War in European History*; Barkawi, *Globalization and War*.
7 Similar themes feature prominently in Chabal and Daloz, *Africa Works*; Clapham, *Africa*; Reno, *Warlord Politics*; Bates, *When Things Fell Apart*.
8 Zeleza, 'Introduction', p. 2.
9 *Human Security Report 2005*, p. 4.
10 *Human Security Brief 2007*, p. 26.
11 Harbom and Wallensteen, 'Patterns', p. 71. The thirteen were Algeria, Angola, Burundi, the DRC, Republic of Congo, Eritrea–Ethiopia, Guinea-Bissau, Liberia, Rwanda, Sierra Leone, Somalia, Sudan and Uganda.
12 *Human Security Brief 2007*.
13 Harbom and Wallensteen, 'Patterns', p. 70.
14 The Uppsala Conflict Data Programme defines non-state armed conflicts as those where organized, collective armed violence occurs but where a recognized government is not one of the parties. One-sided violence refers to 'the use of armed force by the government of a state or by a formally organized group against civilians which results in at least 25 deaths. Extrajudicial killings in custody are excluded.' Harbom and Wallensteen, 'Patterns', pp. 75–6.
15 Clausewitz, *On War*.
16 That said, there are some good reasons why Clausewitzean modes of thinking remain relevant even if some of his historical categories do not. See Smith, *The Utility of Force*; Stone, 'Clausewitz's trinity'; Strachan and Herberg-Rothe, *Clausewitz*; Kaldor, 'Inconclusive wars'.
17 See Sambanis, 'What is civil war?'.
18 For example, Goldstone et al., 'A global forecasting model' (2010).
19 The classic discussion of war as a level-of-analysis problem which sees international anarchy as the principal source of war recurrence is Waltz, *Man, the State, and War*. For a view of warfare as the human version of struggles to survive and reproduce in conditions of scarcity, see Gat, *War in Human Civilization*.

20   Brown, 'The causes and regional dimensions', p. 574.

21   Suganami, 'Explaining war', p. 309.

22   Suganami, 'Stories', pp. 410–11.

23   See, for example, ibid.

24   Zeleza, 'Introduction', p. 1.

25   For example, Brown, 'The causes and regional dimensions', pp. 582–3.

26   Commission for Africa, *Our Common Interest*. See also Elbadawi and Sambanis, 'Why', p. 253.

27   Sierra Leone Truth and Reconciliation Commission, *Witness to Truth*, para. 11.

28   Jackson, *Quasi-States*.

29   See Braathen, Bøås and Sæther, *Ethnicity Kills?*.

30   Fujii, *Killing Neighbors*, p. 5.

31   See Collier and Hoeffler, 'On the economic causes'; Collier, 'Rebellion'; Collier and Hoeffler, 'Greed and grievance in civil war'.

32   For critiques of this approach, see Keen, *Complex Emergencies*, chap. 2; Herbst, 'Economic incentives'; Berdal, 'Beyond greed and grievance'.

33   Collier, Hoeffler and Rohner, 'Beyond greed and grievance'.

34   See Sobek, *The Causes of War*, p. 6.

35   Johnson, 'Darfur', p. 93.

36   de Waal, 'Sudan'.

37   Ibid., p. 37.

38   See Nicholas Kristof's articles 'Ethnic cleansing, again', *New York Times*, 24 March 2004; 'Will we say "never again" yet again?', *New York Times*, 27 March 2004; 'Cruel choices', *New York Times*, 14 April 2004; and Samantha Power, 'Dying in Darfur', *New Yorker*, 30 August 2004.

39   See, for example, ICG, *Darfur Rising*, pp. 8–9; Prunier, *Darfur*, p. 93.

40   See El Din, 'Islam', pp. 92–112; Flint and de Waal, *Darfur*, pp. 17–18.

41   See, for example, Burr and Collins, *Darfur*; Tubiana, *The Chad–Sudan Proxy War*.

42   Faris, 'The real roots', p. 69.

43   The Atlantic Council of the United States Global Leadership Series, 'Remarks by Jan Eliasson, UN Special Envoy to Darfur' (Washington, DC: 16 May 2007), p. 5, at www.acus.org/files/070516-Jan%20Eliasson%20-%20transcript.pdf.

44   Ban Ki-moon, 'A climate culprit in Darfur', *Washington Post*, 16 June 2007.

Chapter 1   Counting Africa's Conflicts

1   The data-set is available at http://globalpolicy.gmu.edu/pitf.

2   For statistical purposes I take 1963 as the start of the postcolonial era because it was the year that the Organization of African Unity was established. I define the post-Cold War era as the period 1990–2009.

3   There are two minimum thresholds for including an armed conflict in the PITF data-set: a mobilization threshold, wherein each party must mobilize 1,000 or more people (armed agents, demonstrators, troops), and a conflict intensity threshold, whereby there must be at least 1,000 direct conflict-related deaths over the full course of the armed conflict and at least one year when the annual conflict-related death toll exceeds 100 fatalities.

4   Keen, 'War and peace'.

5   Marshall, *Conflict Trends*.

6   The data-set can be found at www.ucdp.uu.se.

7   *Human Security Brief 2007*, p. 23.

8   Clapham, *Africa*; Callaghy, Kassimir and Latham, *Intervention and Transnationalism*.

9   Johnson, *The Root Causes*, p. 143.

10 GAO, *Darfur Crisis*, p. 17.

11 Degomme and Guha-Sapir, 'Patterns'.

12 Lacina and Gleditsch, 'Monitoring trends', p. 162.

13 Marshall, *Conflict Trends*, p. 26.

14 Lacina and Gleditsch, 'Monitoring trends', p. 160.

15 IRC, *Mortality in Eastern DRC* (2000).

16 Ibid., p. 13.

17 Ibid., p. 14.

18 Ibid., pp. 11, 15.

19 IRC, *Mortality in Eastern DRC* (2001).

20 IRC, *Mortality in the DRC* (2003).

21 Ibid., p. 13.

22 Coghlan et al., 'Mortality'.

23 Ibid., p. 44

24 Ibid., p. 48.

25 IRC, *Mortality in the Democratic Republic of Congo* (2007).

26 *Human Security Report 2009*.

27 Ibid., pp. 5, 39–41.

28 Ibid., p. 39.

29 See, respectively, Roberts, 'Death rates', and Human Security Report Project, *Overview*.

Chapter 2   The Terrain of Struggle

1   Barkawi, *Globalization and War*, p. xiii.

2   Howard, *War in European History*, p. xi.

3   See, for example, Richards, *No Peace*.

4   Nordstrom, *Shadows of War*, pp. 46, 53.

5   Jackson, 'Africa's Wars', p. 25.

6   See Cox with Sinclair, *Approaches to World Order*. Cox defines historical structures broadly as 'a particular configuration of forces', while the essence of state–society complexes is that states are always embedded in society, which is why different forms of state emerge in different parts of the world. Within any given historical structure, Cox argued, there are three broad categories of forces (expressed as potentials) that interact: material capabilities, ideas and institutions. Material capabilities are productive and destructive potentials that exist in their dynamic form as technological and organizational capabilities and in their accumulated forms as natural resources which technology can transform, as stocks of equipment, and as the wealth which can command these. Ideas come in broadly two forms: (1) intersubjective meanings – that is, broadly shared notions about the nature of social relations; and (2) collective images of a social order held by different groups of people. Institutions are particular amalgams

of ideas and material capabilities which in turn influence the development of ideas and capabilities.

7 Chazan et al., *Politics and Society*, p. 23.

8 Bøås, 'Marginalized youth', p. 40.

9 The classic statements are Singer, 'The level-of-analysis problem'; Waltz, *Man, the State, and War*.

10 Buzan, 'The level of analysis problem', p. 204.

11 Ibid., p. 199.

12 Wight, *Agents*, p. 105.

13 In this sense, I agree with Bøås and Dunn, 'Introduction', p. 3.

14 Wight, *Agents*, p. 111.

15 Kassimir and Latham, 'Toward a new research agenda', p. 270.

16 See Appadurai, *Modernity at Large*, p. 33. Other analysts have made similar points. Barry Buzan wrote about the 'seamless web' of real life to emphasize that the levels were heuristic devices rather than accurate reflections of reality. Buzan, *People, States and Fear*, pp. 187–8. Similarly, Heikki Patomaki argued that analysis should be based on 'interpenetrating contexts' rather than separate levels. Patomaki, 'How to tell better stories', p. 108.

17 Buzan, 'The level of analysis problem', p. 213.

18 See, for example, Buzan and Wæver, *Regions and Powers*, p. 223; Straus, *The Order of Genocide*; Lubkemann, *Culture in Chaos*, chap. 5; Autesserre, 'The trouble with Congo'. This point is not unique to Africa. See Kalyvas, *The Logic of Violence*.

19 Østby, Nordås and Rød, 'Regional inequalities'.

20 See, for example, Peters and Richards, 'Why we fight'; Keen, *Conflict and Collusion*; Weinstein, *Inside Rebellion*.

21 Buhaug and Rød, 'Local determinants'.

22 Verwimp, Justino and Brück, 'The analysis of conflict'; Fujii, *Killing Neighbors*.

23 Autesserre, 'Hobbes and the Congo', p. 259.

24 See Johnson, *The Root Causes*.

25 Tanner and Tubiana, *Divided They Fall*.

26 Thus, contra Kassimir and Latham, it is not necessarily the case that states remain 'key players in transboundary formations' (Kassimir and Latham, 'Toward a new research agenda', p. 274).

27 See Herbst, *States and Power*.

28 Clapham, 'Comments'.

29 Cederman, Wimmer and Min, 'Why do ethnic groups rebel?'.

30 Goldstone et al., 'A global forecasting model' (2010).

31 Reno, 'Patronage politics', pp. 328–9. See also Keen, *Conflict and Collusion*.

32 See, for example, Chabal and Daloz, *Africa Works*.

33 Clapham, *Africa*, p. 20.

34 Reno, 'Patronage politics', p. 329.

35 Ibid., p. 330.

36 Ibid., p. 336.

37 Ibid., p. 332.

38 See, for example, Buzan, *People, States and Fear*, pp. 186–229; Lake and Morgan, *Regional Orders*; Hettne, Inotai and Sunkel, *The New Regionalism*; DFID, *The Causes of Conflict*; Buzan and Wæver, *Regions and Powers*; Pugh and Cooper with Goodhand, *War Economies*.

39 Buzan and Wæver, *Regions and Powers*, p. 45. See also Bøås and Dunn, 'African guerrilla politics', pp. 35–6.
40 See Stedman, 'Conflict and conciliation', pp. 245–9, and, more generally, Salehyan, *Rebels without Borders*.
41 Prunier, *Africa's World War*.
42 See Howe, *Ambiguous Order*, chap. 2.
43 Buzan and Wæver, *Regions and Powers*, p. 232.
44 Transnational relations refer to 'regular interactions across national boundaries when at least one actor is a non-state agent or does not operate on behalf of a national government or an intergovernmental organization.' Risse-Kappen, 'Introduction', p. 3.
45 Saideman, *The Ties*; Lemke, *Regions*.
46 For a discussion of why ethnic conflicts become transnationalized, see Keller, 'Transnational ethnic conflict'.
47 HRW, *Youth, Poverty and Blood*.
48 Press statement by UN Special Rapporteur on extrajudicial executions, Mission to the Democratic Republic of the Congo, 5–15 October 2009, p. 4, at www2.ohchr.org/english/issues/executions/docs/PressStatement_SumEx_DRC.pdf
49 See Bayart, 'Africa in the world'; Austen, 'Africa and globalization'.
50 Hironaka, *Neverending Wars*, p. 11. Ideas about global culture have also affected how international peacekeeping missions have responded to Africa's wars. See Paris, 'Peacekeeping'.
51 Callaghy et al., *Intervention and Transnationalism*.
52 de Waal, *Famine Crimes*; Terry, *Condemned to Repeat?*; Duffield, *Global Governance*.
53 For an enlightening analysis of the global nature of the trade in conflict goods emanating from the DRC, see UN Security Council, *Final Report of the Panel of Experts on the Illegal Exploitation*. Details about all the UN's sanctions committees can be accessed at www.un.org/sc/committees/.
54 See, for example, Combating Terrorism Center, *Al-Qa'ida's (Mis)Adventures*.
55 Keen, *Complex Emergencies*, p. 12.
56 Clausewitz, *On War*, p. 87.
57 Peters and Richards, 'Understanding', p. 451.
58 HRW, *Nigeria*; HRW, *Criminal Politics*, p. 18.
59 Cited in the documentary *Liberia: Murder of a Country* (VBS Television, 1995).
60 Keen, *Conflict and Collusion*.
61 Reno, *Warlord Politics*, pp. 139, 35.
62 de Waal, 'Contemporary warfare', pp. 291–2.
63 See Clapham, *African Guerrillas*; Bøås and Dunn, *African Guerrillas*.
64 Salehyan, *Rebels without Borders*.
65 Clapham, 'Degrees of statehood', p. 153.
66 Ellis, *The Mask*, pp. 90–1.
67 Ibid., p. 14.
68 Clapham, 'Degrees of statehood', p. 157.
69 Keen, 'War and peace'.
70 See Johnston, 'The geography'.
71 Dowden, *Africa*, pp. 185, 183.
72 Bob, *The Marketing of Rebellion*.

73 Weinstein, *Inside Rebellion*.
74 Conibere et al., 'Appendix 1'.
75 de Waal, 'Contemporary warfare', pp. 314–15.
76 See Utas, 'War, violence and videotapes'.
77 For the view that unprotected camps for the displaced are 'the primary deter-minant of child soldier recruitment rates', see Achvarina and Reich, 'No place to hide'.
78 See de Waal, *Demilitarizing the Mind*.

Chapter 3 Neopatrimonialism

1   See, for example, Le Vine, 'African patrimonial regimes'; Bratton and van de Walle, 'Neopatrimonial regimes'; Bratton and van de Walle, *Democratic Experiments*; Chabal and Daloz, *Africa Works*; van de Walle, *African Economies*; Hyden, *African Politics*, chap. 5. Most analyses employing this concept have built on the work of the German sociologist Max Weber and his distinctions between systems of authority based on legal, traditional and charismatic sources. See Weber, *Economy and Society*.
2   See, for example, Erdmann and Engel, 'Neopatrimonialism reconsidered'; Pitcher, Moran and Johnston, 'Rethinking patrimonialism'.
3   Some analysts have suggested that it can also help us understand the dynamics of how these wars unfold, but this is not the focus of this chapter. Reno, 'Patronage politics'; Murphy, 'Military patrimonialism'.
4   Reno, 'Patronage politics', pp. 328–9.
5   Clientalism is the exchange or brokerage of specific services and resources between individuals for political support, often in the form of votes. Patronage 'is the politically motivated distribution of "favours" not to individuals (as in clientalism) but essentially to groups, which in the African context will be mainly ethnic or sub-ethnic groups.' It is usually considered a tool of high-level politics used to create or maintain political order. Erdmann and Engel, 'Neopatrimonialism reconsidered', pp. 106–7.
6   This formulation draws on Kenneth Boulding's distinction between stable and unstable peace. See his *Stable Peace*.
7   Kaarsholm, 'States of failure', p. 4.
8   Ibid., p. 4; Bratton and van de Walle, 'Neopatrimonial regimes', p. 459.
9   Chabal and Daloz, *Africa Works*, p. xix.
10 For a discussion, see Le Vine, 'African patrimonial regimes'. For a contrasting view which defines Botswana's polity in neopatrimonial terms, see Pitcher et al., 'Rethinking patrimonialism'.
11 Clapham, *Third World Politics*, p. 48.
12 van de Walle, *African Economies*, p. 16. Chabal and Daloz made a similar point when they declared that in most African countries the state is 'a pseudo-Western façade masking the realities of deeply personalized political relations'. *Africa Works*, p. 16.
13 Subsequent quotations are from Erdmann and Engel, 'Neopatrimonialism reconsidered', pp. 105–6 and 111.
14 Hyden, *African Politics*, p. 98.
15 Posner and Young, 'The institutionalization', p. 126.

16 The nine presidents that left office were Kérékou of Benin, Monteiro of Cape Verde, Rawlings of Ghana, Moi of Kenya, Konaré of Mali, Chissano of Mozambique, Trovoada of São Tomé and Principe, René of Seychelles and Mkapa of Tanzania. The three that tried to stay but failed were Muluzi of Malawi, Obasanjo of Nigeria and Chiluba of Zambia. The six that succeeded in staying were Déby of Chad, Bongo of Gabon, Conté of Guinea, Nujoma of Namibia, Eyadéma of Togo and Museveni of Uganda.

17 Posner and Young, 'The institutionalization', p. 134.

18 Chabal and Daloz, *Africa Works*, pp. xviii, xix.

19 Erdmann and Engel, 'Neopatrimonialism reconsidered', p. 114.

20 Toft, 'Ending civil wars', pp. 22–3. Toft's conclusion is based on using Polity IV project data to examine the level of authoritarianism five years before the outbreak of armed conflict in all civil wars worldwide during the period 1940–2002.

21 Pitcher et al., 'Rethinking patrimonialism', pp. 148–9.

22 Richards, *Fighting for the Rain Forest*, p. 162.

23 Cited in Dowden, *Africa*, p. 69.

24 Ibid., p. 69.

25 Reno, *Warlord Politics*, p. 2.

26 Omeje, 'Understanding conflict resolution', p. 78.

27 Dowden, *Africa*, p. 72.

28 Ibid.

29 Bates, *When Things Fell Apart*, p. 38.

30 Chabal and Daloz, *Africa Works*, p. 42.

31 Bates, *When Things Fell Apart*, pp. 38–9.

32 Chabal and Daloz, *Africa Works*, p. 39.

33 Reno, 'The changing nature', p. 323.

34 Hyden, *African Politics*, pp. 114–15.

35 Posner and Young, 'The institutionalization', p. 130.

36 van de Walle, *African Economies*, p. 115. For a more sympathetic view of the economic abilities of some neopatrimonial regimes, see Pitcher et al., 'Rethinking patrimonialism', pp. 133–5.

37 Bates, *When Things Fell Apart*.

38 See Reno, *Warlord Politics*, pp. 87–92; Keen, *The Economic Functions of Violence*, chap. 3.

39 Bratton and van de Walle, *Democratic Experiments*, p. 83.

40 Chabal and Daloz, *Africa Works*, p. 37.

41 Ibid., p. 37.

42 On the idea of relative deprivation, see the discussion in chapter 4.

43 Commission for Africa, *Our Common Interest*.

44 Smith, *Political Violence*, p. 8.

45 Clapham, 'Comments'.

46 Clapham, 'Introduction', p. 5. See also Reno, 'The changing nature', p. 332.

47 Bøås and Dunn, 'African guerrilla politics', p. 10.

48 Ibid., pp. 14–15.

49 Bøås, 'Marginalized youth', p. 46.

50 Chabal and Daloz, *Africa Works*, p. 15.

51 Herbst, 'Economic incentives', pp. 282–3.

52 Sasha Lezhnev, presentation at the Elliott School of International Affairs, Washington, DC, 16 April 2008.

53 Brabazon, *Liberia*, p. 6.

54 Collins, 'Disaster in Darfur', p. 9.

55 Ulph, 'GSPC rival leader'.

56 Balint-Kurti, *Côte d'Ivoire's Forces Nouvelles*, pp. 18–19.

57 Hanson, *MEND*.

58 On the CNDP, see UN Security Council, *Final Report of the Group of Experts on the DRC*, para. 20. On the FDLR, see Romkema de Veenhoop, *Opportunities and Constraints*, p. 47.

59 Herbst, 'Economic incentives', p. 283.

60 Reno, 'The changing nature', p. 328.

61 Prunier, *Africa's World War*, p. 128.

62 In this context, marginalization was understood in a Coxian sense to refer to people who were not employed in the formal economy, had low or no education/ skills, were engaged in base occupations and suffered from irregularity of, or no, cash income. See Cox, 'Civil society'.

63 Leysens, 'Social forces', p. 52.

64 Goldstone et al., 'A global forecasting model' (2005). See also Goldstone et al., 'A global forecasting model' (2010).

65 Goldstone et al. (2005), p. 8.

66 Goldstone et al. (2010), p. 197.

67 Goldstone et al. (2005), p. 18. See also Goldstone et al. (2010), p. 197.

68 Marshall and Cole, 'Global report', p. 6.

69 Goldstone et al. (2005), p. 17. See also Goldstone et al. (2010), p. 197.

70 Goldstone et al. (2005), p. 28. Two other important factors were infant mortality levels and neighbourhood politics, especially where four or more neighbouring states are experiencing armed conflict.

71 Ibid., pp. 24–5.

72 Ibid., p. 25.

73 In this sense, Africa caught the tail end of the so-called third wave of democratization which began in the mid-1970s. See Huntington, *The Third Wave*.

74 *Human Security Brief 2007*, p. 26.

75 Goldstone et al. (2005), pp. 28–9.

76 Kandeh, 'Ransoming the state', pp. 351–8.

77 Reno, *Corruption*.

78 Abdullah, 'Bush path', p. 206.

79 See Reno, *Corruption*, pp. 72–5, 89–90, 109–12, 143, 149–52; Kandeh, 'Ransoming the state', pp. 351–2.

80 My account draws upon Reno, *Corruption*; Reno, *Warlord Politics*; and Richards, *Fighting for the Rain Forest*.

81 Reno, *Warlord Politics*, p. 116.

82 Reno, 'Economic reform', p. 27.

83 Keen, *Conflict and Collusion*, pp. 70–3.

84 The Sierra Leonean military grew from about 4,000 in 1990 to 12,000 by 1993. Cited in Howe, *Ambiguous Order*, p. 57.

85 World Bank, *Sierra Leone*, para. 5.1.

86 Keen, *Conflict and Collusion*, pp. 36, 56.

87   The best overall account of this process is ibid.

88   For details, see Musah, 'A country under siege'.

89   Reno, 'Ironies', p. 15.

90   See Richards, *Fighting for the Rain Forest*; Abdullah, 'Bush path'; Keen, *Conflict and Collusion*; Humphreys and Weinstein, 'Who fights?'.

91   Keen, *Conflict and Collusion*, p. 47.

92   Richards, *Fighting for the Rain Forest*, p. 177.

93   Cited in Keen, *Conflict and Collusion*, p. 45.

94   See Gberie, *A Dirty War*.

95   Adebajo and Keen, 'Banquet for warlords', p. 8; Abdullah, 'Bush path', pp. 222–7.

96   Conibere et al., 'Appendix 1'.

97   The database for the TRC included 40,242 violations suffered by 14,995 victims. These were coded into the seventeen types of violation listed in chapter 2: p. 49.

98   Cited in Kandeh, 'Ransoming the state', p. 349.

99   See Reno, *Warlord Politics*, p. 8.

100   Clapham, 'Comments'.

101   Keen, *Conflict and Collusion*, p. 64.

102   Gberie, *A Dirty War*.

Chapter 4   Resources

1   UNEP, *From Conflict*, p. 5.

2   Keen, *The Economic Functions of Violence*, p. 23.

3   Collier and Hoeffler, 'Greed and grievance in civil war', p. 564.

4   Collier, 'Rebellion'.

5   Abdullah, 'Bush path', pp. 207–8.

6   Uvin, *Aiding Violence*, p. 219. See also Mueller, 'The banality', pp. 58–62.

7   Mamdani, *Saviors and Survivors*, pp. 69, 249, and also 256–9.

8   Keen, *The Economic Functions of Violence*, p. 11.

9   Ali, 'The economics', p. 242.

10   The phrase is from Ballentine and Nitzschke, 'Introduction', p. 4.

11   Herbst, 'Economic incentives', pp. 276–7.

12   Global Witness website, www.globalwitness.org/pages/en/definition_of_conflict_resources.html

13   UNEP, *From Conflict*, pp. 8, 11.

14   Humphreys, 'Natural resources'.

15   See, for example, Thayer, *Darwin*; Gat, *War in Human Civilization*.

16   Mkutu, *Guns and Governance*.

17   'DRC: fish war prompts thousands to flee', *IRIN*, 5 November 2009, at www.irinnews.org/Report.aspx?ReportId = 86898.

18   'Congo army retakes stronghold of western uprising', *Reuters*, 14 December 2009, http:// af.reuters.com/article/topNews/idAFJOE5BE01R20091215 (accessed 24 January 2011)..

19   Moisés Naím, 'Oil can be a curse on poor nations', *Financial Times*, 18 August 2009, p. 7; emphasis added.

20   Ballentine and Nitzschke, 'Introduction', p. 3; emphasis added.

21   See Le Billon, 'The political ecology'.

22   Collier and Hoeffler, 'The political economy of secession'.

23   Ross, 'How do natural resources', p. 56.

24   Ibid., p. 58.

25   Ibid., p. 59.

26   Ross, 'A closer look', p. 267.

27   For evidence, see Nest with Grignon and Kisangani, *The Democratic Republic of Congo*.

28   See UN Security Council, *Final Report of the Panel of Experts on the Illegal Exploitation*.

29   Collier and Hoeffler, 'On the economic causes', pp. 568–9.

30   Cramer, *Civil War*, pp. 121–2.

31   The six emergencies in non-mineral dominant economies were Rwanda, Burundi, Mozambique, Sudan, Somalia and South Africa. The highest casualty figures of all the African cases were in Rwanda and Burundi.

32   Le Billon, 'The political ecology', p. 564.

33   Ibid., pp. 568, 575–6.

34   Garrett, Mitchell and Lintzer, *Promoting Legal*, p. 35.

35   Østby, Nordås and Rød, 'Regional inequalities'.

36   Gurr, *Why Men Rebel*, p. 24.

37   Kahl, 'Population growth'.

38   On the specific case of oil wealth and governance, see Soares de Oliveira, *Oil and Politics*, pp. 32–5.

39   See also the findings of the Political Instability Task Force discussed in chapter 3.

40   Englebert and Ron, 'Primary commodities', pp. 75–6.

41   See Grant and Taylor, 'Global governance'.

42   See, for example, Buhaug and Rød, 'Local determinants', p. 332; Østby et al., 'Regional inequalities', p. 315; Dixon, 'What causes civil wars?', p. 714.

43   Le Billon, 'Diamond wars?', p. 350.

44   Ibid., p. 365.

45   Richards, 'Green book millenarians?', p. 120.

46   Sierra Leone Truth and Reconciliation Commission, *Witness to Truth*, para. 17.

47   Cramer, *Civil War*, p. 124.

48   Global Witness, *A Rough Trade*.

49   Cramer, *Civil War*, p. 156.

50   See, for example, de Soysa, 'Paradise is a bazaar?'; Fearon and Laitin, 'Ethnicity'; Collier and Hoeffler, 'Greed and grievance in civil war'; Dixon, 'What causes civil wars?', p. 714.

51   Ross, 'A closer look', pp. 267, 280.

52   Ibid., p. 286.

53   See also Soares de Oliveira, *Oil and Politics*, p. 6.

54   Cramer, *Civil War*, p. 120. See also Soares de Oliveira, *Oil and Politics*, pp. 36–7, 55–6, 79–83. Fearon and Laitin also speculate that 'Oil producers tend to have weaker state apparatuses than one would expect given their level of income because rulers have less need for a socially intrusive and elaborate bureaucratic system to raise revenues.' Fearon and Laitin, 'Ethnicity', p. 81.

55   This section draws heavily from Cramer, *Civil War*, chap. 4.

56   Cater, 'Rethinking', p. 29.

57   Cramer, *Civil War*, p. 160. The risk of this type of reverse causality is recognized in the general literature. Michael Ross, for instance, has asked whether 'civil

wars might produce resource dependence by forcing a country's manufacturing sector to flee while leaving its resource sector – which is location-specific and cannot depart – as the major force in the economy by default.' Ross, 'How do natural resources', p. 36.

58 Watts, 'Petro-insurgency', p. 639.

59 Cited ibid., p. 641.

60 Ibid., p. 641; Watts, 'Resource curse?', p. 51.

61 Since 2004, the four largest producing oil states have received more than $2 billion annually. Watts, 'Petro-insurgency', p. 643. Nigeria's current constitution establishes that at least 13 per cent of revenues should be allotted to the Delta. In 2008, a government-appointed panel, the Niger Delta Technical Committee, recommended raising that figure to 25 per cent. MEND's demand is 50 per cent. ICG, *Nigeria*, p. 14.

62 This is the case in the oil sector throughout the Gulf of Guinea more generally. See Soares de Oliveira, *Oil and Politics*, p. 77.

63 Watts, 'Petro-insurgency', p. 640.

64 Ibid., p. 653.

65 Cited ibid., p. 656.

66 ICG, *Nigeria*, p. 2.

67 Watts, 'Resource curse?', pp. 54, 60; Watts, 'Petro-insurgency', p. 643. This concept has applicability well beyond the Niger Delta. See Soares de Oliveira, *Oil and Politics*.

68 Iliffe, *Africans*, p. 5.

69 Ibid., p. 4.

70 Brunborg and Tableau, 'Demography of conflict', p. 132.

71 Kaplan, 'The coming anarchy'.

72 Clapham, 'The political economy'.

73 Dixon, 'What causes civil wars?', pp. 709–10.

74 Collier and Hoeffler, 'On the economic causes', p. 569.

75 Kahl, 'Population growth'.

76 Boone, 'Africa's new territorial politics'.

77 Kraxberger, 'Strangers'.

78 Wood, Tappan and Hadj, 'Understanding the drivers'.

79 Green, 'Democracy'.

80 See Brunborg and Tableau, 'Demography of conflict', p. 136.

81 Goldstone, 'Population and security'.

82 Urdal, 'People vs. Malthus', p. 428. Urdal noted that, during the 1990s, urbanization was associated with 'a significantly decreased risk of conflict'.

83 Urdal, 'A clash of generations?'.

84 IISS, *Strategic Survey 2007*, pp. 61–2.

85 Burke et al., 'Warming increases'.

86 This was based on a study of civil war onset between 1981 and 2002. Hendrix and Glaser, 'Trends and triggers', p. 710.

87 Dixon, 'What causes civil wars?', p. 713.

88 Leach and Mearns, *The Lie of the Land*.

89 UNDP, *Human Development Report 2006*, p. 156; UNEP, *Sudan*.

90 UNEP, *Sudan*, pp. 81–2.

91 Mazo, *Climate Conflict*, p. 74. See also the AU Assembly Decision, 29–30 January 2007, Addis Ababa, Assembly/AU/Dec.134 (VIII); Ban Ki-moon, 'A climate culprit in Darfur', *Washington Post*, 16 June 2007.

92 CNA Corporation, *National Security*, p. 16.

93 Mazo, *Climate Conflict*, p. 76.

94 Faris, 'The real roots'.

95 de Waal, 'Is climate change the culprit'.

96 As Mazo acknowledges in *Climate Conflict*, p. 85.

97 This is the argument of ibid. and the CNA Corporation, *National Security*.

98 Salehyan, 'From climate change to conflict?', p. 317.

99 UNDP, *Human Development Report 2006*, p. 57.

100 For a good overview, see Kagwanja, 'Calming the waters'.

101 McNeill, 'Can history help', p. 40.

102 Delli Priscoli, cited in Toulmin, *Climate Change*, p. 47.

103 McNeill, 'Can history help', p. 40.

104 Cramer, *Civil War*, p. 115.

105 Reno, *Warlord Politics*, pp. 139, 35.

106 Alao, *Natural Resources*, p. 63.

107 Ibid., pp. 64–110.

108 AUPD, *Darfur*, para. 136(vi).

109 Le Billon, 'The political ecology', p. 565.

Chapter 5   Sovereignty

1 Englebert, *Africa*, p. 95.

2 Lowe, *International Law*, chap. 4.

3 Weber, *The Theory*, pp. 155–6.

4 See Jackson and Rosberg, 'Why Africa's'; Krasner, *Sovereignty*, especially chap. 1.

5 See Clapham, 'Degrees of statehood'.

6 Englebert, *Africa*. But see also Jackson and Rosberg, 'Why Africa's'; Clapham, *Africa*; Reno, *Warlord Politics*; Ellis, *The Mask*, p. 187.

7 Higgins, *Problems and Process*, p. 111.

8 Ibid., pp. 113–14.

9 Ibid., p. 115.

10 Ibid., pp. 119–20.

11 Ibid., p. 124.

12 Ibid., p. 125.

13 Ibid., p. 121.

14 Cited in Kornprobst, 'The management', p. 375.

15 See, for example, the International Court of Justice opinions on Namibia (1971), Western Sahara (1975) and East Timor (1995).

16 Klabbers, 'The right to be taken seriously', p. 189.

17 Hughes, 'Decolonizing Africa', p. 864.

18 This is undoubtedly not a comprehensive list, but it seems to me they are the cases which have generated the most armed conflict.

19 Iyob, 'Regional hegemony', p. 274.

20 See Englebert, *Africa*, p. 171.

21 Ibid., p. 172.
22 Iyob, 'Regional hegemony'.
23 Ibid., pp. 266–8.
24 Keller, *Revolutionary Ethiopia*, chap. 1 and pp. 150ff.
25 Cited in Iyob, *The Eritrean Struggle*, p. 127; emphasis in original.
26 Ibid., p. 139.
27 Adebjao, 'Ethiopia/Eritrea', p. 581.
28 Lyons, *Avoiding Conflict*, p. 8.
29 Cited in Adebajo, 'Ethiopia/Eritrea', p. 584.
30 Lyons, *Avoiding Conflict*, p. 8.
31 UN Secretary-General, *Report*, p. 5.
32 Ibid., p. 15.
33 Ibid., pp. 16–23.
34 Bradbury, *Becoming Somaliland*, pp. 2–3, 245.
35 Ibid., p. 4.
36 Ibid., p. 253.
37 Ibid., p. 6.
38 AU, 'Resume'.
39 Cited in ICG, *Somaliland*, p. 2.
40 See Higgins, *Problems and Process*, pp. 127–8; Roussellier, 'Quicksand'.
41 Roussellier, 'Quicksand', p. 320.
42 Interestingly, Baker accused Morocco of sabotaging his plans, his lack of means
    to impose a solution on the parties, and his lack of support from Zapatero's new
    Spanish government. Martin, 'Briefing', p. 658.
43 Roussellier, 'Quicksand', p. 324.
44 See ICG, *Western Sahara*.
45 HRW, *Angola*, p. 8.
46 Ibid., p. 7.
47 Englebert, *Africa*, pp. 156, 168.
48 My account relies on FCO, *The Casamance Conflict*; Evans, *Senegal*.
49 FCO, *The Casamance Conflict*, p. 9.
50 Evans, *Senegal*, p. 6.
51 Ibid., p. 4.
52 FCO, *The Casamance Conflict*, p. 3.
53 Evans, *Senegal*, p. 17.
54 Ibid., p. 16.
55 Ibid., p. 3.
56 Englebert, *Africa*, pp. 158, 160.
57 Evans, *Senegal*, p. 16.
58 Englebert, *Africa*, p. 160.
59 Graeber, Harris and Hotra, 'A strategic conflict'.
60 Englebert, *Africa*, p. 162.
61 Ibid., p. 161.
62 Graeber et al., 'A strategic conflict', pp. 9–10.
63 Ibid., pp. 11–12.
64 'Niger seeks mediation with Tuareg rebels', *Reuters*, 3 April 2009, at
    http://af.reuters.com/article/idAFJOE53301T20090404 (accessed 24 January
    2011).

65 Englebert, *Africa*, p. 164

66 For an overview of the competing visions of Sudan's political future, see Deng, *War of Visions*.

67 Ken Crossley, cited in Englebert, *Africa*, p. 168.

68 For an overview of trends on the continent between 1960 and 2006, see ibid., pp. 182–3.

69 Ibid., p. 180.

70 Ibid.

71 Clapham, 'Comments'.

72 Hagmann, 'Beyond clannishness'.

73 Shinn, 'Ethiopian armed groups'.

74 Hagmann, 'Beyond clannishness', p. 525.

75 ONLF website, www.onlf.org (accessed 5 June 2010).

76 In an interview with the BBC World Service, at www.bbc.co.uk/worldservice/africa/2010/07/100729_ethiopia_rebels.shtml

77 Kamanu, 'Secession'.

Chapter 6 Ethnicity

1 Wolf, *Ethnic Conflict*, p. 10.

2 Hyden, *African Politics*, p. 204.

3 Fujii, *Killing Neighbors*.

4 Hale, 'Explaining ethnicity', p. 463.

5 Ibid., p. 473. See also Fearon and Laitin, 'Violence', p. 848.

6 Horowitz, *Ethnic Groups*, p. 53.

7 Mamdani, *When Victims Become Killers*, p. 22.

8 Anderson, *Imagined Communities*.

9 Esman, *An Introduction*, p. 47.

10 Daley, 'Ethnicity', pp. 666–9, 677.

11 Lemarchand, *Burundi*.

12 Esman, *An Introduction*, p. 29.

13 Berman, 'Ethnicity', especially pp. 317–22.

14 Ibid., p. 326.

15 See Fenton, *Ethnicity*, chap. 4.

16 See Lake and Rothchild, 'Spreading fear'; Fearon and Laitin, 'Violence'; Gagnon, *The Myth*.

17 Kaufman, 'Symbolic politics'.

18 Cederman, Wimmer and Min, 'Why do ethnic groups rebel?', p. 88.

19 Brown, 'The causes of internal conflict', pp. 6–7.

20 Ibid., p. 7.

21 Wolf, *Ethnic Conflict*, p. 50.

22 Brown, 'The causes of internal conflict', p. 17. This view is shared by writers who point to particular 'catalysts' for armed conflict, who usually appear in the form of leaders such as 'ethnic activists' or 'political entrepreneurs'. Wolf, *Ethnic Conflict*, p. 83.

23 Wolf, *Ethnic Conflict*, p. 88.

24 Fearon and Laitin, 'Violence', pp. 853–4.

25 See Mueller, 'The banality'; Fujii, *Killing Neighbors*, p. 5.

26 Kaufman, 'Symbolic politics', p. 52.

27 Fujii, *Killing Neighbors*, p. 5.

28 Collier and Hoeffler, 'On the incidence', pp. 17–18, 25.

29 Ibid., p. 25.

30 These pathways are similar to those identified by Fearon and Laitin, 'Violence', p. 865.

31 These variants are taken from Byman, *Keeping the Peace*, chap. 2.

32 Zartman, 'Preventing identity conflicts'. As the UCDP data-set on one-sided violence confirms, non-state actors also engage in such activity.

33 Fujii, *Killing Neighbors*, pp. 11–12.

34 de Waal, 'Counter-insurgency'.

35 Flint, *Beyond 'Janjaweed'*, p. 13.

36 Ibid., p. 17.

37 Ibid., p. 23.

38 Ibid., pp. 24, 29.

39 Fearon and Laitin, 'Violence', p. 865.

40 Ibid., p. 864.

41 Daley, 'Ethnicity', p. 671.

42 Uvin, *Aiding Violence*, pp. 205–23.

43 The *akazu* (meaning 'little house') was a core group of individuals within the larger network that supported President Habyarimana. Madame Habyarimana, her relatives and others from the president's home region played a major role within it.

44 For details, see Des Forges, *Leave None*; Melvern, *Conspiracy to Murder*.

45 Des Forges, *Leave None*, p. 32.

46 Ibid., p. 35.

47 Fujii, *Killing Neighbors*, pp. 115–16.

48 According to Prunier, approximately 20,000 Tutsis were killed during and after the 'Hutu revolution' and some 300,000 were forced to flee the country. Prunier, *The Rwanda Crisis*, p. 62.

49 Des Forges, *Leave None*, p. 37.

50 Fujii, *Killing Neighbors*, p. 108.

51 Prunier, *The Rwanda Crisis*, p. 75.

52 Fujii, *Killing Neighbors*, p. 110.

53 Ibid., p. 6.

54 In the mid-1980s, the drop in coffee prices saw Rwanda's coffee sales decline from 14 billion Rwanda francs in 1986 to 5 billion the following year. At the government's request, in 1990 Rwanda underwent a World Bank structural adjustment programme, the national currency was devalued by over 50 per cent and many people experienced a dramatic decline in health services. Hintjens, 'Explaining', pp. 256–7.

55 Straus, *The Order of Genocide*. In Giti, the only government-controlled commune in which genocide did not occur, for instance, the RPF arrived before the interim government officials (p. 65).

56 Ibid., p. 154.

57 To emphasize the point, government and militia forces periodically staged fake attacks on Kigali in order to create a sense of panic. Hintjens, 'Explaining', pp. 264, 267.

58   Des Forges, 'Burundi'.
59   Fujii, *Killing Neighbors*, p. 12.
60   Zartman, 'Preventing identity conflicts'. See also Kaufman, 'Symbolic politics', pp. 52–3.
61   Des Forges, *Leave None*, p. 184.
62   Ibid., p. 198.
63   Melvern, *Conspiracy to Murder*.
64   Prunier, *Africa's World War*, p. 1.
65   This is Linda Melvern's figure in *A People Betrayed*. Others give higher figures, e.g. 1,500 in Kuperman, *The Limits*, p. 41; 1,000 to 1,500 in Des Forges, *Leave None*, pp. 39, 152; and 700 to 1,500 in Mueller, 'The banality', p. 61.
66   Des Forges, *Leave None*, p. 48.
67   Melvern, *A People Betrayed*. The plan was to have 200 in each of Rwanda's 146 communes, but the plan was never completed.
68   Ibid.; Kuperman, *The Limits*, p. 41.
69   This term is from Fujii, *Killing Neighbors*.
70   Mueller, 'The banality', p. 61.
71   Ibid., p. 42.
72   Straus, 'How many'.
73   Mueller, 'The banality', p. 43.
74   Fujii, *Killing Neighbors*, pp. 119–20.
75   Des Forges, *Leave None*, p. 589.
76   Ibid., p. 182.
77   Ibid., p. 198.
78   One estimate suggests that between 10,000 and 30,000 'opposition Hutu' were killed during the massacres. Prunier, *The Rwanda Crisis*, p. 265.
79   Des Forges, *Leave None*, p. 33.
80   Ibid., p. 32.
81   Fujii, *Killing Neighbors*, p. 126.
82   Ibid., p. 121.
83   Ibid., p. 13.

Chapter 7   Religion

1   See Huntington, 'The clash' and *The Clash*.
2   Huntington, *The Clash*, pp. 254–7, 267.
3   For the argument that Islam has played a larger role in contemporary religious civil wars than either Christianity or Judaism, see Toft, 'Getting religion?'.
4   Cavanagh, *The Myth*.
5   ter Haar, 'Religion'.
6   Cavanagh, *The Myth*.
7   Cited in de Waal and Abdel Salam, 'Africa', p. 255.
8   Seul, 'Ours is the way'.
9   Ellis and ter Haar, 'Religion and politics' (1998). See also their *Worlds of Power* and 'Religion and politics' (2007).
10   Durkheim, *The Elementary Forms*, p. 6.
11   See Ellis and ter Haar, *Worlds of Power*; Toft, 'Getting religion?', p. 99.

12 Ellis and ter Haar, *Worlds of Power*, p. 14. This is based on the work of the nineteenth-century anthropologist E. B. Tylor, who defined religion as 'the belief in Spiritual Beings'.

13 Ellis and ter Haar, 'Religion and politics' (2007), p. 396.

14 Zeleza, 'Introduction', p. 25.

15 Jackson, 'Are Africa's wars', p. 279.

16 Ellis, *The Mask*, pp. 264–5.

17 Ibid, p. 304.

18 Ibid, p. 116.

19 Wild, 'Is it witchcraft?'.

20 Collier and Hoeffler, 'On the incidence', p. 22.

21 The PITF reached a similar conclusion. See Goldstone et al., 'A global forecasting model' (2005), p. 25.

22 Basedau and De Juan, *The 'Ambivalence of the Sacred'*, p. 8. Of course, focusing on populations of equivalent size begs the question of what level of analysis one is talking about. In Nigeria, for instance, at the national level Muslims and Christians might be roughly equal in numbers, but in particular towns where violence has erupted, such as Jos, the groups may be heavily skewed, with a dominant majority and small minority.

23 Ibid., p. 8.

24 An alternative data-set of civil wars from 1940 to 2000 compiled by Monica Duffy Toft concluded that forty-two out of 133 cases (32 per cent) could be classified as religious civil wars (of these, religion was a 'central issue' in twenty-five and a 'peripheral issue' in the remaining seventeen). Only seven of these religious civil wars were in Africa and only two occurred in the period after 1990: Algeria (1992) and Sudan (1983). Toft, 'Getting religion?'.

25 Basedau and De Juan, *The 'Ambivalence of the Sacred'*, p. 16.

26 Ibid., pp. 20, 23.

27 Møller, *Religion and Conflict*, p. 5.

28 Ellis and ter Haar, *Worlds of Power*, pp. 106–7.

29 Gurr, *Minorities at Risk*, p. 317.

30 HRW, *Arbitrary Killings*, p. 3; Committee on the Elimination of Racial Discrimination, 76th Session, Decision 1(76) Situation in Nigeria, 11 March 2010 (UN doc. CERD/C/NGA/DEC/1, 14 June 2010).

31 'Nigeria: Plateau State violence claimed 53,000 lives – report', *IRIN News*, 8 October 2004, www.irinnews.org/report.aspx?reportid = 51641.

32 See, respectively, Danfulani and Fwatshak, 'Briefing', p. 243; HRW, *Arbitrary Killings*; 'Nigeria ethnic violence "leaves hundreds dead"', *BBC News Online*, 8 March 2010, http://news.bbc.co.uk/2/hi/8555018.stm; and 'Nigeria religious riot bodies found in village wells', *BBC News Online*, 23 January 2010, http://news.bbc.co.uk/2/hi/africa/8476534.stm.

33 See Danfulani and Fwatshak, 'Briefing'; Last, 'Muslims and Christians'.

34 Smock, 'Mediating', p. 17.

35 HRW, *Arbitrary Killings*, p. 3.

36 Danfulani and Fwatshak, 'Briefing', pp. 247–8.

37 Ibid., p. 255.

38 Martinez, *The Algerian Civil War*, p. 246.

39 Ibid., p. 21.

40   Ibid., pp. 21–2.
41   Ibid., p. 92.
42   Ibid., pp. 93, 251.
43   Abdel Salama and de Waal, 'On the failure', p. 32.
44   Martinez, *The Algerian Civil War*, pp. 7, 10–11. Militarism is also central in the analysis of the war provided by Turshen, 'Militarism'.
45   Martinez, *The Algerian Civil War*, p. 247.
46   Ibid., pp. 75–6, 100, 248.
47   Ibid., pp. 15, 17.
48   Deng, *War of Visions*.
49   Johnson, *The Root Causes*, pp. xviii–xix.
50   For an overview of the project and al Turabi's influential position in it, see de Waal and Abdel Salam, 'Islamism', pp. 71–113.
51   See de Waal, 'The politics'.
52   O'Fahey, 'Islam', p. 258.
53   Deng, *War of Visions*, pp. 13, 16.
54   Johnson, *The Root Causes*, p. xviii.
55   de Waal and Abdel Salam, 'Islamism,' p. 73.
56   Ibid., p. 73.
57   Toft, 'Getting religion?', p. 103.
58   Ibid., p. 128.
59   Wheeler, 'Finding meaning', p. 58.
60   Ibid., pp. 74–5.
61   Ibid., p. 76.
62   O'Fahey, 'Islam', p. 262.
63   de Waal, 'Introduction', p. 1.
64   Connell, 'Eritrea', p. 78.
65   Gunaratna, *Inside Al Qaeda*, p. 152.
66   The interview transcript is at www.fas.org/irp/world/para/docs/eritrea.htm (accessed 7 March 2010).
67   Connell, 'Eritrea', p. 78.
68   Marchal, 'Islamic political dynamics', pp. 125–8.
69   Gérard Prunier, 'Sudan's regional war', *Le Monde Diplomatique* (English edn), February 1997, at http://mondediplo.com/1997/02/02sudan (accessed 18 July 2010).
70   de Waal, 'The politics', pp. 43, 215.
71   Ibid., p. 206.
72   Ibid., pp. 198–200.
73   Ibid., p. 209.
74   Cited in Møller, *Religion and Conflict*, p. 89.
75   Doom and Vlassenroot, 'Kony's message', p. 29.
76   Møller, *Religion and Conflict*, p. 7 and also p. 66.
77   See, for example, ICG, *Darfur Rising*, pp. 8–9; Prunier, *Darfur*, p. 93.
78   *Al-Shabaab* was formally renamed *Harakat Al-Shabaab al-Mujahidin* in 2009 to buttress its jihadist identity and the global nature of its aspirations.
79   My account of these groups draws from ICG, *Somalia's Divided Islamists*.
80   Cited in Jeffrey Gettleman, 'For Somalia, chaos breeds religious war,' *New York Times*, 23 May 2009.
81   The most detailed account is Behrend, *Alice Lakwena*.

82 Doom and Vlassenroot, 'Kony's message', pp. 7–8, 17.
83 Ibid., p. 16.
84 Ibid., p. 18.
85 See Dunn, 'Uganda', p. 137.
86 Doom and Vlassenroot, 'Kony's message', p. 23.
87 Ibid., p. 25.
88 Ibid., pp. 28–30.
89 Ibid., p. 25.
90 Dunn, 'Uganda', p. 140.
91 Rosa Ehrenreich, cited ibid., p. 141.
92 Ibid., p. 145.
93 Religion also appeared in another sense inasmuch as some ordinary Rwandans believed their society was threatened 'not only by political and military upheaval, but by malevolent spiritual forces also [specifically that emanating from the mystical force of *imaana*].' Ellis and ter Haar, 'Religion and politics' (2007), pp. 398–9.
94 Des Forges, *Leave None*, p. 61.
95 See Prunier, *The Rwanda Crisis*, pp. 81, 125; Des Forges, *Leave None*, p. 39.
96 Longman, 'Church politics'; Prunier, *The Rwanda Crisis*, p. 351.
97 Longman, 'Church politics', pp. 166–7.
98 See Des Forges, *Leave None*, pp. 189–90.
99 Longman, 'Churches and social upheaval', p .85.
100 Ibid., p. 86.
101 Longman, 'Church politics', p. 184.

Chapter 8   Organization-Building

1   'Hopeless Africa', *The Economist*, 13–19 May 2000, front cover and p. 15.
2   Malan, 'Africa', p. 90.
3   Cited ibid., p. 89.
4   See Mays, *Africa's First*.
5   See Muyangwa and Vogt, *An Assessment*.
6   Berman and Sams, 'The peacekeeping potential', p. 55.
7   Ibid., pp. 54–6; Franke, *Security Cooperation*, p. 89.
8   From 1 June 1993 to 31 March 2001, the Peace Fund received nearly US$ 41 million, roughly two-thirds of which came from non-African sources. Berman and Sams, 'The peacekeeping potential', p. 55.
9   Ibid., p. 54.
10 Franke, *Security Cooperation*, p. 90.
11 Berman and Sams, 'The peacekeeping potential', p. 54.
12 Interview with AU Commission official, Addis Ababa, May 2007.
13 See van Walraven, *Dreams of Power*.
14 *Declaration on the Framework for an OAU Response to Unconstitutional Changes in Government*, OAU doc. AHG/Decl.5 (XXXVI), 10–12 July 2000. This drew upon the earlier decision on unconstitutional changes of government taken by the heads of state and government of the OAU at the Algiers Summit, 12–14 July 1999.
15 McGowan, 'African military coups'. McGowan classifies 'displacements of government personnel or constitutional relationships lasting at least one week' as 'successful coups d'état'.

16 The likely catalyst for the inclusion of this clause was the assassination of President Sylvanus Olympio of Togo in an army coup d'état in January 1963 as the OAU was being assembled.

17 McGowan, 'African military coups', p. 348.

18 Decisions adopted by the 66th Ordinary Session of the OAU Council of Ministers, CM/Dec.330–363 (LXVI), Dec.356 (1997).

19 See UN Security Council Resolution 841 (1993) and subsequent resolutions on the situation in Haiti.

20 AU, *Draft Background Paper*, p. 20.

21 *Ezulwini Framework for the Enhancement of the Implementation of Measures of the African Union in Situations of Unconstitutional Changes of Government in Africa* (AU doc. PSC/PR/2(CCXIII), 27 January 2010).

22 Haggis, *The African Union*.

23 *Protocol on Amendments to the Constitutive Act of the African Union*, adopted at Addis Ababa, 3 February 2003, at www.africa-union.org/root/au/Documents/Treaties/Text/Protocol%20on%20Amendments%20to%20the%20Constitutive%20Act.pdf.

24 It shall enter into force thirty days after the deposit of instruments of ratification by a two-thirds majority of the AU member states.

25 The preamble to Article 4 (Principles) of the *PSC Protocol* explicitly states that the Council 'shall be guided by the principles enshrined in the . . . Charter of the United Nations'. In addition, the preparatory materials for the OAU Charter indicate that the organization was intended to be one of the 'regional arrangements' referred to in Chapter VIII of the UN Charter. See Henrikson, 'The growth', pp. 130ff. For more details, see Williams, 'The Peace and Security Council', pp. 610–11.

26 AU, *Roadmap*, p. 5.

27 The AU's Operation Democracy in the Comoros (March 2008) was conducted with the consent of the *de jure* authorities and in the name of defending democracy rather than of civilian protection.

28 For the details, see AU doc. EX/CL/Dec.34 (III), Assembly/AU/Dec.22, 4–8 July 2003.

29 The portfolios are peace and security, political affairs, infrastructure and energy, social affairs, human resources, science and technology, trade and industry, farming and agricultural economics, and economic affairs.

30 Engel and Porto, 'The African Union's'.

31 Makinda and Okumu, *The African Union*, p. 51.

32 Malan, 'Africa', p. 113.

33 Interviews with PSC officials, Addis Ababa, May 2007, May 2010.

34 This section draws upon Williams, 'The Peace and Security Council'.

35 Article 2(1) of the *Protocol Relating to the Establishment of the Peace and Security Council of the African Union*. This was signed in Durban on 9 July 2002 and came into force on 26 December 2003 (after ratification by twenty-seven of the fifty-three AU members). The PSC officially began its work on 16 March 2004, at the ministerial level, at the margins of the 4th Ordinary Session of the AU Executive Council.

36 Franke, *Security Cooperation*, p. 97.

37 Ibid., p. 97.

38 Rwanda appears in 'east Africa' as the result of a formal change by the RPF government, while Burundi remains in 'central Africa'.

39 See Sturman and Hayatou, 'The Peace and Security Council'. The so-called Arria formula started in 1992, when the Venezuelan Permanent Representative to the UN Security Council, Diego Arria, invited fellow members of the Security Council to meet away from the Council's chambers with independent experts on the Balkans.

40 The AU authorized the creation of the AU Mission in Burundi (AMIB) in 2003, before the PSC was formally established.

41 AU, *Draft Background Paper*, p. 1; see also p. 18.

42 Franke, *Security Cooperation*, p. 186.

43 Ibid., p. 187.

44 For an overview, see AU, *African Union Continental Early Warning System*.

45 *Protocol Relating to the Establishment of the Peace and Security Council of the African Union* (hereafter *PSC Protocol*), adopted Durban, South Africa, 9 July 2002, Article 12.2b.

46 Wane, 'From concept', p. 6.

47 In the first half of 2010 the CEWS began using a software system called the African Reporter, which had been developed in collaboration with Doug Bond at Harvard University. It was also developing the African Prospectus to forecast risk and vulnerability.

48 These missions and offices were not part of the CEWS but were set up for political reasons by the PSC, usually to monitor areas of ongoing conflict, such as Côte d'Ivoire, DRC, Chad, Comoros, Sudan, Liberia, and Ethiopia–Eritrea. Most of them consisted of only two or three people.

49 For details of the sub-regional mechanisms as of early 2008, see Franke, *Security Cooperation*, pp. 191–206.

50 *Protocol on the Establishment of a Conflict Early Warning and Response Mechanism*, signed by the IGAD heads of state and government, Khartoum, Sudan, January 2002. The protocol entered into force in July 2003 after ratification by Eritrea, Kenya, Ethiopia and Sudan.

51 Franke, *Security Cooperation*, p. 210 n. 36.

52 These offices are in Cotonou (covering Benin, Nigeria and Togo), Ouagadougou (covering Burkina Faso, Côte d'Ivoire, Mali and Niger), Monrovia (covering Liberia, Sierra Leone, Guinea and Ghana) and Banjul (covering the Gambia, Cape Verde, Guinea-Bissau and Senegal).

53 This paragraph is based on the author's discussion with CEWS staff, Washington, DC, 2 July 2009.

54 Franke, *Security Cooperation*, p. 153.

55 Malan, 'Africa', pp. 108–9. Each brigade is supposed to have a headquarters unit, four infantry battalions, an engineer battalion, a reconnaissance element, an aviation element, a communications element, a military police element, a forward logistics element, a medical element, military observers and a civil support element.

56 Franke, *Security Cooperation*, pp. 157–8.

57 Cilliers, *The African Standby Force*, p. 17.

58 Malan, 'Africa', pp. 109, 115.

59 AU, *Roadmap*.

60 One AU document stated: 'Nothing precludes the ASF from deploying outside Africa, either as a contribution to a UN force or as a rapid reaction capability.' AU, *Harmonized Doctrine*, chap. 5, para. 12c.

61 For details, see Franke, *Security Cooperation*, pp. 165–76.

62 Cilliers, *The African Standby Force*, p. 7; Marshall, *Building an Effective*, p. 5.

63 Marshall, *Building an Effective*, p. 19.

64 AU, *A Concept Paper*, para. 11.

65 Cilliers, *The African Standby Force*, p. 4.

66 Marshall, *Building an Effective*, p. 13.

67 For example, ibid., p. 7.

68 There are three obvious alternatives to such donor support. One is that the AU could use the existing lift assets from countries such as Kenya, Nigeria and South Africa and hope that these states will align their priorities with those of the AU. A second is that the AU could investigate hiring private contractors to provide airlift. NATO's Strategic Airlift Interim Solutions (SALIS) might be an option, but contractors are expensive, donors will probably continue to pay for strategic lift capabilities (at least for the foreseeable future) and this option will not build the AU's own capacities in the long term. A third option would be for the AU to start building its own airlift capability. Ibid, p. 15.

69 See Cilliers, *The African Standby Force*, pp. 6–7; Marshall, *Building an Effective*.

70 Franke, *Security Cooperation*, p. 176.

71 Cilliers, *The African Standby Force*, p. 16.

72 Marshall, *Building an Effective*, p. 18.

73 See Nathan, 'Mediation'.

74 Franke, *Security Cooperation*, pp. 144–5.

75 Interviews with AU and independent analysts, Addis Ababa, May 2010.

76 Aboagye, 'Global and regional'.

77 Malan, 'Africa', p. 111.

78 Ibid., p. 116. With regard to the issue of 'ownership', it is notable that Western military officers acting as 'advisors' have been accused of 'exerting considerable influence on the concepts, standards and decisions taken at every level. Only SADC has resisted such an infiltration.' Cilliers, *The African Standby Force*, p. 18.

79 UN Security Council, *Report of the African Union–United Nations Panel*, para. 15.

80 See Herbst, 'Crafting regional cooperation'.

Chapter 9 Peacemaking

1   Harbom, Högbladh and Wallensteen, 'Armed conflict'.

2   Wallensteen, *Understanding*, p. 77. See also Toft, 'Ending civil wars', p. 14.

3   Brahimi and Ahmed, *In Pursuit*, p. 5.

4   See, for example, Crocker, Hampson and Aall, *Taming Intractable Conflicts*.

5   Luttwak, 'Give war a chance'.

6   Tull and Mehler, 'The hidden costs', p. 394.

7   Keen, *Complex Emergencies*, p. 171.

8   Clapham, 'Rwanda'. See also Spears, 'Understanding inclusive'; Tull and Mehler, 'The hidden costs', p. 376.

9   See Lyons, *Demilitarizing Politics*.

10 The Arusha Accords gave the ruling *Mouvement révolutionnaire national pour le développement et la Démocratie* and the Rwanda Patriotic Front five cabinet positions each, the *Mouvement démocratique républicain* four, the *Parti social démocrate* and the *Parti libéral* three each, and the *Parti démocrate chrétien* one. The extremist

Convention pour la défense de la république was excluded from the transitional government. The armed forces were divided on a fifty–fifty basis for the troops, with Hutu elements retaining 60 per cent of the senior officers. For an excellent discussion, see Jones, *Peacemaking*.

11   Lijphart, *Democracy* and 'The power-sharing approach'.

12   Lemarchand, 'Consociationalism', p. 2.

13   Walter, 'The critical barrier'.

14   Ottaway, 'Democratization', p. 248.

15   Spears, 'Understanding inclusive', p. 116.

16   Tull and Mehler, 'The hidden costs', p. 386.

17   Lemarchand, 'Consociationalism', pp. 7–12.

18   Ibid., p. 11.

19   Ibid., p. 19.

20   Mehler, 'Peace and power sharing', p. 453.

21   Analysts differ on how likely negotiated settlements are to break down. Using a data-set of ninety-one civil wars between 1945 and 1993, Roy Licklider concluded that, of those which were brought to a close by negotiated settlement, war restarted within five years in 50 per cent of cases compared with only 15 per cent of the wars which ended in military victory by one side (Licklider, 'The consequences'). Suhrke and Samset, on the other hand, concluded that the rate for this type of risk of civil war recurrence was only 20 to 26 per cent. They do not appear to confine their analysis to civil wars that were terminated by negotiated settlements (Suhrke and Samset, 'What's in a figure?'). Based on an analysis of civil wars between 1940 and 2007, Monica Toft concluded that negotiated settlements increase the chances of war recurrence by 27 per cent, relative to all other types of civil war termination (Toft, 'Ending civil wars', p. 16).

22   Zartman, 'The timing'.

23   Bigombe, Collier and Sambanis, 'Policies'.

24   Sawyer, 'Violent conflicts', p. 451.

25   See Lyons, *Demilitarizing Politics*; Toft, *Securing the Peace*.

26   *Mixage* referred to troops of different ethnicities serving in the same units, whereas *brassage* was when troops were stationed in areas of the country well away from their ethnic homeland.

27   See Adebajo, 'Liberia'.

28   See Walter, 'The critical barrier', p. 361; Stedman, 'Spoiler problems'; Walter, 'Designing transitions'.

29   Bentley and Southall, *An African*.

30   See Melvern, *A People Betrayed*; Dallaire, *Shake Hands*.

31   See also Keen, *Complex Emergencies*, pp. 183–91.

32   See Anderlini, *Women*, pp. 61–3.

33   Mehler, 'Peace and power sharing', p. 472.

34   Spears, 'Understanding inclusive', p. 110.

35   Keen, *Complex Emergencies*, p. 183.

36   Keen, *Conflict and Collusion*, pp. 253–66.

37   Richards and Vincent, 'Sierra Leone'.

38   Tull and Mehler, 'The hidden costs', p. 395.

39   Ibid., p. 375. See also Keen, *Complex Emergencies*, pp. 184–5.

40   Tull and Mehler, 'The hidden costs', p. 388. See also Clapham, 'Rwanda'.

41 Stedman, 'Spoiler problems', p. 11.
42 Tull and Mehler, 'The hidden costs', p. 394.
43 Keen, *Complex Emergencies*, p. 193.
44 Walter, 'The critical barrier' and 'Designing transitions'; Stedman, 'Spoiler problems'.
45 Lyons, *Demilitarizing Politics*, p. 11.
46 Doyle, 'Strategy', p. 79.
47 Patrick Johnston's study of rebel groups in Liberia and Sierra Leone makes the same point. Johnston, 'The geography', pp. 136–6.
48 The quotations are from de Waal, 'Mission without end?', pp. 105, 99, 106, 107, 108 and 112, respectively.
49 See Keen, *Complex Emergencies*, pp. 11–24.
50 Crocker et al., *Taming Intractable Conflicts*, p. 106.
51 See de Waal, *War in Darfur*, especially chaps 8–12.
52 See the figures for 2008 at http://hdr.undp.org/en/statistics/.
53 Hanlon, 'Is the international community'.
54 See de Waal, *Demilitarizing the Mind*; Lyons, *Demilitarizing Politics*.
55 The transformation of African military organizations into political parties has been patchy at best. On the one hand, some defeated insurgencies, notably the RUF and UNITA, clearly failed to gain popular support at the ballot box after the war's end. In Mozambique, however, RENAMO did undergo a significant transition which allowed it to compete in postwar politics. Perhaps more worrying was the reluctance to shed military habits within insurgencies which became governing regimes (or part of governing regimes), such as the RPF in Rwanda, the SPLM in Sudan, the EPLF in Eritrea and ZANU-PF in Zimbabwe. See de Zeeuw (ed.), *From Soldiers*, pp. 55–102, 157–78; Prunier, *Africa's World War*, pp. 22–4.
56 Lyons, *Demilitarizing Politics*, p. 5. See also Toft, *Securing the Peace*.
57 This paragraph relies on Brahimi and Ahmed, *In Pursuit*. Quotations are from pp. 6 and 9.
58 Patrick Mazimhaka, cited in Prunier, *Africa's World War*, p. 224.
59 Ibid., p. 225.
60 *The Economist*, 17 July 1999.
61 Crocker et al., *Taming Intractable Conflicts*, p. 76. See also Downs and Stedman, 'Evaluation issues'.
62 Crocker et al., *Taming Intractable Conflicts*, p. 25.
63 Brahimi and Ahmed, *In Pursuit*, p. 4.
64 Crocker et al., *Taming Intractable Conflicts*, p. 89.
65 Toft, 'Ending civil wars'.
66 See Booth and Wheeler, *The Security Dilemma*, especially part 3.
67 See Murithi, 'African indigenous'.

Chapter 10 Peacekeeping

1 See Bellamy and Williams, *Understanding Peacekeeping*, chaps 4–5.
2 See Berman and Sams, *Peacekeeping*, chap. 3.
3 For overviews of these activities, see ibid, chaps 4–7; Boulden, *Dealing with Conflict*; Coleman, *International Organisations*, chaps 3–5.
4 Boulden, 'UN Security Council'.

5   Khadiagala, 'Burundi', p. 218.

6   Boulden, 'UN Security Council', p. 29.

7   Coleman, *International Organisations*, chaps 3–5.

8   For details, see ibid., chaps 4–5; Howe, *Ambiguous Order*, chap. 4; Adebajo, *Building Peace*.

9   See Ellis, *The Mask*, p. 173; Howe, *Ambiguous Order*, chap. 4; Adebajo, *Liberia's Civil War*.

10   See UN Security Council, *Addendum* and *Final Report of the Panel of Experts on the Illegal Exploitation*.

11   This operation also cost Nigeria an estimated $5 billion and the lives of some 500 troops. Malan, 'Africa', p. 91.

12   For more details, see Williams, 'The African Union's'.

13   For details, see Bellamy and Williams, *Understanding Peacekeeping*, chap. 4.

14   See Melvern, *A People Betrayed*; Dallaire, *Shake Hands*.

15   US Presidential Decision Directive 25 determined that peacekeeping operations should be authorized only when there was a genuine threat to peace and security; regional or sub-regional organizations could assist in resolving the situation; a ceasefire existed and the parties had committed themselves to a peace process; a clear political goal existed and was present in the mandate; a precise mandate had been formulated; and the safety of UN personnel could be reasonably assured.

16   Goulding, *Peacemonger*, p. 217.

17   Cited in Susan E. Rice, 'Why Darfur can't be left to Africa', *Washington Post*, 7 August 2005.

18   Cited in Williams, 'Keeping the peace', p. 311.

19   Tony Blair, May 2007, cited ibid, p. 311. Interestingly, between 2004 and 2007 the AU's Peace Fund received between $109 and $183 million per year, less than 2 per cent of which were contributions from AU member states. Franke, *Security Cooperation*, p. 146.

20   For a critique of this idea, see Williams, 'Keeping the peace'.

21   For a more general defence of pluralism, see Jackson, *The Global Covenant*.

22   IISS, *Strategic Survey 1996/97*, p. 223.

23   Commission for Africa, *Our Common Interest*, p. 167.

24   Williams, 'Fighting for Freetown'.

25   See Bellamy and Williams, *Understanding Peacekeeping*, chap. 5.

26   Jones et al., *Building on Brahimi*, p. 2.

27   Spoilers are 'leaders and parties who believe that peace emerging from negotiations threatens their power, worldview, and interests, and use violence to undermine attempts to achieve it.' Stedman, 'Spoiler problems', p. 5.

28   Downs and Stedman, 'Evaluation issues', pp. 55–9.

29   Ibid., pp. 44, 58, 65–6.

30   See Jones, 'The challenges'.

31   Five institutions in Africa are marketed as centres of excellence for peacekeeping training: SADC's Regional Peacekeeping Training Centre in Harare, Zimbabwe (opened October 1996); the Peace Support Training Centre in Kenya (established August 2001); the Peacekeeping School at Bamako, Mali (inaugurated March 2007); the African Centre for Strategic Research and Studies in Abuja, Nigeria (opened August 2004); and the Kofi Annan International Peacekeeping Training

Centre in Accra, Ghana (opened January 2004). They were funded almost entirely by external donors (and often staffed by seconded foreign personnel). In addition, one respected analyst concluded that none of them was really worthy of the label 'centre of excellence'. For details, see Malan, 'Africa', pp. 103–7.

32   Cited in Roessler and Prendergast, 'Democratic Republic of the Congo', p. 259.

33   Ibid., p. 256.

34   Tull, 'Peacekeeping', p. 218.

35   These included the G8's Global Peace Operations Initiative; Washington's African Crisis Response Initiative and the African Contingency Operations Training Assistance; Paris's Reinforcement of African Peacekeeping Capacities programme; and London's peacekeeping training initiatives.

36   Roessler and Prendergast, 'Democratic Republic of the Congo', p. 253.

37   UN doc. S.PV/6153 (Resumption 1), 29 June 2009, p. 13.

38   HRW, '*You Will be Punished*', p. 141.

39   Jones et al., *Building on Brahimi*, p. 12.

40   UN doc. S.PV/6153, 29 June 2009, p. 3.

41   Letter from Dallaire to Col. Nazrul Islam, 17 April 1994, p. 1. Copy in author's possession.

42   Code cable, 'The military assessment of the situation as of 17 April 1994', para. 17. Copy in author's possession. See also Melvern, *A People Betrayed*, p. 187.

43   Melvern, *A People Betrayed*, pp. 194–5.

44   Wiharta, 'The legitimacy', pp. 102–3.

45   Holt and Berkman, *The Impossible Mandate?*, p. 165.

46   Ibid., pp. 166–7.

47   For more details, see Holt, Taylor and Kelly, *Protecting Civilians*; Williams, *Enhancing Civilian Protection*.

48   Holt and Berkman, *The Impossible Mandate?*, pp. 160–1.

49   Ibid., p. 166.

50   Des Forges, *Leave None*, p. 689. The difficulty with this figure is that many of these people were located within the RPF zone. Consequently, the extent to which UNAMIR was responsible for saving them is not entirely clear.

51   Holt et al., *Protecting Civilians*, pp. 12, 211.

52   Wiharta, 'The legitimacy', p. 115.

53   UN Security Council, *Report of the Monitoring Group*.

54   Wiharta, 'The legitimacy', p. 113.

55   UN, *Investigation*.

56   UN Secretary-General, *Special Measures*.

57   Autesserre, 'Hobbes', pp. 272, 276.

58   See Fortna, *Does Peacekeeping Work?*.

Chapter 11   Aid

1   de Waal, *Famine Crimes*, p. xv.

2   Cited in Goodhand, *Aiding Peace?*, p. 88.

3   Macrae et al., *Uncertain Power*, p. 3.

4   For example, some of the big US players, such as CARE, Catholic Relief Services and World Vision, received large amounts of their funding from USAID.

5   Cited in Goodhand, *Aiding Peace?*, p. 89.

6   Weiss, 'Principles'. See also Goodhand, *Aiding Peace?*, pp. 92–6.
7   Bradol, 'Introduction', p. 6.
8   Weiss, 'Principles', p. 19.
9   de Waal, *Famine Crimes*, p. 148.
10   Keen, *Complex Emergencies*, p. 130.
11   Terry, *Condemned to Repeat?*, p. 39.
12   Ibid., pp. 2, 213.
13   Keen, *Complex Emergencies*, pp. 116–19.
14   Ibid., pp. 122–7.
15   Terry, *Condemned to Repeat?*, p. 38.
16   Forsythe, *The Humanitarians*, pp. 119–20.
17   Terry, *Condemned to Repeat?*, pp. 9–10.
18   Keen, *Complex Emergencies*, pp. 127–36.
19   Cited in Goodhand, *Aiding Peace?*, p. 91.
20   Keen, *Complex Emergencies*, pp. 143, 128; Achvarina and Reich, 'No place to hide'.
21   Messiant, 'Angola', p. 118.
22   Lavergne and Weissman, 'Sudan', pp. 153–5.
23   Anderson, *Do No Harm*, chaps 4–5.
24   Terry, *Condemned to Repeat?*, p. 39.
24   Shearer, 'Aiding'.
26   Terry, *Condemned to Repeat?*, p. 218.
27   Rieff, 'Charity', p. 137.
28   Keen, *Complex Emergencies*, p. 121. See also de Waal, *Famine Crimes*.
29   de Waal, *Famine Crimes*, p. 221.
30   Shearer, 'Aiding', p. 198.
31   Terry, *Condemned to Repeat?*, p. 219.
32   Shearer, 'Aiding', p. 189.
33   Terry, *Condemned to Repeat?*, p. 229.
34   de Waal, *Famine Crimes*, p. 217.
35   See Riddell, *Does Foreign Aid*, chaps 4, 5, 16 and 17.
36   See Hancock, *The Lords*, pp. 42ff; de Haan, *How the Aid Industry Works*; Mosse, *Cultivating Development*. This 'business' spends roughly $100 billion per year and between 1956 and 2006 is estimated to have spent a total of approximately $2.3 trillion (measured in 2006 dollars), much of it in Africa. Easterly and Pfutze, 'Where does the money go?', pp. 29, 51.
37   Collier and Hoeffler, 'On the economic causes', pp. 568, 570–1. See also Dixon, 'What causes civil wars?', p. 714.
38   Dixon, 'What causes civil wars?', p. 714. See also Rice, Graff and Lewis, *Poverty and Civil War*, pp. 6–8.
39   Collier and Hoeffler, 'On the incidence', p. 14.
40   DFID, *Eliminating World Poverty*, p. 22.
41   Uvin, *Aiding Violence*, p. 41.
42   Ibid., p. 41.
43   Prunier, *The Rwanda Crisis*, p. 77.
44   Chossudovsky, *The Globalization of Poverty*.
45   Storey, 'Structural adjustment', p. 366.
46   Some 80 per cent of the total investment budget of the government and a significant fraction of its operating budget. Uvin, *Aiding Violence*, pp. 226–7.

47 Ibid., pp. 7, 231.
48 Adelman and Suhrke, *Early Warning*; Uvin, *Aiding Violence*, pp. 70–81, 94.
49 Uvin, *Aiding Violence*, p. 8.
50 Ibid., pp. 40–2; Storey, 'Structural adjustment', p. 370.
51 World Bank, *Implementation*, p. iv. This was putting it mildly: Rwanda's government had clearly not implemented the adjustment programmes. Uvin, *Aiding Violence*, pp. 58–9.
52 Adelman and Suhrke, *Early Warning*.
53 World Bank, *Rwanda*, para. viii. This is not unique to Rwanda. Paul Collier estimated that 40 per cent of Africa's military spending has been inadvertently financed by aid. Collier, *The Bottom Billion*, p. 103.
54 In contrast to official policy, the Bank's staff working on Rwanda recognized the need to consult RPF representatives during the SAC negotiations and held joint meetings with the government and RPF after the Arusha negotiations from March to August 1993.
55 Uvin, *Aiding Violence*, p. 3.
56 Cited in Adebajo, 'Ending', p. 33.
57 Joseph and Gillies, 'Smart aid', p. 2.
58 Benin, Burkina Faso, Burundi, Cameroon, Central African Republic, Republic of Congo, Ethiopia, Gambia, Ghana, Madagascar, Malawi, Mali, Mauritania, Mozambique, Niger, Rwanda, São Tomé and Príncipe, Senegal, Sierra Leone, Tanzania, Uganda and Zambia.
59 Reno, 'Uganda's politics'.
60 See Callaghy 'The search', pp. 87–102.
61 Sachs, 'The strategic significance', pp. 8–9.
62 See Bradbury, *Becoming Somaliland*.
63 The key document with regard to Africa was the so-called Berg Report (World Bank, *Accelerated Development*). For overviews of structural adjustment in Africa, see van de Walle, *African Economies*; Mkandawire and Soludo, *Our Continent*.
64 van de Walle, *African Economies*, p. 7.
65 Clapham, *Africa*, pp. 196–7.
66 Ibid., p. 195.
67 UN Secretary-General, *The Causes*, para. 67. See also Stevenson, *Preventing Conflict*, pp. 12–13.
68 See Paris, *At War's End*.
69 *USAID Primer*, p. 38.
70 See van de Walle, *Overcoming Stagnation*, p. 43.
71 Ibid., pp. 41–2.
72 Ibid., pp. 1–2; Burnside and Dollar, 'Aid, policies and growth'.
73 van de Walle, *Overcoming Stagnation*, p. 5.
74 The survey measures freedom – the opportunity to act spontaneously in a variety of fields outside the control of the government and other centres of potential domination – according to two broad categories: political rights and civil liberties. Freedom House, *Freedom in the World*, at www.freedomhouse.org.
75 Easterly and Pfutze, 'Where does the money go?', pp. 41–2.
76 Commission for Africa, *Our Common Interest*, p. 61.
77 Richard Dowden, 'Can Gordon save Africa?', *The Observer*, 9 January 2005.
78 van de Walle, *African Economies*, pp. 7–8.

79 See, for example, Reno, 'Old brigades'; Reno, *Corruption*; Reno, 'Ironies'. See also Clapham, *Africa*, pp. 250–1.
80 OECD, 'Paris'.
81 These ideas were not new. See Riddell, *Does Foreign Aid*, chap. 2.
82 See the list in van de Walle, *Overcoming Stagnation*, pp. 7–11. The exceptions were new democracies (Mali and São Tomé and Príncipe) and the other two African states awarded a 'free' rating by Freedom House: Senegal and Ghana.
83 By 2008–9 roughly 27 per cent of UK aid was delivered via budget support.
84 Barkan, 'Rethinking', p. 68.
85 Ibid., p. 72.
86 Ibid., p. 75.
87 de Waal, *Famine Crimes*, pp. 220–1.

Conclusion

1 Clapham, 'Comments'.
2 Zartman, *Governance*, p. 1.
3 Lyons, *Demilitarizing Politics*.
4 See Herbst, *States and Power*, pp. 251–72; Englebert, *Africa*, pp. 250–61.
5 Bates, *When Things Fell Apart*.

References

Abdel Salama, A. H., and Alex de Waal, 'On the failure and persistence of *jihad*', in Alex de Waal (ed.), *Islamism and its Enemies in the Horn of Africa* (Bloomington: Indiana University Press, 2004).

Abdullah, Ibrahim, 'Bush path to destruction: the origin and character of the Revolutionary United Front/Sierra Leone', *Journal of Modern African Studies*, 36/2 (1998): 203–35.

Aboagye, Festus B., 'Global and regional approaches to peacekeeping and security in Africa', presentation to the Potsdam Spring Dialogue, 4–5 April 2008, at www.sef-bonn. org/download/veranstaltungen/2008/2008_pfg_presentation_aboagye_en.pdf.

Achvarina, Vera, and Simon F. Reich, 'No place to hide: refugees, displaced persons, and the recruitment of child soldiers', *International Security*, 31/1 (2006): 127–64.

Adebajo, Adekeye, *Building Peace in West Africa* (Boulder, CO: Lynne Rienner, 2002).

Adebajo, Adekeye, 'Liberia: a warlord's peace', in Stephen J. Stedman, Donald Rothchild and Elizabeth M. Cousens (eds), *Ending Civil Wars* (Boulder, CO: Lynne Rienner, 2002).

Adebajo, Adekeye, *Liberia's Civil War* (Boulder, CO: Lynne Rienner, 2002).

Adebjao, Adekeye, 'Ethiopia/Eritrea', in David M. Malone (ed.), *The UN Security Council* (Boulder, CO: Lynne Rienner, 2004).

Adebajo, Adekeye, 'Ending global apartheid', in Adekeye Adebajo (ed.), *From Global Apartheid to Global Village* (Scottsville: University of KwaZulu Natal Press, 2009).

Adebajo, Adekeye, and David Keen, 'Banquet for warlords', *The World Today*, 56/7 (2000).

Adelman, Howard, and Astri Suhrke, *Early Warning and Conflict Management*, Study 2 of *The International Response to Conflict and Genocide: Lessons from the Rwanda Experience* (Copenhagen: DANIDA, 1996).

Alao, Abiodun, *Natural Resources and Conflict in Africa* (Rochester, NY: University of Rochester Press, 2007).

Ali, Abdel Gadir Ali, 'The economics of conflicts in Africa: an overview', *Journal of African Economies*, 9/3 (2000): 235–43.

Anderlini, Sanam N., *Women Building Peace* (Boulder, CO: Lynne Rienner, 2007).

Anderson, Benedict, *Imagined Communities: Reflections on the Origins and Spread of Nationalism* (London: Verso, 1994).

Anderson, Mary B., *Do No Harm* (Boulder, CO: Lynne Rienner, 1999).

Appadurai, Arjun, *Modernity at Large* (Minneapolis: University of Minnesota Press, 1996).

AU (African Union), *Roadmap for the Operationalization of the African Standby Force* (AU doc. EXP/AU-RECs/ASF/4(I), Addis Ababa, 22–3 March 2005).

AU, 'Resume: AU fact-finding mission to Somaliland (30 April to 4 May 2005)' (Addis Ababa: unpublished AU Commission document, 2005).

AU, *Harmonized Doctrine for Peace Support Operations* (AU doc., Oct. 2006).

AU Assembly Decision, 29–30 January 2007, Addis Ababa, Assembly/AU/Dec.134 (VIII).

AU, *Draft Background Paper on the Review of the Methods of Work of the Peace and Security Council of the African Union* (AU doc. interoffice memorandum, 27 April 2007).

AU, *African Union Continental Early Warning System: The CEWS Handbook* (AU doc. PSD/EW/ CEWS Handbook, 7th draft, 12 February 2008).

AU, *A Concept Paper for the Development of a Rapid Deployment Capability for the ASF* (draft as at 16 April 2010).

AUPD (African Union High-Level Panel on Darfur), *Darfur: The Quest for Peace, Justice and Reconciliation* (Addis Ababa: AU, October 2009).

Austen, Ralph A., 'Africa and globalization: colonialism, decolonization and the post-colonial malaise', *Journal of Global History*, 1/3 (2006), 403–8.

Autesserre, Séverine, 'The trouble with Congo – how local disputes fuel regional violence', *Foreign Affairs*, 87/3 (2008): 94–110.

Autesserre, Séverine, 'Hobbes and the Congo: frames, local violence, and international intervention', *International Organization*, 63/2 (2009): 249–80.

Balint-Kurti, Daniel, *Côte d'Ivoire's Forces Nouvelles* (London: Chatham House Programme Paper, September 2007).

Ballentine, Karen, and Heiko Nitzschke, 'Introduction', in Karen Ballentine and Heiko Nitzschke (eds), *Profiting from Peace* (Boulder, CO: Lynne Rienner, 2005).

Barkan, Joel, 'Rethinking budget support for Africa', in Richard Joseph and Alexandra Gillies (eds), *Smart Aid for Development in Africa* (Boulder, CO: Lynne Rienner, 2009).

Barkawi, Tarak, *Globalization and War* (Lanham, MD: Rowman & Littlefield, 2006).

Basedau, Matthias, and Alexander De Juan, *The 'Ambivalence of the Sacred' in Africa: The Impact of Religion on Peace and Conflict in Sub-Saharan Africa* (Hamburg: GIGA Working Paper No.70, 2008).

Bates, Robert H., *When Things Fell Apart: State Failure in Late-Century Africa* (Cambridge: Cambridge University Press, 2007).

Bayart, Jean-François, 'Africa in the world: a history of extraversion', *African Affairs*, 99/395 (2000): 217–67.

Behrend, Heike, *Alice Lakwena and the Holy Spirits* (Oxford: James Currey, 1999).

Bellamy, Alex J., and Paul D. Williams, *Understanding Peacekeeping*, 2nd edn (Cambridge: Polity, 2010).

Bentley, Kristina A., and Roger Southall, *An African Peace Process: Mandela, South Africa and Burundi* (Pretoria: HSRC Press, 2005).

Berdal, Mats, 'Beyond greed and grievance – and not too soon . . .', *Review of International Studies*, 31 (2005): 687–98.

Berman, Bruce J., 'Ethnicity, patronage and the African state: the politics of uncivil nationalism', *African Affairs*, 97/388 (1998): 305–41.

Berman, Eric G., and Katie E. Sams, *Peacekeeping in Africa: Capabilities and Culpabilities* (Geneva: UNIDIR, 2001).

Berman, Eric G., and Katie E. Sams, 'The peacekeeping potential of African regional organizations', in Jane Boulden (ed.), *Dealing with Conflict in Africa* (New York: Palgrave, 2003).

Bigombe, Betty, Paul Collier and Nicholas Sambanis, 'Policies for building post-conflict peace', *Journal of African Economies*, 9/3 (2000): 323–48.

Bøås, Morten, 'Marginalized youth', in Morten Bøås and Kevin C. Dunn (eds), *African Guerrillas* (Boulder, CO: Lynne Rienner 2007).

Bøås, Morten, and Kevin C. Dunn (eds), *African Guerrillas* (Boulder, CO: Lynne Rienner, 2007).

Bøås, Morten, and Kevin C. Dunn, 'African guerrilla politics', in Morten Bøås and Kevin C. Dunn (eds), *African Guerrillas* (Boulder, CO: Lynne Rienner 2007).

Bøås, Morten, and Kevin C. Dunn, 'Introduction', in Morten Bøås and Kevin C. Dunn (eds), *African Guerrillas* (Boulder, CO: Lynne Rienner 2007).

Bob, Clifford, *The Marketing of Rebellion* (Cambridge: Cambridge University Press, 2005).

Boone, Catherine, 'Africa's new territorial politics: regionalism and the open economy in Côte d'Ivoire', *African Studies Review*, 50/1 (2007): 59–81.

Booth, Ken, and Nicholas J. Wheeler, *The Security Dilemma* (Basingstoke: Palgrave, 2008).

Boulden, Jane (ed.), *Dealing with Conflict in Africa* (New York: Palgrave, 2003).

Boulden, Jane, 'UN Security Council policy on Africa', in Jane Boulden (ed.), *Dealing with Conflict in Africa* (New York: Palgrave, 2003).

Boulding, Kenneth, *Stable Peace* (Austin: University of Texas Press, 1979).

Braathen, Einar, Morten Bøås and Gjermund Sæther (eds), *Ethnicity Kills? The Politics of War, Peace and Ethnicity in Sub-Saharan Africa* (Basingstoke: Palgrave Macmillan, 2000).

Brabazon, James, *Liberia: Liberians United for Reconciliation and Democracy* (London: Chatham House Briefing Paper, February 2003).

Bradbury, Mark, *Becoming Somaliland* (Oxford: James Currey, 2008).

Bradol, Jean-Hervé, 'Introduction', in Fabrice Weissman (ed.), *In the Shadow of Just Wars'* (Ithaca, NY: Cornell University Press, 2004).

Brahimi, Lakhdar, and Salman Ahmed, *In Pursuit of Sustainable Peace: The Seven Deadly Sins of Mediation* (New York: New York University, Centre on International Cooperation, May 2008).

Bratton, Michael, and Nicolas van de Walle, 'Neopatrimonial regimes and political transitions in Africa', *World Politics*, 46/4 (1994): 453–89.

Bratton, Michael, and Nicolas van de Walle, *Democratic Experiments in Africa* (Cambridge: Cambridge University Press, 1997).

Brown, Michael E., 'The causes and regional dimensions of internal conflict', in Michael E. Brown (ed.), *The International Dimensions of Internal Conflict* (Cambridge, MA: MIT Press, 1996).

Brown, Michael E., 'The causes of internal conflict: an overview', in Michael E. Brown (ed.), *Nationalism and Ethnic Conflict*, rev. edn (Cambridge, MA: MIT Press, 2001).

Brunborg, Helge, and Ewa Tabeau, 'Demography of conflict and violence: an emerging field', *European Journal of Population*, 21/2–3 (2005): 131–44.

Buhaug, Halvard, and Jan K. Rød, 'Local determinants of African civil wars, 1970–2001', *Political Geography*, 25/3 (2006): 315–35.

Burke, Marshall B., Edward Miguel, Shanker Satyanath, John A. Dykema and David B. Lobell, 'Warming increases the risk of civil war in Africa', *Proceedings of the National Academy of Sciences*, 106/49 (2009).

Burnside, Craig, and David Dollar, 'Aid, policies and growth', *American Economic Review*, 90/4 (2000): 847–68.

Burr, J. Millard, and Robert O. Collins, *Darfur: The Long Road to Disaster* (Boulder, CO: Westview Press, 2006).

Buzan, Barry, *People, States and Fear*, 2nd edn (Hemel Hempstead: Harvester Wheatsheaf, 1991).

Buzan, Barry, 'The level of analysis problem in international relations reconsidered', in Ken Booth and Steve Smith (eds), *International Relations Theory Today* (Cambridge: Polity, 1995).

Buzan, Barry, and Ole Wæver, *Regions and Powers: The Structure of International Security* (Cambridge: Cambridge University Press, 2003).

Byman, Daniel, *Keeping the Peace: Lasting Solutions to Ethnic Conflict* (Baltimore: Johns Hopkins University Press, 2002).

Callaghy, Thomas M., 'The search for smart debt relief', in Richard Joseph and Alexandra Gillies (eds), *Smart Aid for Development in Africa* (Boulder, CO: Lynne Rienner, 2009).

Callaghy, Thomas, Raymond Kassimir and Robert Latham (eds), *Intervention and Transnationalism in Africa* (Cambridge: Cambridge University Press, 2001).

Cater, Charlie, 'Rethinking the critical cases of Africa', in Karen Ballentine and Jake Sherman (eds), *The Political Economy of Armed Conflict* (Boulder, CO: Lynne Rienner, 2003).

Cavanagh, William T., *The Myth of Religious Violence* (Oxford: Oxford University Press, 2009).

Cederman, Lars-Erik, Andreas Wimmer and Brian Min, 'Why do ethnic groups rebel?', *World Politics*, 62/1 (2010): 87–119.

Chabal, Patrick, and Jean-Pascal Daloz, *Africa Works* (Oxford: James Currey, 1998).

Chazan, Naomi, Peter Lewis, Robert Mortimer, Donald Rothchild and Stephen J. Stedman, *Politics and Society in Contemporary Africa*, 3rd edn (Boulder, CO: Lynne Rienner 1999).

Chossudovsky, Michel, *The Globalization of Poverty: Impacts of IMF and World Bank Reforms* (London: Zed Books, 1997).

CIJ (Coalition for International Justice), *Chronology of Reporting on Events Concerning the Conflict in Darfur, Sudan* (CIJ, February 2006), at www.africaaction.org/resources/darfur_chronology/CIJ_Complete_Darfur_Chronology.pdf.

Cilliers, Jackie, *The African Standby Force: An Update on Progress* (Pretoria: ISS Paper 160, March 2008).

Clapham, Christopher, *Third World Politics: An Introduction* (Abingdon: Routledge, 1985).

Clapham, Christopher, *Africa and the International System* (Cambridge: Cambridge University Press, 1996).

Clapham, Christopher (ed.), *African Guerrillas* (Oxford: James Currey, 1998).

Clapham, Christopher, 'Degrees of statehood', *Review of International Studies*, 24 (1998): 143–57.

Clapham, Christopher, 'Introduction', in Christopher Clapham (ed.), *African Guerrillas* (Oxford: James Currey, 1998).

Clapham, Christopher, 'Rwanda: the perils of peacemaking', *Journal of Peace Research*, 35/2 (1998): 193–210.

Clapham, Christopher, 'Comments on the Ethiopian crisis', unpublished paper, 7 November 2005, at www.ethiomedia.com/fastpress/clapham_on_ethiopian_crisis.html.

Clapham, Christopher, 'The political economy of African population change', *Population and Development Review*, 32 (2006): 96–114.

Clausewitz, Carl von, *On War*, ed. and trans. Michael Howard and Peter Paret (Princeton, NJ: Princeton University Press, 1976).

CNA Corporation, *National Security and the Threat of Climate Change* (Alexandria, VA: CNA Corporation, 2007).

Coghlan, Benjamin, et al., 'Mortality in the Democratic Republic of Congo: a nationwide survey', *The Lancet*, 367 (2006): 44–51.

Coleman, Katharina P., *International Organisations and Peace Enforcement* (Cambridge: Cambridge University Press, 2007).

Collier, Paul, 'Rebellion as a quasi-criminal activity', *Journal of Conflict Resolution*, 44/6 (2000): 839–53.

Collier, Paul, *The Bottom Billion* (Oxford: Oxford University Press, 2007).

Collier, Paul, and Anke Hoeffler, 'On the economic causes of civil war', *Oxford Economic Papers*, 53/4 (1998): 563–73.

Collier, Paul, and Anke Hoeffler, 'On the incidence of civil war in Africa', *Journal of Conflict Resolution*, 46/1 (2002): 13–28.

Collier, Paul, and Anke Hoeffler, 'Greed and grievance in civil war', *Oxford Economic Papers*, 56/4 (2004): 563–95.

Collier, Paul, and Anke Hoeffler, 'The political economy of secession', in Hurst Hannum and Eileen Babbitt (eds), *Negotiating Self-Determination* (Lanham, MD: Lexington Books, 2005).

Collier, Paul, Anke Hoeffler and Dominic Rohner, 'Beyond greed and grievance: feasibility and civil war', *Oxford Economic Papers*, 61/1 (2009): 1–27.

Collins, Robert O., 'Disaster in Darfur: historical overview', in Samuel Totten and Eric Markusen (eds), *Genocide in Darfur* (New York: Routledge, 2006).

Combating Terrorism Center, *Al-Qa'ida's (Mis)Adventures in the Horn of Africa* (West Point, CT: Combating Terrorism Center, 2007), at http://ctc.usma.edu/aq/aqII.asp.

Commission for Africa, *Our Common Interest* (London: TSO/DFID, 2005).

Conibere, Richard, Jana Asher, Kristen Cibelli, Jana Dudukovitch, Rafe Kaplan and Patrick Ball, 'Appendix 1: statistical appendix to the report of the Truth and Reconciliation Commission of Sierra Leone', 5 October 2004, at www.sierra-leone.org/TRCDocuments.html.

Connell, Dan, 'Eritrea: on a slow fuse', in Robert I. Rotberg (ed.), *Battling Terrorism in the Horn of Africa* (Washington, DC: Brookings Institution, 2005).

Cox, Robert W., 'Civil society at the turn of the millennium: prospects for an alternative world order', *Review of International Studies*, 25/1 (1999): 3–28.

Cox, Robert W., with Timothy Sinclair, *Approaches to World Order* (Cambridge: Cambridge University Press, 1996).

Cramer, Christopher, *Civil War is Not a Stupid Thing* (London: Hurst, 2006).

Crocker, Chester, Fen Osler Hampson and Pamela Aall, *Taming Intractable Conflicts* (Washington, DC: US Institute of Peace Press, 2004).

Daley, Patricia, 'Ethnicity and political violence in Africa: the challenge to the Burundian state', *Political Geography*, 25/6 (2006): 657–79.

Dallaire, Roméo, *Shake Hands with the Devil* (Toronto: Random House, 2003).

Danfulani, Umar Habilar Dadem, and Sati U. Fwatshak, 'Briefing: the September 2001 events in Jos, Nigeria', *African Affairs*, 101 (2002): 243–55.

de Haan, Arjan, *How the Aid Industry Works* (Sterling, VA: Kumarian Press, 2009).

de Soysa, Indra, 'Paradise is a bazaar? Greed, creed, and governance in civil war, 1989–99', *Journal of Peace Research*, 39 (2002): 395–416.

de Waal, Alex, 'Contemporary warfare in Africa', in Mary Kaldor and Basker Vashee (eds), *Restructuring the Global Military Sector*, Vol. 1 (London: Pinter, 1997).

de Waal, Alex, *Famine Crimes: Politics and the Disaster Relief Industry in Africa* (Oxford: James Currey, 1997).

de Waal, Alex (ed.), *Demilitarizing the Mind: African Agendas for Peace and Security* (Trenton, NJ: Africa World Press, 2002).

de Waal, Alex, 'Counter-insurgency on the cheap', *London Review of Books*, 26/15 (2004).

de Waal, Alex, 'Introduction', in Alex de Waal (ed.), *Islamism and its Enemies in the Horn of Africa* (Bloomington: Indiana University Press, 2004).

de Waal, Alex, 'The politics of destabilization in the Horn, 1989–2001', in Alex de Waal (ed.), *Islamism and its Enemies in the Horn of Africa* (Bloomington: Indiana University Press, 2004).

de Waal, Alex, 'Is climate change the culprit for Darfur?', *SSRC Blogs: Making Sense of Darfur* (June 2007), at www.ssrc.org/blogs/darfur/2007/06/25/is-climatechange-the-culprit-for-darfur/.

de Waal, Alex 'Sudan: the turbulent state', in Alex de Waal (ed.), *War in Darfur* (Cambridge, MA: Harvard University Press, 2007).

de Waal, Alex (ed.), *War in Darfur and the Search for Peace* (Cambridge, MA: Harvard University Press, 2007).

de Waal, Alex, 'Mission without end? Peacekeeping in the African marketplace', *International Affairs*, 85/1 (2009): 99–113.

de Waal, Alex, and A. H. Abdel Salam, 'Africa, Islamism and America's "War on Terror"', in Alex de Waal (ed.), *Islamism and its Enemies in the Horn of Africa* (Bloomington: Indiana University Press, 2004).

de Waal, Alex, and A. H. Abdel Salam, 'Islamism, state power and *jihad* in Sudan', in Alex de Waal (ed.), *Islamism and its Enemies in the Horn of Africa* (Bloomington: Indiana University Press, 2004).

de Zeeuw, Jeroen (ed.), *From Soldiers to Politicians* (Boulder, CO: Lynne Rienner, 2008).

Degomme, Olivier, and Debarati Guha-Sapir, 'Patterns of mortality rates in Darfur conflict', *The Lancet*, 375 (23 January 2010): 294–300.

Deng, Francis M., *War of Visions: Conflict of Identities in the Sudan* (Washington, DC: Brookings Institution, 1996).

Des Forges, Alison, 'Burundi: failed coup or creeping coup?, *Current History*, 93/583 (1994): 203–7.

Des Forges, Alison, *Leave None to Tell the Story: Genocide in Rwanda* (New York: Human Rights Watch, 1999).

DFID (Department for International Development), *The Causes of Conflict in Africa: Consultation Document* (London: DFID, 2001).

DFID, *Eliminating World Poverty: Building our Common Future*, Cm. 7656 (London: The Stationery Office, 2009).

Dixon, Jeffrey, 'What causes civil wars? Integrating quantitative research findings', *International Studies Review*, 11 (2009): 707–35.

Doom, Ruddy, and Koen Vlassenroot, 'Kony's message: a new Koine? The Lord's Resistance Army in Northern Uganda', *African Affairs*, 98 (1999): 5–36.

Dowden, Richard, *Africa* (London: Portobello Books, 2008).

Downs, George, and Stephen J. Stedman, 'Evaluation issues in peace implementation', in Stephen J. Stedman, Donald Rothchild and Elizabeth M. Cousens (eds), *Ending Civil Wars* (Boulder, CO: Lynne Rienner, 2002).

Doyle, Michael W., 'Strategy and transitional authority', in Stephen J. Stedman, Donald Rothchild and Elizabeth M. Cousens (eds), *Ending Civil Wars* (Boulder, CO: Lynne Rienner, 2002).

Duffield, Mark, *Global Governance and the New Wars* (London: Zed Books, 2001).

Dunn, Kevin C., 'Uganda: the Lord's Resistance Army', in Morten Bøås and Kevin C. Dunn (eds), *African Guerrillas* (Boulder, CO: Lynne Rienner, 2007).

Durkheim, Emile, *The Elementary Forms of Religious Life* (Oxford: Oxford University Press, 2001).

Easterly, William, and Tobias Pfutze, 'Where does the money go? Best and worst practices in foreign aid', *Journal of Economic Perspectives*, 22/2 (2008): 29–52.

Eck, Kristine, Joakim Kreutz and Ralph Sundberg, 'Introducing the UCDP non-state conflict dataset', unpublished manuscript, Uppsala University, 2010.

El Din, Ahmed Kamal, 'Islam and Islamism in Darfur', in Alex de Waal (ed.), *War in Darfur* (Cambridge, MA: Harvard University Press, 2007).

Elbadawi, Ibrahim, and Nicholas Sambanis, 'Why are there so many civil wars in Africa?', *Journal of African Economies*, 9/3 (2000): 244–69.

Ellis, Stephen, *The Mask of Anarchy: The Destruction of Liberia and the Religious Dimension of an African Civil War* (London: Hurst, 1999).

Ellis, Stephen, and Gerrie ter Haar, 'Religion and politics in sub-Saharan Africa', *Journal of Modern African Studies*, 36/2 (1998): 175–201.

Ellis, Stephen, and Gerrie ter Haar, *Worlds of Power: Religious Thought and Political Practice in Africa* (New York: Oxford University Press, 2004).

Ellis, Stephen, and Gerrie ter Haar, 'Religion and politics: taking African epistemologies seriously', *Journal of Modern African Studies*, 45/3 (2007): 385–401.

Engel, Ulf, and Joao G. Porto, 'The African Union's new peace and security architecture', *African Security*, 2/2–3 (2009): 82–96.

Englebert, Pierre, *Africa: Unity, Sovereignty and Sorrow* (Boulder, CO: Lynne Rienner, 2009).

Englebert, Pierre, and James Ron, 'Primary commodities and war: Congo-Brazzaville's ambivalent resource curse', *Comparative Politics*, 37/1 (2004): 61–81.

Erdmann, Gero, and Ulf Engel, 'Neopatrimonialism reconsidered', *Commonwealth & Comparative Politics*, 45/1 (2007): 95–119.

Esman, Milton J., *An Introduction to Ethnic Conflict* (Cambridge: Polity, 2004).

European Development Report, *Overcoming Fragility in Africa* (San Domenico di Fiesole: Robert Schuman Centre for Advanced Studies, European University Institute, 2009).

Evans, Martin, *Senegal: Mouvement des Forces Démocratiques de la Casamance (MFDC)* (London: Chatham House, AFP BP 04/02, December 2004).

Faris, Stephen, 'The real roots of Darfur', *Atlantic Monthly*, 299/3 (2007): 67–9.

FCO (Foreign and Commonwealth Office), *The Casamance Conflict 1982–1999* (London: FCO African Research Group, August 1999).

Fearon, James D., and David D. Laitin, 'Violence and the social construction of ethnic identity', *International Organization*, 54/4 (2000): 845–77.

Fearon, James D., and David D. Laitin, 'Ethnicity, insurgency, and civil war', *American Political Science Review*, 91/1 (2003): 75–90.

Fenton, Steve, *Ethnicity* (Cambridge: Polity, 2004).

Flint, Julie, *Beyond 'Janjaweed': Understanding the Militias of Darfur* (Geneva: Small Arms Survey, HSBA Working Paper 17, 2009).

Flint, Julie, and Alex de Waal, *Darfur: A Short History of a Long War* (London: Zed Books, 2005).

Forsythe, David P., *The Humanitarians: The International Committee of the Red Cross* (Cambridge: Cambridge University Press, 2005).

Fortna, Virginia P., *Does Peacekeeping Work?* (Princeton, NJ: Princeton University Press, 2008).

Franke, Benedikt, *Security Cooperation in Africa: A Reappraisal* (Boulder, CO: Lynne Rienner, 2009).

Fujii, Lee Ann, *Killing Neighbors: Webs of Violence in Rwanda* (Ithaca, NY: Cornell University Press, 2009).

Gagnon, Valère P., *The Myth of Ethnic War: Serbia and Croatia in the 1990s* (Ithaca, NY: Cornell University Press, 2004).

Garrett, Nicholas, Harrison Mitchell and Marie Lintzer, *Promoting Legal Mineral Trade in Africa's Great Lakes Region* (London: Resource Consulting Services, May 2010), at www. resourceglobal.co.uk (accessed 10 July 2010).

Gat, Azar, *War in Human Civilization* (Oxford: Oxford University Press, 2006).

Gberie, Lansana, *A Dirty War in West Africa: The RUF and the Destruction of Sierra Leone* (London: Hurst, 2005).

Global Witness, *A Rough Trade: The Role of Companies and Governments in the Angolan Conflict* (London: Global Witness, 1999).

Goldstone, Jack A., 'Population and security: how demographic change can lead to violent conflict', *Journal of International Affairs*, 56/1 (2002): 3–21.

Goldstone, Jack, et al., 'A global forecasting model of political instability', paper presented at the annual meeting of the American Political Science Association, Washington, DC, 1–4 September 2005.

Goldstone, Jack, et al., 'A global forecasting model of political instability', *American Journal of Political Science*, 54/1 (2010): 190–208.

Goodhand, Jonathan, *Aiding Peace? The Role of NGOs in Armed Conflict* (Boulder, CO: Lynne Rienner, 2006).

Goulding, Marrack, *Peacemonger* (London: John Murray, 2002).

Graeber, John, Laura Harris and Larissa Hotra, 'A strategic conflict and peace assessment of the Tuareg rebellions in Mali and Niger', unpublished paper, George Washington University, April 2009.

Grant, Andrew J., and Ian Taylor, 'Global governance and conflict diamonds', *The Round Table*, 93/375 (2004): 385–401.

Green, Elliott D., 'Democracy, diversity and nativism in contemporary Uganda', *Nations and Nationalism*, 13/4 (2007): 717–36.

Gunaratna, Rohand, *Inside Al Qaeda* (New York: Columbia University Press, 2002).

Gurr, Ted Robert, *Why Men Rebel* (Princeton, NJ: Princeton University Press, 1970).

Gurr, Ted Robert, *Minorities at Risk: A Global View of Ethnopolitical Conflicts* (Washington, DC: US Institute of Peace Press, 1993).

Haggis, Carolyn, 'The African Union and intervention: the origins and implications of Article 4(h) of the 2001 Constitutive Act', unpublished DPhil thesis, University of Oxford, 2009.

Hagmann, Tobias, 'Beyond clannishness and colonialism: understanding political disorder in Ethiopia's Somali region, 1991–2004', *Journal of Modern African Studies*, 43/4 (2005): 509–36.

Hale, Henry, 'Explaining ethnicity', *Comparative Political Studies*, 37/4 (2004): 458–85.

Hancock, Graham, *The Lords of Poverty: The Power, Prestige and Corruption of the International Aid Business* (New York: Atlantic Monthly Press, 1989).

Hanlon, Joseph, 'Is the international community helping to recreate the preconditions for war in Sierra Leone?', *The Round Table*, 94/381 (2005): 459–72.

Hanson, Stephanie, *MEND: The Niger Delta's Militant Umbrella Group* (Council on Foreign Relations, 22 March 2007), at www.cfr.org/publication/12920/.

Harbom, Lotta, and Peter Wallensteen, 'Patterns of major armed conflicts, 1999–2008', in *The SIPRI Yearbook 2009* (Cambridge: Cambridge University Press, 2009).

Harbom, Lotta, Stina Högbladh and Peter Wallensteen, 'Armed conflict and peace agreements', *Journal of Peace Research*, 43/5 (2006): 617–31.

Hendrix, Cullen S., and Sarah M. Glaser, 'Trends and triggers: climate, climate change and civil conflict in sub-Saharan Africa', *Political Geography*, 26/6 (2007): 695–715.

Henrikson, Alan, 'The growth of regional organizations and the role of the United Nations', in Louise Fawcett and Andrew Hurrell (eds), *Regionalism in World Politics* (Oxford: Oxford University Press, 1995).

Herbst, Jeffrey, 'Economic incentives, natural resources and conflict in Africa', *Journal of African Economies*, 9/3 (2000): 270–94.

Herbst, Jeffrey, *States and Power in Africa* (Princeton, NJ: Princeton University Press, 2000).

Herbst, Jeffrey, 'Crafting regional cooperation in Africa', in Amitav Acharya and Alastair I. Johnston (eds), *Crafting Cooperation: Regional International Institutions in Comparative Perspective* (Cambridge: Cambridge University Press, 2007).

Hettne, Björn, András Inotai, and Osvaldo Sunkel (eds), *The New Regionalism and the Future of Security and Development* (New York: St Martin's Press, 2000).

Higgins, Rosalyn, *Problems and Process: International Law and How We Use It* (Oxford: Oxford University Press, 1994).

Hintjens, Helen, 'Explaining the 1994 genocide in Rwanda', *Journal of Modern African Studies*, 37/2 (1999): 241–86.

Hironaka, Ann, *Neverending Wars: The International Community, Weak States, and the Perpetuation of Civil War* (Cambridge, MA: Harvard University Press, 2005).

Holt, Victoria K., and Tobias C. Berkman, *The Impossible Mandate? Military Preparedness, the Responsibility to Protect and Modern Peace Operations* (Washington, DC: Henry L. Stimson Center, 2006).

Holt, Victoria K., and Glyn Taylor with Max Kelly, *Protecting Civilians in the Context of UN Peacekeeping Operations* (New York: UN DPKO/OCHA, November 2009).

Horowitz, Donald, *Ethnic Groups in Conflict* (Berkeley: University of California Press, 1985).

Howard, Michael, *War in European History*, updated edn (Oxford: Oxford University Press, [1976] 2009).

Howe, Herbert M., *Ambiguous Order: Military Forces in African States* (Boulder, CO: Lynne Rienner, 2001).

HRW (Human Rights Watch), *Angola: Between War and Peace in Cabinda* (New York: HRW Briefing Paper, 2004), at www.hrw.org/sites/default/files/related_material/Angola%20 Between%20War%20and%20Peace%20in%20Cabinda.pdf.

HRW, *Youth, Poverty and Blood: The Lethal Legacy of West Africa's Regional Warriors* (New York: HRW, 2005).

HRW, *Criminal Politics: Violence, 'Godfathers' and Corruption in Nigeria* (New York: HRW, Vol. 19, No. 16(A), October 2007).

HRW, *Arbitrary Killings by Security Forces: Submission to the Investigative Bodies on the November 28–29, 2008 Violence in Jos, Plateau State, Nigeria* (New York: HRW, 2009).

HRW, *Nigeria: Investigate Widespread Killings by Police* (New York: HRW, 18 November 2007), at http://hrw.org/english/docs/2007/11/16/nigeri17361.htm.

HRW, *'You Will be Punished': Attacks on Civilians in Eastern Congo* (New York: HRW, December 2009).

Hughes, Arnold, 'Decolonizing Africa: colonial boundaries and the crisis of the (non) nation state', *Diplomacy and Statecraft*, 15/4 (2004): 833–66.

Human Security Brief 2007 (Vancouver: Simon Fraser University, 2008).

Human Security Report 2005 (New York: Oxford University Press, 2005).

Human Security Report 2009: The Shrinking Costs of War (Vancouver: Simon Fraser University, 2010).

Human Security Report Project, *Overview to the Debate Generated by the 'Shrinking Costs of War', 14 April 2010 – updated 7 May 2010* (Vancouver: HSR Project, 2010), at www.humansecurityreport.info.

Humphreys, Macartan, 'Natural resources and armed conflicts', in Karen Ballentine and Heiko Nitzschke (eds), *Profiting from Peace* (Boulder, CO: Lynne Rienner, 2005).

Humphreys, Macartan, and Jeremy M. Weinstein, 'Who fights? The determinants of participation in civil war', *American Journal of Political Science*, 52/2 (2008): 436–55.

Huntington, Samuel P., 'The clash of civilizations?', *Foreign Affairs*, 72/3 (1993): 22–49.

Huntington, Samuel P., *The Third Wave: Democratization in the Late Twentieth Century* (Norman: University of Oklahoma Press, 1993).

Huntington, Samuel P., *The Clash of Civilizations and the Remaking of World Order* (New York: Simon & Schuster, 1998).

Hyden, Goren, *African Politics in Comparative Perspective* (Cambridge: Cambridge University Press, 2006).

ICG (International Crisis Group), *Darfur Rising: Sudan's New Crisis*, Africa Report no. 76 (Brussels: ICG, 24 March 2004).

ICG, *Somaliland: Time for African Union Leadership*, Africa Report no.110 (Brussels: ICG, 23 May 2006).

ICG, *Western Sahara: Out of the Impasse*, North Africa Report no.66 (Brussels: ICG, 11 June 2007).

ICG, *Nigeria: Seizing the Moment in the Niger Delta*, Africa Briefing no.60 (Brussels: ICG, 30 April 2009).

ICG, *Somalia's Divided Islamists*, Africa Briefing no.74 (Brussels: ICG, 18 May 2010).

IISS (International Institute for Strategic Studies), *Strategic Survey 1996/97* (Oxford: Oxford University Press, 1997).

IISS, *Strategic Survey 2007* (London: Taylor & Francis, 2007).

Iliffe, John, *Africans: The History of a Continent* (Cambridge: Cambridge University Press, 1995).

IRC (International Rescue Committee), *Mortality in Eastern DRC: Results from Five Mortality Surveys* (New York: IRC, May 2000), at www.theirc.org/resources/mortality_I_report.pdf.

IRC, *Mortality in Eastern DRC: Results from Eleven Mortality Surveys* (New York: IRC, 2001), at www.theirc.org/resources/mortII_report.pdf.

IRC, *Mortality in the DRC: Results from a Nationwide Survey* (New York: IRC, April 2003), at www.theirc.org/resources/drc_mortality_iii_full.pdf.

IRC, *Mortality in the Democratic Republic of Congo: An Ongoing Crisis* (New York: IRC, 2007), at www.theirc.org/resources/2007/2006-7_congomortalitysurvey.pdf.

Iyob, Ruth, 'Regional hegemony: domination and resistance in the Horn of Africa', *Journal of Modern African Studies*, 31/2 (1993): 257–76.

Iyob, Ruth, *The Eritrean Struggle for Independence* (Cambridge: Cambridge University Press, 1995).

Jackson, Paul, 'Are Africa's wars part of a fourth generation of warfare?', *Contemporary Security Policy*, 28/2 (2007): 267–85.

Jackson, Richard, 'Africa's wars', in Oliver Furley and Roy May (eds), *Ending Africa's Wars* (Aldershot: Ashgate, 2006).

Jackson, Robert H., *Quasi-States: Sovereignty, International Relations and the Third World* (Cambridge: Cambridge University Press, 1990).

Jackson, Robert H., *The Global Covenant* (Oxford: Oxford University Press, 2000).

Jackson, Robert H., and Carl G. Rosberg, 'Why Africa's weak states persist: the empirical and juridical in statehood', *World Politics*, 35/1 (1982): 1–24.

Johnson, Douglas H., *The Root Causes of Sudan's Civil Wars* (Oxford: James Currey, 2003).

Johnson, Douglas, 'Darfur: peace, genocide and crimes against humanity in Sudan', in Preben Kaarsholm (ed.), *Violence, Political Culture and Development in Africa* (Oxford: James Currey, 2006).

Johnston, Patrick, 'The geography of insurgent organization and its consequences for civil wars', *Security Studies*, 17/1 (2008): 107–37.

Jones, Bruce D., *Peacemaking in Rwanda* (Boulder, CO: Lynne Rienner, 2001).

Jones, Bruce D., 'The challenges of strategic coordination', in Stephen J. Stedman, Donald Rothchild and Elizabeth M. Cousens (eds), *Ending Civil Wars* (Boulder, CO: Lynne Rienner, 2002).

Jones, Bruce, Richard Gowan, Jake Sherman et al., *Building on Brahimi: Peacekeeping in an era of Strategic Uncertainty* (New York: Center on International Cooperation, April 2009).

Joseph, Richard, and Alexandria Gillies, 'Smart aid', in Richard Joseph and Alexandra Gillies (eds), *Smart Aid for Development in Africa* (Boulder, CO: Lynne Rienner, 2009).

Kaarsholm, Preben, 'States of failure, societies in collapse? Understandings of violent conflict in Africa', in Preben Kaarsholm (ed.), *Violence, Political Culture and Development in Africa* (Oxford: James Currey, 2005).

Kagwanja, Peter, 'Calming the waters: the East African community and conflict over the Nile resources', *Journal of Eastern African Studies*, 1/3 (2007): 321–37.

Kahl, Colin, 'Population growth, environmental degradation and state-sponsored violence: the case of Kenya, 1991–93', *International Security*, 23/2 (1998): 80–119.

Kaldor, Mary, 'Inconclusive wars: is Clausewitz still relevant in these global times?', *Global Policy*, 1/1 (2010): 271–81.

Kalyvas, Stathis N., *The Logic of Violence in Civil War* (Cambridge: Cambridge University Press, 2006).

Kamanu, Onyeonoro S., 'Secession and the right of self-determination: an OAU dilemma', *Journal of Modern African Studies*, 12/3 (1974): 355–76.

Kandeh, Jimmy D., 'Ransoming the state: elite origins of subaltern terror in Sierra Leone', *Review of African Political Economy*, 26/81 (1999): 351–8.

Kaplan, Robert, 'The coming anarchy', *Atlantic Monthly*, 273/2 (1994): 44–76.

Kassimir, Ronald, and Robert Latham, 'Toward a new research agenda', in Thomas Callaghy, Ronald Kassimir and Robert Latham (eds), *Intervention and Transnationalism in Africa* (Cambridge: Cambridge University Press, 2001).

Kaufman, Stuart J., 'Symbolic politics or rational choice? Testing theories of extreme ethnic violence', *International Security*, 30/4 (2006): 45–86.

Keen, David, *The Economic Functions of Violence in Civil Wars*, Adelphi Paper 320 (Oxford: Oxford University Press, 1998).

Keen, David, 'War and peace: what's the difference?', *International Peacekeeping*, 7/4 (2001): 1–22.

Keen, David, *Conflict and Collusion in Sierra Leone* (Oxford: James Currey, 2005).

Keen, David, *Complex Emergencies* (Cambridge: Polity, 2008).

Keller, Edmund, *Revolutionary Ethiopia* (Bloomington: Indiana University Press, 1991).

Keller, Edmund, 'Transnational ethnic conflict in Africa', in David A. Lake and Donald S. Rothchild (eds), *The International Spread of Ethnic Conflict* (Princeton, NJ: Princeton University Press, 1998).

Khadiagala, Gilbert M., 'Burundi', in Jane Boulden (ed.), *Dealing with Conflict in Africa* (New York: Palgrave, 2003).

Klabbers, Jan, 'The right to be taken seriously: self-determination in international law', *Human Rights Quarterly*, 28/1 (2006): 186–206.

Kornprobst, Markus, 'The management of border disputes in African regional subsystems', *Journal of Modern African Studies*, 40/3 (2002): 369–93.

Krasner, Stephen D., *Sovereignty: Organized Hypocrisy* (Princeton, NJ: Princeton University Press, 1999).

Kraxberger, Brennan 'Strangers, indigenes and settlers: contested geographies of citizenship in Nigeria', *Space and Polity*, 9/1 (2005): 9–28.

Kuperman, Alan, *The Limits of Humanitarian Intervention* (Washington, DC: Brookings Institution Press, 2001).

Lacina, Bethany Ann, and Nils Petter Gleditsch, 'Monitoring trends in global combat: a new dataset of battle deaths', *European Journal of Population*, 21/2–3 (2005): 145–66.

Lake, David A., and Patrick M. Morgan (eds), *Regional Orders: Building Security in a New World* (University Park: Pennsylvania State University Press, 1997).

Lake, David A., and Donald Rothchild, 'Spreading fear' in David A. Lake and Donald Rothchild (eds), *The International Spread of Ethnic Conflict* (Princeton, NJ: Princeton University Press, 1998).

Lasswell, Harold D., *Politics: Who Gets What, When, How* (New York: McGraw-Hill, 1936).

Last, Murray, 'Muslims and Christians in Nigeria: an economy of political panic', *The Round Table*, no. 392 (2007): 605–16.

Lavergne, Marc, and Fabrice Weissman, 'Sudan', in Fabrice Weissman (ed.), *In the Shadow of Just Wars'* (Ithaca, NY: Cornell University Press, 2004).

Le Billon, Philippe, 'The political ecology of war: natural resources and armed conflicts', *Political Geography*, 20 (2001): 561–84.

Le Billon, Philippe, 'Diamond wars? Conflict diamonds and geographies of resource wars', *Annals of the Association of American Geographers*, 98/2 (2008): 345–72.

Le Vine, Victor, 'African patrimonial regimes in comparative perspective', *Journal of Modern African Studies*, 18/4 (1980): 657–73.

Leach, Melissa, and Robin Mearns (eds), *The Lie of the Land: Challenging Received Wisdom on the African Environment* (Oxford: James Currey, 1996).

Lemarchand, René, *Burundi: Ethnic Conflict and Genocide* (Cambridge: Cambridge University Press, 1996).

Lemarchand, René, 'Consociationalism and power sharing in Africa', *African Affairs*, 106/422 (2006): 1–20.

Lemke, Douglas, *Regions of War and Peace* (Cambridge: Cambridge University Press, 2002).

Leysens, Anthony, 'Social forces in southern Africa: transformation from below?', *Journal of Modern African Studies*, 44/1 (2006): 31–58.

Licklider, Roy, 'The consequences of negotiated settlements in civil wars, 1945–1993', *American Political Science Review*, 89/3 (1995): 681–90.

Lijphart, Arend, *Democracy in Plural Societies* (New Haven, CT: Yale University Press, 1977).

Lijphart, Arend, 'The power-sharing approach', in Joseph V. Montville (ed.), *Conflict and Peace-Making in Multiethnic Societies* (New York: Lexington Books, 1990).

Longman, Timothy, 'Church politics and the genocide in Rwanda', *Journal of Religion in Africa*, 31/2 (2001): 163–86.

Longman, Timothy, 'Churches and social upheaval in Rwanda and Burundi', in Niels Kastfelt (ed.), *Religion and African Civil Wars* (New York: Palgrave Macmillan, 2005).

Lowe, Vaughan, *International Law* (Oxford: Clarendon Press, 2007).

Lubkemann, Stephen C., *Culture in Chaos: An Anthropology of the Social Condition in War* (Chicago: University of Chicago Press, 2008).

Luttwak, Edward, 'Give war a chance', *Foreign Affairs*, 78/4 (1999): 36–44.

Lyons, Terrence, *Demilitarizing Politics* (Boulder, CO: Lynne Rienner, 2005).

Lyons, Terrence, *Avoiding Conflict in the Horn of Africa* (Washington, DC: Council on Foreign Relations, 2006).

Macrae, Joanna et al., *Uncertain Power: The Changing Role of Official Donors in Humanitarian Action*, HPG Report 12 (London: Overseas Development Institute, December 2002).

Makinda, Samuel M., and F. Wafula Okumu, *The African Union* (London: Routledge, 2008).

Malan, Mark, 'Africa: building institutions on the run', in Donald Daniel, Patricia Taft and Sharon Wiharta (eds), *Peace Operations* (Washington, DC: Georgetown University Press, 2008).

Mamdani, Mahmoud, *When Victims Become Killers: Colonialism, Nativism, and the Genocide in Rwanda* (Oxford: James Currey, 2001).

Mamdani, Mahmoud, *Saviors and Survivors: Darfur, Politics and the War on Terror* (New York: Pantheon, 2009).

Marchal, Roland, 'Islamic political dynamics in the Somali civil war', in Alex de Waal (ed.), *Islamism and its Enemies in the Horn of Africa* (Bloomington: Indiana University Press, 2004).

Marshall, Jeffrey E., *Building an Effective African Standby Force to Promote African Stability, Conflict Resolution and Prosperity*, Crisis States Discussion Papers no.16 (London: London School of Economics, April 2009).

Marshall, Monty G., *Conflict Trends in Africa, 1946–2004: A Macro-Comparative Perspective* (London: Department for International Development, 2006).

Marshall, Monty G., and Benjamin R. Cole, 'Global report on conflict, governance and state fragility, 2008', *Foreign Policy Bulletin*, 18/1 (2008): 3–21.

Martin, Pablo San, 'Briefing: Western Sahara: road to perdition?', *African Affairs*, 103/413 (2004): 651–63.

Martinez, Luis, *The Algerian Civil War 1990–1998* (New York: Columbia University Press, 2000).

Mays, Terry M., *Africa's First Peacekeeping Operation* (Westport, CT: Praeger, 2002).

Mazo, Jeffrey, *Climate Conflict*, Adelphi Paper 409 (Abingdon: Routledge, 2009).

McGowan, Patrick J., 'African military coups d'états, 1956–2001', *Journal of Modern African Studies*, 413 (2003): 339–70.

McNeill, J. R., 'Can history help with global warming', in Kurt M. Campbell (ed.), *Climatic Cataclysm* (Washington DC: Brookings Institution Press, 2008).

Mehler, Andreas, 'Peace and power sharing in Africa', *African Affairs*, 108/432 (2009): 453–73.

Melvern, Linda, *Conspiracy to Murder: The Rwandan Genocide*, rev. edn (London: Verso, 2006).

Melvern, Linda, *A People Betrayed*, rev. edn (London: Zed Books, 2009).

Messiant, Christine, 'Angola', in Fabrice Weissman (ed.), *In the Shadow of Just Wars'* (Ithaca, NY: Cornell University Press, 2004).

Mkandawire, Thandika, and Charles C. Soludo, *Our Continent, Our Future: African Perspectives on Structural Adjustment* (Dakar: CODESRIA, 1998).

Mkutu, Kennedy Agade, *Guns and Governance in the Rift Valley* (Oxford: James Currey, 2008).

Møller, Bjørn, *Religion and Conflict in Africa*, Report 2006:6 (Copenhagen: Danish Institute for International Studies, 2006).

Mosse, David, *Cultivating Development* (London: Pluto Press, 2005).

Mueller, John, 'The banality of ethnic war', *International Security*, 25/1 (2000): 42–70.

Murithi, Tim, 'African indigenous and endogenous approaches to peace and conflict resolution', in David J. Francis (ed.), *Peace and Conflict in Africa* (London: Zed Books, 2008).

Murphy, William, 'Military patrimonialism and child soldier clientalism in the Liberian and Sierra Leonean civil wars', *African Studies Review*, 46/2 (2003): 61–87.

Musah, Abdel-Fatau, 'A country under siege', in Abdel-Fatau Musah and J. Kayode Fayemi (eds), *Mercenaries: An African Security Dilemma* (London: Pluto Press, 2000).

Muyangwa, Monde, and Margaret A. Vogt, *An Assessment of the OAU Mechanism for Conflict Prevention, Management and Resolution, 1993–2000* (New York: International Peace Academy, 2000).

Nathan, Laurie, 'Mediation and the African Union's Panel of the Wise', submission to the Commission for Africa, 15 July 2004, at www.commissionforafrica.org/english/consultation/submissions/before/sb-jul-aug04-007.pdf.

Nest, Michael, with François Grignon and Emizet F. Kisangani, *The Democratic Republic of Congo: Economic Dimensions of War and Peace* (Boulder, CO: Lynne Rienner, 2006).

Nordstrom, Carolyn, *Shadows of War: Violence, Power, and International Profiteering in the Twenty-First Century* (Berkeley: University of California Press, 2004).

O'Fahey, R. S., 'Islam and ethnicity in the Sudan', *Journal of Religion in Africa*, 26/3 (1996): 258–67.

OECD (Organization for Economic Cooperation and Deveopment), 'Paris declaration on aid effectiveness: ownership, harmonization, alignment, results and mutual accountability', statement by High Level Forum of the OECD, Paris, March 2005, at www.oecd.org/dataoecd/11/41/34428351.pdf.

Omeje, Kenneth C., 'Understanding conflict resolution in Africa', in David J. Francis (ed.), *Peace and Conflict in Africa* (London: Zed Books, 2008).

Østby, Gudrun, Ragnhild Nordås and Jan Ketil Rød, 'Regional inequalities and civil conflict in sub-Saharan Africa', *International Studies Quarterly*, 53 (2009): 301–24.

Ottaway, Marina, 'Democratization in collapsed states', in I. William Zartman (ed.), *Collapsed States* (Boulder, CO: Lynne Rienner, 1995).

Paris, Roland, 'Peacekeeping and the constraints of global culture', *European Journal of International Relations*, 9/3 (2003): 441–73.

Paris, Roland, *At War's End: Building Peace after Civil Conflict* (Cambridge: Cambridge University Press, 2004).

Patomaki, Heikki, 'How to tell better stories about world politics', *European Journal of International Relations*, 2/1 (1996): 105–33.

Peters, Krijn, and Paul Richards, 'Why we fight: voices of youth combatants in Sierra Leone', *Africa*, 68/2 (1998): 183–210.

Peters, Krijn, and Paul Richards, 'Understanding recent African wars', *Africa*, 77/3 (2007): 442–54.

Pitcher, Anne, Mary H. Moran and Michael Johnston, 'Rethinking patrimonialism and neopatrimonialism in Africa', *African Studies Review*, 52/1 (2009): 125–56.

Posner, Daniel N., and Daniel J. Young, 'The institutionalization of political power in Africa', *Journal of Democracy*, 18/3 (2007): 126–40.

Prunier, Gérard, *The Rwanda Crisis 1959–1994* (London: Hurst, 1998).

Prunier, Gérard, *Darfur: The Ambiguous Genocide* (Ithaca, NY: Cornell University Press, 2005).

Prunier, Gérard, *Africa's World War* (Oxford: Oxford University Press, 2009).

Pugh, Michael, and Neil Cooper with Jonathan Goodhand, *War Economies in a Regional Context* (Boulder, CO: Lynne Rienner, 2004).

Reno, William, 'Economic reform and the strange case of "liberalization" in Sierra Leone', *Governance*, 6/1 (1993): 23–42.

Reno, William, 'Old brigades, money bags, new breeds, and the ironies of reform in Nigeria', *Canadian Journal of African Studies*, 27/1 (1993): 66–87.

Reno, William, *Corruption and State Politics in Sierra Leone* (Cambridge: Cambridge University Press, 1995).

Reno, William, 'Ironies of post-Cold War structural adjustment in Sierra Leone', *Review of African Political Economy*, 23/67 (1996): 7–18.

Reno, William, *Warlord Politics and African States* (Boulder, CO: Lynne Rienner, 1998).

Reno, William, 'Uganda's politics of war and debt relief', *Review of International Political Economy*, 9/3 (2002): 415–35.

Reno, William, 'The changing nature of warfare and the absence of state-building in West Africa', in Diane E. Davis and Anthony W. Pereira (eds), *Irregular Armed Forces and their Role in Politics and State Formation* (Cambridge: Cambridge University Press, 2003).

Reno, William, 'Patronage politics and the behavior of armed groups', *Civil Wars*, 9/4 (2007): 324–42.

Rice, Susan E., Corinne Graff and Janet Lewis, *Poverty and Civil War: What Policymakers Need to Know*, Working Paper #02 (Washington, DC: Brookings Institution, 2006).

Richards, Paul, *Fighting for the Rain Forest: War, Youth and Resources in Sierra Leone* (Oxford: James Currey, 1996).

Richards, Paul, 'Green book millenarians? The Sierra Leone war within the perspective of an anthropology of religion', in Niels Kastfelt (ed.), *Religion and African Civil Wars* (New York: Palgrave Macmillan, 2005).

Richards, Paul (ed.), *No Peace, No War: An Anthropology of Contemporary Armed Conflicts* (Oxford: James Currey, 2005).

Richards, Paul, and James Vincent, 'Sierra Leone', in Jeroen de Zeeuw (ed.), *From Soldiers to Politicians* (Boulder, CO: Lynne Rienner, 2008).

Riddell, Roger C., *Does Foreign Aid Really Work?* (Oxford: Oxford University Press, 2007).

Rieff, David, 'Charity on the rampage', *Foreign Affairs*, 76/1 (1997): 132–8.

Risse-Kappen, Thomas, 'Introduction', in Thomas Risse-Kappen (ed.), *Bringing Transnational Relations Back In* (Cambridge: Cambridge University Press, 1995).

Roberts, Leslie F., 'Death rates don't actually decline during wars', *Informed Comment*, blog, posted 27 January 2010, at www.juancole.com/2010/01/roberts-death-rates-dont-actually.html.

Roessler, Philip, and John Prendergast, 'Democratic Republic of the Congo', in William J. Durch (ed.), *Twenty-First-Century Peace Operations* (Washington, DC: US Institute of Peace Press, 2006).

Romkema de Veenhoop, Hans, *Opportunities and Constraints for the Disarmament & Repatriation of Foreign Armed Groups in the Democratic Republic of Congo* (Washington, DC: World Bank Multi-Country Demobilization and Reintegration Program, June 2007), at www.kongo-kinshasa.de/dokumente/divers/MDRP_DRC_COFS_Study_Final_EN.pdf.

Ross, Michael L., 'How do natural resources influence civil war? Evidence from thirteen cases', *International Organization*, 58/1 (2004): 35–67.

Ross, Michael L., 'A closer look at oil, diamonds, and civil war', *Annual Review of Political Science*, 9 (2006): 265–300.

Roussellier, Jacques Eric, 'Quicksand in the Western Sahara? From referendum stalemate to negotiated solution', *International Negotiation*, 10 (2005): 311–36.

Sachs, Jeffrey, 'The strategic significance of global inequality', *Washington Quarterly*, 24/3 (2001): 187–98.

Saideman, Stephen M., *The Ties that Divide* (New York: Columbia University Press, 2001).

Salehyan, Idean, 'From climate change to conflict? No consensus Yet', *Journal of Peace Research*, 45/3 (2008): 315–26.

Salehyan, Idean, *Rebels without Borders: Transnational Insurgencies in World Politics* (Ithaca, NY: Cornell University Press, 2009).

Sambanis, Nicholas, 'What is civil war?', *Journal of Conflict Resolution*, 48/6 (2004): 814–58.

Sawyer, Amos, 'Violent conflicts and governance challenges in West Africa', *Journal of Modern African Studies*, 42/3 (2004): 437–63.

Seul, Jeffrey R., '"Ours is the way of God": religion, identity, and intergroup conflict', *Journal of Peace Research*, 36/5 (1999): 553–69.

Shearer, David, 'Aiding or abetting? Humanitarian aid and its economic role in civil war', in Mats Berdal and David M. Malone (eds), *Greed and Grievance: Economic Agendas in Civil Wars* (Boulder, CO: Lynne Rienner, 2000).

Shinn, David H., 'Ethiopian armed groups', paper presented at conference 'The Future of Armed Groups in Africa', Garmisch, Germany, 13–14 November 2009.

Sierra Leone Truth and Reconciliation Commission, *Witness to Truth*, Volume 1 (October 2004), at http://reliefweb.int/rw/rwb.nsf/db900sid/EVOD-73HJHY/$File/full_report.pdf.

Singer, J. David, 'The level-of-analysis problem in international relations', *World Politics*, 14/1 (1961): 77–92.

Smith, Lara, *Political Violence and Democratic Uncertainty in Ethiopia*, Special Report no. 192 (Washington, DC: US Institute of Peace Press, August 2007).

Smith, Rupert, *The Utility of Force* (London: Allen Lane, 2005).

Smock, David R., 'Mediating between Christians and Muslims in Plateau State, Nigeria', in David R. Smock (ed.), *Religious Contributions to Peacemaking*, Peaceworks no. 55 (Washington, DC: US Institute of Peace Press, January 2006).

Soares de Oliveira, Ricardo, *Oil and Politics in the Gulf of Guinea* (London: Hurst, 2007).

Sobek, David, *The Causes of War* (Cambridge: Polity, 2008).

Spears, Ian S., 'Understanding inclusive peace agreements in Africa', *Third World Quarterly*, 21/1 (2000): 105–18.

Stedman, Stephen J., 'Conflict and conciliation in sub-Saharan Africa', in Michael E. Brown (ed.), *The International Dimensions of Internal Conflict* (Cambridge, MA: MIT Press, 1996).

Stedman, Stephen J., 'Spoiler problems in peace processes', *International Security*, 22/2 (1997): 5–53.

Stevenson, Jonathan, *Preventing Conflict: The Role of the Bretton Woods Institutions* (London: Oxford University Press for the IISS, 2000).

Stone, John, 'Clausewitz's trinity and contemporary conflict', *Civil Wars*, 9/3 (2007): 282–96.

Storey, Andy, 'Structural adjustment, state power and genocide: the World Bank and Rwanda', *Review of African Political Economy*, no. 89 (2001): 365–85.

Strachan, Hew, and Andreas Herberg-Rothe (eds), *Clausewitz in the Twenty-First Century* (Oxford: Oxford University Press, 2007).

Straus, Scott, 'How many perpetrators were there in the Rwandan genocide? An estimate', *Journal of Genocide Research*, 6/1 (2004): 85–98.

Straus, Scott, *The Order of Genocide* (Ithaca, NY: Cornell University Press, 2006).

Sturman, Kathryn, and Aissatou Hayatou, 'The Peace and Security Council of the African Union: from design to reality', in Ulf Engel, Joao G. Porto and Doug Bond (eds), *Africa's New Peace and Security Architecture* (Aldershot: Ashgate, 2010).

Suganami, Hidemi, 'Stories of war origins: a narrativist theory of the causes of war', *Review of International Studies*, 23 (1997): 401–18.

Suganami, Hidemi, 'Explaining war: some critical observations', *International Relations*, 16/3 (2002): 307–26.

Suhrke, Astri, and Ingrid Samset, 'What's in a figure? Estimating recurrence of civil war', *International Peacekeeping*, 14/2 (2007): 195–203.

Tanner, Victor, and Jerome Tubiana, *Divided They Fall: The Fragmentation of Darfur Rebel Groups*, HSBA Working Paper no. 6 (Geneva: Small Arms Survey, 2007).

ter Haar, Gerrie, 'Religion: source of conflict or resource for peace?', in Gerrie ter Haar and James J. Busuttil (eds), *Bridge or Barrier: Religion, Violence and Visions for Peace* (Leiden: Brill, 2005).

Terry, Fiona, *Condemned to Repeat? The Paradox of Humanitarian Action* (Ithaca, NY: Cornell University Press, 2002).

Thayer, Bradley A., *Darwin and International Relations* (Lexington: University Press of Kentucky, 2004).

Toft, Monica Duffy, 'Getting religion? The puzzling case of Islam and civil war', *International Security*, 31/4 (2007): 97–131.

Toft, Monica Duffy, 'Ending civil wars: a case for rebel victory', *International Security*, 34/4 (2010): 7–36.

Toft, Monica Duffy, *Securing the Peace* (Princeton, NJ: Princeton University Press, 2010).

Toulmin, Camilla, *Climate Change in Africa* (London: Zed Books, 2009).

Tubiana, Jerome, *The Chad–Sudan Proxy War and the 'Darfurization' of Chad*, HSBA Working Paper no. 12 (Geneva: Small Arms Survey, 2008).

Tull, Denis, 'Peacekeeping in the Democratic Republic of Congo', *International Peacekeeping*, 16/2 (2009): 215–30.

Tull, Denis, and Andreas Mehler, 'The hidden costs of power sharing: reproducing insurgent violence in Africa', *African Affairs*, 104/416 (2005): 375–98.

Turshen, Meredeth, 'Militarism and Islamism in Algeria', *Journal of Asian and African Studies*, 39/1–2 (2004): 119–32.

Ulph, Stephen, 'GSPC rival leader Hattab reclaims title', *Terrorism Focus*, 2/21 (2005).

UN (United Nations), *Investigation by the Office of Internal Oversight Services into Allegations of Sexual Exploitation and Abuse in the United Nations Organization Mission in the Democratic Republic of the Congo* (UN doc. A/59/661, 5 January 2005).

UNDP (United Nations Development Programme), *Human Development Report 2003* (Oxford: UNDP/Oxford University Press, 2003).

UNDP, *Human Development Report 2006* (New York: UNDP, 2006).

UNEP (United Nations Environment Programme), *Sudan: Post-Conflict Environmental Assessment: Synthesis Report* (Nairobi: UNEP, 2007).

UNEP, *From Conflict to Peacebuilding: The Role of Natural Resources and the Environment* (Nairobi: UNEP, 2009).

UN Secretary-General, *The Causes of Conflict and the Promotion of Durable Peace and Sustainable Development in Africa* (New York: United Nations, April 1998).

UN Secretary-General, *Special Measures for Protection from Sexual Exploitation and Sexual Abuse* (UN doc. A/59/782, 15 April 2005).

UN Secretary-General, *Report of the Secretary-General on Ethiopia and Eritrea* (UN doc. S/2008/40, 23 January 2008).

UN Security Council, *Addendum to the Report of the Panel of Experts on the Illegal Exploitation of Natural Resources and Other Forms of Wealth of the Democratic Republic of the Congo* (UN doc. S/2001/1072, 13 November 2001).

UN Security Council, *Final Report of the Panel of Experts on the Illegal Exploitation of Natural Resources and Other Forms of Wealth of the Democratic Republic of the Congo* (UN doc. S/2002/1146, 16 October 2002).

UN Security Council, *Final Report of the Group of Experts on the DRC* (UN doc. S/2008/773, 12 December 2008).

UN Security Council, *Report of the African Union–United Nations Panel on Modalities for Support to African Union Peacekeeping Operations* (UN doc. A/63/666-S/2008/813, 31 December 2008).

UN Security Council, *Report of the Monitoring Group on Somalia pursuant to Security Council resolution 1766 (2007)* (UN doc. S/2008/274, 24 April 2008).

Urdal, Henrik, 'People vs. Malthus: population pressure, environmental degradation, and armed conflict revisited', *Journal of Peace Research*, 42/4 (2005): 417–34.

Urdal, Henrik, 'A clash of generations? Youth bulges and political violence', *International Studies Quarterly*, 50/3 (2006): 607–29.

US GAO (Government Accountability Office), *Darfur Crisis: Death Estimates Demonstrate Severity of the Crisis, but their Accuracy and Credibility Could Be Enhanced*, GAO-07-24 (Washington, DC: GAO, November 2006).

USAID Primer: What We Do and How We Do It (Washington, DC: USAID, January 2006).

Utas, Mats, 'War, violence and videotapes', in Preben Kaarsholm (ed.), *Violence, Political Culture and Development in Africa* (Oxford: James Currey, 2006).

Uvin, Peter, *Aiding Violence: The Development Enterprise in Rwanda* (West Hartford, CT: Kumarian Press, 1998).

van de Walle, Nicolas, *African Economies and the Politics of Permanent Crisis, 1979–1999* (Cambridge: Cambridge University Press, 2001).

van de Walle, Nicolas, *Overcoming Stagnation in Aid-Dependent Countries* (Washington, DC: Center for Global Development, 2005).

van Walraven, Klaas, *Dreams of Power: The Role of the OAU in the Politics of Africa, 1963–1993* (Aldershot: Ashgate, 1999).

Verwimp, Philip, Patricia Justino and Tilman Brück, 'The analysis of conflict: a micro-level perspective', *Journal of Peace Research*, 46/3 (2009): 307–14.

Wallensteen, Peter, *Understanding Conflict Resolution*, 2nd edn (London: Sage, 2006).

Walter, Barbara F., 'The critical barrier to civil war', *International Organization*, 51/3 (1997): 335–64.

Walter, Barbara F., 'Designing transitions from civil war', *International Security*, 24/1 (1999): 127–55.

Waltz, Kenneth N., *Man, the State, and War* (New York: Columbia University Press, 1965).

Wane, El Ghassim, 'From concept to implementation: the establishment of the CEWS of the African Union' (2008), at www.africa-union.org/root/AU/AUC/Departments/PSC/PSC/CD/2_From%20Concept%20to%20Implementation.pdf.

Watts, Michael, 'Resource curse? Governmentality, oil and power in the Niger Delta, Nigeria', *Geopolitics*, 9/1 (2004): 50–80.

Watts, Michael, 'Petro-insurgency or criminal syndicate? Conflict and violence in the Niger Delta', *Review of African Political Economy*, 34/114 (2007): 637–60.

Weber, Max, *The Theory of Social and Economic Organization*, ed. Talcott Parsons (New York: Free Press, 1964).

Weber, Max, *Economy and Society*, ed Guenther Roth and Claus Wittich (Berkeley: University of California Press, 1978).

Weinstein, Jeremy M., *Inside Rebellion* (Cambridge: Cambridge University Press, 2007).

Weiss, Thomas G., 'Principles, politics and humanitarian action', *Ethics and International Affairs*, 13/1 (1999): 1–22.

Wheeler, Andrew C., 'Finding meaning amid the chaos', in Niels Kastfelt (ed.), *Religion and African Civil Wars* (New York: Palgrave Macmillan, 2005).

Wight, Colin, *Agents, Structures and International Relations* (Cambridge: Cambridge University Press, 2006).

Wiharta, Sharon, 'The legitimacy of peace operations', in *SIPRI Yearbook 2009* (Cambridge: Cambridge University Press, 2009).

Wild, Emma, '"Is it witchcraft? Is it Satan? It is a miracle": Mai-Mai soldiers and Christian concepts of evil in North-East Congo', *Journal of Religion in Africa*, 28/4 (1998): 450–67.

Williams, Paul, D. 'Fighting for Freetown: British military intervention in Sierra Leone', *Contemporary Security Policy*, 22/3 (2001): 140–68.

Williams, Paul D., 'Keeping the peace in Africa: why "African" solutions are not enough', *Ethics and International Affairs*, 22/3 (2008): 309–29.

Williams, Paul D., 'The African Union's peace operations: a comparative analysis', *African Security*, 2/2–3 (2009): 97–118.

Williams, Paul D., 'The Peace and Security Council of the African Union: evaluating an embryonic institution', *Journal of Modern African Studies*, 47/4 (2009): 603–26.

Williams, Paul. D., *Enhancing Civilian Protection in Peace Operations: Insights from Africa* (Washington, DC: Africa Center for Strategic Studies, 2010).

Wolff, Stefan, *Ethnic Conflict: A Global Perspective* (Oxford: Oxford University Press, 2007).

Wood, E. C., G. G. Tappan and A. Hadj, 'Understanding the drivers of agricultural land use change in South-Central Senegal', *Journal of Arid Environments*, 59/3 (2004): 565–82.

World Bank, *Accelerated Development in Sub-Saharan Africa: An Agenda for Action* (Washington DC: World Bank, 1981).

World Bank, *Rwanda: Poverty Reduction and Sustainable Growth*, Report no. 12465-RW (Washington DC: World Bank, 16 May 1994).

World Bank, *Sierra Leone: Public Expenditure Policies for Sustained Economic Growth and Poverty Alleviation*, Report no. 2618-SL (Washington, DC: World Bank, 16 February 1994) [Berg Report].

World Bank, *Implementation Completion Report: Rwandese Republic: SAC No.2271-RW*, Report no. 14873 (Washington, DC: World Bank, 19 July 1995).

Zartman, I. William (ed.), *Governance as Conflict Management* (Washington, DC: Brookings Institution, 1997).

Zartman, I. William, 'The timing of peace initiatives: hurting stalemates and ripe moments', *Global Review of Ethnopolitics*, 1/1 (2001): 8–18, at www.ethnopolitics.org/ethnopolitics/archive/volume_I/issue_1/zartman.pdf.

Zartman, I. William, 'Preventing identity conflicts leading to genocide and mass killings', 23 June 2010, at http://www.allianceforpeacebuilding.org/news/44386/Preventing-Identity-Conflicts-leading-to-Genocide-and-Mass-Killings.htm.

Zeleza, Paul Tiyambe, 'Introduction', in Alfred Nhema and Paul Tiyambe Zeleza (eds), *The Roots of African Conflicts* (Oxford: James Currey, 2008).

Index

Italicized page numbers refer to illustrations